Oracle JD Edwards EnterpriseOne 9.0: Supply Chain Management Cookbook

Over 130 simple but incredibly effective recipes for configuring, supporting, and enhancing EnterpriseOne SCM

Kashif Rasheed

[PACKT] PUBLISHING enterprise
professional expertise distilled

BIRMINGHAM - MUMBAI

Oracle JD Edwards EnterpriseOne 9.0: Supply Chain Management Cookbook

First published: March 2012

Production Reference: 1210312

Published by Packt Publishing Ltd.
Livery Place
35 Livery Street
Birmingham B3 2PB, UK

ISBN 978-1-84968-196-4

`www.packtpub.com`

Cover Image by Meir Jacob Jacob (`meirjac@netvision.net.il`)

Credits

Author
Kashif Rasheed

Reviewers
David Gamble
Bala Pujari, CSCP
Haytham R. Said

Acquisition Editor
Stephanie Moss

Lead Technical Editor
Alina Lewis
Azharuddin Sheikh

Technical Editors
Joyslita D'Souza
Veronica Fernandes

Copy Editor
Laxmi Subramanian

Project Coordinator
Jovita Pinto

Proofreader
Dirk Manuel

Indexer
Tejal Daruwale
Hemangini Bari

Production Coordinator
Melwyn D'sa
Alwin Roy

Cover Work
Melwyn D'sa

About the Author

Kashif Rasheed started his professional career in April 2000. He was born in Karachi, Pakistan and completed his MBA (MIS) from PAF-KIET, Karachi in January 2007. Previously, he completed a Bachelor's degree in Computer Science (BCS). Since September 2008, he has been working as an Oracle EnterpriseOne Supply Chain Consultant in Saudi Arabia and has implemented various ERP projects. He has also worked as a Project Developer and Application Programmer for PricewaterhouserCooper (PwC) at its Pakistan office.

I would like to thank my parents, friends, and family, who supported me throughout the writing of this book.

About the Reviewers

David Gamble is a Technical Consultant and has been working with JD Edwards Software since 1995; World Software A5, A6 and A73. From 1999 onwards this includes OneWorld and EnterpriseOne up to and including 9.0, JD Edwards EnterpriseOne Tools - Version: 8.93 and later.

Bala Pujari, CSCP is a JD Edwards Supply Chain and Finance Consultant with over 11 years of experience working in various verticals including Pharmaceuticals, Oil and Natural Gas companies, and Publishing houses, and is currently working for one of the biggest real estate services companies as a Transition Lead.

He has worked for Capgemini, one of the Big Four consulting firm, as a Senior Consultant in JD Edwards.

He has worked for Tata Consultancy Services, Asia's largest software export company, as an IT Analyst. He acted as a Practice Lead for a brief duration, where his responsibilities included answering RFPs, Solution Delivery, Resource Management, and Recruitment.

He has provided consulting services to Lafarge, JnJ operating companies, Glaxo, Merck, Exterran, GDF Suez, Pride International, and Wolter Kluwers.

He has provided papers, internal publications to Capgemini on Cold Fusion, Rational Unified Process, and Web Methods.

I would like to extend my thanks to my family and important friend, Vani Venuthurla, who encouraged me during the reviewing process.

Haytham R. Said is an EnterpriseOne CNC Specialist and Technical Project Manager with JD Edwards and has worked on more than 15 implementations, since its original beta release.

Table of Contents

Preface

Oracle's JD Edwards EnterpriseOne Supply Chain Management (SCM) application suite aids your business in enhancing your interactions with Enterprise suppliers, and this practical cookbook provides essential implementation sequences to make the most of the suite. The functionality across the application described in this comprehensive guide allows you to be proactive in reacting to real-time information and in developing procurement strategies and best practices.

Oracle JD Edwards EnterpriseOne 9.0: Supply Chain Management Cookbook explains with step-by-step instructions how to fully implement the EnterpriseOne Supply Chain suite, how to set up Inventory Management, Procurement Management, and Sales Order Management, and much more. Each chapter will provide you the details of setup-related information, and provide instructions that will direct you in configuring your company's business processes.

This business-ready cookbook provides you with all the instructions that you need to set up the SCM application and utilize it based on your company's individual business requirements. It begins by demonstrating how to review inventory quantity information and perform physical inventory through cycle counts and tag counts, and later moves on to explain how to configure the interactive application and how to set up the batch versions. Along the way, it also covers item master information, classification, AAI setup, and system integration. Ultimately, this book equips you with the knowledge to configure and take advantage of the entire SCM system.

What this book covers

Chapter 1, Inventory Management, discusses inventory management, which is the core module of the Supply Chain Management modules. It is necessary to understand how to set up and manage inventory in order to effectively work with all of the other programs in JD Edwards EnterpriseOne. The JD Edwards EnterpriseOne Inventory Management system defines inventory items, which enables you to manipulate inventory throughout the supply chain.

Chapter 2, Inventory Transactions, Item Quantity, and Physical Inventories, shows how to perform inventory transactions, review inventory quantity information, and perform physical inventory through cycle counts and tag counts.

Chapter 3, Updating Costs, Using Kits, and Lot Processing, gets you acquainted with updating item costs, setting up kits items, and using lot processing.

Chapter 4, Understanding and Setting up Procurement, teaches procurement management system setup, including procurement management system integration, setting up different order types, setting up order approval, and receipt routing.

Chapter 5, Understanding Pricing in Procurement and Purchase Orders, discusses procurement management system setup including procurement management system integration, setting up different order types, setup order approval and receipt route.

Chapter 6, Receipt Processing, shows purchase order receipt processing, reviewing receipt journals, standard receipt processing, and receipt routing processing.

Chapter 7, Creating Vouchers and Landed Costs, teaches how vouchers can be created based on invoice and receipt, and based on invoice and purchase order. There are two types of voucher matching, two way voucher matching and three way voucher matching. This chapter covers the voucher matching process. It also covers landed costs (the additional cost incurred during purchasing) during receipt process, and standalone landed costs.

Chapter 8, Processing Special Orders and Approvals, provides a variety of special orders that may be required depending upon the company's business process. For example, some companies require a quotation process and some companies have long-term purchase contract called blanket order with their vendors. In this chapter, you will see the processing of special orders, including requisition orders, quote orders, long term contracts, or blanket orders. This chapter will also cover generating purchase orders, and purchase order approvals including approval route set up.

Chapter 9, Sales Order Management and Additional Orders, explains the Sales Order Management system helps you to review and examine sales order information and review the sales order status, including customer payments and sales invoice standings. It also allows you to plan for future requirements. You can rapidly retrieve information such as item number, availability, quantity, cost, and so on. This chapter provides you with the details of the sales order system.

Chapter 10, Holding, Releasing, and Reviewing, provides you with the details of additional Sales Order Management system processes, which includes the release of held orders that can be set up as per the business needs. It also provides Release Quote Order and Release Blanket Order processes.

Chapter 11, Order Processing, Prepayments, and Invoicing, provides you with the details of Order Processing, which includes printing pick slip documents, running the confirm shipment process, and so on. It also provides details of invoice processing, which covers the pre-payments for advance payment processing.

Chapter 12, Updating Prices, End of Day Processes, and Sales Returns, talks about the Order Management pricing, which includes base price revisions based on customer, items, customer group, and/or item group. It also gives you the details of how to perform End of Day operations, which update the financial modules as per the financial integration setup.

Chapter 13, SCM Customizations, talks about the SCM customized objects, which provides you with the details of supply chain's commonly-used customized objects. The chapter provides both the technical specification and technical coding that the Technical Consultant and Application Programmer require.

Appendix, The Supply Chain Business Process, provides you a live case study of a supply chain implementation of a client. The business analysis document gives you the details of the As-Is and To-Be business process, which is based on JD Edwards EnterpriseOne Supply Chain Management application features.

What you need for this book

The reader of this book should install JDE demo 9.0, Adobe Acrobat Reader, and Microsoft Excel in order to execute all of the instructions provided in this book.

Who this book is for

If you are a Functional Consultant, Technical Consultant/Developer, or Project Manager, and want to improve your business perspective of EnterpriseOne SCM, this book is for you.

You should have basic knowledge of navigating in EnterpriseOne and general supply chain familiarity. Knowledge of the Common Foundation JDE 9.0 module is advantageous; the supply chain business domain knowledge will be an add-on to this.

Conventions

In this book, you will find a number of styles of text that distinguish between different kinds of information. Here are some examples of these styles, and an explanation of their meaning.

Code words in text are shown as follows: "In the `Initialize Section` of the following code, you will initialize the variable."

A block of code is set as follows:

```
rpt_CompanyKey_F0911_KCO
rpt_DocumentType_F0911_DCT
rpt_InvoiceNumber_F0911_DOC
rpt_RevenueAmount_F0911_AA
```

When we wish to draw your attention to a particular part of a code block, the relevant lines or items are set in bold:

```
rpt_CompanyKey_F0911_KCO
rpt_DocumentType_F0911_DCT
rpt_InvoiceNumber_F0911_DOC
rpt_RevenueAmount_F0911_AA
```

New terms and **important words** are shown in bold. Words that you see on the screen, in menus or dialog boxes for example, appear in the text like this: "On the **Update Sales Order - Detail First** form, click on **Find** to search for your order."

[Warnings or important notes appear in a box like this.]

[Tips and tricks appear like this.]

Reader feedback

Feedback from our readers is always welcome. Let us know what you think about this book—what you liked or may have disliked. Reader feedback is important for us to develop titles that you really get the most out of.

To send us general feedback, simply send an e-mail to `feedback@packtpub.com`, and mention the book title via the subject of your message.

If there is a book that you need and would like to see us publish, please send us a note in the **SUGGEST A TITLE** form on `www.packtpub.com` or e-mail `suggest@packtpub.com`.

If there is a topic that you have expertise in and you are interested in either writing or contributing to a book, see our author guide on `www.packtpub.com/authors`.

Customer support

Now that you are the proud owner of a Packt book, we have a number of things to help you to get the most from your purchase.

Errata

Although we have taken every care to ensure the accuracy of our content, mistakes do happen. If you find a mistake in one of our books—maybe a mistake in the text or the code—we would be grateful if you would report this to us. By doing so, you can save other readers from frustration and help us improve subsequent versions of this book. If you find any errata, please report them by visiting `http://www.packtpub.com/support`, selecting your book, clicking on the **errata submission form** link, and entering the details of your errata. Once your errata are verified, your submission will be accepted and the errata will be uploaded on our website, or added to any list of existing errata, under the Errata section of that title. Any existing errata can be viewed by selecting your title from `http://www.packtpub.com/support`.

Piracy

Piracy of copyright material on the Internet is an ongoing problem across all media. At Packt, we take the protection of our copyright and licenses very seriously. If you come across any illegal copies of our works, in any form, on the Internet, please provide us with the location address or website name immediately so that we can pursue a remedy.

Please contact us at `copyright@packtpub.com` with a link to the suspected pirated material.

We appreciate your help in protecting our authors, and our ability to bring you valuable content.

Questions

You can contact us at `questions@packtpub.com` if you are having a problem with any aspect of the book, and we will do our best to address it.

1
Inventory Management

In this chapter, we will cover:

- Inventory management setup
- Setting up branch/plant constants
- Setting up inventory transactions
- Defining item information
- Defining segmented items and templates
- Item classification
- Item Unit of Measure (UOM) conversion
- Item branch/plant setup
- Item costing and pricing

Introduction

Inventory management is a core module of the Supply Chain Management modules. It is necessary to understand how to set up and manage inventory in order to effectively work with all in order the other programs in JD Edwards EnterpriseOne. The JD Edwards EnterpriseOne Inventory Management system defines inventory items, which enables you to manipulate inventory throughout the supply chain. The Inventory Management application integrates with the following EnterpriseOne applications:

- JD Edwards EnterpriseOne Sales Order Management
- JD Edwards EnterpriseOne General Ledger

- JD Edwards EnterpriseOne Advance Pricing
- JD Edwards EnterpriseOne Warehouse Management
- JD Edwards EnterpriseOne Product Data Management
- JD Edwards EnterpriseOne Shop Floor Management
- JD Edwards EnterpriseOne Equipment and Plant Management
- JD Edwards EnterpriseOne Material Planning
- JD Edwards EnterpriseOne Forecast Management
- JD Edwards EnterpriseOne Procurement Management
- JD Edwards EnterpriseOne Manufacturing

Inventory management setup

In this recipe, we will see how to set up the inventory management default options. There are several tasks that need to be completed before you can set up the actual inventory management system setup.

Getting ready

Before you start, you should make sure that the general accounting system has been configured, in order to integrate the inventory management module with the general accounting system. The inventory management default setup can be accessed from the **G4141** menu.

> The general accounting system configuration is a part of the Financials Management system and its setup is available in the financial standard implementation guide.

How to do it...

1. To set up system constants, select **Sys. Constants** from the form menu on the **Work with Branch/Plant Constants** form, in order to access the system constants.
2. Select the checkbox for **Unit of Measure Conversion by Branch** in order for the system to display the item-specific conversion table when you add an item to a specific branch/plant.
3. Select the **Update Average Cost On-Line** checkbox so that the system calculates a new average cost immediately after any transaction that affects the average cost of an item occurs.

4. Select the **Scientific Rounding** checkbox to indicate that scientific rounding should be performed.
5. Select the relevant checkbox to indicate whether the system should apply the **Ship Ascending Date Rule** by customer and by item.
6. Select the appropriate value by clicking on **Visual Assist** for allowing duplicate lots. You can choose from the following options:
    - **Duplicate Lots Not Allowed (is value "1")**: The lot is restricted to one item and one branch/plant
    - **Duplicate Lots Allowed (is value "2")**: Allows you to create a lot that contains multiple items and branches/plants
    - **Duplicate Lots Not Allowed (is value "3")**: The lot is restricted to one item, but can contain quantities in multiple branches/plants
7. To set up warehouse locations, select **Location Def** from the row menu on the **Work with Branch/Plant Constants (P41001)** form.
8. On the **Work With Location Master (P4100)** form, click **Add** to enter locations individually.
9. On the **Work with Default Location & Printers (P400951)** form, click **Add** and then enter the name of the default printer.
10. To set up standard units of measure on **Work With Standard Units of Measure (P41003),** click **Add** to set the unit of measure conversion. You can access the **Standard Unit of Measure Revisions (P41003)** application from **Work With Standard Units**.
11. Item cross reference set-up can be accessed through **Work With Item Cross Reference (P4104)**. Click **Add** to set up item cross referencing.
12. To set up messages, select a record and then select **Revisions** from the row menu on the **Work With Print Message (P40162)**. You can define a print message, which can be attached to different document types, customers, or suppliers.
13. To set up document type information, click **Add** on the **Work With Document Type (P40040)** form. Enter the document type code and description. The document type code should be a two-digit code, and the description should not be greater than 10 characters in length.
14. To set up **Automatic Accounting Instructions**, enter **DMAAI** on the fast path, and access the AAI application, **Work With AAIs (P40950).**

15. Select the AAI that you want to setup, and select AAI details from the row menu on the **Work With AAIs (P40950)** form for entering the financials AAI object account.

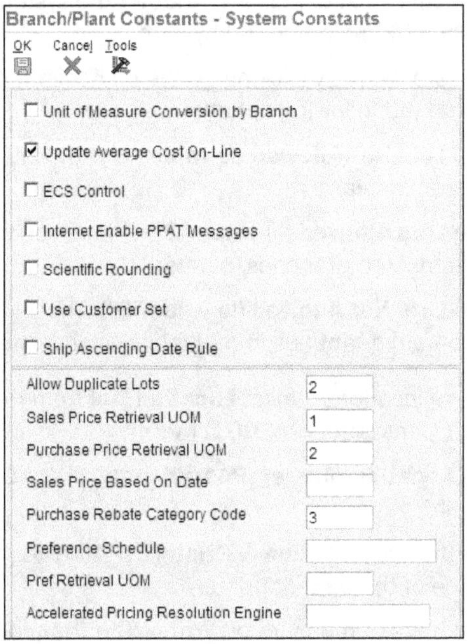

How it works...

Before you can begin with Inventory Management, it is necessary to perform a number of minor setups. You need to set up **System Constants** to specify which functions to perform. For example, assume that you have several branches/plants and you use different units of measure for the items in each branch/plant. You can set a system constant to automatically convert units of measure by branch/plant. A system constant is configured at the branch/plant/company level.

In addition**, Location Control** is required for the EnterpriseOne warehouse management system, but is optional for all other distribution systems. The system stores location information in the F4100 table. The **Speed Location Setup Program (P4100A)** enables you to set up the warehouse quickly by copying an existing location to create new locations. Using this program is much faster than entering locations individually.

In the **Standard Unit of Measure** part of the recipe, you can create any number of conversion factors for any number of units of measure, but they must all be able to convert to the primary unit of measure through either a direct path—for example, 1 box equals 2 each, where each is the primary unit of measure—or an indirect path—for example, 1 box equals 4 each. You can also set up conversion factors that associate each unit of measure with the primary unit of measure.

[You should restart the EnterpriseOne system after setting up the system constants.]

There's more...

A particularly important aspect of these setups to take note of is **Automatic Accounting Instructions**. A company code identifies each specific organization. The company code must already exist in the **Company Constants table (F0010)** and must identify a reporting entity that has a complete balance sheet. The following image shows the **Automatic Accounting Instructions** (AAI) setup.

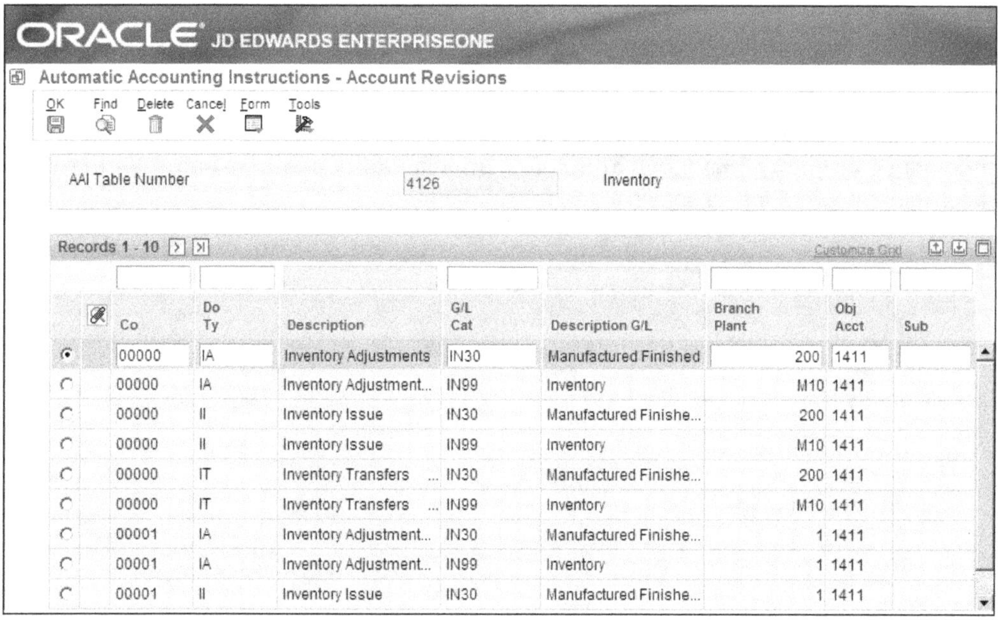

ORACLE JD EDWARDS ENTERPRISEONE

Automatic Accounting Instructions - Account Revisions

OK Find Delete Cancel Form Tools

AAI Table Number 4126 Inventory

Records 1 - 10

Co	Do Ty	Description	G/L Cat	Description G/L	Branch Plant	Obj Acct	Sub
00000	IA	Inventory Adjustments	IN30	Manufactured Finished	200	1411	
00000	IA	Inventory Adjustment...	IN99	Inventory	M10	1411	
00000	II	Inventory Issue	IN30	Manufactured Finishe...	200	1411	
00000	II	Inventory Issue	IN99	Inventory	M10	1411	
00000	IT	Inventory Transfers ...	IN30	Manufactured Finishe...	200	1411	
00000	IT	Inventory Transfers ...	IN99	Inventory	M10	1411	
00001	IA	Inventory Adjustment...	IN30	Manufactured Finishe...	1	1411	
00001	IA	Inventory Adjustment...	IN99	Inventory	1	1411	
00001	II	Inventory Issue	IN30	Manufactured Finishe...	1	1411	

Document type

The document type identifies the origin and purpose of the transaction. The system reserves several prefixes for document types, such as vouchers, invoices, receipts, and time sheets. Document type information is typically set up in a **User-Defined Code (UDC)**. The **Document Type Maintenance** Program (**P40040**) updates the **Document Type Master Table** (**F40039**). This program also updates the **User Defined Codes Table** (**F0005**). The General Ledger category identifies the GL offset that the system uses when it searches for the account to which it posts the transaction. If you do not want to specify a class code, you can enter **** (four asterisks) in this field. You can use **AAIs** to predefine classes of automatic offset accounts for the inventory management, procurement, and sales order management systems.

See also

- *Setting up branch/plant constants*

Setting up branch/plant constants

Branch/plant constants enable you to configure the processing of daily transactions for each branch/plant in the supply chain management systems. Branch plant setup is critical, and each option is significant.

Getting ready

Before setting up branches/plants, you must set up branches/plants in the business unit | application **Work With Business Units (P0006)**.

Select EnterpriseOne menus: **EnterpriseOne menu** | **Inventory management** | **Daily processing** | **Inventory Management Set up** | **Branch Plant Constants** and enter the branch/plant information as shown in the following image:

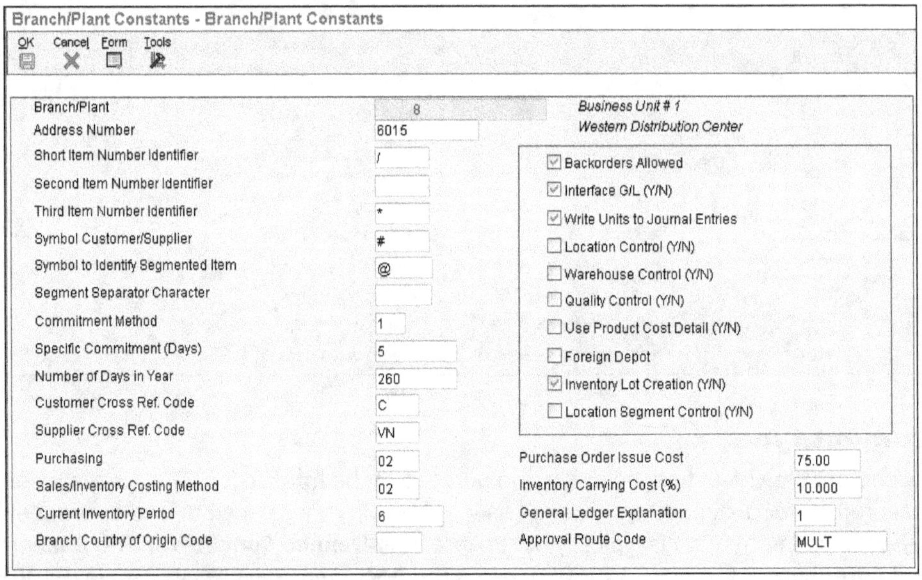

How to do it...

1. Enter each **Branch/Plant** in the address book. The search type of the branch/plant should be **Branch/Plant**. The **Branch Country of Origin Code** is defined in **UDC 40R/CO** and specifies where a part was made.

2. Enter a two-digit code indicating parts made outside of the USA, for example, **SA** refers to **Saudi Arabia**. The **Approval Route Code** determines to whom an order is routed for approval.
3. Select the **Location Control** checkbox to indicate which type of location control the system requires. You should use location control if you want to use only locations that are in the **Location Master Table F4100** table.
4. Select the **Warehouse Control** checkbox to indicate that the system creates warehouse transactions for the branch/plant.
5. The **Quality Control** checkbox indicates that the JD Edwards quality management system is enabled for the branch/plant. In addition to activating quality control for each branch/plant that you want to include in quality tests, you need to activate quality management on the **Quality Management** setup menu **(G3741)**.
6. Use the **Product Cost detail** checkbox to indicate that the distribution programs use the total cost method or the detailed product cost method.
7. Select the **Foreign Depot** checkbox to indicate that another company owns the branch/plant. The **Bulk And Packed Load Confirmation** programs use this code to determine whether the depot from which the product is being loaded is a foreign depot. If it is a foreign depot, you must enter a valid borrow agreement during load confirmation.
8. The **Location Segment Control** checkbox enables the location segment specifications in the **Location Definition Program** (**P41001**). The segment specifications determine how the system segments locations within a branch using **UDC 41/ER**.
9. Enter **User Defined Code 40/CM** to indicate the cost method that the system uses to calculate the cost of goods that are sold for the item.
10. Enter the **Inventory Carrying Cost (%)** percentage of inventory investment that you want the **JD Edwards EnterpriseOne procurement system** to use to calculate **EOQ**. Enter the percentage as a decimal value.

How it works...

A **Short item number** is an eight-character number that you use when you do not want to use it as the primary item number. The short number is a system-generated number that is generated automatically through the next number application. Leave this field blank to indicate that you want to use this item number as the primary number. That is, you use it most often to enter or review information. If this is not the primary number, you must enter a special symbol to identify it. Use a symbol that is not significant for any other purposes of entry, such as /, *, or &.

> Make sure that you do not use a period or a comma as a symbol. The JDE system allows only the characters already described.

In the **Branch Plant Constants** setup, if you leave the second item number field blank then this indicates that you want to use this item number as the primary number. If the second item number is not the primary number, a special symbol should be used to identify it.

The **Third item number** is a number of up to 25 characters in length for when you do not want to use it as the primary number. A blank field indicates that you want to use this item number as the primary number. If this is not the primary number, you must enter a special symbol to identify it. Use a symbol that is not significant for any other purposes of entry such as /, *, or &.

When you enter a number preceded by this character, the system recognizes the number as the customer's or supplier's number. The system then uses the cross-reference table to match the number to the item number. You must complete this field if you want the system to perform cross-referencing.

Setting up **Cross Reference UDC 41/DT** identifies the type of cross-reference setup for this customer. Examples of cross-reference types include substitutes, replacements, and customer and supplier item numbers.

The character or symbol will be used to separate segments within an item number based on the template that is associated with the item number. If this field is left blank, the system displays the segments as one string of characters.

Numbers from 1 - 14 identify the current accounting period. The system uses this number to generate error messages, such as **PBCO (Posted Before Cut Off)** and **PACO (Posted After Cut Off)**.

Inventory commitment involves committing the inventory through sales orders, based on the Branch Plant constants setup. This value in days is added to the current date and compared with the promised ship date for the order line. If the promised date is greater than the calculated date, the order line is future-committed in the **Item Location Table F41021** table.

There's more...

It is suggested that you define how the system should calculate item availability for each branch/plant. Item availability affects how the system calculates back orders, cancellations, and customer delivery time. The following image shows the item availability definition setup.

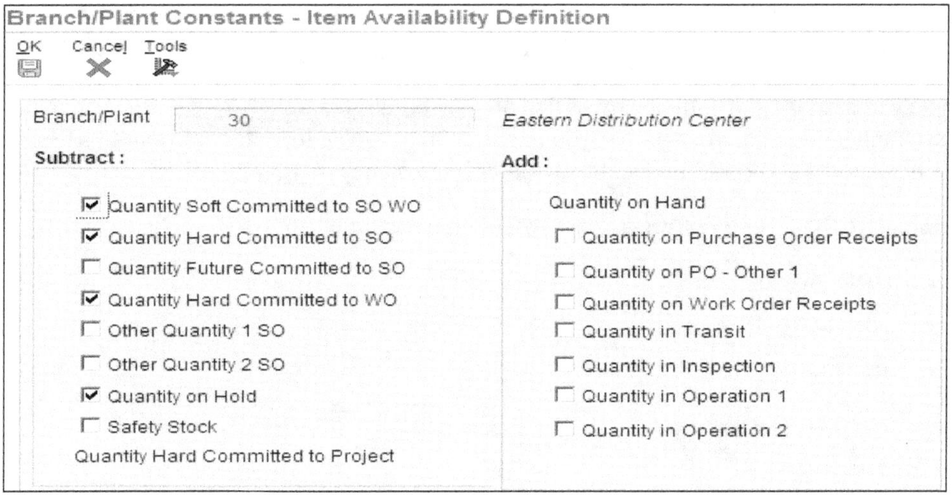

User defined codes for document type setup

Following are the **User Defined Codes (UDC)** used for the document type maintenance program **P40040**.

- Trace/Track Document Types in UDC 40/DC
- Commitment Document Types in UDC 40/CT
- Blanket Order Types in UDC 40/BT
- Inventory Update Types in UDC 40/IU
- Transaction Type in UDC 39/TT
- Nature of Transaction in UDC 40/NT
- Category of Order in UDC 40/OC
- Other Quantity in UDC 40/OQ
- Interbranch Orders in UDC 40/IB
- Service Contract Type in UDC 17/CM
- Work Order Type in UDC 48/OT
- Carton Status in UDC 46/RS

See also

- *Inventory management setup*

Setting up inventory transactions

To help you manage the complex recording and accounting functions that are involved in maintaining an up-to-date inventory, you might need to record inventory movements between branches/plants and between locations in a branch/plant.

Following are the inventory transactions types that need to be set up:

- Issue inventory
- Adjust inventory
- Transfer inventory

Getting ready

For issuing inventory, access the menu from **EnterpriseOne menu | Inventory management | daily processing | Inventory master transaction | Issues.**

How to do it...

1. On the **Work With Inventory Issues (P4112)** form, click on **Add**.
2. Enter the branch/plant, issue date, general ledger date, item number, and item quantity.
3. The document will appear in the application automatically, based on the document type next number application setup.
4. General ledger batches are created automatically once you have saved the transaction. You should review and post general ledger batches from the application **Batches P0011**.

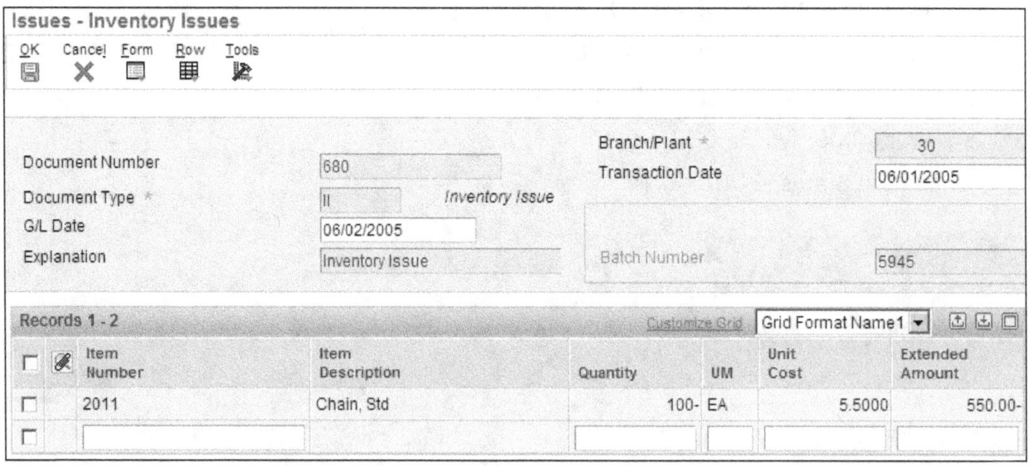

5. For inventory adjustment, access the menu from **EnterpriseOne menu | Inventory Management | Daily Processing | Inventory Master Transaction | Adjustment**.
6. On the **Work With Inventory Adjustment (P4114)** form, click on **add**.
7. Enter branch plant, issue date, GL date, item number, and item quantity.
8. The document will come automatically from the document type next number application.
9. Post the general ledger batches.

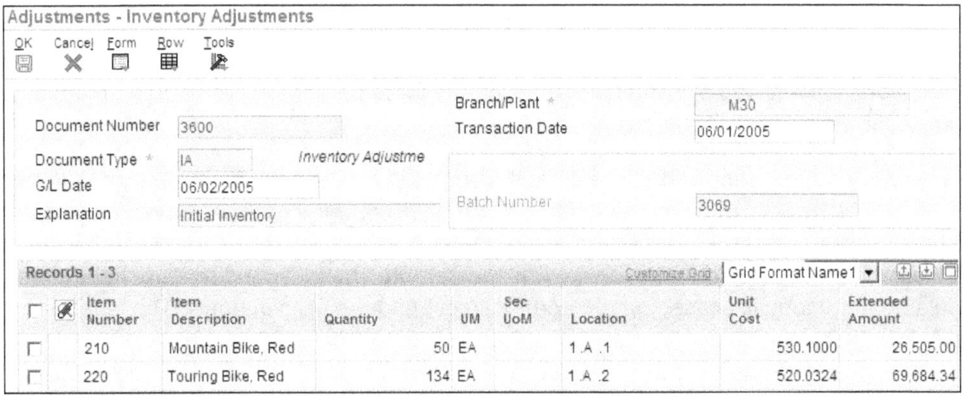

10. For setting up inventory transfers, access the menu from **EnterpriseOne menu | Inventory Management | Daily Processing | Inventory Master Transaction | Transfer**.
11. On the **Work With Inventory Transfer (P4113)** form, click on **Add**.
12. Enter the branch/plant FROM; branch/plant TO, issue date, general ledger date, item number, and item quantity.
13. The document will come automatically through the document type next number application.
14. Post the general ledger batches.

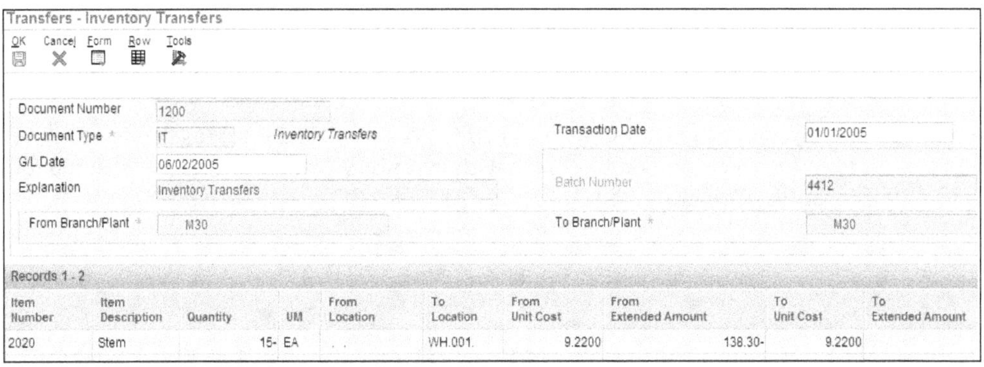

How it works...

Inventory issue setup **UDC 00/DT** specifies the document type. The default document type is typically II (Inventory Issues). If you leave this processing option blank, the system does not provide a default value. The issue type specifies whether or not the equipment and subledger information appears in the detail area of the **Inventory Issues** form. The system requires the entry of account numbers in the detail area of the **Inventory Issues** form. This field is available only when you enter 2 or 3 as the issue type processing option. Allow an issue quantity that is greater than the available quantity, which could result in a negative on-hand quantity. The system enables the issue of lots that are on hold. If the lot status code field on the item/ branch/plant form is blank, the lot is not on hold. Use this processing option to update the **Item History Table (F4115)** if you use the Inventory Management system and do not use the **Sales Order Management system**.

For **Inventory Adjustment Setup**, the default inventory adjustment document type is **IA**. You can use the primary location as the default only if all secondary locations have a physical location (for example, aisle, and bin). If any of the secondary locations have a blank location or lot, you cannot set the primary location as the default. The extended amount field will be calculated automatically based on the item unit cost and the item quantity. The journal entries specify whether detailed or summarized journal entries are created for the general ledger. For summarized journal entries, the system creates a summarized debit total and a summarized credit total by account number for each line in an adjustment. The **Lot** and **Layering** fields determine whether to display the lot information fields on the forms and whether they can be updated. Adjustment quantities specify the way in which the system validates a transaction that results in a negative quantity.

For **Inventory Transfer,** the default document type is typically **IT (inventory transfers).** The journal inventory management system integrates with general accounting through the document type. **From location** is used to issue the quantity from whichever location you want. Once you select the location, the system subtracts the quantity from that location. **To location** is used for receiving the quantity into stock. Once you select the **To Location**, the system adds the quantity upon completion of the transaction.

Journal entries specify the version of the journal entries program to use when you access it from the row menu on the **Work With Inventory Transfer (P4113)** form or from the form menu on the **Inventory Transfers** form. For summarized journal entries, the system creates a summarized debit total and credit total per account number for all lines in a transfer.

Item Ledger specifies the version of the Item Ledger Inquiry (**CARDEX**) program to use when you access it from the row menu on the **Work with Inventory Transfers** form or from the form menu on the **Inventory Transfers** form.

Issuing inventory

Issuing inventory typically involves removing items from a branch/plant or location, adjusting the inventory balance, and recording the transaction in the GL. Setting up inventory issues is done through the **Inventory Issue** application (**P4112**) processing option.

Inventory adjustments

Inventory adjustments are used to increase or decrease the on-hand quantity and the cost of inventory items in a branch/plant without conducting a complete physical inventory. The main setup for inventory adjustment is to set up the processing option of **Inventory Adjustment P4114**.

Transfer transactions

Transfer transactions are used to record two types of inventory movement: movement between different locations in the same branches/plant, and movement between different branch/plants. An inventory transfer creates two journal entries in the **GL**. The first journal entry decreases inventory at the original location. The second entry increases inventory at the destination location. Inventory application is done by using the application **P4113**. The main setup of inventory transaction is the **P4113** processing option.

Defining item information

Before you can work with inventory, you must provide the system with information about the items that you stock. You must enter master information for all stock and non-stock items.

Getting ready

To begin to define an item master, select **EnterpriseOne Menus| Logistics Management | Inventory Management | Daily Processing | Inventory/Master Transactions | Item Master**.

How to do it...

1. On the **Work With Item Master (P4101)** browse form, click on **add**.
2. Enter the **Basic Data Item**, such as the item code, description, GL class, supplier, stocking type, planner number, and buyer number.
3. Enter the item category codes information from **Item Master Revisions** row menu category codes, and enter the item category based on your item master setup.

4. Enter the weights and **Unit of Measure** information, such as **EA** for **Each**, and so on.
5. Enter **Item/Branch**.

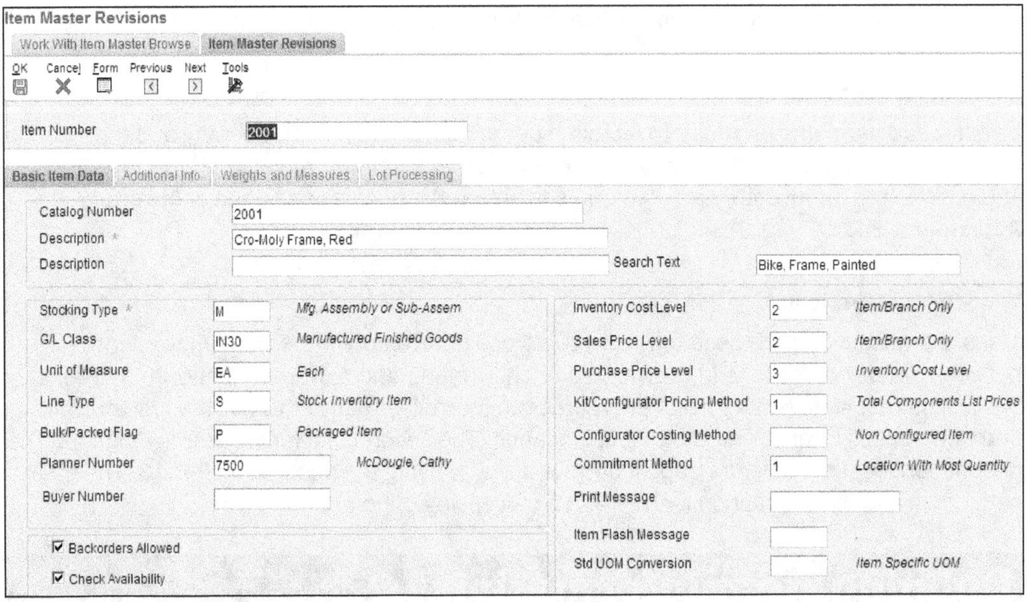

How it works...

The item number is identified based on company business needs.

When you enter the item into the system, the short item number is assigned automatically. The second item number will be entered manually, as per business needs. The system stores the item master in the **Item Master table (F4101)**. The catalog number can be entered as a vendor item number for reference. The catalog number is also stored in the **Sales Order Detail table (F4211)**, along with the second item number.

You can define multiple stocking types, such as **S** for **Stock** and **N** for **Non Stock Item**. The stocking type is a base of all the transactions. The system reads the stocking type of the item from the item master. If the item is stocking type **S**, then you will receive the physical quantity into your stock.

GL/Class controls the general ledger accounts that will receive the monetary amount of inventory transactions for this item.

You can enable back-orders per item using the **Item Master** (**P4101**) program or the **Item Branch (P41026)** program, per customer by using the **Customer Master (P03013)** program, or per branch/plant by using the **Branch/Plant Constants (P41001)** program. You might want to enable availability checking for certain items. For other items, if you assume that an adequate supply is available, leave availability checking disabled.

Advanced serial number processing enables you to use a serial number to track an item through purchasing and sales. The code that specifies whether you must attach a serial number to this item at receipt or sale for basic serial number processing, or whether memo lot information is required for advanced serial number processing.

The lot status code indicates the status of the lot. Leaving this field blank indicates that the lot is approved. All other codes indicate that the lot is on hold. You can assign a different status code to each location in which a lot resides, in the item/location information or location lot status change application.

The commitment date method specifies which date the system uses to commit inventory when an item is committed by date. The default value is 01 (**lot expiration date**).

Shelf life days are the days for which an item can remain in inventory before it expires. The system adds this number to the date on which the item is received, in order to determine the expiration date for the item. If you do not enter a value here, you must enter an expiration date each time you receive the lot item.

The default number of days is the number of days for which an item can remain in inventory before it should be consumed. The system uses the number that you enter to calculate the **Best Before Date** by using one of two different methods, depending on whether the number that you enter in this field is positive or negative. If the value is positive, the system adds the days to the based-on date to determine the best before date for the lot. If the value is negative, the system subtracts the days from the lot expiration date to determine the best before date.

Number of days

The number of days refers to the number of days for which an item must remain in inventory before the system considers the item to be available for sales and manufacturing commitments. To calculate the lot effective date, the system adds the number that you enter in this field to the based-on date that appears in the **Lot Master F4108** table. The system uses this number when calculating and displaying the effective date field in the **Purchase Orders** program (**P4310**) and the **PO Receipts** program (**P4312**).

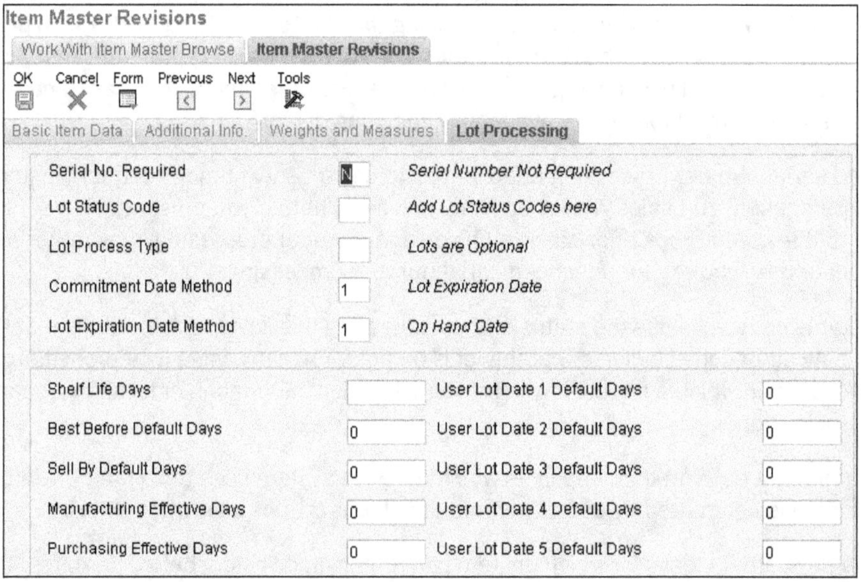

There's more...

- The system uses EA (each) as the primary unit of measure.
- **Category Codes** store additional information for item grouping that is used for reporting and inquiry purposes.
- **Additional System Information** indicates whether the system displays the additional system information form when you add or change information on the **Item Master Revisions (P4101)** form.

See also

- *Item branch/plant setup*

Defining segmented items and templates

Many industries have **base products** that differ from another base product because of packaging components, packaging processes, other attributes, or other differences that can cause costing structures to differ. You are going to create one or more templates for entering **segmented items**.

Getting ready

Before creating the template, you should decide upon the item's segmented category.

How to do it...

1. From the fast path, enter **P410014** and access the **Template Master** application, and then enter the template name.
2. Give a description of the template.
3. Enter the length of a segment.
4. Define the segments.
5. After defining the segments, access **Item Master Processing 11** on the **Process** tab to enable the use of the template.
6. Enter a segmented item.
7. Attach messages to an item, for example any precaution messages or handling notes, and so on.
8. Enter notes for an item.
9. Enter attachments for an item.
10. Assign item responsibility.
11. Enter classification codes.
12. Enter default units of measure for items.
13. Define item unit of measure conversions.
14. Specify a dual unit of measure for an item.
15. Set up the search sequence to use price units of measure.

16. Set up manufacturing information.

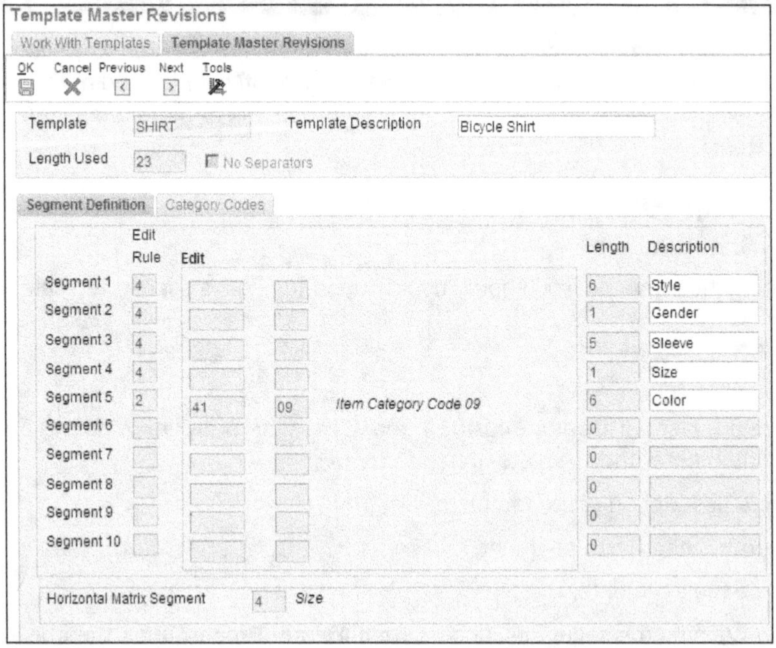

How it works...

You have just created templates for entering segmented items. If the same template is not applicable for all of the segmented items, create a template for each type and name each template appropriately. After you have created a template, you can attach it to the **Item Master Revisions** form if the use templates processing option has been activated.

You can use template names when entering items on the **Item Master Revisions Form**. This name is case-sensitive. If you use any capital letters in the template name when you add it, you must enter those letters in capitals whenever you search for the template or attach it to the **Item Master Revisions Form**.

You should specify whether characters will be used to separate the segments. If you select this control, separators are not used in this template and all 25 character spaces can be allotted to the segmented item number. The length field is used to keep a running total of the number of spaces, including separators, that are used in all of the segments.

See also

- *Defining item information*

Item classification

Items can be classified into groups. The inventory management system provides for numerous purchasing, sales, and distribution classifications. By using these classifications, you can report on purchasing or sales activity using many different facets of item characteristics. These classifications are also used to determine how products move through or reside within the warehouse.

Getting ready

Before defining an item classification, the user-defined codes that are related to the item classification need to be defined in the user-defined codes constants. Define the item category in the **User Defined Codes P0004A** application.

How to do it...

1. Select **EnterpriseOne Menus | Logistics Management | Inventory Management | Daily Processing | Inventory/Master Transactions** | **Item Master.**
2. On the **Work With Item Master (P4101)** browse form, click **Find**.
3. Select the item, and then from the **Row** menu, click on **Category Codes**.
4. Enter the item category codes information.

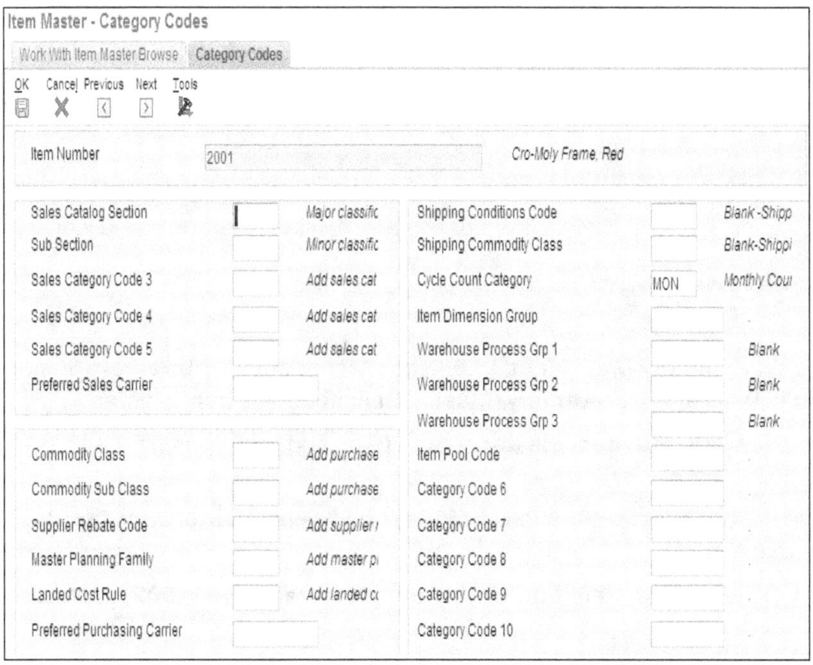

How it works...

The sales catalog and user-defined category code need to be set up for the item property and classification, such as color, material content, brand, and many different classifications. The **User Defined Codes** from **41/S1** to **49/S0** need to be set up. The system uses this code to sort and process like items. This field is one of ten classification categories that are available, primarily for sales purposes. When item classification has been set up you can inquire on a sales order or purchase order based on these category codes. You can make a customized report and also set up standard reports based on the selection of a specific category. These category codes will be stored, including sales order, in the **Sales Order Detail** table F4211, and the **Purchase Order Detail** table F4311, respectively.

There's more...

The **Cycle Count** category represents the family or cycle in which an item is counted. Cycle counting means that you count different inventory items at different times. Cycle codes commonly represent item values, item locations, time frames, or product groups.

Item Unit of Measure (UOM) conversion

It is suggested that you enter the default unit of measure information; it is also required to provide the system with unit of measure conversion information if the item has various units of measure (for example, an item that you stock in both boxes and in crates). You can update conversion information only for items that already exist in the system. For new items, you must select **OK** to save the item, and then select the item on the **Work With Item Master** browse form to return to the item master revisions form.

Getting ready...

You should define the item master before defining any unit of measure conversion information.

How to do it

1. Select **EnterpriseOne Menus | Logistics Management | Inventory Management | Daily Processing | Inventory/Master Transactions | Item Master**.
2. On the **Work With Item Master** browse form, and then search for and select the item number.
3. On the **Item Master Revisions (P4101)** form, select **Conversions** from the form menu.
4. On the **Work With Item Unit of Measure Conversions (P41002)** form, click on **Add**.

5. On the **Item Unit of Measure Conversions** form, click on **Add** and enter the unit of measure From (UoM), Quantity, and Unit of measure To (UoM) in the Item Unit of Measurement Conversion. For example, if you enter EA in the From unit of measure and Box in the To unit of measure then the unit of measure conversion will be Box = 6. (Each is the unit of measurement available in the system, by default.)

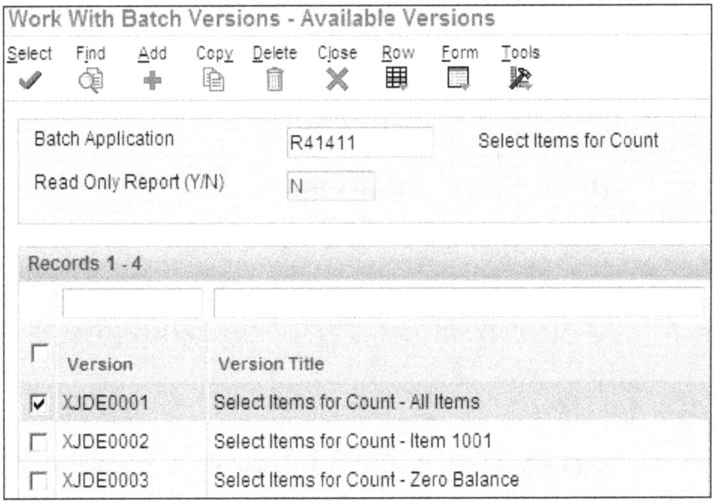

How it works...

After defining a unit of measure conversion, whenever you will create a sales/purchase order. the system will, search the unit of conversion table for the conversion factor. The system stores unit of conversion information in the **Item Unit of Measure Conversion Factors F41002** table. You can search the item quantity by dual unit of measure on item availability. If you change the **UOM (Unit of Measure)** field in the heading area of the **Work With Item Availability (P41202)** form from **EA** (each) to **BX** (boxes), you might expect to see the quantity on hand to be displayed. However, with no display decimals specified, the system does not display decimal quantities. You can also select the price unit of measure during sales order creation. The dual picking process specifies whether the system uses the primary or secondary unit of measure for a dual unit of measure item for picking, sales order availability checking, and splitting purchase order lines. To use the primary unit of measure, do not select this option. To use the secondary unit of measure, select this option.

There's more...

Dual unit of measure Item use specifies whether the system must maintain inventory balances and record transactions for an item in a secondary unit of measure that does not have a fixed conversion to the primary unit of measure. Typically, you select this option when the item is ordered or sold by a packaged quantity and priced by weight or volume.

Item branch/plant setup

Item branch/plant set-up is required for **Item Branch Plant Setup** application in the item master. Non stock items do not require branch/plant set-up. You can also specify the locations within the branch/plant where the item is stored. The JD Edwards EnterpriseOne system retrieves item information from the item **Branch/Plant Information** before searching the item master information.

Getting ready

Before you complete the tasks in this recipe, you must:

- Set up the origin of imported items in UDC 41/L9
- Set up customs codes in UDC 41/LO
- Enter a value in the country of origin field on the item branch/plant Info form

How to do it...

1. Select **EnterpriseOne Menus | Logistics Management | Inventory Management | Daily Processing | Inventory/Master Transactions | Item Branch/Plant.**
2. On the **Work with Item Branch (P41026)** form, enter the item number and item branch.
3. On the **Cost Revisions (P4105)** form, add **Sales/Inventory Price**, **Purchasing Price**, **Cost Method**, **Description**, and **Unit Cost**.
4. Enter the **Lot/ Serial Number**.

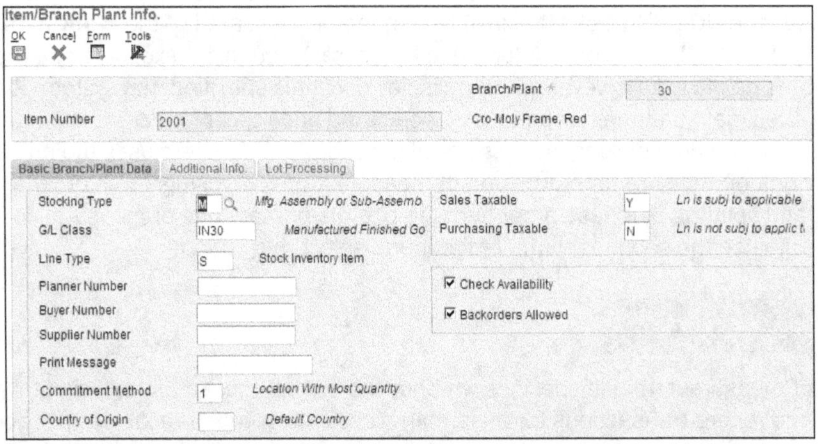

How it works...

We might have item information that applies to items in multiple branches/plants. We can enter item information for one branch/plant and then duplicate the information for as many as ten other branches/plants either by using the **Item Branch Duplication** program (**P41015**) to select individual items for duplication, or by using the batch program **Item Branch Duplication - Batch Selection (R41826)** to define criteria for items that you want to duplicate.

For both actions, we use processing options to specify the branches/plants for which you are duplicating information. We can also specify which information to duplicate, such as costs, prices, units of measure, and so on. For either procedure, the system sends a message to the employee work center when the duplication process is completed.

When you duplicate item information, the system does not duplicate the primary location for an item. The system uses the blank location that you have set up for the branch/plant to which you are duplicating the information.

If you use item branch duplication to select individual items for duplication, you can set processing options to display up to four search fields to enable you to locate items for a particular branch/plant.

There's more...

1. **Category codes** specify whether to display the category codes form when you add or change information.
2. **Quantities** specify whether to display the quantities form when you add or change information.
3. **Additional system information** specifies whether to display the additional system information form when you add or change information.
4. **Item profile revisions** specify whether to display the item profile revisions form when you add or change information.
5. **Cost revisions** specify whether to display the cost revisions form when you add or change information.
6. **Price revisions** specify whether to display the price revisions form when you add or change information.
7. After you assign an item to a branch/plant, you can specify multiple locations in which the item resides. For each branch/plant, it is required to assign the primary location. You can also assign a secondary location for each item.

Item costing and pricing

Cost information determines:

- Whether the system maintains one overall cost for the item or a different cost for each branch/plant
- The cost method that system uses to track inventory costs
- The cost method that system uses for purchase orders

This recipe will provide you with an overview of item cost setup and how to do it.

Getting ready

You should get ready to provide cost information for items in order to track inventory costs.

How to do it...

1. Assign a cost level to an item. From the **Item/Branch (P41026)**, select the item and select the **Cost Revision (P4105)** form row menu.
2. Assign a cost method to an item. Select **Last In**, **Standard** cost, and **Weighted Average** cost on the **item's Cost Revision** application, and enter the item cost.
3. Enter manufacturing setup **Cost Information (09)** for manufacturing items.
4. Set up the costing method for **Sales/Inventory** as *02* and for **Purchasing** as *01* on the **Cost Revisions (P4105)** form.

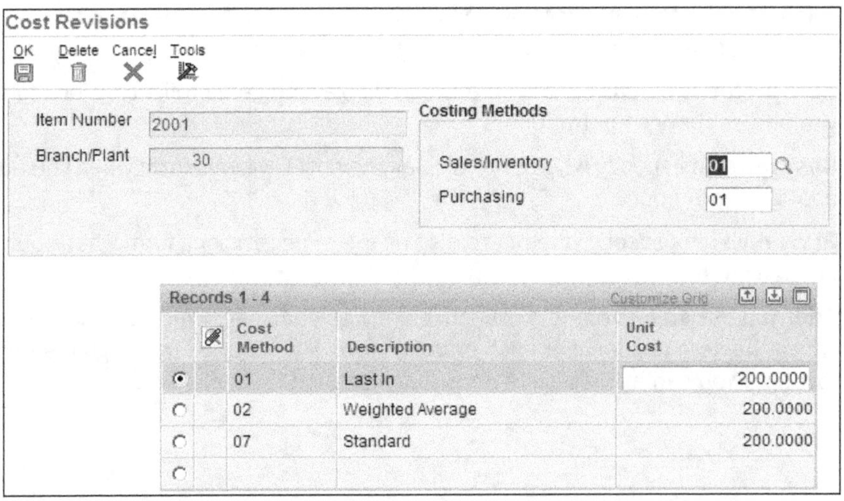

How it works...

For each cost method that you assign to an item, you must also specify a cost. For example, to use the last-in cost method for an item, you must enter an initial cost for that cost method. The system updates the last-in cost based on the cost of the item as of the last receipt date. The system stores inventory cost records in the **F4105** table.

You can also define a different cost for each location and lot within a branch/plant. The level at which you assign a cost to an item determines whether the system maintains costs at the lot, location, branch/plant, or master level. The cost level also determines how you locate the item to which to assign cost methods and enter item costs. For example, you can locate the item based on the item level or based on the item and branch/plant level, or based on the item, branch, and location level.

You can also indicate from which table the system is to retrieve a cost for an item when you enter a purchase order. The purchase price level that you specify for an item indicates which of these costs to use for inventory costs for the item, which are stored in the **Item Cost F4105** table, and supplier's cost for the item, which are stored in the **Supplier Price/Catalog F41061** table.

Cost methods for items should specify the cost method that the system uses to determine an item's cost for sales and cost of goods sold for purchase orders.

The system provides eight predefined cost methods. You can define your own cost methods by using **User-Defined Codes**, although cost methods 01 through 19 are reserved.

If you do not enter an item cost for the cost methods that you assign to sales, inventory, and purchasing, the system displays a warning message. If you ignore the warning, the system assigns a zero cost for the cost method. When you review costs for an item, the system displays only those methods for which you entered an amount.

If you change the amount for the cost method that you use to track costs of goods sold, the system applies the new amount to the on-hand quantity of the item. It also creates journal entries to record the difference between the old and the new amounts. Certain programs update the amount for cost methods 01 through 08. For last-in, or cost method 01, the system interactively updates this amount based on the last cost of the item at the time of receipt. For weighted average, or cost method 02, the system calculates and updates this amount by adding transaction quantities together, adding transaction costs together, and dividing the total cost by the total quantity. You cannot use the weighted average cost method (02) for the sales/inventory cost method with stocking types C or R.

For actual cost, or cost method 09, the system calculates the cost of the product built on a work order or rate schedule based on the actual hours used and the actual quantity of parts issued. The system updates the cost based on the most current information. You cannot use the actual cost method (09) for the sales/inventory cost method with stocking types C or R.

The system also updates last-in, purchasing, and lot costs via the **PO Receipts** program. Purchasing cost is updated by the **Voucher Match Program (P4314)**.

The additional cost methods must be updated manually. You can delete a cost method for an item if it is no longer applicable. If you try to delete the sales, inventory, or purchasing cost method, the system displays a warning message. The system does not delete the cost method, but assigns a zero cost for the cost method.

There's more...

The system also updates these costs:

- Last-in, purchasing, and lot costs are updated by the **PO Receipts program (P4312)**
- Purchasing cost is updated by the **Voucher Match program (P4314)**

If you create additional cost methods, you must update their amounts manually.

See also

- *Item branch/plant setup*

2
Inventory Transactions, Item Quantity, and Physical Inventories

In this chapter, we will cover:

- Issuing inventory
- Adjusting inventory
- Transferring inventory
- Item and quantity information
- Locating item and quantity information
- Defining search criteria
- Item Ledger Inquiry (CARDEX)
- Reviewing supply-and-demand information
- Physical inventory processing with cycle counts
- Processing tag counts

Introduction

In this chapter, you will see how to perform inventory transactions such as inventory issuing (**P4112**), inventory transfers (**P4113**) and adjustments (**P4114**), how to review inventory quantity information, and how to perform physical inventory through cycle count and tag count.

You can accurately plan for future stocking needs by reviewing stock information, reviewing supply/demand information, and reviewing inventory item balances. To help you manage the complex transactions that are involved in maintaining an up-to-date inventory, you might need to record inventory movements between branches/plants and between locations in a branch/plant through an inventory transaction. You can also improve the accuracy of inventory by reducing back orders, reducing monetary amounts of inventory, and increasing on-time deliveries. You can use both cycle and tag counts to satisfy a variety of needs. Both help you to reconcile the online inventory records with the physical inventory.

Issuing inventory

Issuing inventory typically involves removing items from a branch/plant or location, adjusting the inventory balance, and recording the transaction in the GL. Setup for inventory issues is done through the **Inventory Issue Application (P4112)** processing option.

Getting ready

Before you complete the tasks in this recipe, you must:

- Verify the Item and branch/plant information in the item branch file (**F4102**) and the item location file **F41021** tables
- Set up general ledger accounts in the account master **F0901** table
- Set up processing options for **Inventory Issues (P4112)**

How to do it...

1. You can access the processing option of **P4112** by accessing the **EnterpriseOne Menus | Logistics Management | Inventory Management** | **Inventory Management** | **Daily Processing** | **Inventory Master/Transaction** and click on the arrow on **Issues** and then click on **Values**.
2. Enter a code from **UDC 00/DT** that specifies the document type. The default document type is typically **II (Inventory Issues)**. You can enter the document type or select it from the **Select User Defined Code** form. The system does not provide any default value.
3. Specify whether the system supplies default values for the **Location** and **Lot** serial fields.

4. Specify the version of the journal entries program to use when you access the program from the row menu of the **Work With Inventory Issues** form.
5. Specify the version of the item ledger inquiry program to use when you access the program from the row menu of the **Work With Inventory Issues** form.
6. Specify the version of the manual replenishments program to use when you access the program from the form menu of the **Work With Inventory Issues** form.
7. Specify whether equipment and subledger information appears in the detail area of the **Work With Inventory Issues** form.
8. **Issue Quantity** specifies whether to allow an issue quantity that is greater than the available quantity, which could result in a negative on-hand quantity. Leave this processing option blank in order to avoid the **Available** and **On-hand Quantity** becoming negative.
9. **Lots on Hold** specifies whether the system allows the issue of lots that are on hold. If the lot status code field on the item/branch plant information form is blank, then the lot is not on hold. Leave this processing option blank in order to avoid issuing lots that are on hold.
10. Use the **Item Sales History Processing** option to update the **Item History Table (F4115)** if you use the Inventory Management system, and do not use the Sales Order Management system.
11. The **Secondary Quantity Unit of Measure** option in the **Inventory Constants** field appears on data entry screens. For the secondary UOM (Unit of Measure), enter a code from **UDC 00/UM** that indicates an alternate unit of measure for the item.

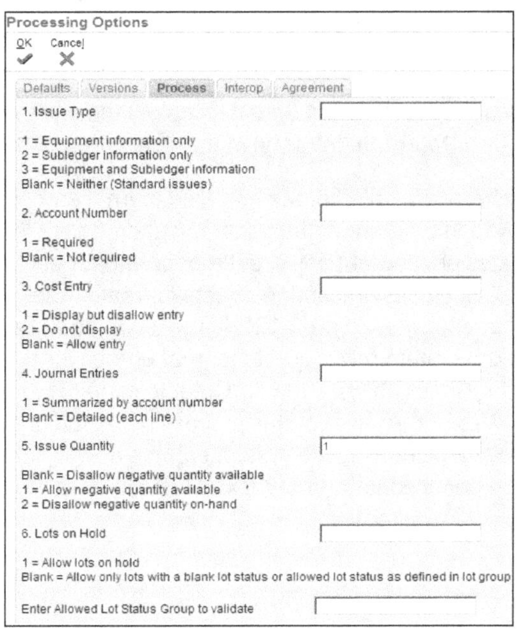
Processing Options

OK Cancel

Defaults | Versions | Process | Interop | Agreement

1. Issue Type

1 = Equipment information only
2 = Subledger information only
3 = Equipment and Subledger information
Blank = Neither (Standard issues)

2. Account Number

1 = Required
Blank = Not required

3. Cost Entry

1 = Display but disallow entry
2 = Do not display
Blank = Allow entry

4. Journal Entries

1 = Summarized by account number
Blank = Detailed (each line)

5. Issue Quantity: 1

Blank = Disallow negative quantity available
1 = Allow negative quantity available
2 = Disallow negative quantity on-hand

6. Lots on Hold

1 = Allow lots on hold
Blank = Allow only lots with a blank lot status or allowed lot status as defined in lot group

Enter Allowed Lot Status Group to validate

How it works...

The system processes the transaction and displays the document number, document type, and batch number for the transaction. For zero unit cost, the system changes the Unit Cost field to zero and the Extended Amount field to blank. The fields are not available for entry. When you move the cursor to the next row, the program uses the default values in the **Item Cost File (F4105)** to complete the unit cost and extended amount fields. To issue inventory, you must enter transaction, item, and accounting information. You can also enter issue-related information for each branch/plant in which an item is stored.

When you enter a transaction, the system displays a document type, batch number, and document number.

> Record the document number so that you can locate the transaction later.

Depending on how you set the processing options, you may be able to issue a quantity that is greater than the on-hand quantity for the parent item in a kit. The system displays the parent quantity as a negative number. You can correct an issue that was made in error by creating a reversing entry. Because records of each inventory transaction are kept for accounting purposes, you cannot delete the record. A reversing entry enters a positive quantity and cost amount back into the item information.

When you select subledger information from the form menu, the account information form displays the fields for account number and subledger information, but does not display the equipment field.

The account number specifies whether the system requires the entry of account numbers (for example, **Business Unit.Object.Subsidiary**) in the detail area of the inventory issues form.

Journal entries specify whether detailed or summarized journal entries should be created from the **Inventory Issues** (**P4112**) program in the general ledger. If detailed journal entries are created, the system creates one journal entry (debit or credit) for each detail line in an issue, using a batch type of **N**. This processing option affects journal entries in the F0911 table only. The AAIs that are most commonly used are 4122 (Inventory) and 4124 (Expense or COGS). If you use standard costs, the system might create journal entries for the variance based on AAI item 4141 (Inventory or Expense COGS). The **F4111** table contains information for each detail line in each issue regardless of the value of this processing option. If summarized journal entries by account number are created, the system creates a summarized debit total and a summarized credit total per account number for all lines in an issue.

There's more...

For example, a company that operates a consignment warehouse might use the **P4112** program only to reduce inventory. However, the company might want to review historical information about issues by reviewing buyer information, which you can access from the **Inventory Inquiries Menu (G41112)**. If you are using the sales order management system, the system can update the **Item History (F4115)** table as a result of sales transactions that are part of the sales updating process.

Tasks that relate to issuing inventory...

- Recording the use of inventory items by an operating department in the company.
- Removing obsolete or damaged goods.
- Issuing inventory to a job.
- Charging inventory that is used for the repair or maintenance of equipment.
- Copying a bill of materials list for an issue.

See also

- *Setting up inventory transactions* in *Chapter 1, Inventory Management*

Adjusting inventory

Inventory adjustments are used to increase or decrease the on-hand quantity and the cost of inventory items in a branch/plant without conducting a complete physical inventory. The major setup for inventory adjustment is, to set up the processing options for the **Inventory Adjustment Application (P4114)**.

Getting ready

Before you complete the tasks in this recipe, you should verify that the following information is set up:

- Item and branch/plant information in the **F4102** and **F41021** tables
- GL accounts in the **F0901** table
- Processing options for **Inventory Adjustment (P4114)**

How to do it...

1. You can access the processing option of P4112 by accessing the **EnterpriseOne Menus | Logistics Management** | **Inventory Management** | **Daily Processing** | **Inventory Master/Transaction** and click on the arrow on **Adjustments** and then click on **Values**.
2. For document type setup, enter a code from **UDC 00/DT** that specifies the default document type for inventory adjustments. Typically, the default is document type **IA (Inventory Adjustments)**. The system does not enter any default document type.
3. Define the primary location as the default location when entering adjustments.
4. Specify the version of the journal entries program to use when you access it from the row menu on the **Work With Inventory Adjustments** form or from the form menu on the **Inventory Adjustments** form.
5. Use the item ledger processing option to determine which version of the **Item Ledger Inquiry (CARDEX)** program **(P4111)** the system uses when you access it from the row menu on the **Work With Inventory Adjustments** form or from the **Form** menu on the **Inventory Adjustments** form. If you leave this processing option blank, the system uses version **ZJDE0001**.
6. Specify the version of the Manual Replenishments program (P46100) to use when you access it from the form menu on the **Inventory Adjustments** form. If you leave the processing option blank, the system will assign version **ZJDE0001** automatically.
7. Cost entry specifies whether to display the unit cost and extended amount fields on the inventory adjustments form and whether they can be updated. Select a value of **1** to display the fields with default values from the **Item Cost Table (F4105)** but not allow them to be updated. A value of **2** displays the field; if you leave this processing option blank the system allows you to override cost information.
8. A Lot and Layering Fields option determine whether to display the lot information fields on the forms and whether they can be updated. Select a value of **1** to Display and Allow Entry or **2** to Display and Protect the field; if you leave this processing option blank the system does not display the field.
9. The adjustment quantity specifies the way the system validates a transaction that results in a negative quantity. Leave this processing option blank. If you select **1** the system allows you to adjust the negative quantity from **Available**; if you select **2** the system will allow you to adjust the negative quantity from **On-hand**.
10. The **Lots on Hold** option specifies whether to enable adjustments to lots that are on hold. If the lot status code field on the item/branch plant information form is blank, the lot is not on hold. Leave this processing option blank in order to avoid issuing lots that are on hold.

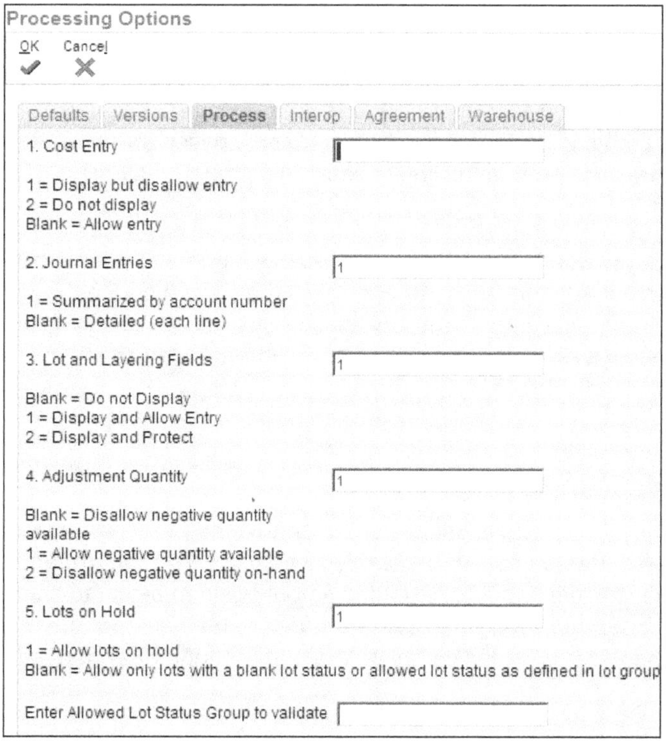

How it works...

The **Inventory Adjustments Program (P4114)** enables you to enter an adjustment for the parent item, although the system does not update quantity information for the components. To adjust inventory, you must enter **Transaction**, **Item**, and **Lot Information**. You can enter adjustment information for each branch/plant in which an item is stored. When you enter a transaction, the system displays a document type, batch number, and document number. Record the document number so that you can locate the transaction later.

You can correct an adjustment that was made in error by entering a **Reversing Entry**. Because the system records each inventory transaction for accounting purposes, you cannot delete the record. A reversing entry enters a negative quantity and cost amount back into the item information.

You can use the primary location as the default only if all secondary locations have a physical location (for example, aisle and bin). If any of the secondary locations have a blank location or lot, you cannot set the primary location as the default.

The **Inventory Adjustments Program (P4114)** creates a transaction with a Batch Type of **N**. This processing option affects journal entries for the **F0911** table only. The **AAIs (Automatic Accounting Instruction)** that are most commonly used are **4122 (Inventory Valuation Account)** and **4124 (Expense or Cost of Goods Sold Account)**. If you use standard costs, the system might create journal entries for the variance, based on **AAI 4141**. The **F4111** table contains entries for each detail line in each adjustment, regardless of how you set this processing option.

Journal entries specify whether detailed or summarized journal entries are created for the general ledger. For summarized journal entries, the system creates a summarized debit total and a summarized credit total by account number for each line in an adjustment. For detailed journal entries, the system creates one journal entry (debit or credit) for each line in an adjustment.

There's more...

The system changes the unit cost field to zero to enable the zero cost, select the row, and select Zero Cost from the row menu. To disable zero cost, select the row and select Cancel Zero Cost from the row menu for the Extended Amount field to be set to blank. The fields are not available for entry. When you move the cursor to the next row, the program uses the default value in the **F4105** table to complete the unit cost and extended amount fields.

You can set up processing options to provide default values and to display cost and lot information. The lot information that appears depends on how you set up duplicate lot processing in **System Constants**.

See also

- *Setting up inventory transactions* in *Chapter 1, Inventory Management*

Transferring inventory

This recipe provides an overview of inventory transfer and discusses how to:

- Set processing options for Inventory Transfers (P4113)
- Transfer inventory

Getting ready

Before you complete the tasks in this recipe, verify that the following information is set up:

- Item and branch/plant information in the F4102 and F41021 tables
- General ledger accounts in the F0901 table
- Processing options for Inventory Transfer (P4113)

How to do it...

1. Enter a code from **UDC 00/DT** that specifies the default document type for transfers. The default document type is typically **IT (Inventory Transfers)**.
2. Specify the **FROM Location/Lot** processing option to define the primary location and lot as the default location that the **Inventory Transfers** Program (P4113) uses for the **From Location** and **From Lot/Serial** fields.
3. Specify the **TO Location/Lot** processing option to define the primary location and lot as the default location that is provided by the **Inventory Transfers Program** (**P4113**), in the **To Location** and **To Lot Number** fields.

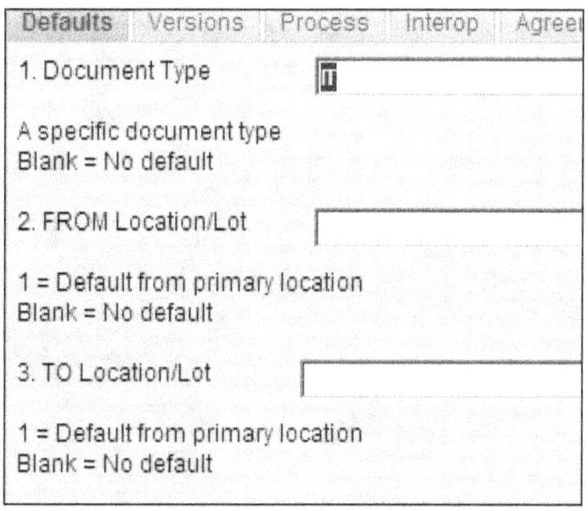

4. For the **Journal Entries** form (P0911), specify the version of the journal entries program to use when you access it from the **Row** menu on the **Work With Inventory Transfers** form or from the **Form** menu on the **Inventory Transfers** form.
5. For the **Item Ledger** form (P4111), specify the version of the **Item Ledger Inquiry** (**CARDEX**) program to use when you access it from the **Row** menu on the **Work With Inventory Transfers** form or from the **Form** menu on the **Inventory Transfers** form.
6. For cost entry, specify whether to display the **To Unit Cost** and **Extended Amount** fields on the inventory transfers form.

7. For **Journal Entries**, specify whether to use detailed or summarized journal entries in the general ledger from inventory transfers.
8. For **Lots on Hold**, specify whether to enable transfers from and to lots that are on hold. If the lot status code field on the item/branch plant information form is blank, the lot is not on hold.
9. Enter the lot group name to process **On-hold** items with an allowed lot status. The system validates the lot status code against the specified lot status group setup in **Allowed Lot Status Setup Program (P41081)**.
10. For transfer quantities, specify whether to enable transfer that result in a negative **On-hand** quantity. These are transfers for which, the quantity of the transfer is greater than the **On-hand** quantity.

> **CARDEX** is an alternate name for the **Item Ledger Inquiry (P4111)** program.

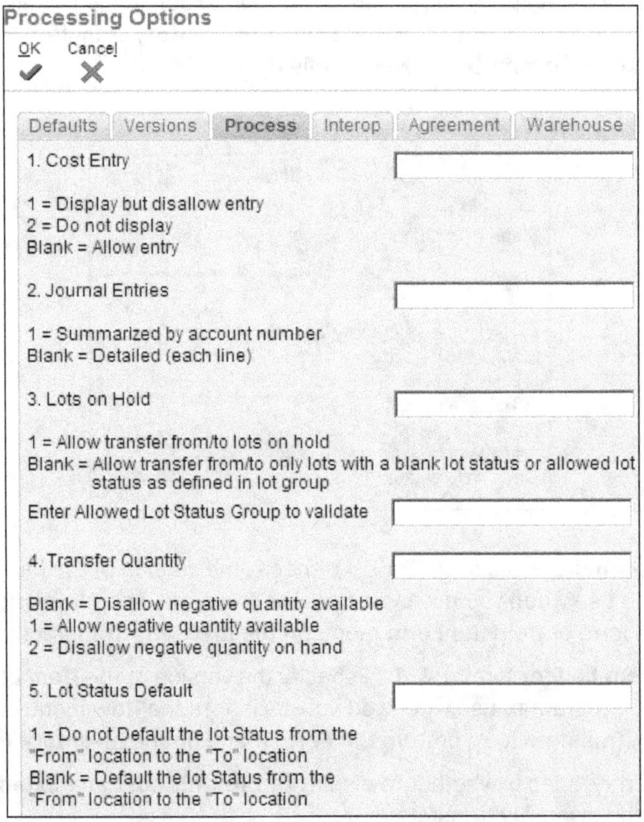

How it works...

An inventory transfer creates two journal entries in the **GL (General Ledger)**. The first journal entry decreases inventory at the original location. The second entry increases inventory at the destination location. Inventory transactions will be performed by using the **P4113** application.

To transfer inventory, you must enter transaction and item information for both the original and destination locations. You can set up processing options to provide default values and to display cost information. If you transfer inventory from a location that results in a quantity of zero but is still associated with an amount, the system automatically creates journal entries to the appropriate accounts to balance the amount to zero.

You can correct a transfer that was made in error by entering a reversing entry. Because the system records each inventory transaction for accounting purposes, you cannot delete the record. A reversing entry enters a positive quantity and cost back into the item information at the original location and a negative quantity and amount to the item at the destination location.

There's more...

You can use the primary location as the default only if all of the secondary locations have a physical location (for example, aisle and bin). If any of the secondary locations have a blank location or lot, you cannot set the primary location as the default.

Summarized journal entries

For summarized journal entries, the system creates a summarized debit total and credit total per account number for all lines in a transfer. For detailed journal entries, the system creates one journal entry (debit or credit) for each detail line in a transfer. The batch type that the inventory transfers program creates is **N**. This processing option affects journal entries for the **F0911** table only. The AAIs (automatic accounting instruction) that are most commonly used are **4122** (Inventory) and **4124** (Expense or COGS). If you use standard costs, the system might create journal entries for the variance, based on AAI **4141** (Inventory or Expense/ COGS). The **F4111** contains entries for each detail line in each transfer regardless of the way that you set this processing option.

See also

- *Setting up inventory transactions in Chapter 1, Inventory Management.*

Item and quantity information

You can accurately plan for future stocking needs by reviewing information that the system provides about both the item and the quantity. For example, you can:

- Access information about stock items
- Access summary and detailed information about on-hand, committed, and available items
- Access item information about previous sales, current inventory quantities, and future receipts
- Review balance forward records for a specific fiscal year
- Reconcile inventory balances with the general ledger (GL), and access detailed item transaction information
- Compare the inventory balances at the end of one period with the same period end for the GL

Getting ready

Before you complete the tasks in this recipe, you must:

- Set up the system to calculate availability for Manufacturing Processes if you are using the JD Edwards EnterpriseOne Product Data Management system
- Set up location segments, in order for information to be available
- Verify that the system is set up to calculate availability for inventory items

How to do it...

1. On the **Work With Item Availability** form from the **Inventory Management Inquiry** menu, enter the item number for reviewing item quantities.
2. Enter the branch/plant number for searching for a specific branch/plant.
3. Review the item quantities, such as **On-hand**, **Available**, **Committed**, and so on.
4. Click on **Summary** to review the quantity at the branch/plant level.

How it works...

Item Availability is the number of items that you can use based on user-defined calculations. You determine how the system calculates item availability by defining the factors that subtract from or add to the available quantity of an item. This calculation can include quantities that do not immediately affect on-hand amounts. For example, you can set up the availability calculation to subtract any quantities that are committed to sales or work orders, and add any quantities that are on purchase orders or in transit.

Available to Promise (ATP) refers to the number of items that are uncommitted (available for sales or distribution) until the next replenishment orders arrive. You select whether to use the basic method or the cumulative method to determine ATP. The basic method assumes customer demand only, such as sales orders. It also fulfills demand for all periods until the next replenishment order arrives, such as purchase orders. You can review the number of items that are in a specific lot, as well as the activity dates, item quantities, and hold statuses that pertain to the lot. The activity date and quantity information reflect transactions such as issues, receipts, and sales. If the same item or lot appears more than once, then the item exists in multiple locations. You can locate the on-hand quantity and accounting information for a specific transaction date and document number in the **Item Ledger Inquiry (CARDEX) (P4111)**. The **Item Ledger Inquiry (CARDEX)** contains transaction history such as sales, receipts, and transfers for each item in inventory. Each entry represents a transaction that affects the on-hand quantity of an item. You can review a transaction to determine both item quantities and the related costs, for any branch, location, or lot as of a particular date. You can also see any transactions for that item that have taken place as of a specific date and locate information about quantities that are deducted from the on-hand quantity.

There's more...

When you create transactions such as issues, transfers, and adjustments, you can locate item information and return this information to the transaction that you are creating. Locating and returning information such as location, lot number, grade, potency, expiration date, and lot status code can save you entry time and reduce errors. Use the **Item Search Returns Quantity Program (P40ITM2)** to locate and return the information for items to the **Transaction Entry** form, that is. **Inventory Issue (P4112)**, and **Inventory Adjustment (P4114)**. If you use quality mode, only branches/plants and grade and potency information that is specified in the customer preferences are available.

Item search

You can locate item information using criteria that you define for each branch/plant. After you locate the item information, you can also access quantity information about the item. You can define specific criteria for an item search. Use this type of search when you know what the item is, but you want to limit the search. For example, you can limit the search for an item to a specific branch/plant and supplier.

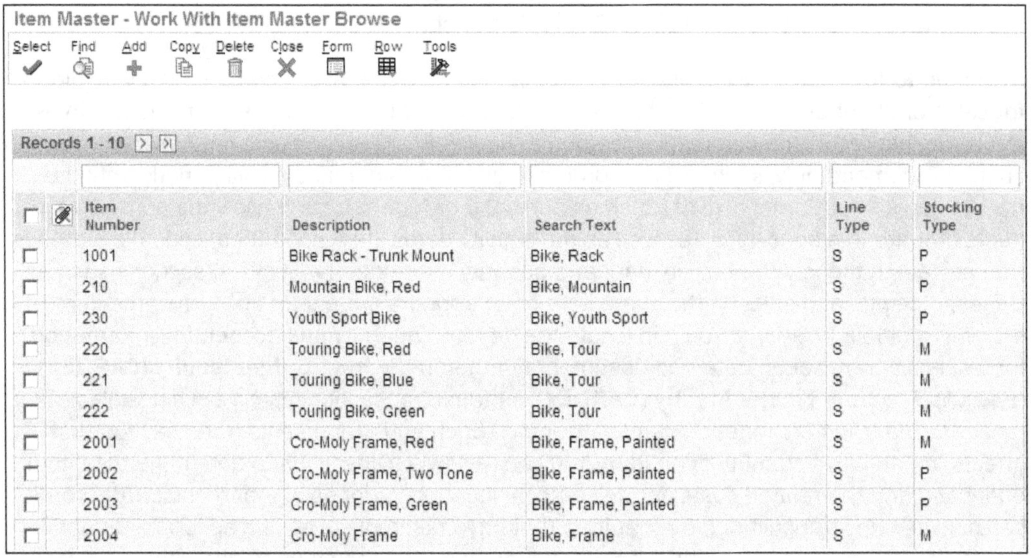

Item Number	Description	Search Text	Line Type	Stocking Type
1001	Bike Rack - Trunk Mount	Bike, Rack	S	P
210	Mountain Bike, Red	Bike, Mountain	S	P
230	Youth Sport Bike	Bike, Youth Sport	S	P
220	Touring Bike, Red	Bike, Tour	S	M
221	Touring Bike, Blue	Bike, Tour	S	M
222	Touring Bike, Green	Bike, Tour	S	M
2001	Cro-Moly Frame, Red	Bike, Frame, Painted	S	M
2002	Cro-Moly Frame, Two Tone	Bike, Frame, Painted	S	P
2003	Cro-Moly Frame, Green	Bike, Frame, Painted	S	P
2004	Cro-Moly Frame	Bike, Frame	S	M

Current inventory levels on the Web

Suppliers can use the Web to enquire about the items that they supply. They can check the availability and on-hand quantity of those items so that they can determine whether to use other programs in supplier self-service to create purchase orders or to issue quotes. Reviewing inventory levels from the Web enables the supplier to maintain a predictable delivery of goods and services, which facilitates better communication and a better working relationship. It also enables the supplier to prepare for future activity, gather information on particular trends, and prepare for surpluses and shortages. Using their item number, suppliers can review information such as **Branch/plant**, **Quantity On-hand**, **Quantity on Purchase Order**, **Location, Lot/Serial Number**, and **Short Item Number**. The supplier can also have the system display the information in detail mode by un-checking the **Summary Only** check box.

Item balance reconciliation with the GL

You can compare the inventory balances to the GL at the end of a period. Because inventory transactions continue after GL periods close, the system provides a method for you to reconcile the inventory balances to the GL for any fiscal period.

See also

- *Locating item and quantity information*

Locating item and quantity information

This recipe provides an outline for locating item and quantity information so that you can:

- Locate item information
- Locate quantity information
- Work with transaction records

Getting ready

For locating item information and quantity you should set up the processing options of **Item Availability Application (P41202)**.

How to do it...

1. From **Inventory Master/Transactions (G4111)** | **Item Master** | **Work with Item Master Browse**, locate Items for Item Master and click **Select** and then **Review Item Master**.
2. On the **Work With Item Master Browse** form, select **Item Word Search** from the **Form** menu | **Item Word Search**, and then enter the item search text.
3. Click **Find** to locate the items.

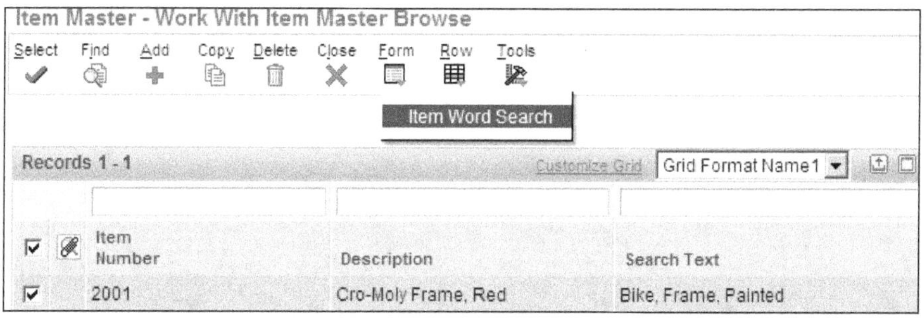

4. Select **Item Search** from the form menu on any of the transaction entry forms, such as **Inventory Adjustments**, **Item Search Returning Quantity (P40ITM2)**, and locate the items for transaction.

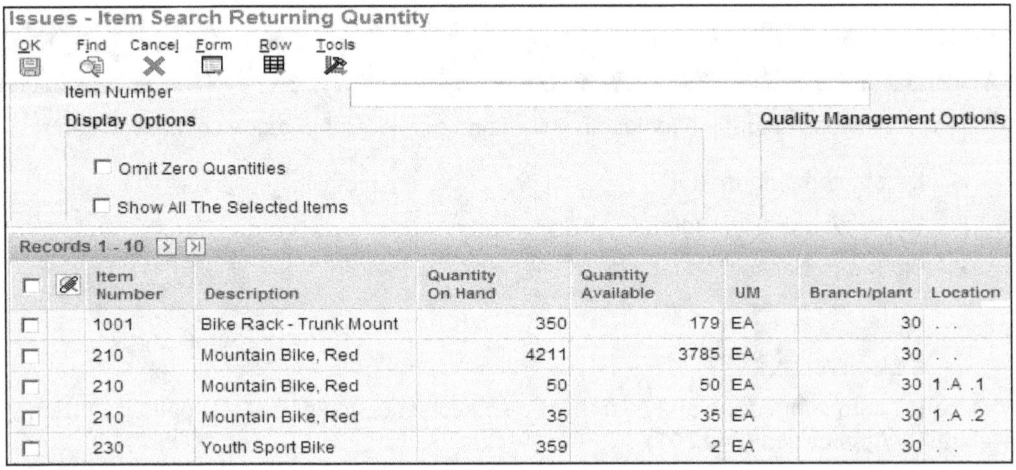

Item Number	Description	Quantity On Hand	Quantity Available	UM	Branch/plant	Location
1001	Bike Rack - Trunk Mount	350	179	EA	30	. .
210	Mountain Bike, Red	4211	3785	EA	30	. .
210	Mountain Bike, Red	50	50	EA	30	1 .A .1
210	Mountain Bike, Red	35	35	EA	30	1 .A .2
230	Youth Sport Bike	359	2	EA	30	. .

5. Select a record from the grid, and then select **Cross Reference** from the **Row** menu on the **Work with Item Search** form. You will see the **Work with Item Cross Reference** for defining the **Search Criteria**.
6. From **Inventory Inquiries (G41112)** | **Item Search** | **Work With Item Search**, enter the search text for finding the correct model and brand of printer.
7. Refer to the following screenshot to set up the processing options for **Item Availability (P41202)**. Click on the arrow for **Summary Availability** and then click on **Values**.

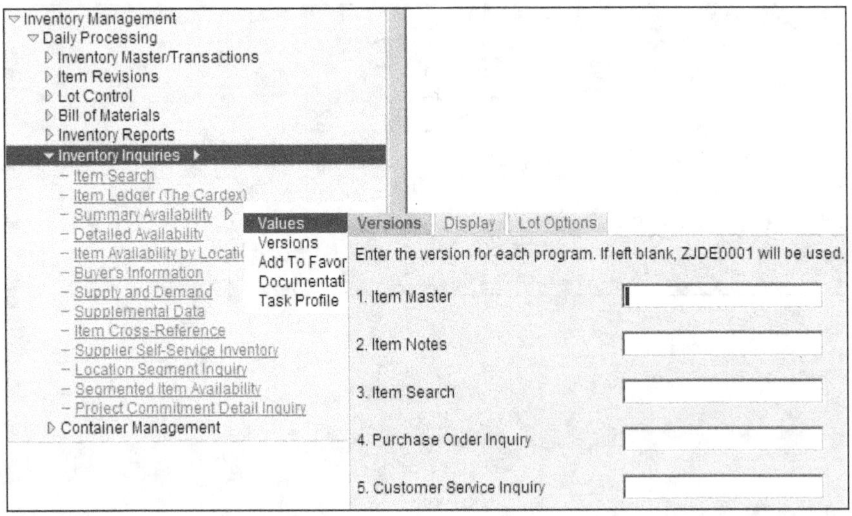

8. On the **Version** tab, leave the processing options blank, and the system will use ZJDE0001 version as a default.
9. On the **Display** tab, select **1** to specify that the system should display quantity information in the primary unit of measure.

How it works...

There are a variety of reasons why you might want to locate item information, such as entering changes to inventory, revising the information that is associated with inventory items, or reviewing available quantities. You can use three methods to locate item information. The method that you select depends on the type of search criteria that you use and where the method is available:

1. The first method is **Locating Items with a Word Search**, which is available when you are using **Item Master** or any transaction entry form (**Issues, Transfers, Adjustments**, and **Reclassifications**).
2. The second method is **Locating and Returning Item Information** which is available when you are using any transaction entry form (**Issues**, **Transfers**, **Adjustments**, and **Reclassifications**).
3. The third method is locating item information with item search, which is available from a search button from the **Item Number** field and from the Inventory Inquiries menu (**G41112**).

The system does not display decimal quantities if the **Display Decimals** field in the **Quantity On Hand-Primary Quantity** (**PQOH**) data item has no display decimals specified. The **Summary Only** checkbox indicates that the system will display information that is summarized by item, company, currency code, and cost rule. If you do not select this checkbox, the system displays individual receipt records. The **Omit Zero Quantities** checkbox indicates that the system does not display information with zero on-hand quantities. If you do not select this checkbox, the system displays information with zero on-hand quantities.

You can locate the item quantity on many different columns of the item availability application.

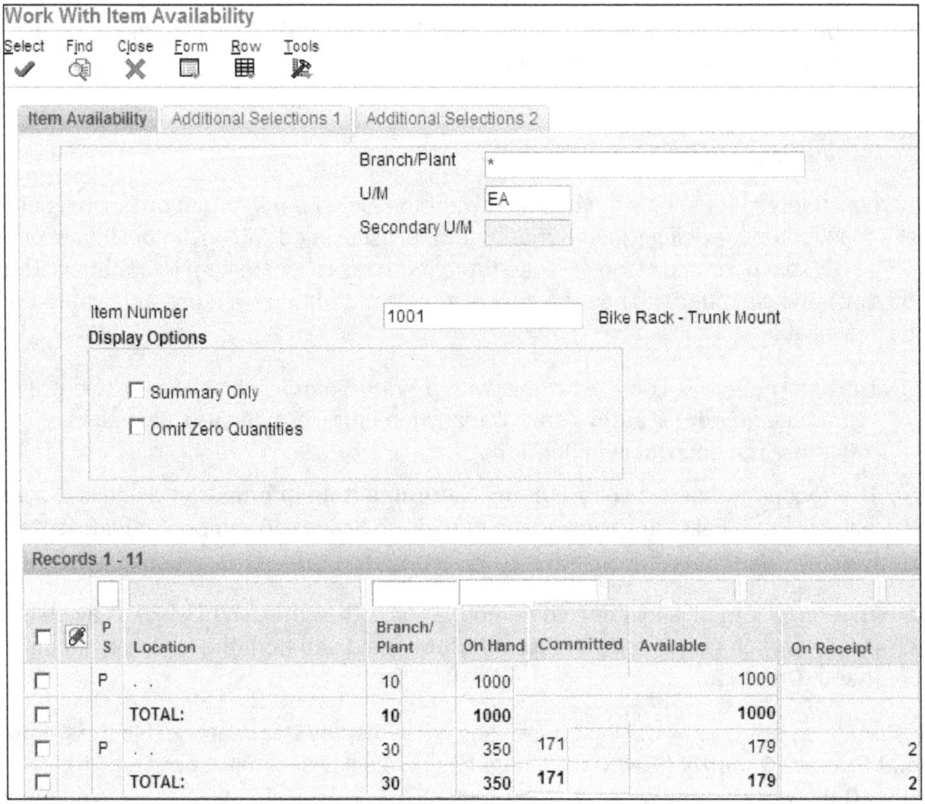

> You can customize the grid to better locate the item and quantity information.

First, you received the quantity at the warehouse, and then you received the quantity in JDE. Through **Receipt Entry**, **Inventory Adjustment**, **Transfer Receipt**, or **Inventory Transfer**, the system will update the on-hand quantity in the **F41021** table. The on-hand inquiry will read the data from **F41021**. The system displays the quantity on-hand in the primary unit of measure. **Committed** shows the total quantity that is committed at a specific location. The total quantity is the sum of all quantities that have been sold, soft committed, or hard committed to sales orders and work orders. You can review the total committed quantity on the **Customer Service Inquiry** form by specifying a status of less than **999**. **Available** shows the quantity that is available. For example, the available quantity might consist of the on-hand quantity minus commitments, reservations, and backorders. Availability is user defined. You can define how availability is calculated in the **Branch/Plant Constants** program (**P41001**).

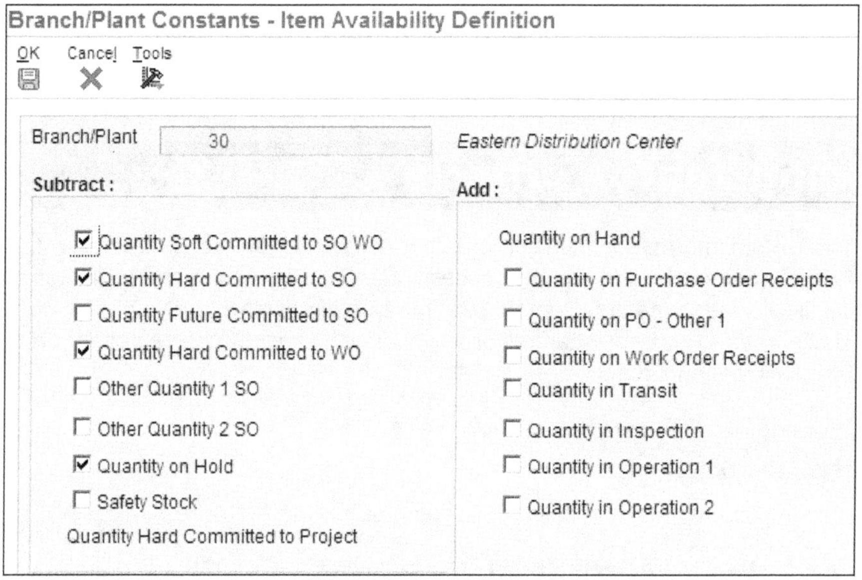

999 is the order activity status that qualifies closed sales orders. If you want to see the open sales orders you need to specify a status of less than 999.

There's more...

Grade Range is a code from **UDC 40/LG** that indicates the minimum grade that is acceptable for an item. The system displays a warning message if you try to purchase or issue items with grades that do not meet the minimum grade acceptable. The system does not allow you to sell items with grades that do not meet the minimum acceptable level.

Potency Range determines whether the system displays the Percent of Life Remaining field. If you do not choose this option, the system does not display the Percent of Life Remaining field.

Location is the only difference between hard commitment and soft commitment. If you issue the quantity from specific location it's called hard commitment, whereas if you issue the quantity from the primary location it's called soft commitment.

See also

- *Item and quantity information*

Defining search criteria

You can locate item information using criteria that you define for each branch/plant. After you locate the item information, you can also access quantity information about the item. You can define specific criteria for an item search. Use this type of search when you know what the item is but you want to limit the search. For example, you can limit the search for an item to a specific branch/plant and supplier.

Getting ready

Before you complete the tasks in this recipe, you must:

- Run the **Item Word Search Build** batch application **(R41829)** to create or update the **Item Word Search table (F41829)**
- Verify that the **Item Cross-Reference** types for cross-reference numbers are set up in **UDC 41/DT**
- Verify that any external item numbers, such as supplier or substitute numbers are set up in the **Item Cross-Reference program (P4104)**
- Verify that you have set up any internal item numbers, such as the second or third item numbers, on the **Item Master Revisions** form
- Set up processing options for **Item Word Search Build (R41829)**

How to do it...

1. For **X-Ref Type**, enter a code from **UDC 41/DT** that identifies the type of cross-reference setup for this customer. The **Cross-Reference** types include substitutes, replacements, and customer or supplier item numbers.
2. On the **Work with Item Cross Reference (P4104)**, click on **Add**, and enter the cross reference type.
3. Enter the Second Item Number for defining the cross reference.
4. Enter the Address Number of the customer or supplier.
5. Enter the **Cross-reference Item Number** that the system assigns to an item number. A cross-reference number enables you to use a supplier's item number if it is different from the own item number when you are processing an order or printing.
6. Enter a **Cross Reference Description** remark about an item.

7. Enter the OEM-assigned **Card Number** value from **UDC 40R/CD** that further describes the part number.

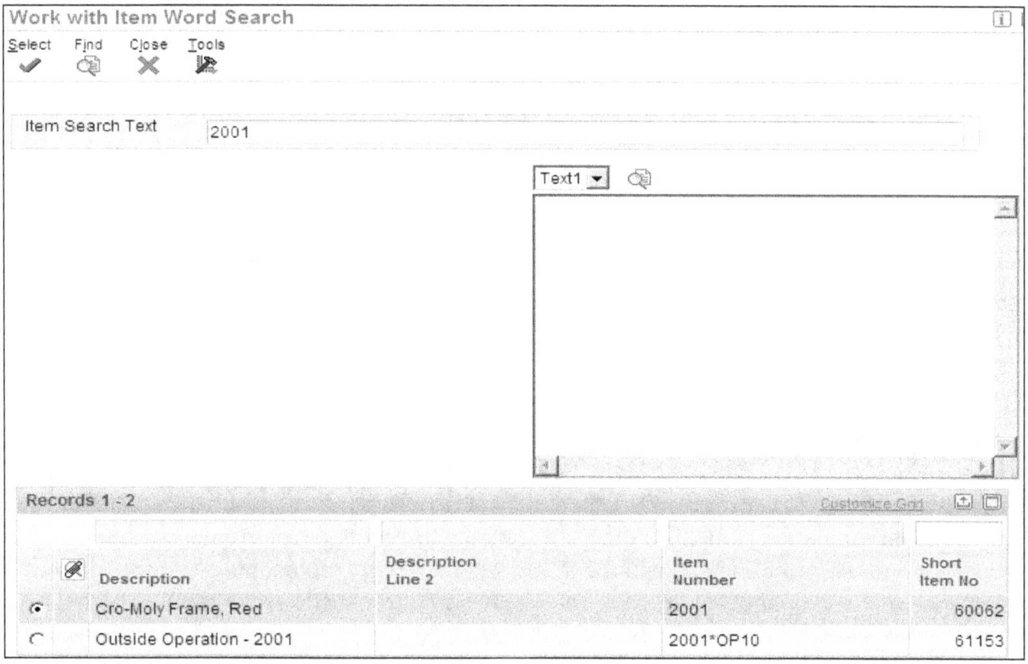

How it works...

When you search for an item using item word search, the system accesses the **Item Word** Search table (**F41829**) for item information. You must run the **Item Word Search Build** (**R41829**) batch application to create and update the **F41829** table. You can run the program for the entire item master or for a specific branch/plant. When you change any of the descriptive (text) information, the system does not update the **Item Word Search** table. The program extracts information from the following tables: **F4101**, **F4102**, **F4100**, **F4108**, **F4101D**, and **F4104**.

You can run the **Item Word Search Build** batch application as often as necessary. For example, you might run the batch application monthly, depending on the number of changes to descriptions. You can set the processing option to clear and completely rebuild the **Item Word Search** table, if appropriate. If you do not clear the table, use data selection to specify the items to update. When you run the report by branch/plant, the processing time is significantly reduced.

There's more...

In order to run the item word search build program you should access batch application (**R41829**) to build the item word search. To run the batch application you should follow the following steps.

1. From the fast path, enter **BV (Batch Version)**.
2. The batch application will open; enter the **Item Word Search** batch application (**R41829**).
3. Click **Select** and then click **Submit**.

See also

- *Item and quantity information*

Item Ledger Inquiry (CARDEX)

The **Item Ledger Inquiry** (**CARDEX**) program contains transaction history such as sales, receipts, or transfers for each item in the inventory. Each entry represents a transaction that affects the on-hand quantity of an item. You can review a transaction to determine both the item quantities and the related costs in any branch, location, or lot as of a particular date. You can also see any transactions for that item that have taken place as of a specific date, and locate information about quantities that are deducted from the **On-Hand** quantity.

Getting ready

Before you complete the tasks in this section, you must:

- Set up the system to calculate availability for manufacturing processes if you are using the JD Edwards EnterpriseOne product data management system
- Set up location segments for information to be available
- Verify that the system is set up to calculate availability for inventory items
- Set up processing options for **Item Ledger Inquiry (P4111)**

How to do it...

1. Enter a code from **UDC 00/DT** that specifies document type. If you leave this processing option blank, * is the default value and all document types appear.
2. In the **Load and Delivery Ledger Inquiry** (**FUTURE**), enter the application or batch version to be used for each program, or leave this processing option blank.

3. Enter *1* on the **Display** tab to show the quantity in the primary units of measure.

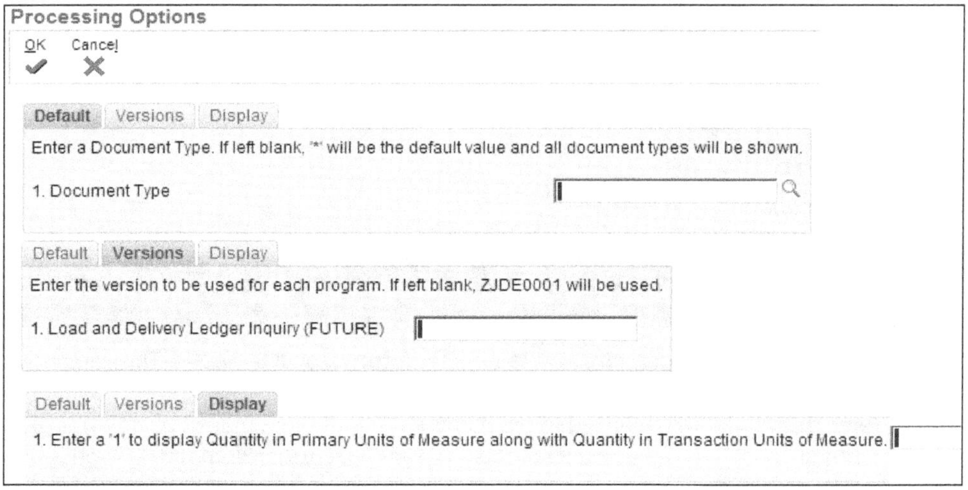

How it works...

The **Item Ledger Inquiry (CARDEX)** contains transaction history, such as sales, receipts, and transfers for each item in inventory. Each entry represents a transaction that affects the on-hand quantity of an item.

You can compare the inventory balances to the GL at the end of a period. Because inventory transactions continue after GL periods close, the system provides a method for you to reconcile the inventory balances to the GL for any fiscal period. The **Item Ledger** fetches the data from the **F4111** table for the **Item Ledger Inquiry** program.

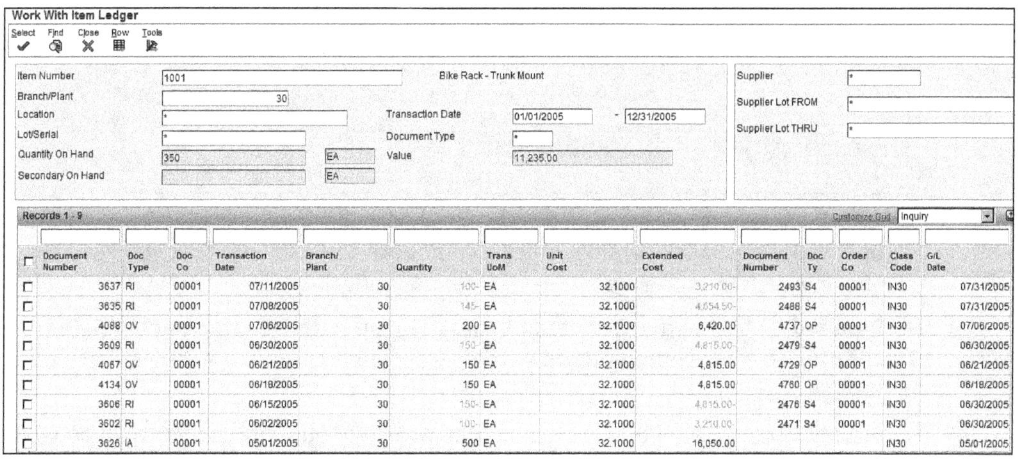

There's more...

Now, let's talk about some other options, or possibly some pieces of general information that are relevant to this task.

See also

- *Item and quantity information*

Reviewing supply-and-demand information

Supply-and-demand information helps you to plan for future stocking needs. This recipe provides a supply-and-demand inquiry to review demand, supply, and available quantities for a specific item. This recipe will help you to provide the general product and item performance for a given branch/plant, as well as past sales performance, current demand, and other item information. The information is based on inventory, purchasing, and sales history.

Getting ready

Before you start, set up processing option for **Supply and Demand Inquiry** (**P4021**).

How to do it...

1. Enter the date that an item is scheduled to arrive or that an action is scheduled for completion.

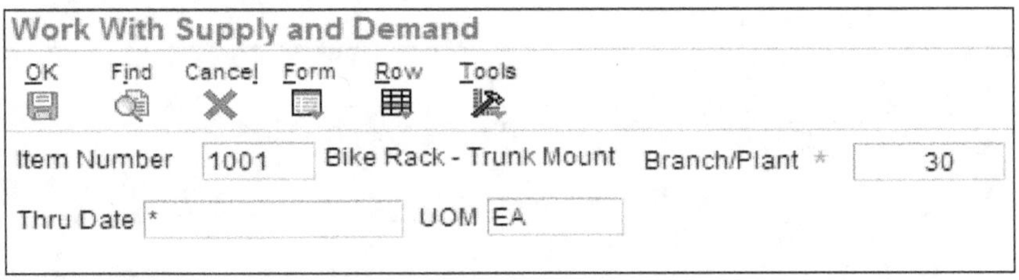

2. For **Unit of Measure Conversion**, enter a code from **UDC 00/UM** that specifies the quantity in which to express an inventory item quantity.
3. For **Demand**, enter the number of units that are committed for shipment in **Sales Order Entry**. Use either the entered or the primary unit of measure that is defined for the item.
4. For **Supply**, enter a value that represents the available quantity, which might consist of the on-hand balance minus commitments, reservations, and backorders. You enter this value in the **Branch/Plant Constants** program (**P41001**).

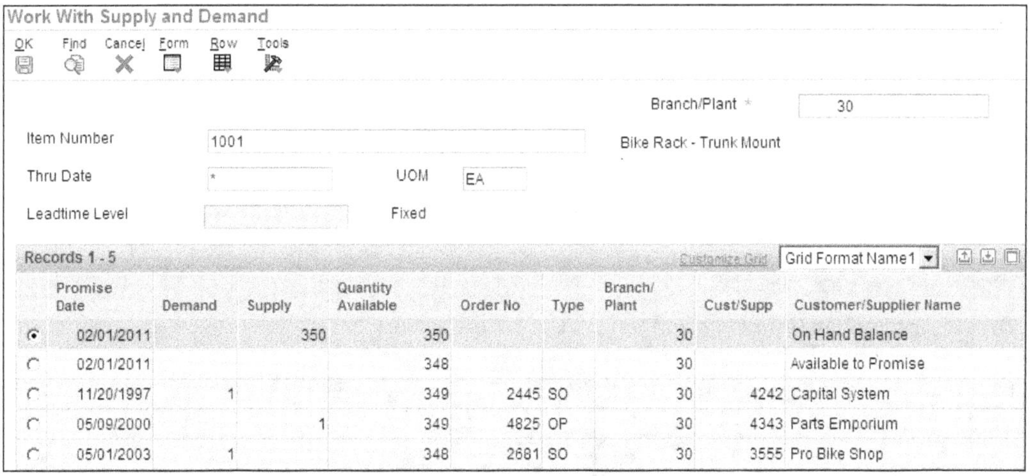

Work With Supply and Demand

OK Find Cancel Form Row Tools

Branch/Plant * 30

Item Number 1001 Bike Rack - Trunk Mount

Thru Date * UOM EA

Leadtime Level Fixed

Records 1 - 5 Customize Grid Grid Format Name1

	Promise Date	Demand	Supply	Quantity Available	Order No	Type	Branch/ Plant	Cust/Supp	Customer/Supplier Name
◉	02/01/2011		350	350			30		On Hand Balance
○	02/01/2011			348			30		Available to Promise
○	11/20/1997	1		349	2445	SO	30	4242	Capital System
○	05/09/2000		1	349	4825	OP	30	4343	Parts Emporium
○	05/01/2003	1		348	2681	SO	30	3555	Pro Bike Shop

5. For **Quantity Available**, enter a number that indicates the quantity that is available. For example, the available quantity might consist of the on-hand quantity minus commitments, reservations, and backorders.
6. For **Order Number**, enter a number that identifies an original document. This document can be a voucher, a sales order, an invoice, unapplied cash, a journal entry, and so on.
7. For **Order Type**, enter a code from **UDC 00/DT** that identifies the type of document. This code also indicates the origin of the transaction.

How it works...

The system considers the Inventory as available based on the planned effective date of the items on the order. When calculating supply from a purchase order, the system calculates availability based on the value in the expected effective date on the purchase order detail line. When calculating supply inventory from a work order, the system calculates availability based on the planned effective date of the work order.

The supply quantities are presented by date and can include on-hand inventory and quantities on purchase orders, manufacturing work orders, planned orders, and rate schedules. Supply quantities without a date or order information represent current availability by branch/plant storage location. The demand quantities are presented by date and can include safety stock, quantities on sales orders, work order parts lists, planned order demand for lower levels, and interplant and forecast demand.

There's more...

The **Available-To-Promise (ATP)** lines on the **Supply/Demand Inquiry** form indicate the company's uncommitted available inventory. Available-to-promise inventory is available for sale or distribution within a specified period. The system displays information from the **F41021, F4211,** and **F4311** tables.

See also

- *Item and quantity information*

Physical inventory processing with cycle counts

Accurate inventories help you to:

- Reduce backorders
- Reduce monetary amounts that are invested in inventory
- Reduce downtime that is attributed to stock outages
- Increase on-time deliveries

Cycle Counts help you to reconcile the online inventory records and the physical inventory. A cycle count is an item-based method of counting inventory. Using the **Cycle Count Process**, you select items to be counted at various intervals throughout the year.

Getting ready

Before you complete the tasks in this section, you must verify that the automatic accounting instructions are set up as follows:

- Maintain the AAI table 4152, which provides the inventory account to offset against any count variance
- Maintain the AAI table 4154, which provides the cost of goods, sold account to update
- Maintain the AAI table 4141, which provides the variance account to update (set up only if you use standard costs)
- Maintain the AAI tables 4122, 4124, 4126, and 4128, which provide the accounts for zero balance adjustments
- Run the select **Select Items for Count (R41411)** batch application

How to do it...

1. Set processing options for **Select Items for Count** (**R41411**).
2. Run the **Select Items for Count** batch application from **Work With Batch Versions - Available Versions (P98305)**.

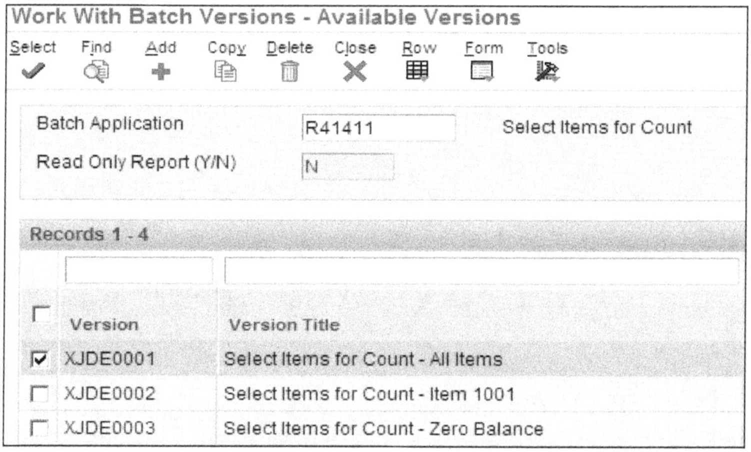

3. Review the output of **R41411**, which generates the selected items for the count report. This lets you compare the actual on-hand quantity with the online records.
4. Select the items to be counted, based on the data selection.
5. Copy the current on-hand balance to the quantity on-hand in the **Count** field in the **F4141** table.
6. Review the cycle count status using **Cycle Count Review (P41240)**, which should be **10**.

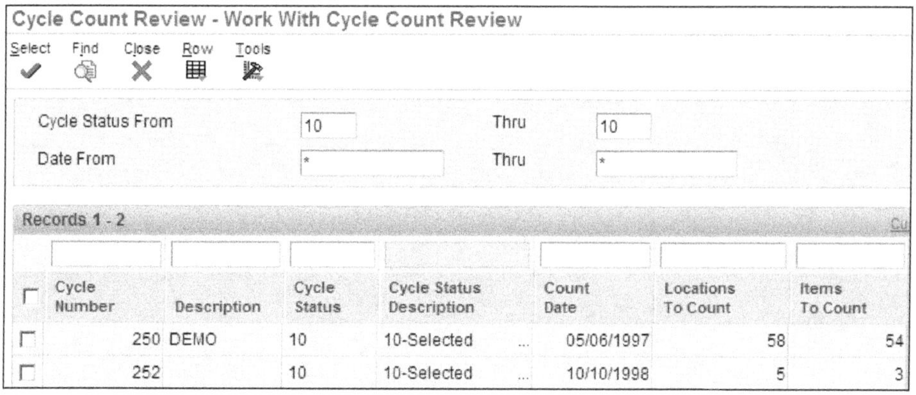

7. Click on **Row** menu **Print Cycle Sheets**.

8. Set processing options for **Print Cycle Count Sheets (R41410A)**.

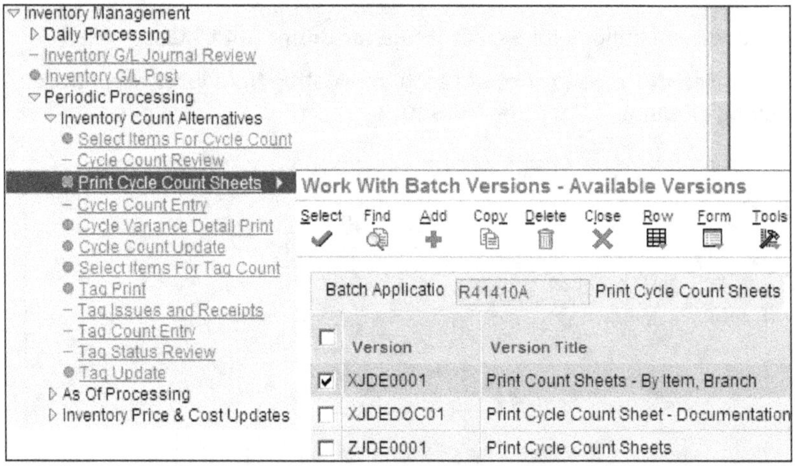

9. On the **Work with Cycle Count Review** form, refresh your screen and review the status of your cycle count.
10. Chose **Enter Cycle Count Results** from the **Row** menu.
11. Click **Find** on the **Menu** option to view all items in the cycle count and enter the counted quantity.
12. Click **Ok** to return to the cycle count review.
13. To review cycle count variances, highlight your cycle count and choose **Cycle Count Detail** from the **Row** menu.
14. Review the quantity counted, which should reflect the numbers that you entered in the previous step.

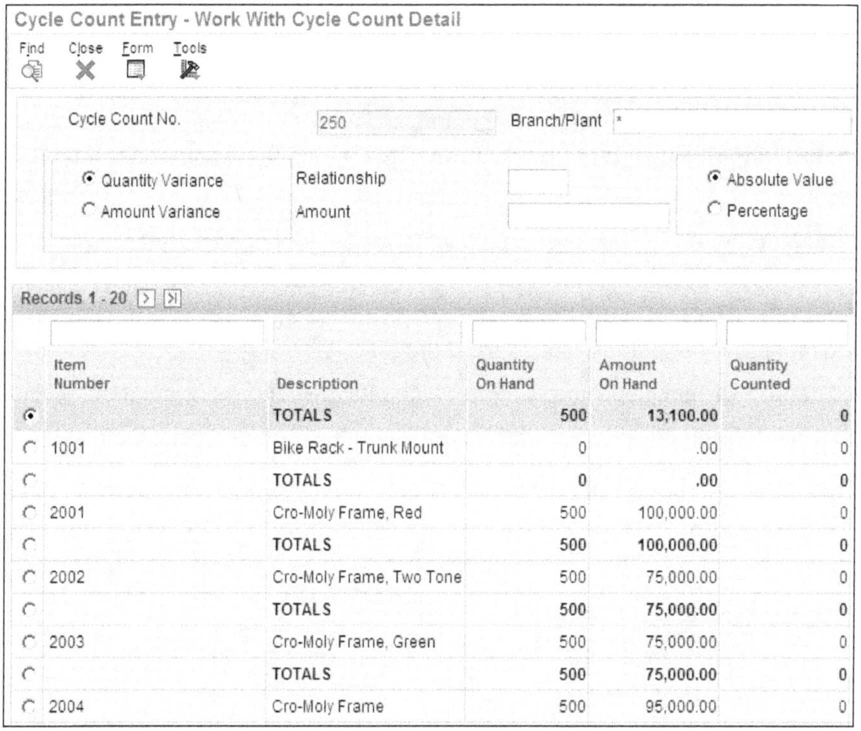

15. To approve the cycle count result, click **Approve Cycle Count** from the **Row** menu.
16. To update the cycle count result on the **Work with Cycle Count Review form**, choose **Update Cycle Count** from the **Row** menu.

How it works...

You can cancel a cycle count at any time before you update it. For example, if several days pass between the times that you print cycle count sheets and actually perform the cycle count, you can cancel the cycle count and reprint it later. After you cancel the cycle count number, the status field displays "Cancelled". After you have performed the cycle count and recorded the information on the cycle count sheets, transfer the results to the online inventory records. Even if the result of the count is zero, you must enter the cycle count results. If the count included an item that is found in a new location, you can add the new location on a blank line of the cycle count entry form, unless the location control constant is turned on for the branch/plant. If the location control constant is turned on, you must set up the new location in the **F4100** table before you can enter the quantity on the **Cycle Count Entry** form.

There's more...

When you run the variance detail report from the **Form** menu, the system uses the variance criteria that are set up on the form and overrides any processing option defaults. When you run the report from the **Inventory Count Alternatives menu**, the system uses the processing options for the version.

- **Absolute Value** specifies whether a variance amount is displayed when it is greater than an absolute value or greater than a percentage of the original
- **Quantity Counted** is the total quantity that has been counted for the item in all locations, in the primary unit of measure
- **Quantity Variance** specifies whether a quantity variance is calculated and displayed
- **Amount Variance** specifies whether an amount variance is calculated and displayed

You can use data selection to group items by cycle count categories (for example, monthly and semiannually—ABC codes for example, count items monthly). You cannot change this sequence for the selected items for count report.

See also

- *Processing tag counts*

Processing tag counts

A **Tag Count** is a location-based method of counting inventory. This recipe provides the details of tag counts and discusses how to:

- Select the items for the count program
- Print inventory tags
- Set processing options for printing inventory tags (**R41607**)
- Record tag distribution and receipt information
- Set processing options for the tag status review (**P41604**)
- Enter the tag count results
- Review tag status summaries
- Review tag count variances
- Run tag count updates

Getting ready

Before you start the tag count process, you must run the select items for **Count-Tag Inventory** (**R416060**) batch application. The select items for the **Count-Tag Inventory** batch application builds a record for each inventory item to be counted, and records the current on-hand quantity and cost for each item.

How to do it...

1. Go to **(G41) Inventory Management** | **Periodic Processing** | **Inventory Count Alternatives**.
2. Run the **print inventory tags program** (**R41607**) to print inventory tags for each location. In the **Processing** option of the **Tag** program, enter the number of tags that you want to print, and enter the branch plant information. Record the tag number for tag updates.
3. Enter the tag count result, which you recorded during the physical inventory count.
4. Review the tag status summaries to verify that you don't have a quantity variance.
5. Compare the online on-hand count to the physical count in the **Tag Variance Review** form.
6. Review the tag count variances as sown in the following example. Variances can be in quantity or amount. If the difference occurs in quantity, it's called a Quantity Variance and if the difference occurs in amount, it's called a Amount Variance.

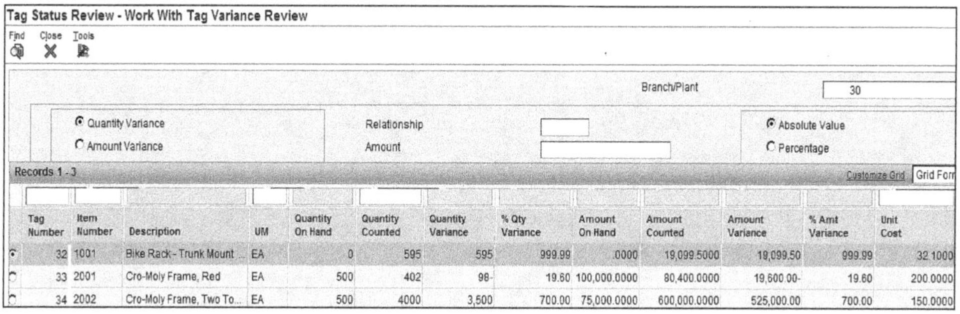

Tag Number	Item Number	Description	UM	Quantity On Hand	Quantity Counted	Quantity Variance	% Qty Variance	Amount On Hand	Amount Counted	Amount Variance	% Amt Variance	Unit Cost
32	1001	Bike Rack - Trunk Mount ...	EA	0	595	595	999.99	.0000	19,099.5000	19,099.50	999.99	32.1000
33	2001	Cro-Moly Frame, Red	EA	500	402	98-	19.60	100,000.0000	80,400.0000	19,600.00-	19.60	200.0000
34	2002	Cro-Moly Frame, Two To...	EA	500	4000	3,500	700.00	75,000.0000	600,000.0000	525,000.00	700.00	150.0000

7. After you have entered the tag count results and reviewed any variances, run the **tag inventory update program**. Select **Inventory Count Alternatives** (**G4121**) and choose **Tag Update**.

8. **On the Tag Update** application, enter the tag number on the data selection where F4160= tag number, which you have already created. Note the following screenshot:

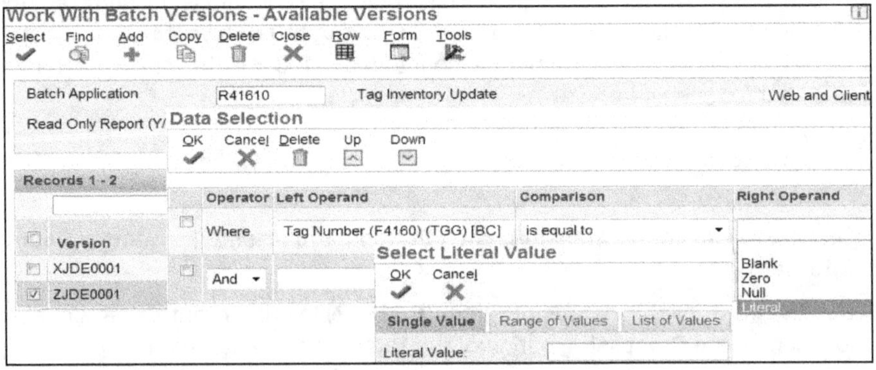

9. Enter the **General Ledger** date in the relevant processing option, and run the batch application **R41610** to update the new quantity information in the **Item Location** record and **Item Ledger**.

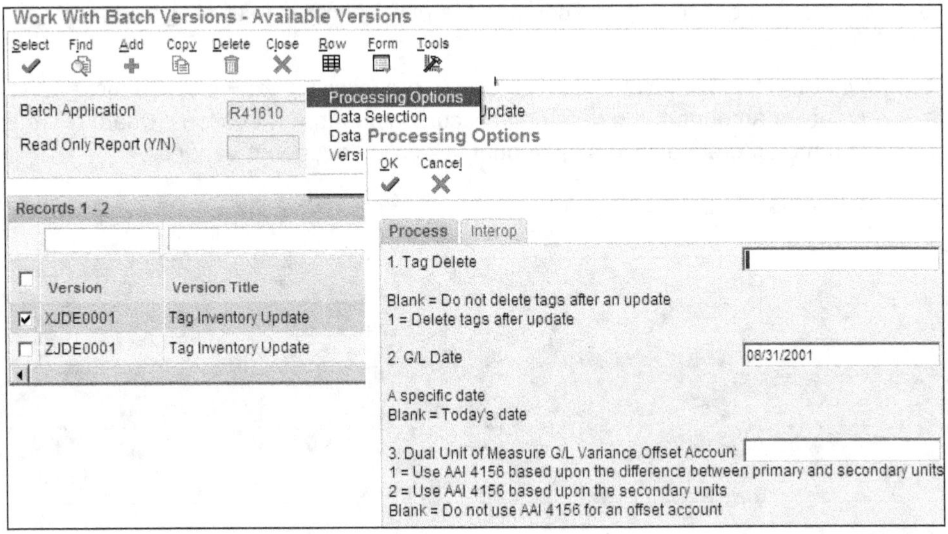

Review the tag status after running the **Tag Update** application. The **Tag Status Description** should show as **Closed**.

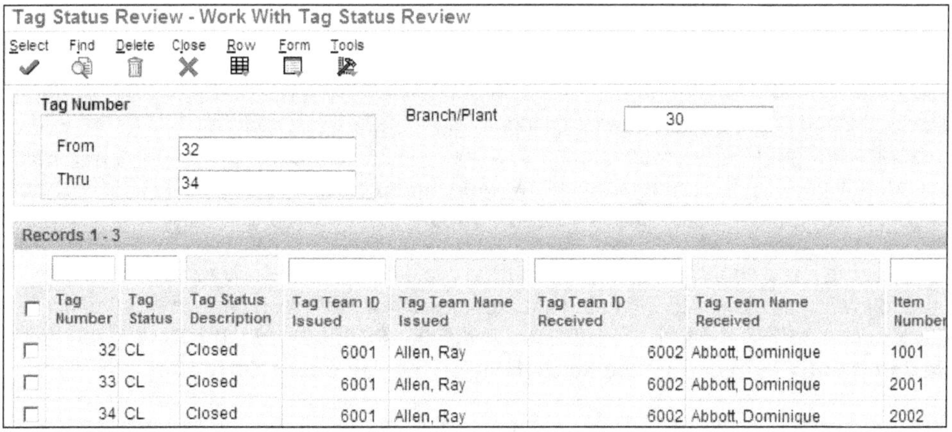

10. Journal entries are created automatically based on the AAI's setup. The **Document Type** created is **PI** and the **Batch Type** is **N**.

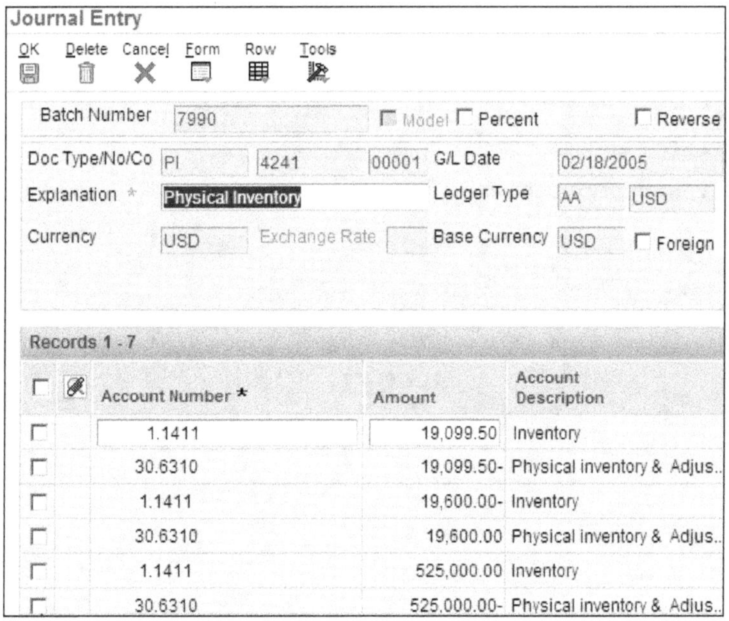

How it works...

A tag count is a method of counting all items in a location. When you perform a **Tag Count**, you physically tag and count all items twice by location. Typically, a tag count occurs at the end of the year or any other frequency scheduled by a company. To complete a tag count, two teams independently perform the same physical inventory and record their data on two different parts of the tag. Later, you use each team's data to compare the results and resolve any variances.

Consider using a tag count in conjunction with a cycle count to ensure accuracy. You also can use the following programs to indicate that a counted quantity is on certain existing license plates. You can access the **LPN Detail Entry Program** (**P46L42**) from the **Row** menu on the **Cycle Count Entry** form or from the **Form** menu on the **Tag Count Entry** form.

Although you can print tags at any time, you typically print tags at the beginning of the tag count process, and distribute them to the teams who are counting items. Run the **Print Inventory Tags** (**R41607**) batch application to print inventory tags for each location. The tag is a two-part form that includes branch/plant, date printed, and tag number.

You can vary the tag's format to accommodate for your individual business needs. The system stores the tag number and tag status in the **F4160** table.

See also

- *Physical inventory processing with cycle counts*

3
Updating Costs, Using Kits, and Lot Processing

In this chapter, we will cover:

- Updating item costs
- Updating average costs for items
- Updating detail costing
- Processing kit components
- Entering bills of material for kit items
- Creating lot processing
- Viewing lot availability
- Reviewing lot quantities
- Revising lot activity dates
- Viewing a lot transaction
- Reclassifying a lot

Introduction

This chapter will get you acquainted with updating item costs, setting up kit items, and using lot processing. **Cost information** determines whether the system maintains one overall cost for the item, or a different cost per branch/plant. **Lot processing** enables you to manage and maintain information about groups of items. For example, you can have the system assign lot numbers to groups of perishable items based on receipt dates, in order to identify the items that you must sell first. You can view current information about each lot, such as the quantity of available items and the transactions that have affected the lot.

Updating item costs

This recipe provides details of item cost updates and discusses how to:

- Set processing options for **Speed Cost Maintenance (P41051)**
- Update costs for an item across multiple branches/plants
- Update costs for multiple items across multiple branches/plants
- Update average costs for items
- Update current item costs with future costs

Getting ready

Before you complete the tasks in this chapter, you must:

- Verify the existence of current cost information for items
- Verify that **AAIs** for changes to inventory costs are set up
- Set processing options for **Batch Cost Maintenance** (**R41802**)
- Set processing options for **Future Cost Update** (**R41052**)

How to do it...

1. To set up processing options for the **Speed Cost Maintenance** application, access the (**G4123**) from the **Fast Path Inventory Price & Cost Updates** | **Speed Cost Maintenance**.
2. Click on the **Speed Cost Maintenance** arrow, and then click **Values**.
3. Enter a code from **UDC 40/CM** that indicates the cost method that the system should use to determine the cost of the item for purchase orders. The system reserves cost methods 01–19.

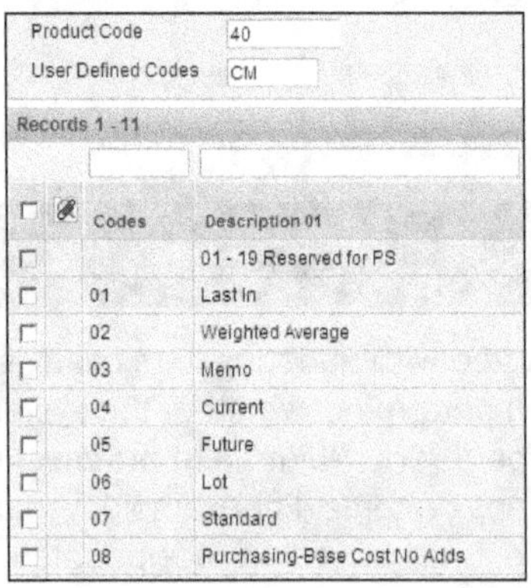

4. From UDC 40/CM, select **02**:

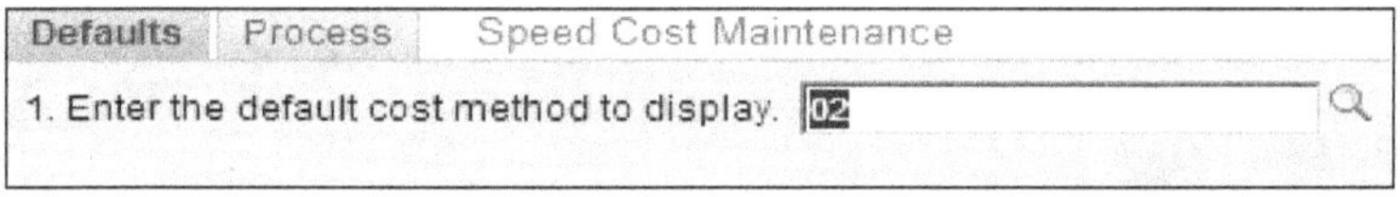

5. Specify whether or not to change the standard cost.
6. From **Inventory Price & Cost Updates (G4123)** | **Speed Cost Maintenance** | **Work with Location Costs**, select **Branch/Plants** to **Work with Costs**.
7. From the **Row** menu click **Cost Revision**.
8. Enter the **Weighted Average Cost 02**, **Last in cost 01**, and **Standard Cost 07** then click **Ok**.

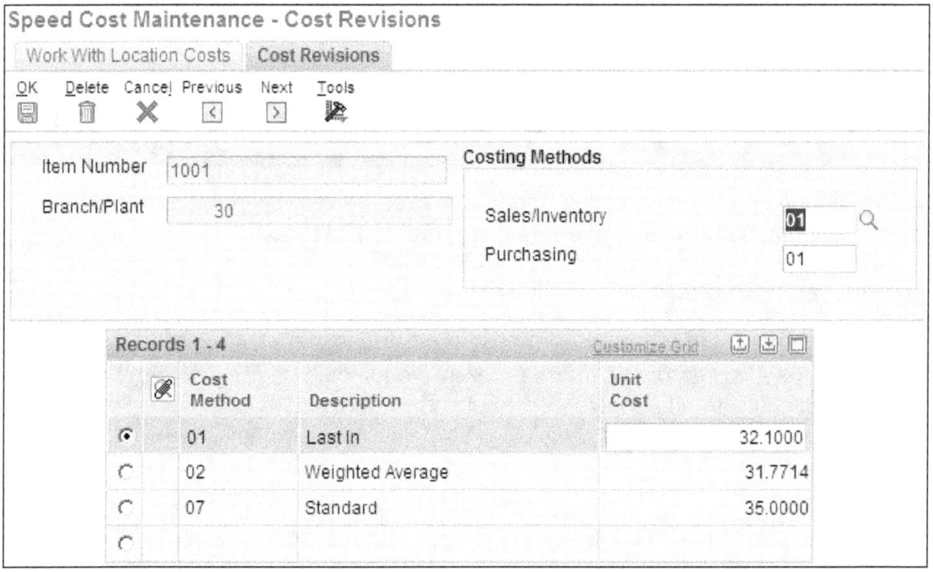

How it works...

Item costs can be updated for branches/plants, locations, and lots that you select. You can increase or decrease costs by a specific percentage or a numeric value, or you can specify a new unit cost. The system will also update the average and future cost for all of the items that you have selected. You can update costs for several items simultaneously, rather than on an individual or cost-by-cost basis. For example, you can implement a percentage increase in the standard cost for a group of items. If you use the average cost method to determine inventory costs, you can update the average cost for all items. Cost maintenance procedures enable you to update costs for individual items, or for multiple items in the branches/plants, locations, and lots that you select.

The system stores item costs in the **Item Cost File (F4105)**. After you update item costs, the system updates the **F4105** table. After you update costs for an item's sales/inventory cost method, the system creates general ledger (GL) and item ledger records.

There's more...

You can update costs for a single item across multiple branches/plants, locations, and lots. You select the cost method for which you want to update item costs. For example, you can update an item's last-in costs, average costs, and so on. Changes that you make to costs take place immediately.

See also

- *Inventory management setup in Chapter 1, Inventory Management*
- *Updating average costs for items*

Updating average costs for items

This recipe demonstrates how you can update the average cost by using an interactive application and batch application **Average Cost Update (R41811)**.

Getting ready

Before you run the **Average Cost Update** program, you should be familiar with the cost level of the items that you want to update. You should consider that:

- For all items with a cost level of 1, it is required to specify the branch/plant and locations
- For all items with a cost level of 2, it is required to specify the locations only
- If you select to run the update for items from all three cost levels, you should select by item number only
- You need to set up **UDC 40/AV to** specify the programs that update the **Average Cost Work File (F41051)**

How to do it...

1. Upload the item cost information into the **F41051** table.
2. Select **Inventory Price & Cost Updates (G4123)** | **Update Average Cost** batch application.

3. Set the data selection, if you want to update the cost for a specific item, and then click **Submit**.

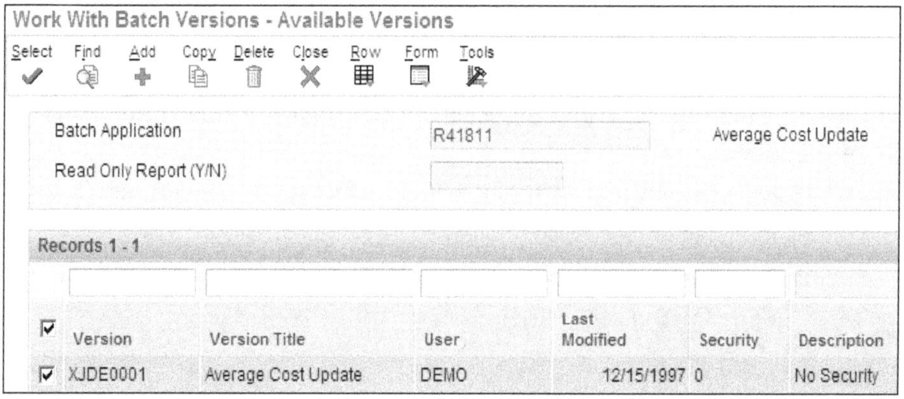

How it works...

When you run the **Average Cost Update** program, the system accesses current cost information from the **F41051 Average Cost Work file** table. It then calculates the average cost for each item and updates the **F4105** table. Each time a transaction affects the current cost of an item, the system updates the **Average Cost Work File**, and then deletes the transaction work file. To specify that the system updates **Average Costs** interactively, use the **System Constants** program. To update average costs in batch mode, use the **Average Cost Update** program. You specify the items, branches/plants, locations, and lots for which to update average costs.

There's more...

You can update item costs through an interactive process. Set up the **Update Average Cost Online** option in the branch plant system constants. The system then calculates a new average cost for an item immediately after any transaction occurs that affects the average cost of the item.

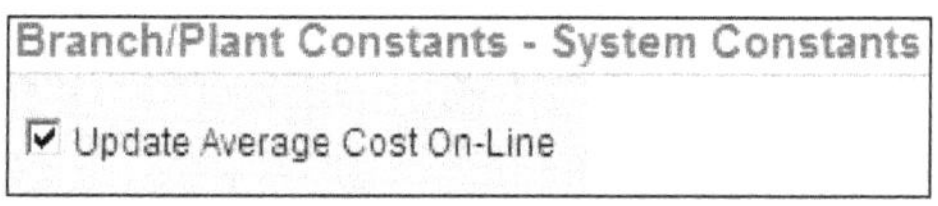

See also

- *Setting up branch/plant constants in Chapter 1, Inventory Management*

Updating detail costing

This recipe will show how to set up and review the costing process. It includes:

- Setting up detail costing in distribution
- Creating simulated costs for distribution to copy costs from the **F4105** table to the **F30026** table
- Setting up processing options for the **Simulated Cost Update program (R30840)**
- Copying manufacturing cost components
- Setting up processing options for the **Copy Cost Components (R41891)**

Getting ready

You need to set up the processing options for the following batch applications:

- Set up the processing option for the **Simulated Cost Update (R30480)**
- Set up processing options for the **Copy Cost Components (R41891)**

How to do it...

1. To set up the processing options for the **Simulated Cost Update** (**R30480**), access the **G4125** menu from the fast path and click on **Simulated Cost Update**.
2. Select the version **ZJDE0001** and click on **Row** and select **Processing Options**.

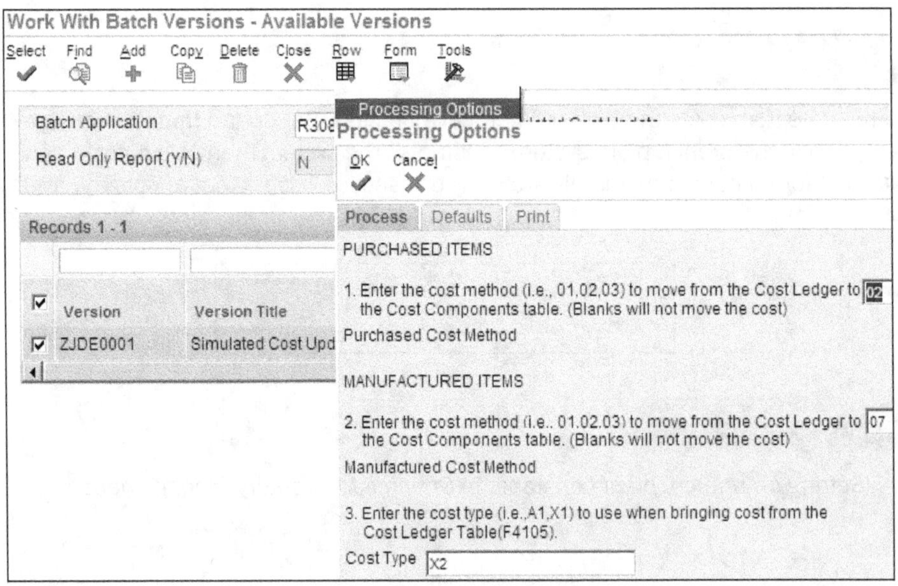

3. Enter the cost method (for example, 01, 02, or 03) to move from the **F4105** to the **F30026** table. If you leave this processing option blank, the system does not move costs.
4. Enter the cost type (for example, A1, or X1) to use when bringing costs from the **F4105** table.
5. Enter the cost method used to calculate the change in cost (for example, 01, 02, or 03). If you leave this processing option blank, the system uses cost method **07** (standard).

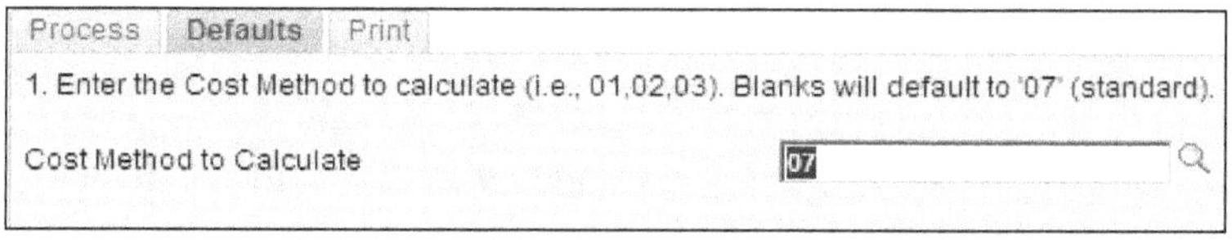

6. To set up the processing option of **Copy Cost Components** (**R41981**), access the **G4125** menu from the fast path and click on **Copy Cost Components**.
7. Click on **Row** and select the processing option **Processing Options** for **R41891**.
8. Enter a code from **UDC 40/CM** that specifies the cost method to copy. If you leave this processing option blank, the system does not copy costs.
9. Specify which costs should be copied.

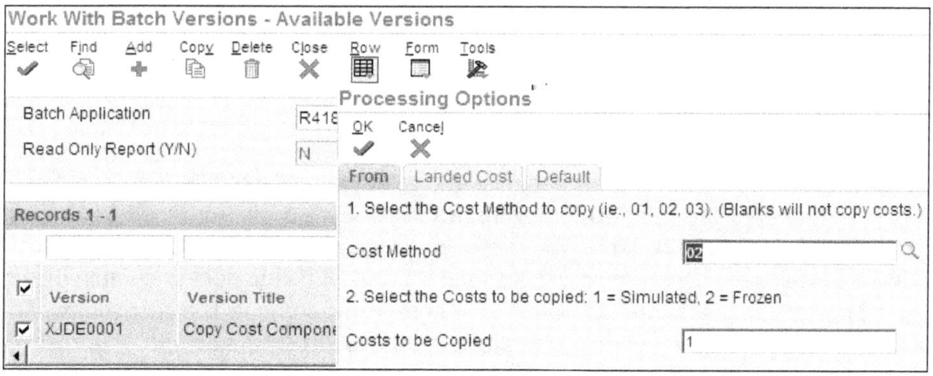

10. Enter the effective from date for the landed cost component. The default is today's date.

11. Enter the effective through date for new landed cost components. The default is December 31st of the century change year (this is the default value from **CENTCHG** in the data dictionary).

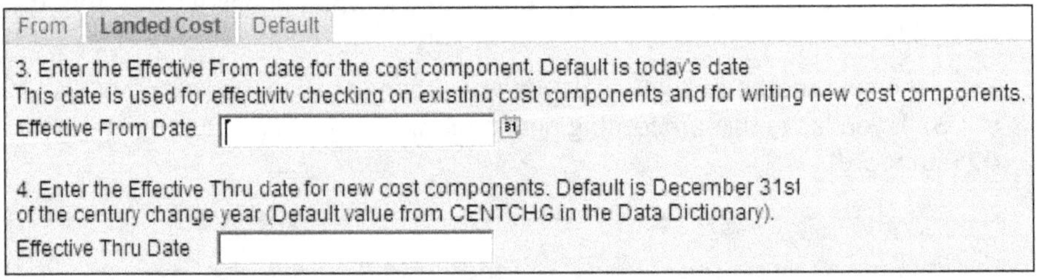

12. Enter a code from **UDC 41/9** that specifies the GL category code, on the **Default** tab.

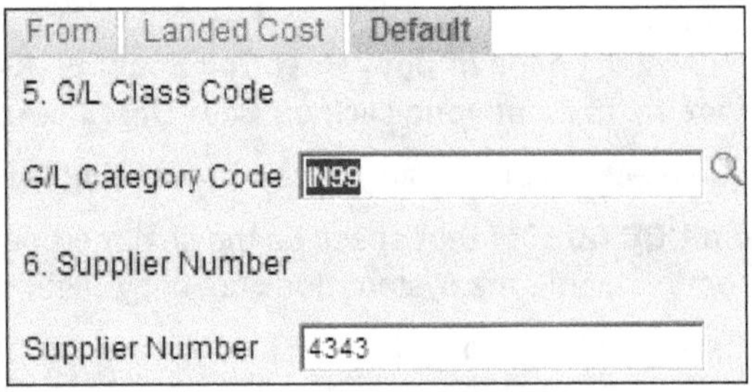

13. Enter an address book number for your supplier, on the **Default** tab.

How it works...

In a distribution environment, you cannot calculate costs from bills of material or routings. Instead, the **Simulated Cost Update Program** (**R30840**) uses costs from the **F4105** table to update costs in the **F30026** table. You can use a processing option to define which cost component contains the costs. You can also specify any cost component to contain the costs. A, B, and C cost components are not hard coded in this environment. The cost components optional add-on computations usually operate with the type Xx extra add-ons. This cost structure allows you to use an unlimited number of cost components to calculate alternative cost rollups. The system then associates these cost components with one of six user-defined summary cost buckets. The **Simulated Cost Update** (**R30840**) program for distribution is similar to the **Cost Simulation** Program for manufacturing. Use the **Simulated Cost Update** program to copy costs from the **F4105** table to the **F30026** table. After you update simulated costs to determine the effect of the changes, you can update the frozen costs with simulated values by running a **Frozen Update**.

> The **Frozen Cost** is a part of the manufacturing system. The only difference between **Frozen Cost** and **Simulated Cost** is engineering variance. The frozen cost comes from the cost component table. You can run the **Item Cost Component - Frozen Update (R30835)** update batch application for updating **Frozen Cost**.

There's more...

Landed cost date is used for effectively checking on existing cost components and for writing new cost components.

See also

- *Setting up branch/plant constants in Chapter 1, Inventory Management*

Processing kit components

A kit is a collection of inventory items that are associated with a parent item. Kits provide a way to:

- Package items together to be sold under a parent name
- Assemble a parent item from multiple inventory items

For example, you might store several computer components together, such as a monitor, hard drive, keyboard, and a mouse. When you sell the items, you might sell them collectively as a computer system. In another example, you might store the same computer components in different locations within a warehouse. By entering the components in the system as kit components, you can easily locate each item and assemble the final product. You do not stock the parent item as an inventory item.

Getting ready

Before setting up kit processing you need to :

- Enter item master records for kits
- Set up locations for kits
- Enter kit pricing information

How to do it...

1. From **Inventory Master/Transactions (G4111)** | **Item Master**, on the **Work With Item Master Browse** form, click **Add**.
2. Enter a code from the user-defined code list **(UDC) 41/I**, which indicates how you stock the item. The kit stocking type should be **K**. The stocking type is hard-coded and you should not change it.

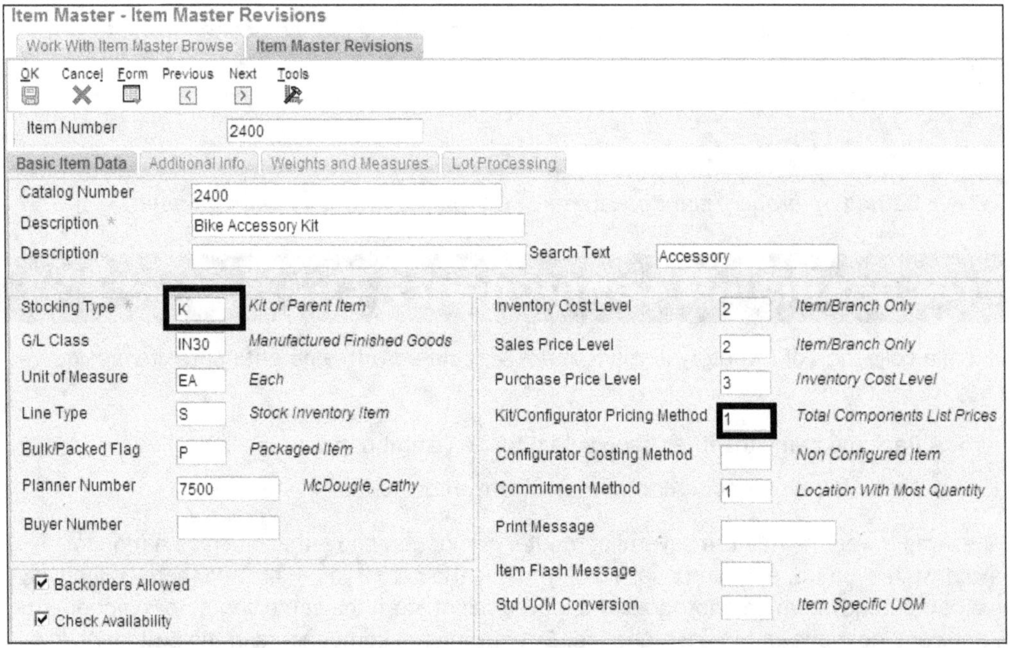

3. Enter a code that determines how the system calculates the price for kit items or configured items. Select the code as per your business requirement. You can see the valid values by pressing *F1* with the cursor on **Kit/Configuration Pricing Method**.
4. Enter a code that indicates whether the system maintains standard sales prices for an item, different sales prices for each branch/plant, or different sales prices for each location and lot within a branch/plant. The system maintains sales prices in the **F4106** table.
5. Select the values as per your business needs. You can see the valid values by pressing *F1* with the cursor on the sales price level.
6. Enter a code that indicates from where to retrieve the purchase price for an item when you enter a purchase order. You can see the valid values by pressing *F1* with the cursor on the **Purchase Price Level**.
7. On the **Work With Item Branch** form, select a component, and then select **Item/ Branch** from the **Row** menu, then **Set up Locations for Kits**.

How it works...

If you assign a line type to a component, feature, or option, then when you enter each kit component, the system checks component item numbers against the **Item Master** (**F4101**) table. Kits can also contain non-stock components. In this case, the system does not validate the item numbers against the **F4101** table. An example of a non-stock component is a flyer or catalog. Kits and bills of material can have up to 999 levels. A **Level** consists of **Components**, **Features**, and **Options.** Each level can consist of various parts. For example, you define a feature in a component of a parent kit and then enter the feature as a parent. The parent of the feature parent is the first level. The feature becomes a second level (a child of the first level).

There's more...

Features and options are additional items for the kit. Feature items have a stocking type of **F** (for **Feature**). The system recognizes feature items as second-level parent items because the system does not carry inventory for the feature items. You set up the actual inventory items in the bill of material.

See also

- *Defining item information in Chapter 1, Inventory Management*

Entering bills of material for kit items

This recipe provides details of bills of material and list prerequisites, and discusses how to:

- Set processing options for **Bill of Material Revisions** (**P3002**)
- Enter bill of material information

Getting ready

Before you complete the tasks in this recipe, you must:

- Verify that the parent, components, features, and options for the kit are set up in **Item Master Information**
- Verify that a valid parent item number exists in the **Item Master (F4101) table**
- Determine whether you need to enter branch/plant information for kits

How to do it...

1. To set up the processing options for **Bill of Material Revision** (**P3002)**, access the **G4114** menu from the fast path, and then click on **Bill of Material menu**.
2. Select the **Bill of Material Revision** (**P3002)** application, click on the arrow, and then click on **Values** and select **Setting Processing Options** for (**P3002**).

   To add a new bill of material by copying an existing bill of material, select the component branch on the **Defaults** tab to specify whether to use the parent branch or a component branch as the default value.

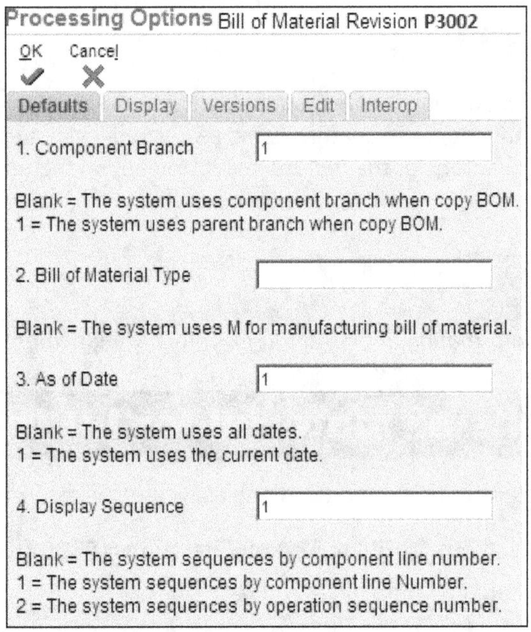

3. Enter a code from **UDC 40/TB** that specifies the bill of material type for the system to use as the default value in the type of bill fields. If you leave this processing option blank, the system uses **M**, for manufacturing bill of material.
4. Specify how the system sorts the information on the **Enter Bill of Material Information** form. You can choose whether to sequence the data by **Component Line Number** or by **Operation Sequence Number**. The component line number indicates the sequence of the components on a bill of material. The operation sequence number indicates the sequence of the fabrication, or the assembly steps, in the manufacture of the item.
5. Specify whether to display the Bill Type field in the header area of both the **Work With Bill of Material** and **Enter Bill of Material Information** forms.

6. Specify whether to display the batch quantity field in the header area of the enter **Bill of Material Information** form. The batch quantity is the quantity of finished units that you expect a specific bill of material to produce.

How it works...

As we have seen earlier, after you enter each kit component, the system checks component item numbers against the **Item Master** (**F4101**) table if you assign a line type to the component, feature, or option. Kits can also contain non-stock components. In this case, the system does not validate the item numbers against the **F4101** table. An example of a non-stock component is a flyer or catalog.

However, the item information must exist in the item master. To enter a bill of material, you must set up the inventory kit, and enter each level in the kit separately. If you are entering a bill of material for a kit that contains a feature, you must first enter the bill of material for all of the kit components except the feature. Then, you enter the bill of material for the feature using the feature as the parent item. If you have set a processing option so that the system does not validate the existence of an item/branch record, you do not have to set up the location of a component in the branch/plant where the kit is created. However, the item information must exist in the item master.

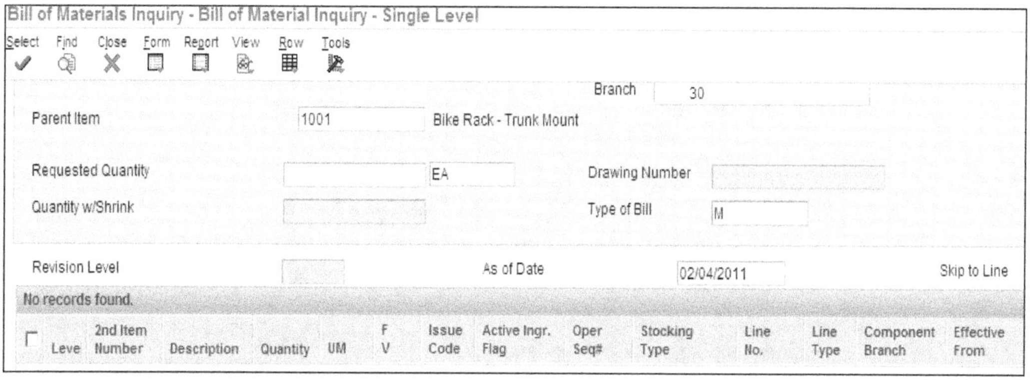

There's more...

By entering a bill of material, you also provide the system with information such as:

- The feature items and options that are included with the kit
- The feature items that are optional
- The number of items that you need in order to assemble the kit

See also

- *Processing kit components*

Creating lot processing

This recipe discusses the creation of lot processing and defining the lot master.

Getting ready

You should set up processing options for **Lot Master** (**P4108**) before creating lot processing.

How to do it...

1. From the **G41 menu**, click on the **Lot Control** menu, and click on the arrow for accessing the processing options for **Lot Master Revision**.

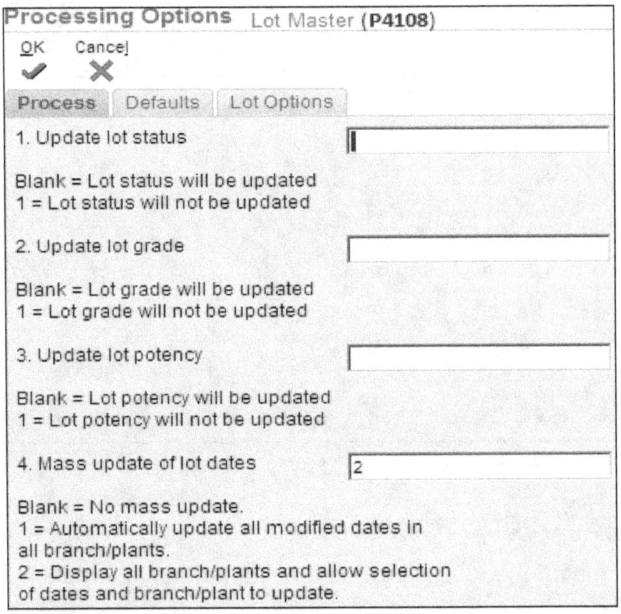

2. Access the **Item Master Revision** program, and then click on the **Lot Processing** tab.
3. Enter a code from **UDC 41/L** that indicates the status of the lot, as shown in the following screenshot. Leaving this field blank indicates that the lot is approved. All other codes indicate that the lot is on hold.

4. You can assign a different status code to each location in which a lot resides, in the **Lot Status Code** field on the **Lot Processing** tab of **Item Master Revision**.
5. On the **Lot Process** tab of **Item Master Revision**, enter a code that indicates whether lot or serial number is assigned on the **Serial Number Required** field. Lot and serial number processes use the **F4108** table.
6. From the **Basic Item Data** tab on the **Item Master Revision (P4101)** application, enter a code that indicates the commitment method that the system uses to commit lot items from inventory, in the **Commitment Data Method** field.
7. Enter a code that specifies whether you must attach a serial number to this item at receipt or sale for basic serial number processing, or whether memo lot information is required for advanced serial number processing. **Advanced Serial Number Processing** enables you to use a serial number to track an item through purchasing and sales.
8. Enter the number of days that an item can remain in inventory before it expires. The system adds this number to the date that the item is received, to determine the expiration date for the item. If you do not enter a value here, you must enter an expiration date each time you receive the lot item.

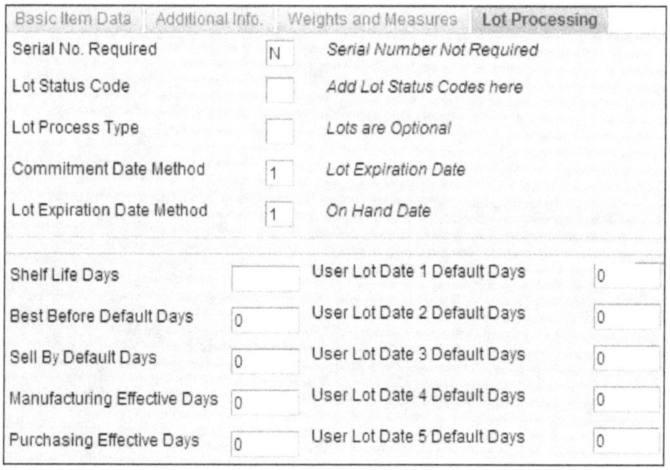

How it works...

Lot processing enables you to manage and maintain information about groups of items. You can view current information about each lot, such as the quantity of available items, and the transactions that have affected the lot. Lot control is beneficial for identifying groups of items that are components of a final product.

For example, if you assign lot numbers to both hard drives and to desktop computers that are assembled using the hard drive, you can identify the lot number for the hard drives that were used to build a specific desktop computer. If you later find that a particular lot of hard drives are defective, you can immediately identify and recall all desktop computers that were assembled with the defective hard drive. A lot usually contains one type of item, but you can set up system constants to enable different types of items in the same lot. If a lot contains different items, the system maintains lot information for each lot number and item combination. You can also set up system constants to restrict a lot to one type of item and still enable that lot to exist in multiple warehouses.

There's more...

You can set up system constants to process a lot that contains only one type of item, but with quantities located in multiple warehouses. For example, say Lot 234 consists of one type of item: bicycle tires. In addition, Warehouse A represents the bulk warehouse, where the majority of the tires are stored. However, Warehouses B and C receive partial quantities of the same item, so that Warehouse A has adequate space. When you receive the tires at warehouses B and C, you can assign them to Lot 234 and track them through the unique lot number.

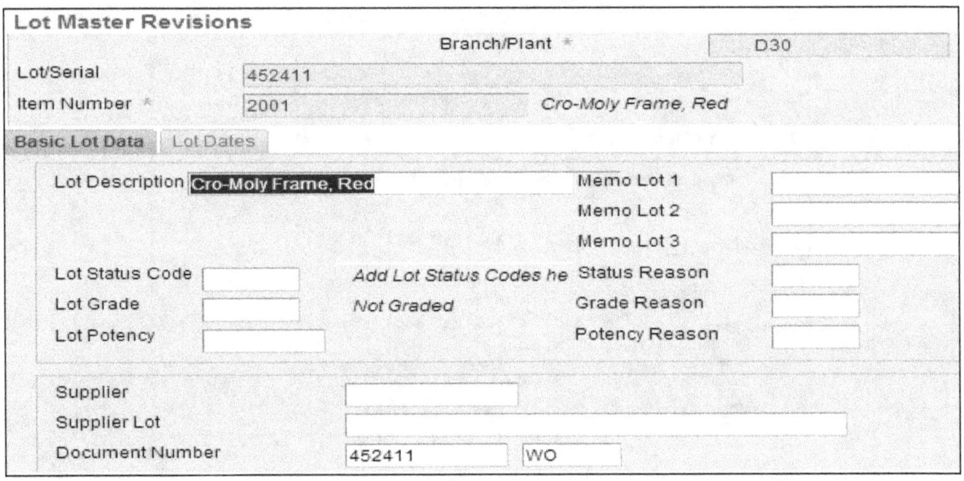

See also

- *Setting up branch/plant constants in Chapter 1, Inventory Management*

Viewing lot availability

This recipe discusses how to view the lot availability information.

Getting ready

You should set up processing options for **Lot Master Availability** (**P41280**).

How to do it...

1. From the **G41 menu**, click on the **Lot Control** menu. Click on the arrow to access the processing option of **Lot Master Availability** (**P41280**), and then set up the processing option.

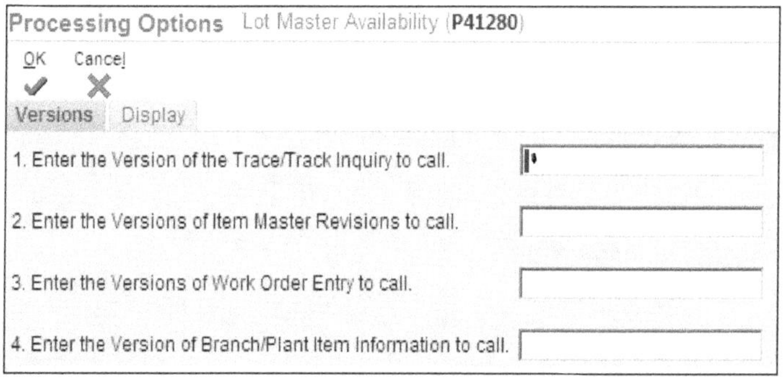

2. Enter an option that indicates whether the system displays all lots, or only lots with quantity on hand. A check mark indicates that the system displays only lots with quantity on-hand.
3. Enter a code from **UDC 41/L** that indicates the status of the lot. Leaving this field blank indicates that the lot is approved. All other codes indicate that the lot is on hold. You can assign a different status code to each location in which a lot resides, in the **Item/Location Information**, or via **Location Lot Status Change**.
4. Enter the date on which a lot of items expire. The system automatically enters this date if you specified the shelf life days for the item in the **Item Master** or **Item Branch/Plant information**.
5. Enter the number of units that are physically in stock. The system displays the quantity on-hand in the primary unit of measure.

6. Enter a number that indicates the quantity that is available. For example, the available quantity might consist of the on-hand quantity minus commitments, reservations, and backorders. Availability is user defined. You can set up availability in the **Branch/Plant Constants** (**P41001**) **program**.

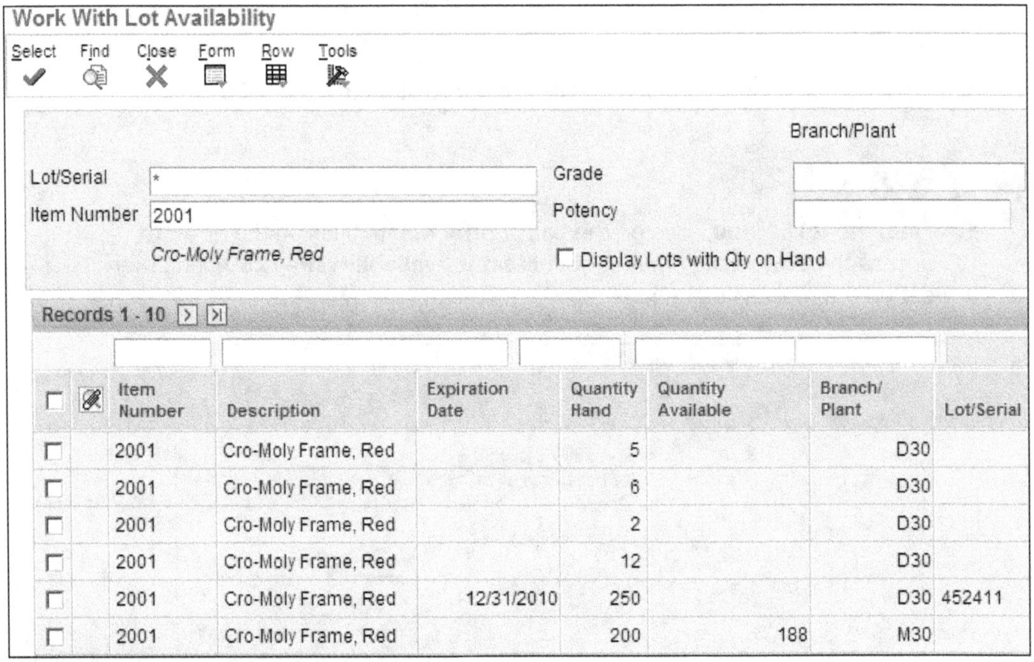

How it works...

You can view the availability of items in a lot as well as the activity dates, item quantities, and hold statuses that pertain to the lot.

Activity dates and item quantities reflect receipts, issues, sales, and so on. For items in a lot, you can view lot the availability for all items in a lot, or all lots that contain a specific item. You can choose to view only those items or lots for which on-hand balances are available. If the same item or lot appears more than once, then each item or lot exists in a different location.

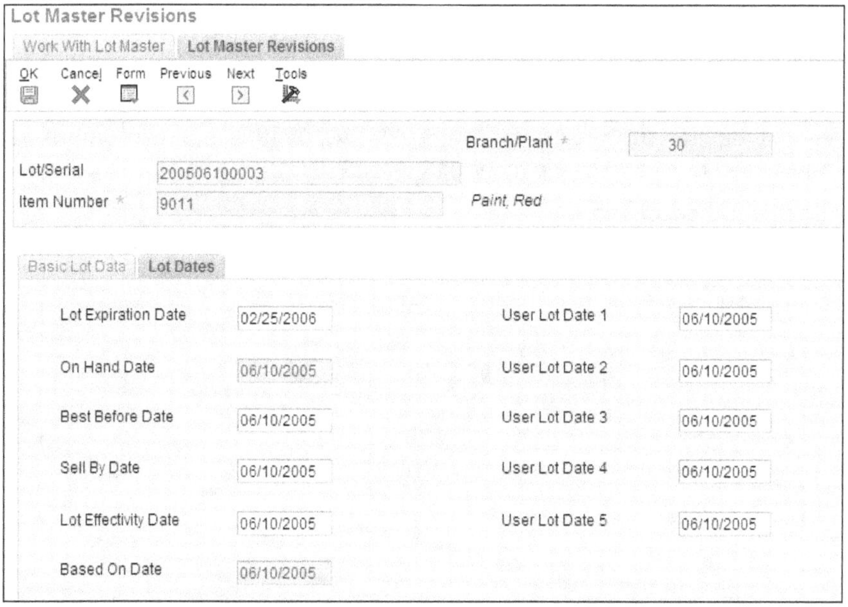

There's more...

The system calculates the expiration date by adding the number of shelf life days to the date on which you received the item. You can commit inventory based on the lot expiration date for items. You select how the system commits inventory for an item in the **Item Master** or **Item Branch/Plant information**.

See also

- *Setting up branch/plant constants in Chapter 1, Inventory Management,*

Reviewing lot quantities

You can view the on-hand quantity, the available quantity, and the quantity held for each lot. You can also view up to six other quantity types, which you set up in the **User-Defined Code** table **UDC (40/LQ)**.

Getting ready

You are going to set up an inventory item quantity review. You need to set up **UDC 40/LQ**.

How to do it...

1. From the fast path, enter **P004A** for setting up the lot quantity review application.
2. Add the required **UDC** codes, for example **IA**, **IC**, **OV** (this is the document type that is used to receive/issue the lot).
3. Add the UDC description.
4. Add all of the document types that will be used for the lot during transactions.

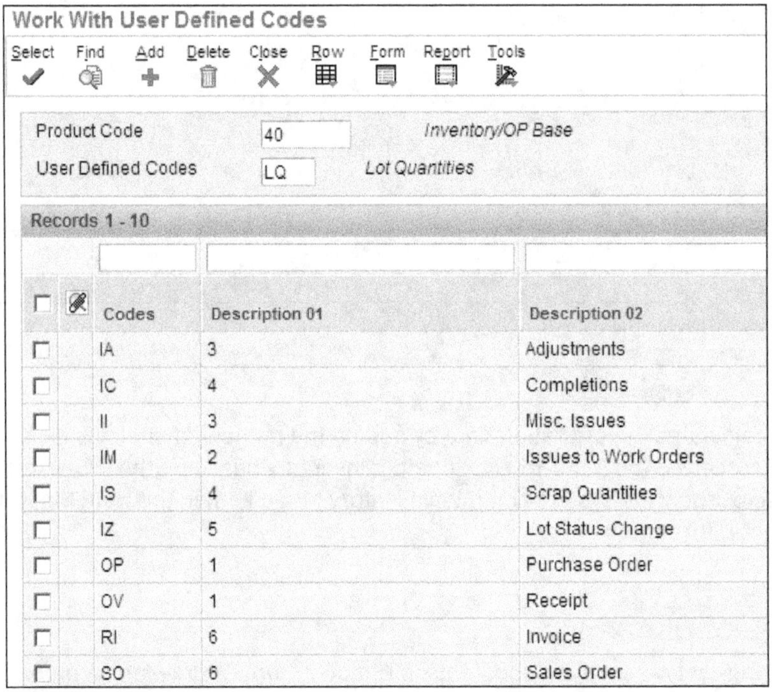

How it works...

UDC 40/LQ indicates for which document type the system will track lot quantities. You must associate each document type with one of the quantity type categories that appears on **Lot Master Revisions**. For example, if you specify the received category for document type **OP** (purchase order type), then each time that you receive items on a purchase order, the system records the quantity to the received category for the lot. For certain items, you should enter grade and potency information. If you do not specify a grade or potency for items that require this information, the system uses the standard grade and potency from **Preference Profile - Grade and Potency (P40308/F40308)**.

See also

- *Revising lot activity dates*

Revising lot activity dates

You can view the on-hand quantity, the available quantity, and the quantity that is held for each lot. You can also view up to six other quantity types, which you set up in **UDC 40/LQ**. These quantity types might reflect the quantity of items in the following categories:

- Received
- Issued
- Adjusted
- Completed
- Approved
- Sold

Getting ready

Before revising the lot activity dates, you should define the **UDC Setup LD/40** in the **Lot Dates Revision** application.

How to do it...

1. You can revise the lot dates by selecting **Inventory Management (G41) Menu** | **Daily Processing** | **Lot Control** | **Lot Master Revision** | **Work with Lot Master**.
2. Select the item, and then select **Qty/ Dates** from the **Row** menu.
3. Enter a type of quantity on the **P4108** application, **Lot Dates and Quantities** form. This field represents quantity category 1. You specify the document types that update this category in **UDC 40/LQ**. The system updates user-defined quantities when it writes **Item Cardex Information** in the **F4111** table.

4. Enter the last date on which a particular activity occurred, for example, the last date the lot was issued, sold, adjusted, completed, and approved, on the **P4108** application, **Lot Dates and Quantities** form. You determine the type of activity that the category represents (for example, issues to work orders). This field represents date category 2. You specify the document types that update this category in **UDC 40/LD**.

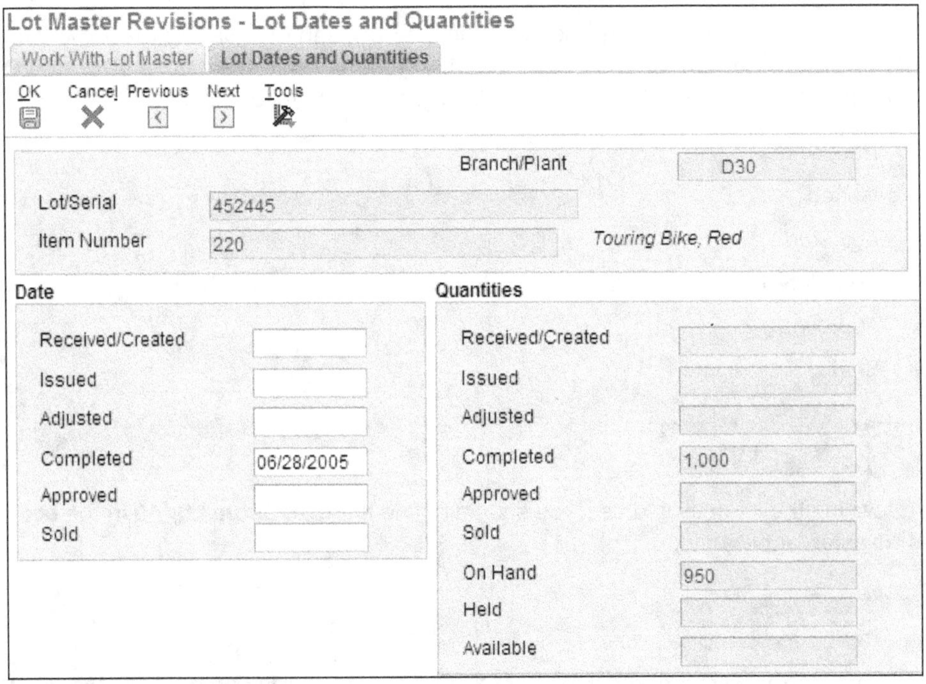

How it works...

When you set up the **UDC 40/LD**, the activity dates appear. These activity dates might reflect the last time that activities such as these occurred for an item. You set up **UDC 40/LD** to indicate for which document type the system will track lot activity dates. It is required that you associate each document type with one of the six activity for date categories. For example, you specify the **Sold Category** for the document type **SO** (Sales Orders). Then, each time that you confirm shipments for a sales order, the system records the date in the sold category for the lot. You can also enter lot activity dates manually, instead of having the system track them for you.

See also

- *Reviewing lot quantities*

Viewing a lot transaction

This recipe provides the information for tracking and tracing a faulty lot, and discusses how to:

- Review lot trace and track information
- Search for lots by supplier or supplier lot number

Getting ready

Before viewing a lot transaction, you must set up the processing option of **Lot Trace/Track Inquiry (P41203)**.

How to do it...

1. From **Inventory Management (G41) Menu** | **Daily Processing** | **Lot Control** | **Trace/ Track Inquiry**, click on the arrow, and then click **Values**.

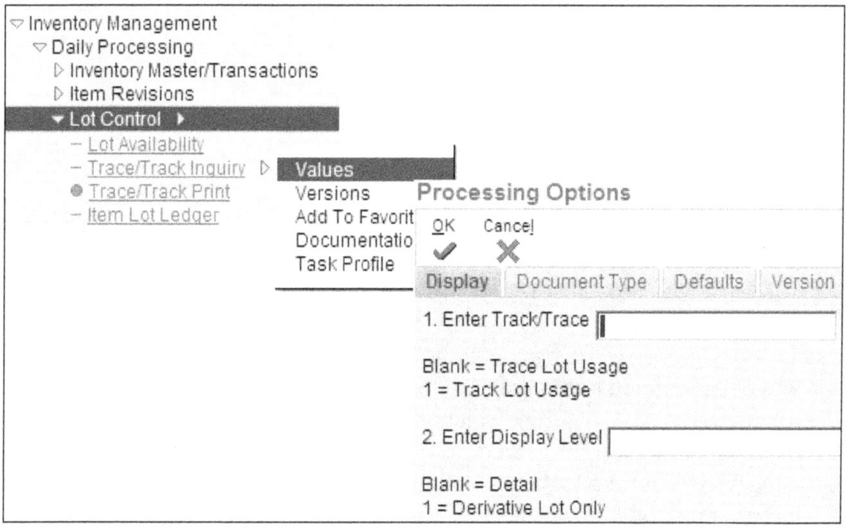

2. On the **Display** tab, specify which method the system uses to trace or track lot usage.
   - If you choose to trace the lot, the system traces, from the time of shipment to the time of manufacture, all of the items that made up the current item.
   - If you choose to track the item, the system determines all of the assemblies of which this item is to be a component, from the time of manufacture to the time of shipment.

3. On the **Display** tab, specify the level at which the **Trace/Track** result is to be displayed.
4. If you leave the **Document Type processing** option blank, the system automatically uses a default document type of **IM**.
5. If you leave the **Defaults** tab processing option blank, the system automatically provides the default document type **OP**.
6. If you leave the **Version** tab processing option blank, the system assigns the **ZJDE0001** version as the default version.
7. View the **Lot Control (G4113), Trace/Track Inquiry** | **Lot Management Workbench,** on the **lot Management Workbench** form select **Supplier Lot Inquiry** from the **Form** menu.

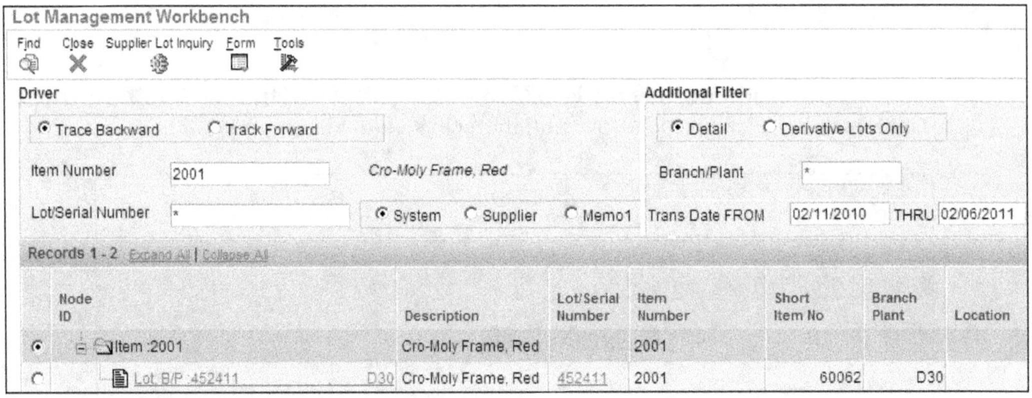

How it works...

You can use lot tracing to view the transactions in which items were assigned to the lot. If the lot contains kits or assembled items, you can identify the parts that were used to assemble items in the lot, as well as the lots from which the parts came. You use lot tracking to view the transactions in which items were removed from the lot. You can identify items that have been assembled using parts from the lot, and the lots to which the assembled items were assigned. You provide information about how you want the system to trace and track lots. For example, you specify the document types that the system monitors to **Trace and Track lots**. You also specify whether you want to view transactions for assembled items or non assembled items, by specifying a **Trace and Track** mode. You can trace a component or ingredient lot back to the immediate supplier in those cases where faults are found with the lot. You must also identify active orders that are associated with lots containing faulty or recalled components, assess the impact, and process product recalls effectively. This procedure lets you reduce unnecessary scrap or recalls on orders that were already shipped to customers.

Trace and track can be reviewed on the **Lot Management Workbench** application.

The **Lot Management Workbench** form enables you to search for an **Internal Lot**, **Supplier Lot**, or **Memo Lot**. After you locate the active orders that are associated with the faulty lot, you can assess the impact of the product recall. You can also access respective order management programs from the **Order** tabs on this form, and make any necessary changes to the order.

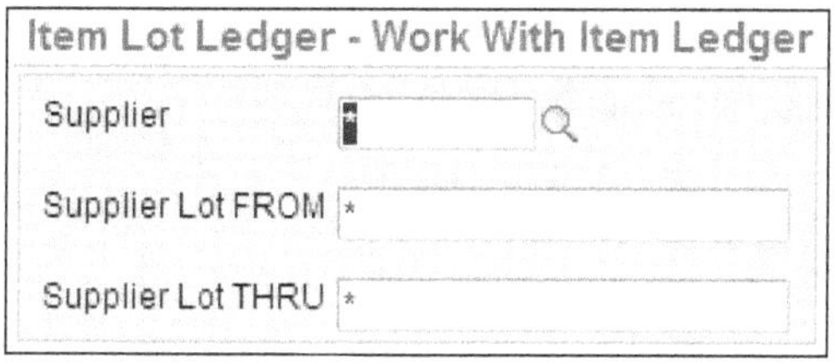

The system stores the supplier and supplier lot number, along with other purchase order receipt information, in the **F4111** table, and displays this information on the **Work with Item Ledger**, **Lot Supplier Inquiry (P4111)**, and **Transaction Information (P4111)** applications. The system also uses the **F4108** table for processing information.

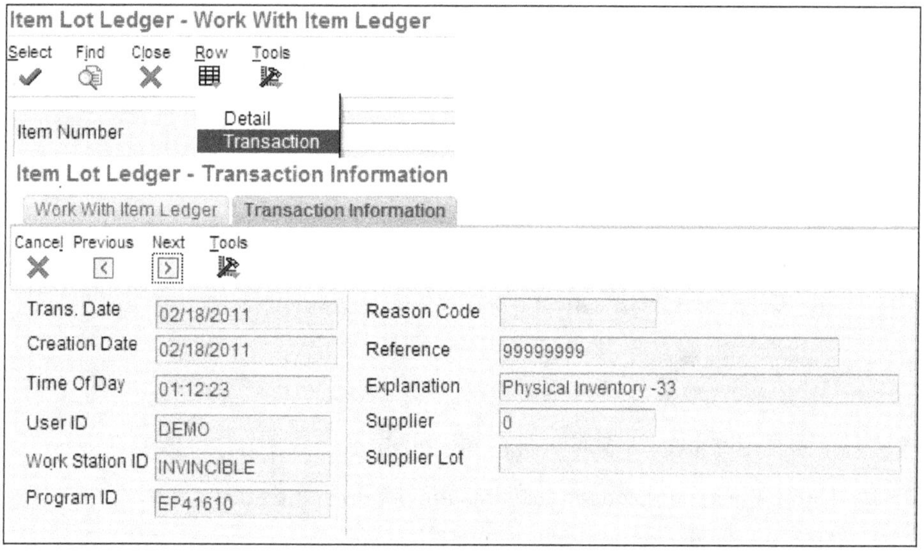

Supplier Lot is also known as **Recall Situation**.

There's more...

You can access the **Lot Supplier Inquiry** form and filter the fields to locate lots based on the supplier or supplier lot number.

Trace/Track inclusion rules

The Trace/Track Inclusion rules are driven by the document type in the **Item Ledger (F4111)** file, which is where the Trace/Track information is stored. This is controlled by the **40/DC UDC** table. The code in the table is the Document Type from the **Item Ledger (F4111)** file and the first character of the second description contains a *B* to trace to the bottom level (**Product's Origin**) or a *C* to track to the top level (**Final Product**). If the document type is an intermediate level, leave the **Description-2** field blank.

See also

- *Reviewing lot quantities*

Reclassifying a lot

This recipe provides information for lot reclassification, lists prerequisites, and discusses how to:

- Reclassify items and lots
- Change a lot and any of the associated items. You can do this in the following ways:
    - Change the item number, location, lot, and lot status
    - Create a new lot from an existing lot
    - Combine several lots into a single lot
    - Split one lot into several lots
    - Combine several lots and create several new lots

Getting ready

Before you complete the tasks in this recipe, you must:

- Verify that the general ledger accounts are set up in the **F0901** table
- Verify that AAIs for distribution are set up
- Review uncommitted quantity information for the item and related lot that you are reclassifying, via **Item Availability**
- Set processing options for **Item Reclassifications (P4116)**

How to do it...

1. From **Inventory Management (G41) Menu | Daily Processing | Inventory Transaction**, click on **Reclassifications**.

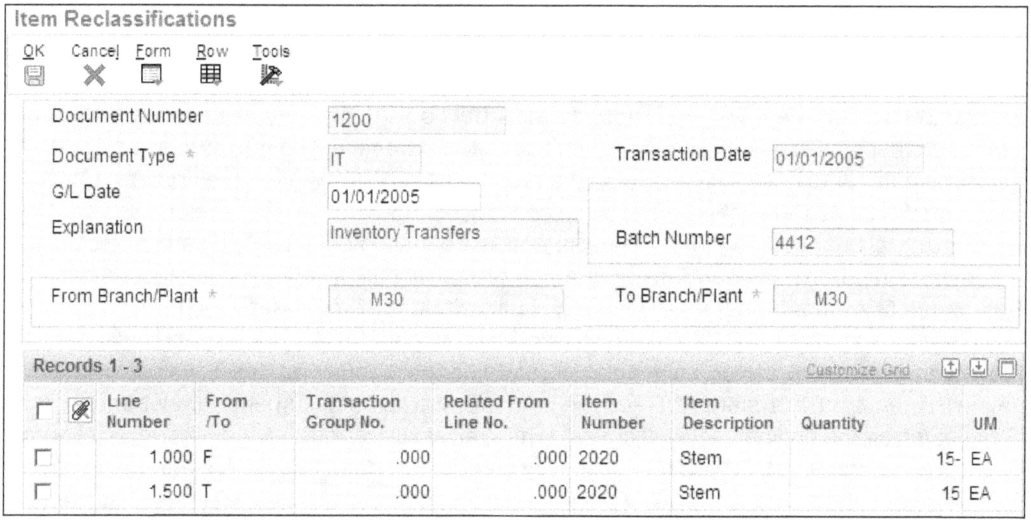

2. Enter the lowest value of the range in the **From Branch/Plant** field that a given user is authorized to view and process data, it is used in conjunction with the business unit through code, which defines the highest value. If no record exists for a user and file, the user is completely authorized to the file. If the file name is blank for a given user, the business unit range applies to all users of the file.
3. Enter an alphanumeric code in the **To Branch/Plant** field that identifies a separate entity within a business for which you want to track costs, for example, a business unit might be a warehouse location, job, project, work center, branch, or plant.
4. Enter a code in the **From/To** field that indicates whether a line in a transaction is a From line or a To line. This field enables you to combine multiple existing products or locations into a single product or location.
5. Enter a value in the **Transaction Group Number** field that identifies the lines that were grouped when the system performed multiple reclassification transactions.
6. In the **Related from Line Number** field, enter the number of the line item from which this line inherits lot and quality data.
7. Enter in the **Lot Effective Date** field date on which a lot becomes available. The system uses this date, for availability and commitment processing, to indicate that the lot is available on or after the date that you specify. You must complete this field when inventory first becomes an on-hand quantity for the lot. If you leave this field blank, the system calculates the effective date of the lot by using the value for effective days in the **F4102** table, or the current date if the value for effective days is zero.

How it works...

When you reclassify a lot, you create new item numbers and combine or split existing lots within locations. For example, property changes that occur over time in technical grade sulfuric acid can result in a less potent grade of acid. You can create a new lot for this acid by specifying a different potency and grade. Similarly, if you blend several lots of sulfuric acid together and dilute them with water, you can create a new lot with a new potency and grade. You can view detailed or summarized journal entries for these transactions on the **Journal Entries** and **Item Ledger Inquiry** forms. After you enter several reclassifications, you can group them together for processing. After you group transactions, the system assigns the same number to each transaction in the group, and processes all of the **From** and **To** lines with the same transaction number. Depending on how you have set the processing options, the system validates that the **From** and **To** quantities balance. You cannot use the **Reclassifications Transactions** program to reclassify bulk inventory. Instead, use the **Bulk Stock Movement** program to reclassify bulk inventory. If you make an error when you reclassify an item or lot, you can correct the mistake by entering a reversing entry. Because the system keeps a record of each reclassification, for accounting purposes, you cannot delete the record. The system reverses the item with the same document number and for the same batch as the original reclassification. When reclassifying lots, you can manually override or enter an effective date. If you do not specify an effective date, the system automatically calculates the effective date by using the default values from the manufacturing effective days and purchasing effective days fields established in the **Item Branch File (F4102)** table. To calculate the value in the **Lot Effective Date** field, the system determines the stocking type of the item being reclassified. The effective date is calculated based on stocking type. If the stocking type is P (Purchased), then the system use the Purchasing effective date. If the stocking type is M (manufactured), then the system uses the manufacturing effective days, and adds those days to the on-hand date to calculate the effective date.

The system calculates effective dates differently when you split, blend, and combine lots. When splitting a lot, you create multiple lots from a single parent lot. Each child lot inherits the effective date and lot creation date from the parent lot. If some properties of the lot have changed to necessitate a different effective date, you can override this date. When combining lots, child lots can inherit the on-hand date and the effective date. For example, when combining lots, you can specify whether child Lot 1 inherits information from original lot A or from lot B. When blending multiple lots into a single lot, you can specify whether the new lot inherits the on-hand date or the effective date.

There's more...

You can also set up the processing options for the **Item Reclassifications (P4116)** program. The system will use the default document type "IT", for **Item Reclassification**. You can also set up the processing option for **Assign Expiration Dates** by specifying **1** if you want to use **Shelf Life Days** as **Expiration Date**, or can leave it blank if you want to enter the lot expiry date manually.

Reclassification

For example, if you want to merge two different lots into one lot, you can enter the two lots in the **From/To** Lot field with **F**, and Target Lot with **T**, including the lot number and expiration date.

See also

- *Creating lot processing*

4
Understanding and Setting up Procurement

In this chapter, we will cover:

- Setting up Automatic Accounting Instructions
- Setting up the document type
- Setting up order activity rules
- Setting up a requisition
- Setting up Request For Quotes (RFQs)
- Setting up contract/blanket orders
- Setting up purchase orders
- Setting up Order Approval
- Setting up a receipt route
- Setting up standard receipts

Introduction

The purchasing department is an integral part of processing purchase orders, credit orders, and returns. Procurement involves everything from purchase order entry through to actual payment for the goods and services that you receive. This chapter will provide you with details of the procurement management system set-up including how the procurement system integrates with other applications. For example, the procurement system integrates with the accounts payable system and creates a payment voucher. It also integrates with inventory management so that when an item is received it will increase the inventory on hand quantity. This chapter also includes the setting up of different order types, the order approval process, and receipt routing.

Setting up Automatic Accounting Instructions

This recipe demonstrates the AAI tables for the procurement system, and discusses how to:

- Set processing options for **Distribution AAIs** (**P40950**)
- Set up distribution AAIs

Getting ready

You should set up the **Processing Options** for **Distribution AAIs (P40950)**.

How to do it...

1. On the **Automatic Accounting Instruction (P40950)** form, click on the arrow and then click on **Values** to access the **Processing Options**.
2. Enter the AAI table number that is used to specify the sequence, and retrieve the accounting information.
3. For availability-to-distribution AAI tables, enter a *1* if the cost type field should be available to the following **Distribution AAI tables: 4122, 4124, 4134, 4136, 4220, 4240, and 4310**.

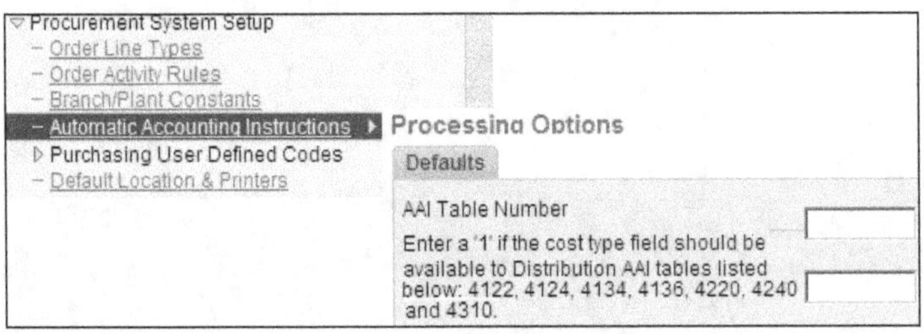

4. After setting the **Processing Options** from the **Procurement System Setup** (**G43A41**), click on **Automatic Accounting Instructions** in order to access **Automatic Accounting Instruction-Work With AAIs**.

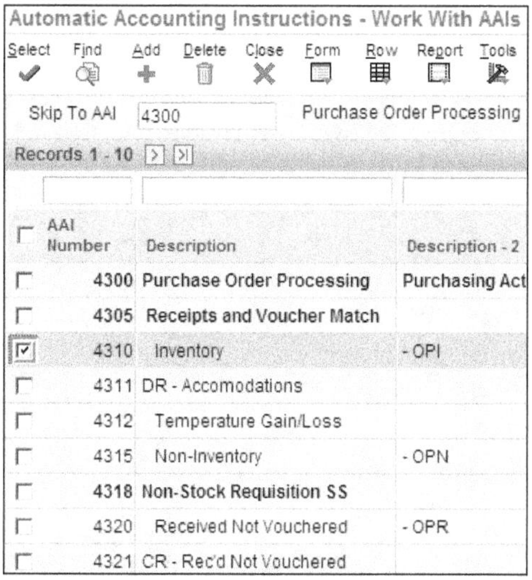

5. Select a row on the **Work With AAIs** form, and then select **Details** from the **Row** menu:

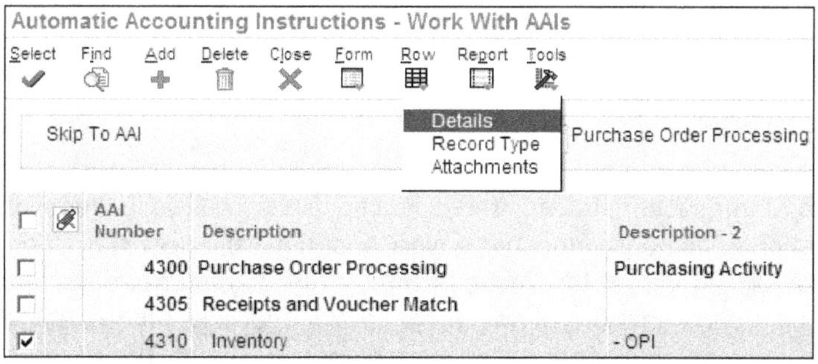

6. Enter the portion of an **Object Account** that refers to the division of the **Subsidiary** (for example, labor, materials, and equipment) into subcategories.

Automatic Accounting Instructions - Account Revisions

OK Find Delete Cancel Form Tools

AAI Table Number 4310 Inventory

Records 1 - 10

Co	Do Ty	Description	G/L Cat	Description G/L	Branch Plant	Obj Acct	Sub
00000	04	Purchase Order -Trans	****			1411	
00000	OK	Purchase Intercompa...	IN30	Manufactured Finishe...		1411	
00000	OM	Purchase Order RMA ...	****			1411	
00000	OZ	EDI Purchase Order ...	****		1	1411	
00001	OP	Purchase Order ...	****		1	1411	
00001	OT	Transfer Order	****		1	1411	
00200	OD	Direct Ship Order ...	****			1462	
00200	OM	Purchase Order RMA ...	IN30	Manufactured Finishe...	S30	1411	

7. If you use a flexible chart of accounts and the object account is set to six digits, you should use all six digits. For example, entering 000456 is not the same as entering 456 because, if you enter 456, the system enters three blank spaces to form a six-digit object.

How it works...

When you set up the procurement system, AAI uses multiple **AAI** tables, each of which applies to a certain type of transaction. In each table, you specify a general ledger account for each unique combination of company, document type, and general ledger class. For example, you can set up an **AAI** table for inventory receipt transactions. Each time you enter a receipt for an inventory item, the system determines the general ledger account to debit, based on the company, document type, and general ledger class for the receipt. The AAI **4310** is set up for **Inventory Item**, **4315** for **Non Stock Item**, and **4320** for **Received Not Vouchered**. The system stores **AAIs** in the **Distribution /Manufacturing - AAI Values (F4095)** table.

> The GL class is very important in the AAI setup. The journal entries that are created during item receipt and voucher matching are based on the GL class setup.

There's more...

You set up AAIs to indicate the accounts for which the system creates the journal entries. You also can enter memo text for each AAI. In the procurement management system, AAIs define the links between the Job Cost and General Accounting systems.

See also

- *Setting up the document type*

Setting up the document type

In this recipe, we will set up the procurement document type by setting up **UDC 00/DT** with the values that you use to indicate the document types to be used for procurement. For example, **OP** indicates a purchase order.

Getting ready

You must set up the document types for **Pre-Encumbrances** and commitments in **UDC 40/CT**.

How to do it...

1. To set up the document type, enter **P0004A** in the fast path **Work With User Defined Codes** application.
2. Enter **Product Code: 00** and **User Defined Codes: DT**, and then click on **Add**.

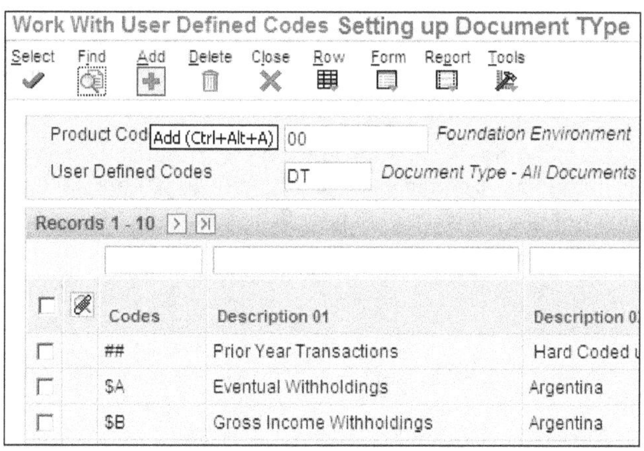

3. Click on the **Go to end** button, as shown in the following screenshot, and then enter the **Code** and **Description**.

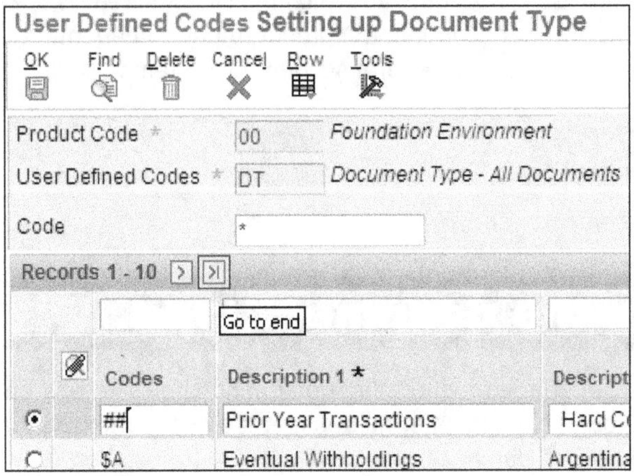

4. Click on **OK** to save the document type.

How it works...

When you enter a value in **UDC 00/DT**, the system identifies this as a document type. **UDC (00/DT**) also indicates the origin of the transaction. The EnterpriseOne system has reserved document type codes for vouchers, invoices, receipts, and time sheets, which create automatic offset entries during the post program. (These entries are not self-balancing when you originally enter them). These document types are defined by JD Edwards EnterpriseOne, and should not be changed. When you create an order detail line, the system verifies that the document type exists in **UDC 40/CT**, that the line type has an inventory interface of A, B, or C, and automatically creates commitments and encumbrances. When you want to define a new **Order Type**, you first need to set up the **Order Type** in **UDC 00/DT**. After that, it is necessary to clear the server cache in order to use that document type in further set up activities.

> The system can create commitments only for document types that you have set up in the **User-Defined Code (UDC)** table **40/CT** and for line types that use an inventory interface of A, B, or C.

There's more...

These are predefined prefixes for document types, and these should not be changed:

- *P: Accounts Payable documents*
- *R: Accounts Receivable documents*

- *T: Payroll documents*
- *I: Inventory documents*
- *O: Purchase Order documents*
- *J: General Ledger/Joint Interest billing documents*
- *S: Sales Order Processing documents*

If you enter a document type, the system displays only the orders of the document type that you specify. You can create different versions that correspond to the different document types that you use.

> A **pre-encumbrance** is the recognition of a future obligation from which you can commit budget amounts based on that request.

See also

- *Setting up Automatic Accounting Instructions*

Setting up order activity rules

This recipe demonstrates and discusses how to set up order activity rules.

Getting ready

In order to set up order activity rules, you must:

- Verify that you have set up the required status codes in the Activity/Status Codes **(40/AT)** UDC table
- Verify that you have set up the required order types in the Document Type (**00/DT**) UDC table
- Verify that the correct order line types exist

How to do it...

1. To define **Procurement System Setup**, enter **G43A41** on the fast path, in order to access the **Order Activity Rules** application.
2. Click on the **Add** button for the **Order Activity Rules Revision** program **(P40204)**.
3. Enter the **Order Type**, which you have already created in the **Document Type** set-up.
4. Enter the **Line Type**, which is S for a **Stock Item** and *N* for a **Non Stock Item**.

5. Enter a code in the **Order Type Next Number** field that tells the system which next number series to use when creating order numbers for this order type. Ten **Next Number** series' are available. Enter the order activity **Last Status** and **Next Status** based on your required setup. The following screenshot show the order activity set-up for a stock item with document type *OP* and line type *S:*

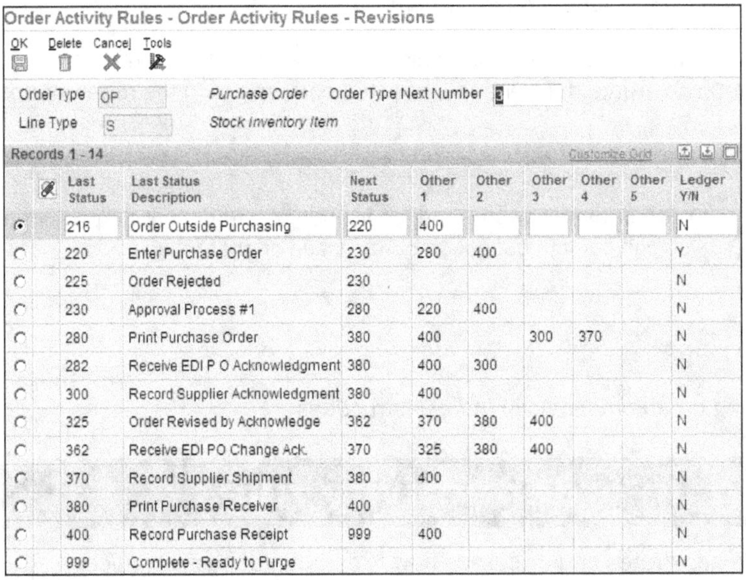

Order Activity Rules - Order Activity Rules - Revisions

OK Delete Cancel Tools

Order Type OP Purchase Order Order Type Next Number 3

Line Type S Stock Inventory Item

Records 1 - 14

Last Status	Last Status Description	Next Status	Other 1	Other 2	Other 3	Other 4	Other 5	Ledger Y/N
216	Order Outside Purchasing	220	400					N
220	Enter Purchase Order	230	280	400				Y
225	Order Rejected	230						N
230	Approval Process #1	280	220	400				N
280	Print Purchase Order	380	400		300	370		N
282	Receive EDI P O Acknowledgment	380	400	300				N
300	Record Supplier Acknowledgment	380	400					N
325	Order Revised by Acknowledge	362	370	380	400			N
362	Receive EDI PO Change Ack.	370	325	380	400			N
370	Record Supplier Shipment	380	400					N
380	Print Purchase Receiver	400						N
400	Record Purchase Receipt	999	400					N
999	Complete - Ready to Purge							N

6. On the **Other 1** to **Other 5** fields, enter additional statuses that can be performed as the next step in the order process. These fields are optional. Although this is not the preferred or the expected next step, this field is an allowed override. The system does not allow you to initiate an order line step or status not defined as either the expected next status or an allowed status. Other allowed status codes let you bypass processing steps. These codes are often referred to in processing options as **override next status codes**.

7. Enter *Y* or *N* in the **Ledger** field (*Y* will write the record to the **Purchase Order History Table F43199**).

> The procurement system is based on the line type. There are four types of procurement:
>
> - **Stock Based** uses line type **S**
> - **Non Stock** uses line type **N**
> - The services or projects and **Subcontract Management** uses line type **J**
> - Project Based Purchasing

How it works...

When you set up the order activity rule, for each item or service that you enter into the purchase order, you must enter an order line with detailed information that describes the order item or service. This includes the item number, item quantity, and item cost. The system then processes the steps based on the order activity rule set-up. For example, you can specify that a set of activity rules apply only to purchase order detail lines that have a line type of S (stock items). Status codes identify the current status of a detail line and the next status into which the line should be advanced. You must define status codes in ascending numerical order. The purchase order, requisition, quote order, and blanket order will follow the order activity set-up.

> Purchase requisitions that carry order numbers different from quote request, purchase orders, and blanket sales orders are numbered in a different number range from standard sales orders.

There's more...

You must set up order activity rules to establish the sequence of steps through which you process each detail line, that is, enter order, approve order, print order, and receive order. You can set up multiple sets of activity rules. You must assign each set of rules to a certain order type (purchase order, requisition, and so on) and line type.

You can set up status codes for purchase order stock line types as follows:

Last	Next	Description
220	230	Enter Order
230	280	Approval Process
280	400	Print Purchase Order
400	999	Receive Order

Non-Stock setup

The following screenshot show the order activity setup for a Non-Stock Item with document type **OP** and line type **N**.

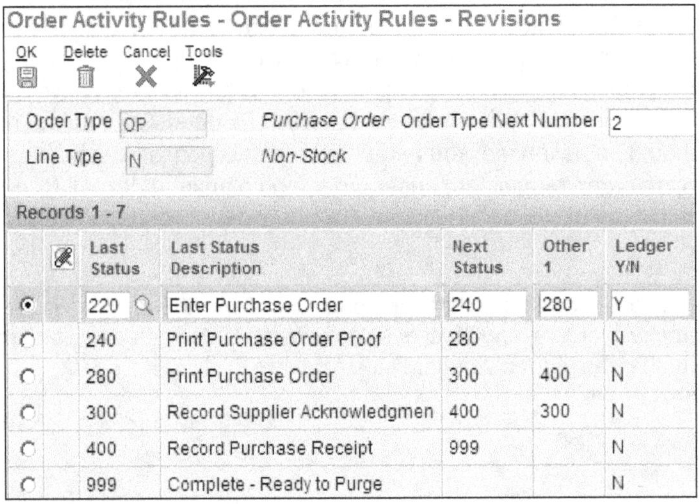
Order Activity Rules - Order Activity Rules - Revisions

OK Delete Cancel Tools

Order Type OP Purchase Order Order Type Next Number 2

Line Type N Non-Stock

Records 1 - 7

Last Status	Last Status Description	Next Status	Other 1	Ledger Y/N
220	Enter Purchase Order	240	280	Y
240	Print Purchase Order Proof	280		N
280	Print Purchase Order	300	400	N
300	Record Supplier Acknowledgmen	400	300	N
400	Record Purchase Receipt	999		N
999	Complete - Ready to Purge			N

See also

- *Setting up the document type*

Setting up a requisition

This recipe demonstrates setting up purchase requisition order activity and purchase requisition application processing options.

Getting ready

You should set up the order activity rule for purchase requisitions in order to set up the processing option of the **Purchase Requisition Entry** application **P4310**.

How to do it...

1. Set up the **Order Activity Rule** for **Purchase Requisition** on the **G43A41** menu.
2. Enter the **Document Type** for purchase requisition as **OR**, and the Line Type as **S**.
3. Enter **Order Activity** for Purchase Requisition; the following screenshot shows the standard purchase requisition **Order Activity Rule**:

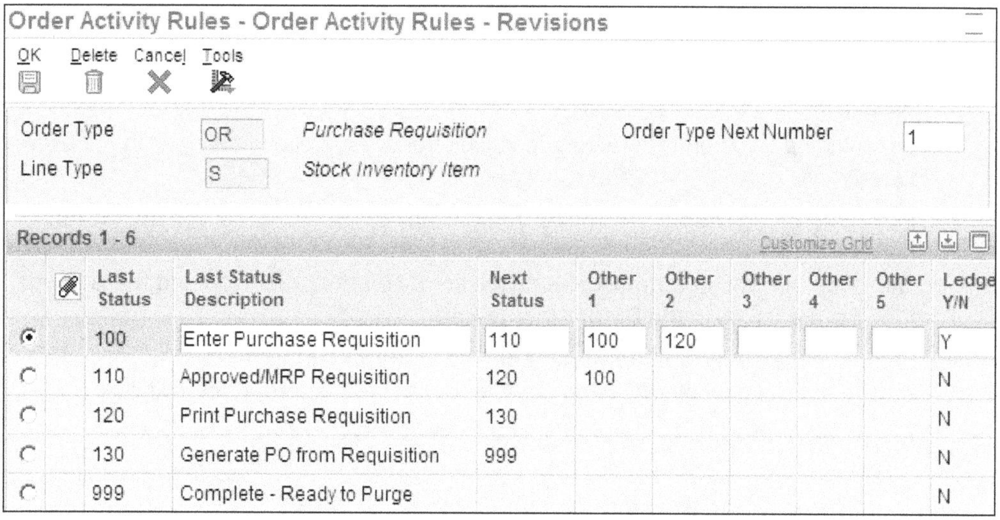

4. Select **Procurement and Subcontract Management** | **Daily Processing** | **Stock Based Purchasing** | **Requisition and Quote Management,** and then click the arrow next to **Enter Requisitions** (**P4310**).
5. Select **Values.**

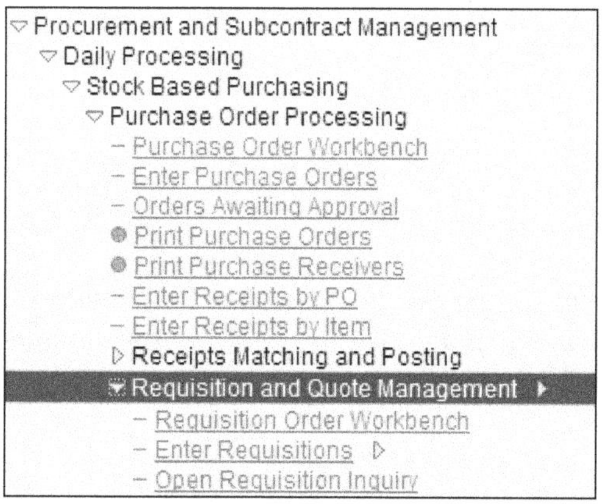

6. Enter **Order Type** *OR* in the **Order Type** field in the **Default** tab that exists in the **Document Type - All Documents (00/DT)** UDC to specify the default value for the order type. The system populates the **Order Type** field on the **Order Header** form with this value.

7. Enter **Line Type** S in the **Line Type** field in the **Default** tab, to specify how the system processes lines on a transaction. The line type affects the systems with which the transaction interfaces (General Ledger, Job Cost, Accounts Payable, Accounts Receivable, and Inventory Management). The line type also specifies the conditions for including a line on reports and in calculations. You define line types in the **Order Line Types** program (**P40205**).
8. Enter **Beginning Status** *100* in the **Default** tab that exists in the **Activity/Status** Codes (**40/AT**) UDC to specify the default value for the beginning status of the order. The value that you enter must already be set up for the order type and the line type that you are using, in the **Order Activity Rule**.
9. Enter *1* in the **Line Number Increment** field in the **1 - Defaults** tab. This tells the system to automatically increase the line number on the order detail line.

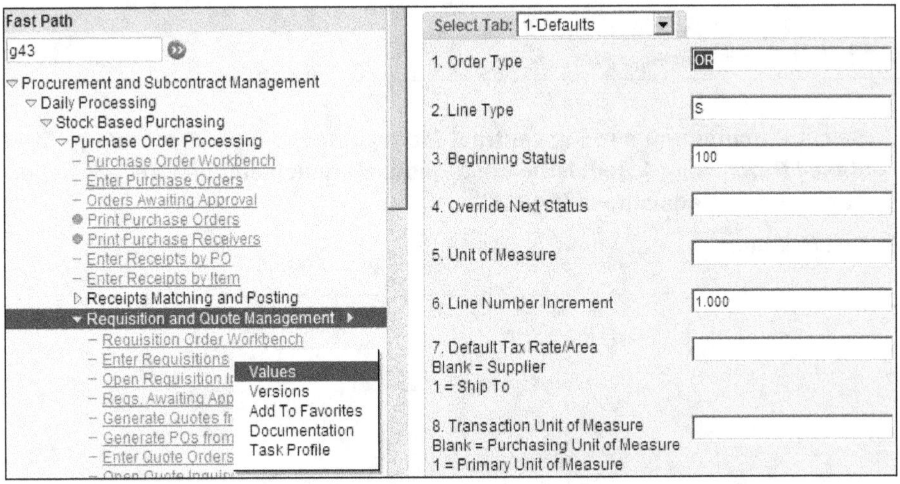

10. On the **Interface** tab, enter **1** in the **Business Unit Validation**, **PBCO Warning**, **PACO Warning**, and **Quantity Update** fields. These are the recommended settings for the **Purchase Requisition** application:

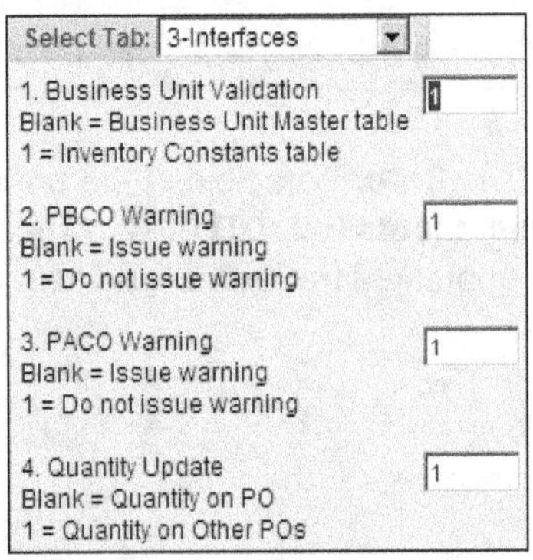

11. On the **Duplication** tab, enter **Duplicate Order Type** *OR*, **Beginning Status Code** *100*, **Next Status Code** *110*, and **Copy Selection** *2*.

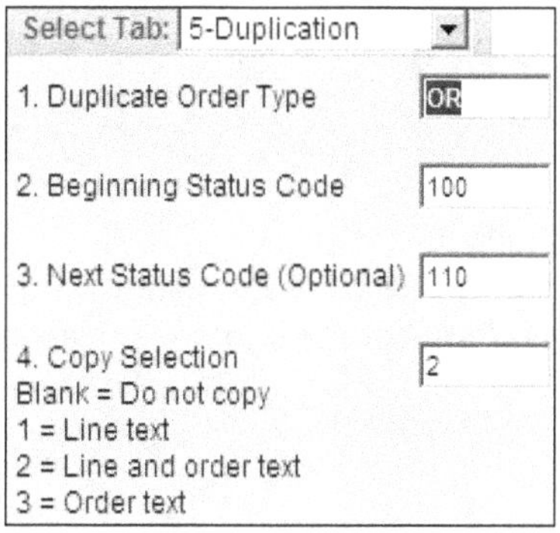

12. On the **Order Inquiry** tab, enter *110* in the **From Status Code** and *999* in the **Thru Status Code**.

How it works...

When you set up the **Processing Options** for **P4310** enter requisition, the system distinguishes a requisition by its order type and order activity rules. For example, when you work with a requisition, you usually enter an order type of **OR** (**Requisition Order**). The system's working is based on the document types, line types, activity rules, and status codes that you set up in the requisition **Processing Options**. The system reads the set-up information from **Processing Options**. When you set up the **Processing Option** document type *OR*, the system gets the information from the order activity set-up and processes the purchase requisition as per the order activity set-up. On the **Interface** tab, you set the quantity update to *1*, which indicates that when you enter the requisition, the system will store the item quantity on the **Other OP** field in the item location table for the location item quantity in the **Item Availability Inquiry**.

There's more...

There are some reserved document type codes for vouchers, invoices, and receipts for which the system creates automatic offset entries during the post program.

See also

- *Setting up order activity rules*

Setting up Request For Quotes (RFQs)

This recipe demonstrates setting up the Request for Quote activity rule and quote request application processing options.

Getting ready

You should set up the order activity rule for the **Request for Quote** application in order to set up the processing options for the **Request for Quote** application **P4310**.

How to do it...

1. Set up the **Order Activity Rule** for **Request for Quote** via the **G43A41** menu.
2. Enter the **Document Type** for **Request for Quote** as *OQ*, and the **Line Type** as *S*.
3. Enter the **Order Activity** for **Request for Quote**. The following screenshot shows the standard purchase requisition **Order Activity Rule**:

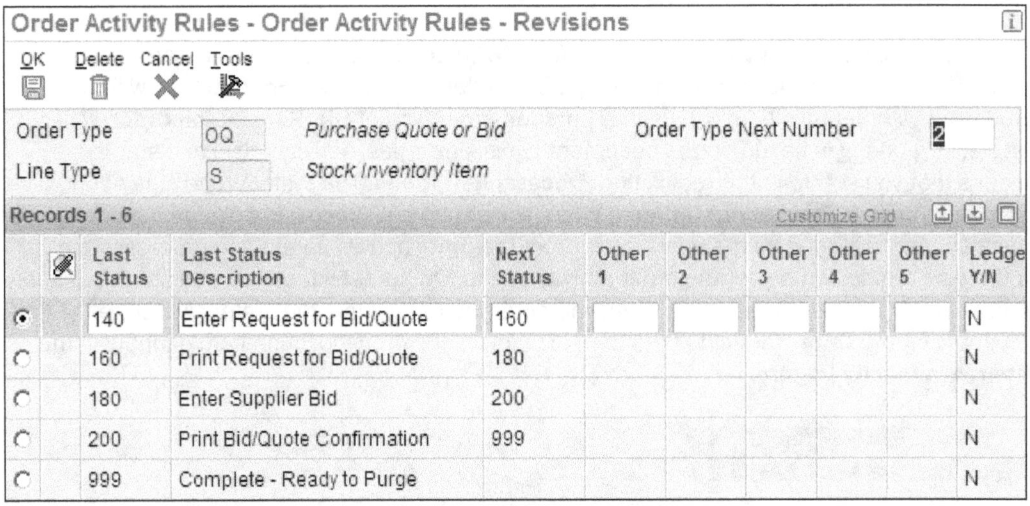

4. Select **Procurement and Subcontract Management** | **Daily Processing** | **Stock Based Purchasing** | **Requisition and Quote Management**, click the arrow next to **Enter Quote Order (P4310)**, and then select **Values**.
5. Enter **Order Type** *OQ* in the **Order Type** field in the **Default** tab that exists in the **Document Type - All Documents (00/DT) UDC** to specify the default value for the order type. The system populates the **Order Type** field of the **Order Header** form with this value.

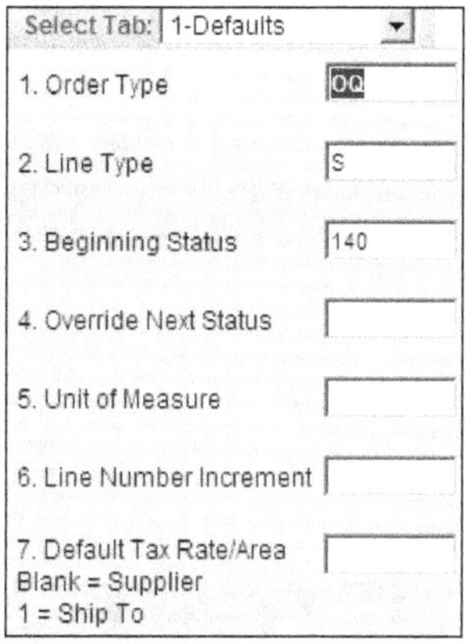

6. Enter **Line Type** *S* in the **Line Type** field in the **Default** tab to specify how the system processes lines on a transaction. The line type affects the systems with which the transaction interfaces (General Ledger, Job Cost, Accounts Payable, Accounts Receivable, and Inventory Management). The line type also specifies the conditions for including a line on reports and in calculations. You define line types in the **Order Line Types** program **(P40205)**.
7. Enter **Beginning Status** *140* in the **Default** tab that exists in the **Activity/Status Codes (40/AT) UDC** to specify the default value for the beginning status of the order. The value that you enter must be set up for the order type and the line type.
8. On the **Order Inquiry** tab, enter *110* in the **From Status Code,** and *999* in the **Thru Status Code**.

How it works...

When you set up the **Processing Options** for the **Enter Quote Order** application (**P4310**), the system distinguishes a quote by its order type and the order activity rules. For example, when you work with a quote, you usually enter an order type of *OQ* (**Quote Order**). The quote order application reads the document type *OQ* from the processing options, and then gets the information from the order activity set-up. On the **Interface** tab, you set up the quantity update with *1*, which indicates that the quotation will store the **Other OP** field in the item location table.

> Using the preceding activity rules, you can bypass the print quote request step. To do this, you must assign an alternative next status code.

There's more...

When you set up the order activity rule for a quote order, you should set up the order activity for the quote request to be after the requisition order activity - for example, set the **Requisition Order Last Status** to start with *100*, and **Quote Order Last Status** to start from *140*.

See also

- *Setting up order activity rules*

Setting up contract/blanket orders

This recipe demonstrates setting up the **Blanket Order** activity rule and **Blanket Order** application **Processing Options**.

Getting ready

You should set up the order activity rule for **Blanket Order** in order to set up the processing options for the **Blanket Order Entry** application **P4310**.

How to do it...

1. Set up the **Order Activity Rule** for Purchase Requisition via the **G43A41** menu.
2. Enter the **Document Type** for **Blanket Order** as *OB*, and the **Line Type** as *S*.
3. Enter **Order Activity** for **Blanket Order**; the following screenshot shows the standard purchase requisition **Order Activity Rule**.

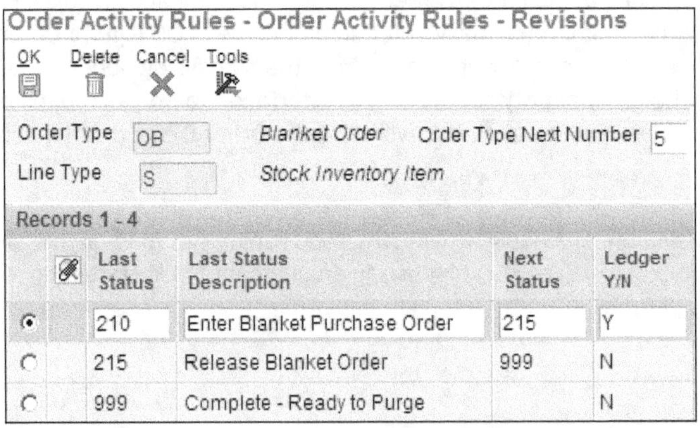

4. Select **Procurement and Subcontract Management** | **Daily Processing** | **Stock Based Purchasing** | **Purchase Order Processing**, click the arrow next on **Enter Blanket Order (P4310)**, and then select **Values**.
5. Enter **Order Type** *OB* in the **Order Type** field in the **Default** tab that exists in the **Document Type - All Documents (00/DT) UDC** to specify the default value for the order type. The system populates the **Order Type** field of the **Order Header** form with this value.
6. Enter **Beginning Status** *210* in the **Default** tab that exists in the **Activity/Status** Codes (**40/AT**) UDC, in order to specify the default value for the beginning status for the order. The value that you enter must be set up for the order type and the line type.
7. On the **Order Inquiry** tab, enter *210* in the **From Status Code** field, and *999* in the **Thru Status Code** field.

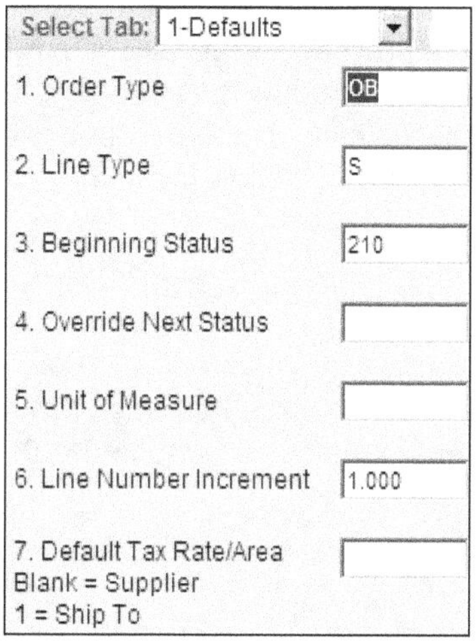

How it works...

When you set up the **Processing Options** for **P4310 Enter Blanket Order**, the system distinguishes a blanket order by its order type and the order activity rules. For example, when you work with a blanket order, you usually enter an order type of *OB* (**Blanket Order**). The system is working based on the document type, line types, activity rules, and status codes that you set up for requisition processing options. The system reads the set-up information from the processing options. On the **Default** tab, when you enter a **Beginning Status** of *210* the system will pick the **Next Status** from **Order Activity Setup**. On the **Interface** tab, you set the quantity update to 1, which indicates that when you enter the blanket order, the system will store the item quantity on the **Other OP** field in the item location table for location item quantity in the **Item Availability Inquiry**.

There's more...

You can use the **Override Next Status** field if you want to skip the status in the **Order Activity** table.

See also

- *Setting up order activity rules*

Setting up purchase orders

This recipe demonstrates setting up a **Purchase Order** activity rule and the **Purchase Order** application processing options. You need to set up a Purchase Order rule for each individual item or service that you enter on a purchase order, and you must enter a line of detailed information that describes the order, including the quantity and cost of the item or service. You must set up order activity rules to establish the sequence of steps through which you progress. The Order Activity forces users to follow the same sequence that was specified in the the Order Activity set-up.

Getting ready

You should set up the order activity rule for the **Purchase Order** application in order to set up the processing options for **Purchase Order** application **P4310**.

How to do it...

1. Set up the **Order Activity Rule** for Purchase Requisition via the **G43A41** menu.
2. Enter the **Document Type** for purchase orders as *OP*, and the **Line Type** as S.
3. Enter the **Order Activity** for **Purchase Order**; the following screenshot shows the standard purchase requisition **Order Activity Rule**:

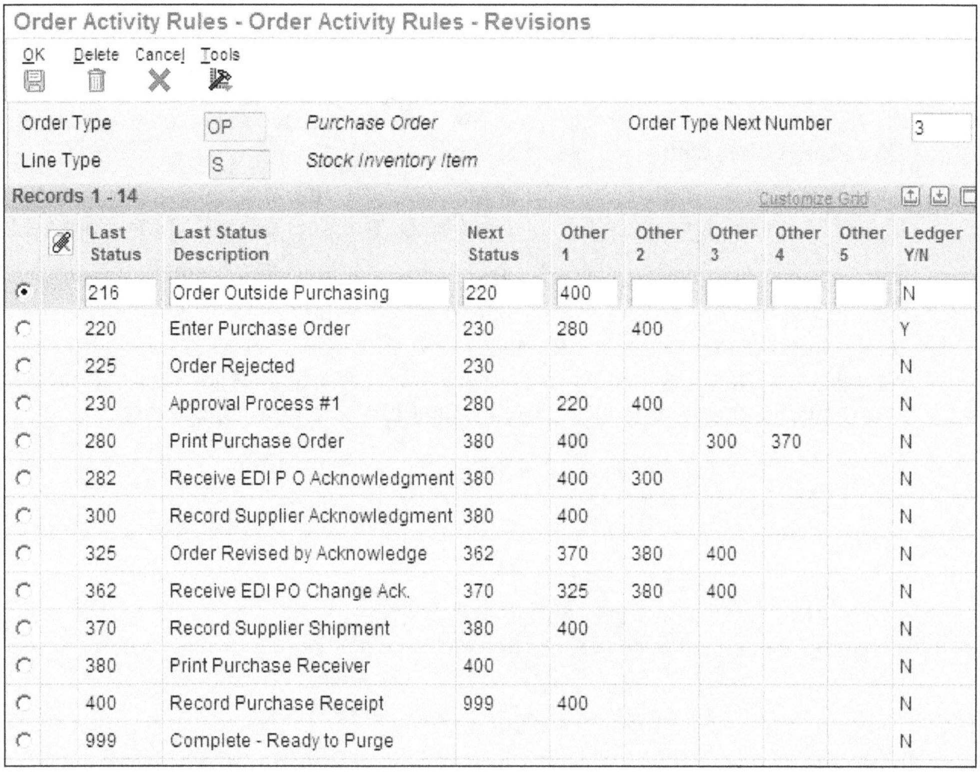

Last Status	Last Status Description	Next Status	Other 1	Other 2	Other 3	Other 4	Other 5	Ledger Y/N
216	Order Outside Purchasing	220	400					N
220	Enter Purchase Order	230	280	400				Y
225	Order Rejected	230						N
230	Approval Process #1	280	220	400				N
280	Print Purchase Order	380	400		300	370		N
282	Receive EDI P O Acknowledgment	380	400	300				N
300	Record Supplier Acknowledgment	380	400					N
325	Order Revised by Acknowledge	362	370	380	400			N
362	Receive EDI PO Change Ack.	370	325	380	400			N
370	Record Supplier Shipment	380	400					N
380	Print Purchase Receiver	400						N
400	Record Purchase Receipt	999	400					N
999	Complete - Ready to Purge							N

4. Select **Procurement and Subcontract Management** | **Daily Processing** | **Stock Based Purchasing** | **Purchase Order Processing**, click the arrow next on **Enter Purchase Order (P4310)**, and then select **Values**.
5. Enter **Order Type** *OP* in the **Order Type** field in the **Default** tab. See the Order Activity rule set up screenshots, shown earlier.

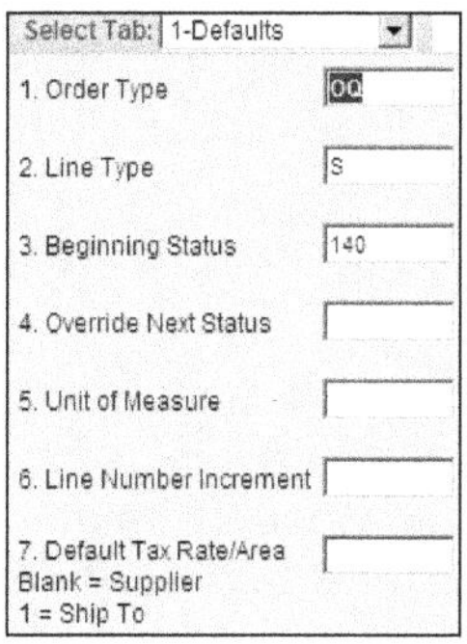

6. Enter **Beginning Status** *220* in the **Default** tab that exists in the **Activity/Status Codes (40/AT) UDC** to specify the default value for the beginning status for the order. The value that you enter must be set up for the Order Type and the Line Type.
7. On the **Order Inquiry** tab, enter *220* in the **From Status Code** field**,** and *999* in the **Thru Status Code** field.
8. Enter a value that exists in the **Unit of Measure** (**00/UM**) UDC to specify the default **Unit of Measure** that the system displays in the **Transaction Unit of Measure** field.
9. Enter a whole number that the system uses to automatically increment the order lines on the order.
10. On the **Interface** tab, leave the **Business Unit Validation**, **PBCO Warning**, **PACO Warning**, and **Quantity Update** fields blank, as shown in the following screenshot. These are the recommended settings for the **Purchase Order** application.

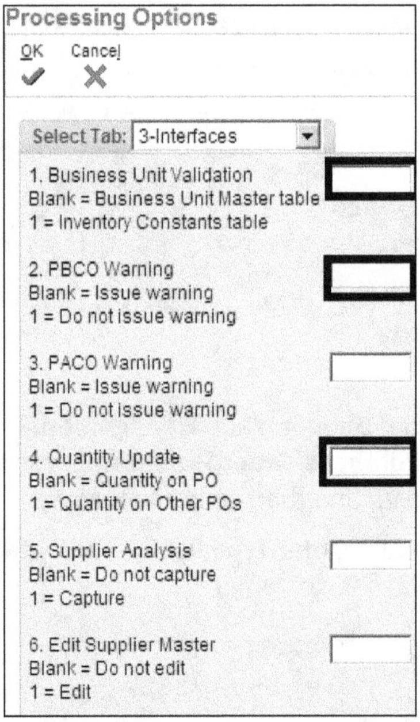

11. On the **Order Revision** tab, specify whether the system allows revisions to an order. Enter *1* in the **Processing Option**.
12. Specify the **Next Status Code** at which the system begins tracking order revision audit information. The system does not record revisions to a detail line if the line's status precedes the status code that you enter in this **Processing Option**. The system stores revision information in the **P.O. Detail Ledger File - Flexible Version (F43199)**. You can access this table through the **Order Revision Inquiry program (P4319)**.
13. Specify whether the system allows you to enter text when you are entering a revision.

How it works...

The system populates the **Order Type** field of the **Order Header** form with the order type processing option for the **P4310** application. When you set up the Line Type in the processing options, the systems affects with the transaction interfaces (General Ledger, Job Cost, and Accounts Payable) based on line type setup. The **Line Type** also specifies the conditions for including a line on reports and in calculations. You define line types in the **Order Line Types** program (**P40205**). The value that you enter must be set up for the order type and the line type that you are using.

The system gets the next status codes for combinations of order type and line type by using the **Order Activity Rules** program (**P40204**). When you leave this processing option blank, the system uses the **Next Status** code in the **Order Activity Rules** as the default value.

The system uses the **Purchasing Unit of Measure** from the **F4101** table. The transaction unit of measure directly relates to the number that you have entered in the **Quantity** field on the **Purchase Order Entry** form. If you select an item from a catalog in **Purchase Order Entry**, the unit of measure in the catalog overrides the value that you enter in this field. If you have entered a value in the **Unit of Measure** field, you should not enter a value in this field.

The system hides cost information. The cost field does not appear, although the system still writes the cost information to the **F4311** table. The system uses cost information from the cost tables as the default. Examples of the cost tables are the **F4105** table and the **F41061** table. The cost table that the system uses for the default information depends on the way that the system is set up.

The system also validates the branch/plant against the **F0006** table. Typically, you use this **Processing Option** when you are performing services expenditure purchasing. When you leave this processing option blank, the **Ship To** address book number from the address book number in the **F0006** table is used. You can access the **Business Unit Master** table through the **Revise Business Unit (P0006)** program.

There's more...

Using the **Processing Options** for **Order Entry**, you can display a header form before the detail form. Depending on how you set the **Processing Options**, certain fields can display on the header form. If you bypass the header form, you must enter limited header information on the detail form. Based on the supplier and branch/plant that you enter, the system applies default values to the fields on the header form.

See also

- *Setting up order activity rules*

Setting up Order Approval

In order to activate Order Approval, you should set up the processing options to enable approval processing. It is also required that you set up the order activity rule to activate **Order Approval.** The **Order Approval** is based on the **Approval Route**, which can be activated through **Originator's address**, **Originator's User Profile**, **Branch Plant**, or **Default Location**.

Getting ready

You should set up the following application **Processing Options** before performing this task:

- Processing Options for **Purchase Order (P4310)**
- Processing Options for **Purchase Order Approvals (P43081)**

How to do it...

1. Select **Procurement and Subcontract Management** | **Daily Processing** | **Stock Based Purchasing** | **Purchase Order Processing**, click the arrow next to **Enter Purchase Order** (**P4310**), and then select **Values**.

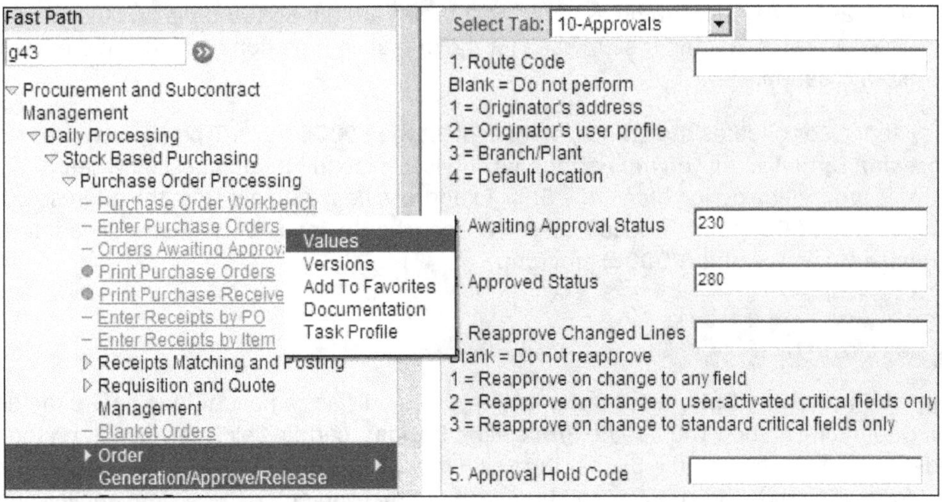

2. On the **Approvals** tab, enter a **Route Code** to specify which code the system uses for approval processing. The system provides various options depending on business needs.
3. For **Order Awaiting Approval Status**, enter the **Next Status** for the system to use when the order enters the **Approval Route**.

4. Enter the **Approved Status** for **Next Status as per order activity rule setup** for the system to use when the order is automatically approved, for example *280*.
5. Specify whether the system activates approval processing for certain types of modifications to a purchase order line that has already been approved.
6. Specify the **Approval Hold Code** that the system uses when placing the order on hold for the approval process. If you leave this **Processing Option** blank, the system does not place the order on hold.
7. Select **Procurement and Subcontract Management | Daily Processing | Stock Based Purchasing | Order Generation/Approval/Release**, click the arrow next to **Order Awaiting for Approval (P43081)**, and then click on **Values**.

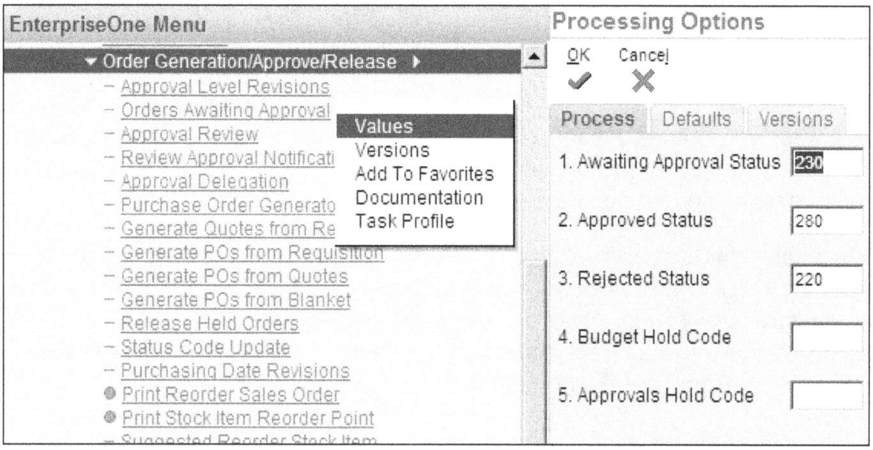

8. On the **Process** tab, enter a value from **UDC 40/AT** that specifies the **Awaiting Approval Status** in the processing cycle for this order type. You set up the steps for the processing cycle on the **Order Activity Rules** form.
9. Enter the **Approved Status** from **UDC 40/AT** that indicates the next step in the order flow of the line type.
10. Enter the **Rejected Status** from **UDC 40/AT** that indicates the last step that this order line has rejected in the processing option.
11. Enter the **Budget Hold Code** from **UDC 42/HC** that identifies why an order is on budget hold.
12. Enter the **Approvals Hold Code** from **UDC 42/HC** that identifies why an order is on approval hold.
13. On the **Default** tab, enter the **Order Type** from **UDC 00/DT** that identifies the type of document. This codec also indicates the origin of the transaction. There are document type codes for Vouchers, invoices, receipts, and time sheets, which create automatic offset entries during the post program.

14. The **Enter '1' to protect address number from input** field enables you to prevent other users from entering or changing the address number.

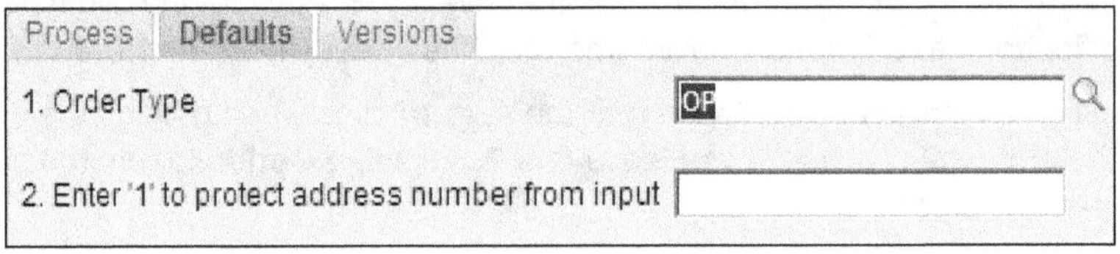

How it works...

When you set up the approval route, the system notifies those persons responsible for approving the order. The system sends a notification e-mail to the first authorized person for approval If the person approves the order, the system either sends a message to the next person responsible for approving the order, or updates the order to an approved status (if no other approvals are necessary) and sends an approval message to the order originator. If a person rejects the order, the system returns a rejection message to the originator. If the originator amends the order, the system restarts the approval process.

You can use e-mail for the approval process even if you do not use the electronic mail system from Oracle on a company-wide basis. You can access the messages from the e-mail form that is set up specifically for approval processing, or from any e-mail form on which you have a mailbox. If you use the approval processing e-mail form, processing options enable you to determine which mailboxes appear on the form.

There's more...

If a person assigned to multiple approval routes leaves the company or goes on a vacation, you can transfer approval authority to another person. After you create an approval route, you can assign it to an order. The system does not allow further processing of the order until it is fully approved.

Locate Purchase Order Approvals

You can locate all orders that are awaiting approval and select individual orders to review for approval or rejection. You can also locate all orders that you originated, in order to review the status of each, such as **Approved**, **Rejected**, or **Pending**. You locate orders based on the address book number. You can also locate orders based on the age of the order, in order to identify orders that require immediate attention. If you originate orders, you can specify that only approved or rejected orders appear. You can access an order's status summary to identify who is responsible for approving the order, and to review a history of the actions that have occurred for that order.

See also

- *Setting up purchase orders*

Setting up a receipt route

This recipe demonstrates receipt routing definition and activation, lists a prerequisite, and discusses how to assign receipt routes to items.

Getting ready

You should set up the operation code on **UDC 43/RC** in the **P0004A** application **Work with User Defined Codes**.

How to do it...

1. Select **Procurement and Subcontract Management** | **Daily Processing** | **Stock Based Purchasing** | **Receipt Routing**, and then click on **Receipt Routing Definition**.
2. Enter a value in the **Route Code** field by selecting the value from **UDC 43/RC** that identifies a receipt route. Each receipt route consists of a series of operations through which the system directs items upon receipt.

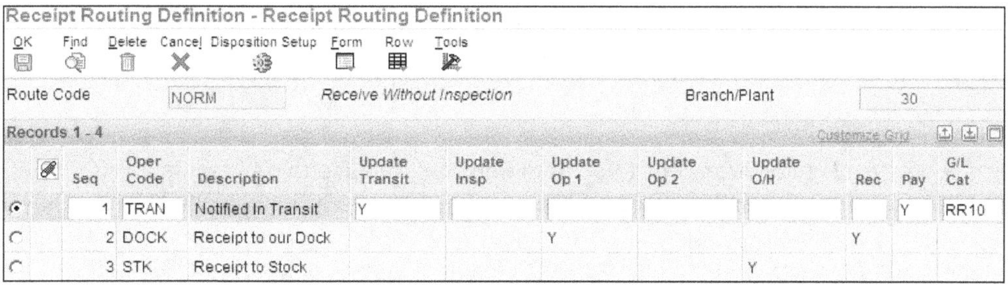

		Seq	Oper Code	Description	Update Transit	Update Insp	Update Op 1	Update Op 2	Update O/H	Rec	Pay	G/L Cat
		1	TRAN	Notified In Transit	Y						Y	RR10
		2	DOCK	Receipt to our Dock			Y			Y		
		3	STK	Receipt to Stock					Y			

3. Enter the **Operation Sequence** in which the system performs the operations or steps of the route.
4. Enter an **Oper Code** (operation code) from UDC **43/OC** that represents an operation or step within the receipt route.
5. Enter *Y* in **Update Transit field**, to indicate that the system should update the quantity in transit field in the **F41021** table.
6. Enter *Y* in the **Update Insp**, if you want to update the inspection information.
7. Enter a value that indicates whether to update the **Quantity in Inspection** field in the **F41021** table as soon as a quantity moves into this operation.

8. Enter Y in **Update Op 1** and **Update Op 2** if you want to update operation 1 and Update Op 2.
9. Enter a value that indicates whether to update the quantity in the **Operation 1** field in the **F41021** table as soon as a quantity moves into this operation.
10. You can enter *Y* in this column only once for each route code. For **Update O/H** (update on hand), enter a value that indicates whether to update the **Quantity on Hand** field in the **F41021** table as soon as a quantity moves into this operation. You can enter *Y* for the last operation only.
11. Enter *Y* in **Rec** (receipt acknowledgement) if you want receipt acknowledgement.

How it works...

You can monitor items from the moment that they leave a supplier's warehouse. You create receipt routes to determine the series of operations through which you process items until the items become part of the inventory. You must define the operations that make up each receipt route. You must also determine the updates that occur as you transfer items to each operation. For example, you specify the operation at which items become on-hand inventory. When you enter items at the on-hand operation, the system creates journal entries to reflect the items in inventory, and you can create a voucher to pay for the items.

You can direct the system to create journal entries each time that you transfer items to and from an operation in a receipt route. You do this so that the value of the items at each operation appears in the general ledger. For example, you might want the general ledger to reflect the value of items currently at the dock. When you create a receipt route, you must indicate whether to pay for items that you remove (disposition) from the route, based on the reason for which you remove them. For example, you might want to pay for items that you rework but not for items that you return.

Each update field on the **Work With Receipts Routing Codes** form represents a field in the **F41021** table. The system maintains balances of inventory items in this table. You can have the system update the availability of an item at any operation in a receipt route. For example, you might want the ability to promise items to customers (enter sales orders) when the items arrive at the dock instead of waiting until the items are in stock. You access the **Item Availability Definition** form from the **Branch/Plant Constants** form to indicate which fields the system uses to calculate item availability. For example, you can specify that the system add the balance in the **Update Transit Quantity** field to the current on-hand balance, in order to calculate availability. You must specify at which operation the system records the receipt date for items. For example, you can specify that the system record the receipt date when items arrive at the dock. The system compares the receipt date to the date that the supplier promised to deliver the items, in order to determine supplier performance. You must specify at which operation the item is eligible for payment. When you transfer items to the payment eligible operation, the system creates journal entries to reflect a liability for the items, and you can create a voucher to pay for the items.

Based on the receipt date, the system calculates supplier performance information such as lead time days for an item, and on-time deliveries. **Pay** (payment eligible) indicates at which operation the goods are eligible for payment. The system automatically updates the **Pay** (payment eligible) field for the same operation at which you update the on-hand balance. When quantity is moved to this operation, the system updates the open quantity and open amount in the **Purchase Order Receiver** file (**F43121**) table so that it can voucher in the **Voucher Match** program. The system uses this field to determine whether the quantity is eligible for payment when the quantity is disposition it out of the routing process. Each quantity disposition has its own set-up. This must be the last operation in the route. You can enter a sequence number if the sequence in which you want the operations to occur differs from the sequence in which you enter the operations.

There's more...

When you create a receipt route, you must indicate whether you want to pay for items that you remove (disposition) from the route, based on the reason these which you remove them. For example, you might want to pay for items that you rework, but not pay for items that you return. You must specify the removal categories (returns, reworks, scrap, rejects, or adjustments) for which items are payable. For example, if you specify that the scrap category is payable, the system determines that you must pay for items that you classify as scrap. If items that you remove from a receipt route are payable, the system creates journal entries to reflect a liability for the items. The system credits a received account, and not a voucher account, and debits a disposition account, based on the general ledger category that you specify for the removal category.

Receipt route

A **Receipt route** is a series of operations through which you process items upon receipt. To create a receipt route, you must define the series of operations that make up the route. For example, you can create a receipt route that is made up of two operations–staging area and stock–and another receipt route that is made up of three operations–staging area, inspection, and stock. You determine the updates that the system performs as you progress items through a receipt route by specifying at which operation.

See also

- *Setting up order activity rules*

Setting up standard receipts

This recipe provides details of receipt information, lists a prerequisite, and discusses how to process standard receipts.

Getting ready

You should set up the **Processing Option** for the **PO Receipt** application (**P4312**) and also review the order activity rules for Purchase Order.

How to do it...

1. In the **Default** tab, specify the type of document for inquiry. This **UDC (00/DT)** also indicates the origin of the transaction. Document type codes are reserved for vouchers, invoices, receipts, and time sheets, which create automatic offset entries during the post program.
2. In the **Default** tab, specify the type of document for receipt. This **UDC (00/DT)** also indicates the origin of the transaction. Document type codes are reserved for vouchers, invoices, receipts, and time sheets, which create automatic offset entries during the post program.

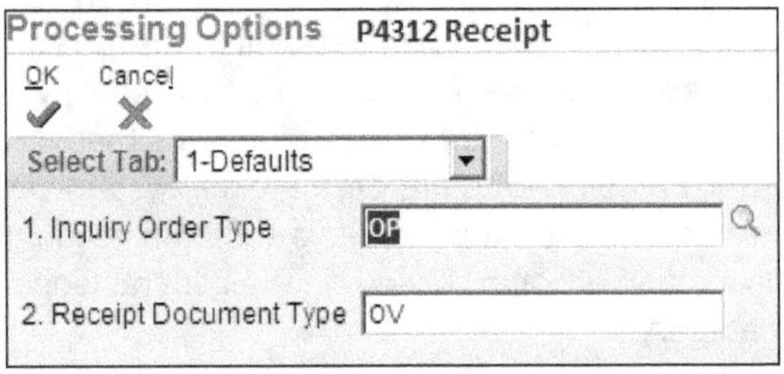

3. On the **Status Default** tab, set the next incoming status in the **Acceptable Incoming Status Code 1** to **Acceptable Incoming Status Code 4** for those orders that are eligible for receipt.
4. In the **Status Default** tab, specify the next outgoing status in the **Outgoing Status for Partial Receipts** for the order that has been received partially.
5. In the **Status Default** tab, specify the next outgoing status in the **Outgoing Status for Closing** for those orders that has been received completely.
6. In the **Status Default** tab, specify the next outgoing status in the **Outgoing Status for Cancelling** for those orders where the order detail line has been canceled.

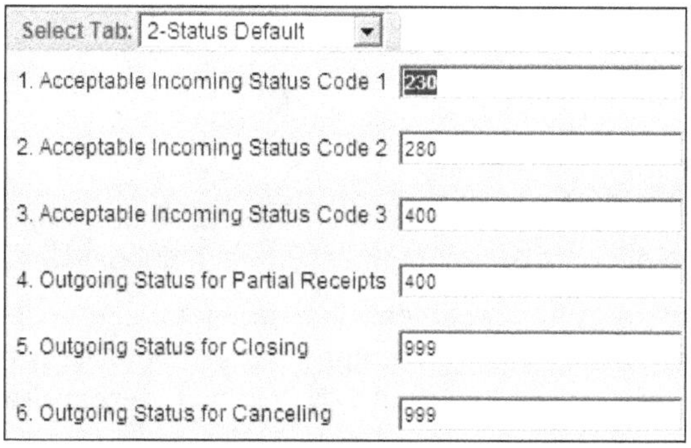

7. The **Display** tab specifies how you want to release backorders, in the **Sales Order Backorders**. If you enter *1*, the system will display the **Backorder Release** form. If you leave this blank, it will not display the **Backorder Release** form.
8. On the **Display** tab, specify whether the system displays lot information, such as the **Lot** field and the **Expiration Date** field, in the **Lot Information** field. If you select *1*, the system will display this information, and if you leave it blank, the system will not display the lot information.
9. On the **Display** tab, specify whether you want to allow users to change costs. If you select *1* in the **Cost Protection** field, the system will disable this field. If you leave this field blank, the system will display the cost field.
10. Specify the **Receiving Mode** that the system uses to receive detail lines, as either based on purchase order or based on item number. You can see the Receiving options in the following screenshot, and can select the correct option as per your business needs.

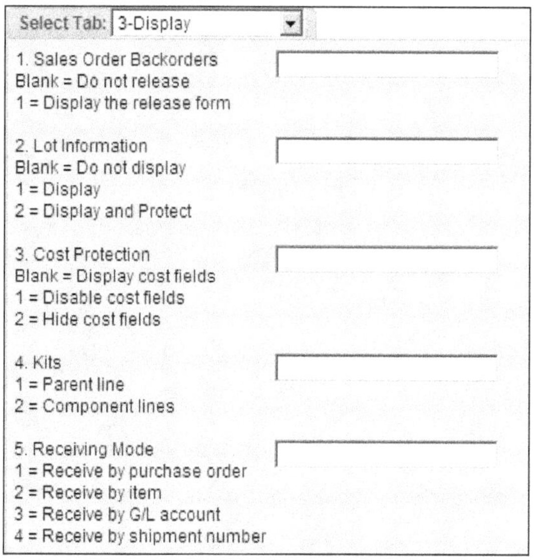

11. On the **Process** tab, specify whether the system updates the supplier number in the **F4102** table.
12. Specify whether the system uses default lot and location information in the **Purchase Order Receipts** program (**P4312**).
13. Specify whether the system automatically selects all detail lines for receipt, which prevents you from having to manually select each detail line.
14. Specify whether the system enables you to enter serial number information. Note that before you enter serial number information, you should verify that you have entered *Y* (Yes) in the **Serial Number Required Y/N** field on the **Item Branch Revisions** form.
15. Specify manual or automatic entry of quantity information. Enter *1* if you want to enter the quantity manually; leaving this blank will pick the open quantity from the purchase order.
16. Specify whether to manually apply landed costs or whether the system should automatically apply landed costs. Note that you can manually apply landed costs after a receipt, via the **Receipts Inquiry** form, which you access through the **Standalone Landed Cost** program (**P43214**).
17. Specify whether the system prints a receipt traveler document after each receipt. The system uses the version that you specified on the **Versions** tab.
18. Specify whether the system captures supplier analysis information.
19. Specify whether to activate **Receipt Routing**.
20. Enter a code that qualifies the routing for an item and supplier combination. Examples would include specific routing types for ASNs (**EDI 856** Ship Notice/ Manifest transactions) and for transfers.
21. Specify whether the system will price at receipt.
22. Specify whether the system will continue processing a receipt if the system calculates a negative **On-Hand Quantity**.

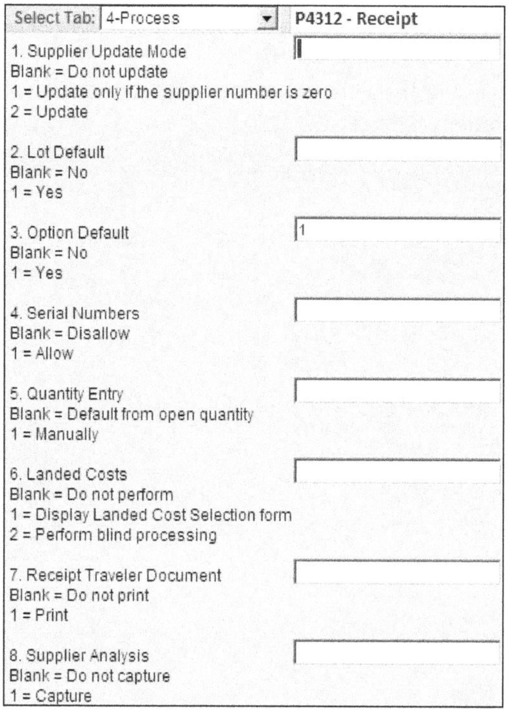

23. On the **Tolerance** tab, specify whether the system should check whether a detail line's quantity or amount exceed the tolerance percentage. To check the tolerance, you can access the **Purchasing Tolerance Setup** program (**P4322**).
24. In the **Tolerance** tab, specify whether the system checks to determine whether a detail line's date is outside of the tolerance date range. To check the tolerance date range, you can access the **Supplier/Item Relationships** program (**P43090**).

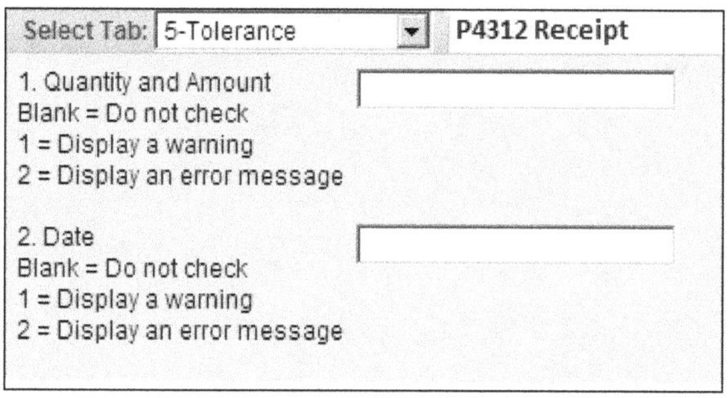

25. Specify the recipient of the e-mail that the system automatically sends when goods are received.

26. Specify the recipient of the e-mail that the system automatically sends when the unit cost/lump sum changes on a purchase order detail line during receipt.
27. Specify the recipient of the e-mail that the system automatically sends when the quantity on the order changes.

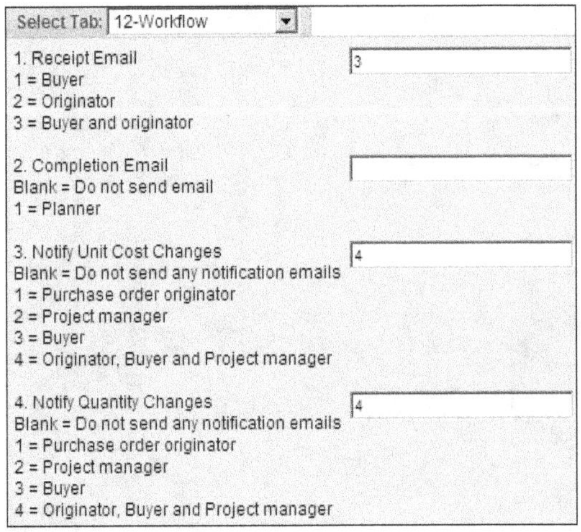

How it works...

When you receive goods, you must verify that the details of the receipt correspond to the information on the purchase order. You must verify item numbers, quantities, units of measure, costs, and so forth. If the receipt details differ from those on the purchase order, you must adjust the purchase order detail lines to reflect the receipt. For example, if landed costs, such as delivery charges or import taxes, apply to the item's purchase price, you enter these costs for the order during the receipt process. The system also enables the pricing and re-pricing of purchase order items at receipt. Pricing and re-pricing at receipt time for matrix items and quality attributes enables you to account for price changes that must be reflected when an item is received.

When you select only one detail line on the **Work With Receipts** menu, the system displays all of the detail lines on the **Receipt Revisions** menu that meet the criteria of the mode that you have entered. For example, if you enter *1* for the receiving mode and select one detail line on the **Work With Receipts** form, then the system displays all of the lines for the purchase order. If you enter *2* for the receiving mode and select one detail line on the **Work With Receipts** form, the system displays all of the lines for the selected item. If you enter *3* for the receiving mode and select one detail line on the **Work With Receipts** form, then the system displays all of the lines for the general ledger account. If you enter *4* for the receiving mode and select one detail line on the **Work With Receipts** form, then the system displays all of the lines for the shipment number.

If you work in an inventory environment, you can specify the warehouse location in which to store items upon receipt. If a certain location is full, you can assign items to multiple locations. If you group items by lot, you can assign items to a single lot or to multiple lots. If necessary, you can specify serial numbers for these items. If the receiving branch/plant has license plate functionality activated, you can use the processing options on the **Warehouse** tab, and license plate branch/plant constants, to process license plate information for adding inventory to the location.

There's more...

When a direct ship order is created in Sales Order Management, the system automatically creates a corresponding purchase order. For a direct ship order, you must enter a receipt in order to update the corresponding sales order with the new status information. However, if you enter a partial receipt, the system splits the corresponding order detail lines on the direct ship sales order, and updates only the order detail line that was received.

See also

- *Setting up purchase orders*

5
Understanding Pricing in Procurement and Purchase Orders

In this chapter, we will cover:

- Setting up pricing in procurement
- Creating stock/non stock-based purchase orders
- Creating discount terms
- Creating tax information
- Creating substitute or replacement items
- Creating kits orders
- Change orders
- Printing orders
- Creating orders for multiple suppliers
- Creating supplier catalogs
- Entering order using order templates
- Creating order from quote order
- Setting an order on hold
- Entering and releasing order holds

Introduction

As pricing is probably one of the most complex aspects of the business, planning, setting up, and maintaining pricing information might take a considerable amount of time. When you enter a purchase order, the system retrieves the unit cost for the item based on characteristics such as the branch/plant, the supplier, and the quantity.

Setting up pricing in procurement

Procurement provides flexibility when defining pricing. Setting up procurement pricing enables you to price items by using a procurement pricing structure, and enables you to streamline pricing set up and maintenance. You can easily adjust prices for each purchase order, and then combine the adjustments into a pricing structure or schedule. In EnterpriseOne Advanced Pricing, price set-up is based on the quantity, weight, or amount of an item that is entered on an order. Pricing can also be based on quality attributes of the product that is purchased.

Getting ready

Verify that the pricing hierarchy is defined in **Preference Hierarchy (P40073)** application. Select the **Pref Type 51 Base Price** and review.

How to do it...

1. Access the **Base Price Revisions (P4106)** application from **Fast Path,** and then click on **Add** to set up the **Item Base Price.**
2. Select in **Preference Hierarchy** the type of price that you want to enter:

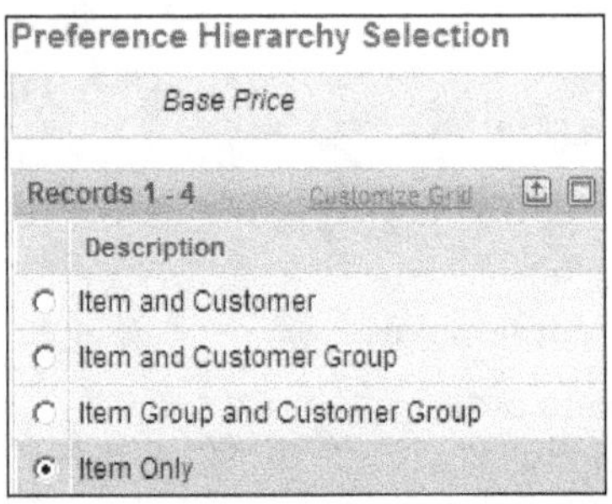

3. Enter the **Item Number**, **UOM**, **Currency Code**, **Unit Price**, **Effective From Date**, and **Effective To Date**.

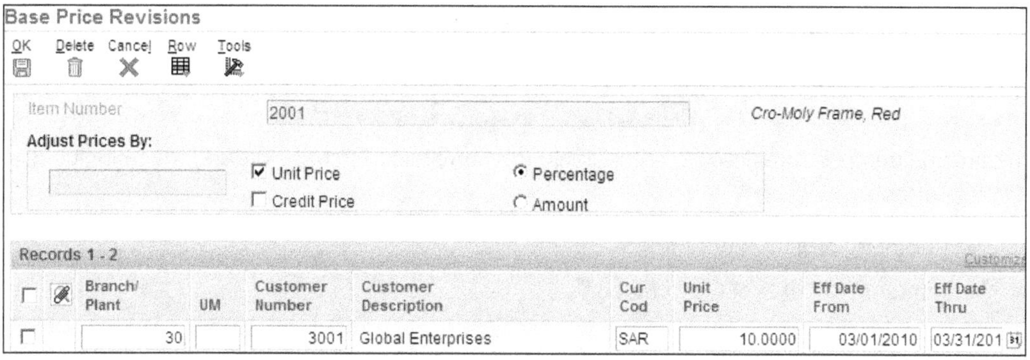

How it works...

When you enter a purchase order, the system retrieves the unit cost for the item based on characteristics such as the branch/plant, the supplier, the quantity, and the item, or a contract. Before the system processes any type of advanced price adjustment to the purchase order, it must first retrieve the unit cost. Depending on the purchase price level for the item, the system retrieves the unit cost from either the **Supplier Price/Catalog** file (**F41061**) table or the **Item Cost** (**F4105**) table. After the system retrieves the unit cost, it verifies that **Advanced Procurement Pricing** is active. Quality attribute pricing is a quality level-break adjustment. Therefore, for quality level-break type adjustments, the system will not process adjustments that use the quantity, weight, or amount entered for the order. If **Advanced Procurement Pricing** is active, the system bypasses the standard price adjustments that you set up in procurement and searches for applicable schedules and adjustments in advanced pricing.

There's more...

To enter a credit order, use a line type for which the **Reverse Sign** Flag is set to *Y* in the **F40205** table. The system stores all credit prices in the **F4106** table.

> The minimum or maximum price adjustment enables you to adjust the unit price of a particular item, customer, item group, customer group, or combinations of these. The sequence of the minimum or maximum price adjustment on the adjustment schedule determines what the price will be at that point in the schedule.

See also

- *Creating supplier catalogs*

Creating stock/non stock-based purchase orders

This recipe demonstrates how to enter stock and non stock purchase orders, which includes the following:

- Entering order header information
- Entering order detail information

Getting ready

You should set up the processing options for **Purchase Orders** (**P4310**) in order to enter the purchase order.

How to do it...

1. Select **Procurement and Subcontract Management** | **Daily Processing** | **Stock Based Purchasing**, and then click on **Purchase Order Processing**.
2. On the **Work With Order Headers form**, click **Add,** and then enter the following information:

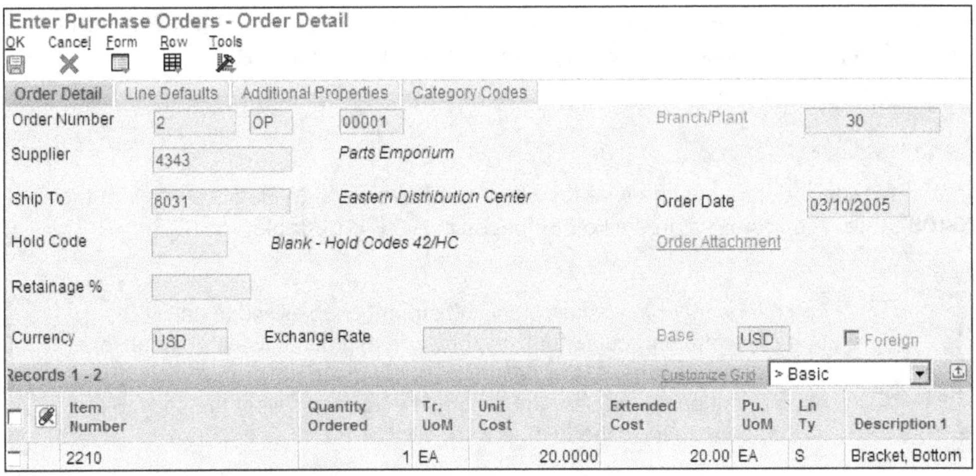

3. Enter the **Supplier** information.
4. Enter the **Branch/Plant** information.
5. Enter the **Order Date**.
6. Enter the **Requested Date**.

7. Enter the **Promise Delivery Date** and then click **OK**.
8. On the **Order Detail** form, click the **Line Defaults** tab and enter the **G/L Date**.
9. Enter the **Item Number** on the detail line.
10. Enter the **Quantity Ordered**.
11. Enter the **Transaction UOM**.
12. Enter the **Unit Cost;** the **Extended Cost** will be calculated automatically based on the **Quantity Ordered**.
13. For **Non Stock Item** select **Procurement and Subcontract Management | Daily Processing | Non Stock Purchasing,** and then click on **Purchase Order Processing**.
14. Enter the **Account Number** for **Non Stock Item**.
15. Enter the **Quantity Ordered**.
16. Enter the **Unit Cost**; the **Extended Cost** will be calculated automatically based on the **Quantity Ordered**.

How it works...

When you enter the order header to generate an order, you must provide information about the supplier who is to fill the order, the branch/plant that is requesting the order, and the shipping address for the order. The header information that you enter determines how the system processes the order. For example, supplier information determines the address to which the order is sent, the payment terms for the order, and so forth. Origination information determines the business unit accountable for the order and the address to which the goods and services are to be delivered. Tax information determines how the system calculates taxes for the order. Header information also includes the date on which the order is placed, the date on which the order is due, and reference information such as the employee entering the order. Using the **Processing Options** for Order Entry, you can display a header form before the detail form. Depending on how you set the processing options, certain fields can display on the header form. If you bypass the header form, you must enter limited header information on the detail form. Based on the supplier and branch/plant that you enter, the system applies default values to the fields on the header form. After you enter an item number on a detail line, the system validates that the item exists in the **Inventory Management** system. The system retrieves information for the item from the **Inventory Management** system. The system provides default values for detail lines based on the header information on an order. The system retrieves information such as the cost, description, and unit of measure for the item, and enters it on the detail line. You can add and change the information for each detail line based on what is relevant to the purchasing process. For example, if you purchase items for inventory, you must specify the unit of measure for the item. You can also specify the location where the item is stored upon receipt, and the weight, volume, lot, and manufacturing information for the item. You can specify an asset identifier and landed cost rules. You also can attach notes, or narrative text, to each detail line.

The **Item Number** is optional for a **Non Stock Purchase Order**.

There's more...

If you purchase goods or services from international suppliers, you might need to enter order amounts in different currencies, such as Canadian dollars, Japanese yen, and the Euro. Before you can do this, you must specify on the header form if the supplier uses a foreign currency. The system completes the currency field on the **Order Header** form with the default currency, if any, that you establish for the supplier.

See also

- *Setting up purchase orders* in *Chapter 4, Understanding and Setting up Procurement*

Creating discount terms

The system applies a discount factor to the unit price in order to determine the net price. The system retrieves this value from the inventory pricing rules, if you have assigned a rule to this item. The pricing rule set-up determines whether the system multiplies the unit price by this value or adds it to or deducts it from the unit price.

Getting ready

Define the **Item Price Group** in the Inventory management system in order to set up the discount terms.

How to do it...

1. Access the **Inventory Pricing Rules** application from the **G43A17** menu, and then click on **Inventory Price Rule**.

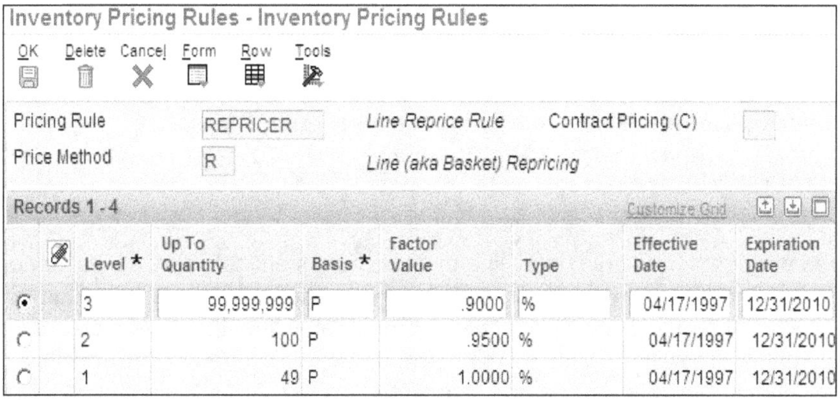

2. Enter a value in the **Pricing Rule** field, taken from the **Item Price Groups (40/PI) UDC** that the system uses to classify inventory by pricing rules.
3. Enter *P* for purchase order discounts in the **Price Method** field from the **(42/CT) UDC** that indicates the basis for the price rule. *P* for purchase order discounts.
4. Enter a value in the **Contract Pricing** field, taken from the **Pricing Type (42/PT) UDC,** to specify a special pricing relationship between the item and one or more of the customers. The inventory pricing rule code for a contract is the item number.
5. Enter an alphanumeric code in the **Level** field that determines the sequence in which the system displays the rules within the pricing group. You define levels when you set up the pricing groups. You must enter a value in the **Level** field for each discount that is applicable to the rule.
6. Enter an **Up To Quantity** value for the volume or quantity breaks commonly used in pricing tables. For example, if the quantity on the first level of a rule is 5, then the pricing logic on this level applies only to sales of five or fewer items. If the quantity on the next level is 10, then the pricing logic applies to sales of six through ten items. 99,999,999 indicates all quantities.
7. Enter a value in the **Basis** field from the **Cost/Price Basis (H42/CB) UDC**.
   The system uses the value that you enter to determine the order's net price.
8. In sales order repricing, the system bases all reprice calculations on either the unit cost or the price in the sales detail. Specify *P* if you want the system to use the unit price in the sales order as the basis for reprice calculations. Otherwise, specify a value between *1* and *8* to use the unit cost in the sales detail as the base on value for all reprice calculations.
9. Enter a **Factor Value** for the discount that the system uses when it calculates the price of an item attached to this inventory pricing rule. Discounts can be expressed as multipliers, additional amounts, or deductible amounts. For example, a *10* percent discount would be expressed as *.90*. You can use the same factor for markups over cost. For example, a 10 percent markup would be expressed as *1.10*.

10. Enter a **Type** value from the **FVTY (H00/FV) UDC** that indicates whether the factor value is a multiplier (percentage) or an additional/deductible cash amount (USD) when applied to an order's price.
11. Enter an **Override Price** that overrides all other rules or prices.

How it works...

You entered discount terms on a detail line to have the system calculate a discount on the items that you purchase. For example, a supplier might offer a *10* percent discount on certain items. When you enter a specific discount factor for a detail line, the system enters a cost for the item on the detail line based on the discount factor. For example, to specify a 10 percent discount for an item, you enter a discount factor of 0.*90*. If the unit cost for the item is usually *10*.00, the system enters a unit cost of 9.00. You can also specify a discount for an item based on a price rule. The system applies a discount to the unit cost of the item based on the discount that has been set up for the price rule. The system retrieves a default price rule for an item for which you have attached a price rule to the branch/plant level information for the item, or for which you have attached the price rule to the supplier from whom you are purchasing the item (or to the price group for the supplier).

There's more...

You can set up as many detail categories as you need. A single code can be used for sales, purchasing, order/basket, and contract pricing. If you set up a contract rule, it must equal the short number for the item under contract. If you indicate that a pricing type is a contract, you must enter the quantity that may be sold at this contract price, and the contract number if there is one. You must also attach the contract pricing rule to the customer or customer group for the rule to become effective.

See also

- *Setting up pricing in procurement*

Creating tax information

This tax information determines whether taxes apply to the items or services on the detail line, and how the system calculates the taxes.

Getting ready

You should set up the **UDC 00/EX** in order to set up the Tax Information.

How to do it...

1. On the **Purchase Order Detail** revision (**P4310**), enter a taxable code that indicates whether the item is subject to sales tax when you purchase it. The system calculates tax on the item only if the supplier is also taxable.
2. Enter **Expl Code** from the hard-coded **UDC 00/EX** that controls the algorithm that the system uses to calculate tax and general ledger distribution amounts. The system uses the tax explanation code in conjunction with the tax rate area and tax rules to determine how the tax is calculated. Each transaction pay item can be defined with a different tax explanation code.
3. Enter a code that identifies a tax or geographic area that has common tax rates and tax authorities. The system validates the code that you enter against the **F4008** table. The system uses the tax rate area in conjunction with the tax explanation code and tax rules to calculate tax and general ledger distribution amounts when you create an invoice or voucher.

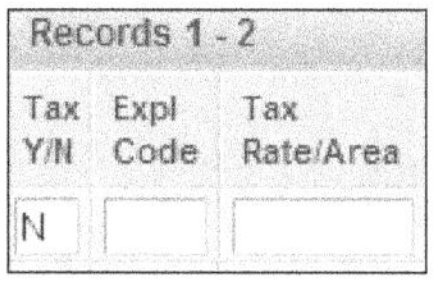

How it works...

When you enter tax information into the **Purchase Order** detail, the system retrieves the default tax information for each detail line based on the tax information that you entered for the order. If tax information for the detail line differs from that of the rest of the order, you can change the tax information to accommodate the detail line. If you are using the **Vertex Sales Tax Q Series** system in conjunction with EnterpriseOne software, the system retrieves the default **GeoCodes** in order to determine the tax rate to apply to the order.

> The taxation set-up is optional and is based on the country's taxation laws. It varies from country to country, and even from state in then U.S. to state. Each country/state has its own taxation law.

See also

- *Setting up purchase orders* in *Chapter 4, Understanding and Setting up Procurement*

Creating substitute or replacement items

You might enter an order for an item, but the supplier does not have the quantity available to fill the order. If the system notifies you that the item on a detail line is obsolete, you can review and select a replacement for the item.

Getting ready

Set up the processing options of the **P4310** application in order to activate the item cross reference.

How to do it...

1. From the **P4310** application **Processing** option, access the **Cross Ref** tab.

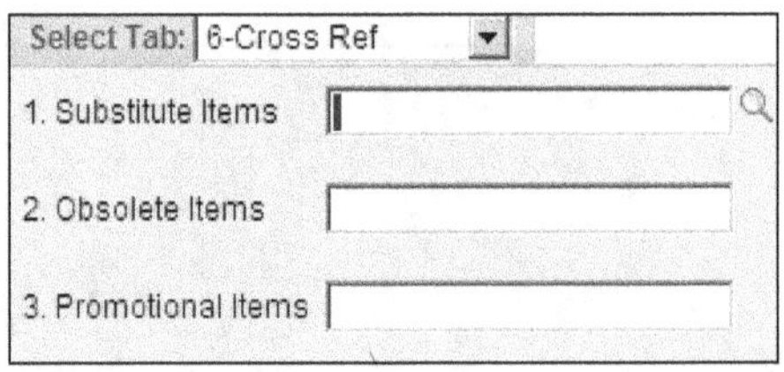

2. Specify the default **Cross-Reference** code that the system uses to retrieve **Substitute Items**. The value that you enter is used as the default on the **Substitute Item Search and Select** form.
3. Specify the **Cross-Reference** code that the system uses to retrieve item replacements for **Obsolete Items**. The system uses the value that you enter as the default on the **Substitute Item Search and Select** form.

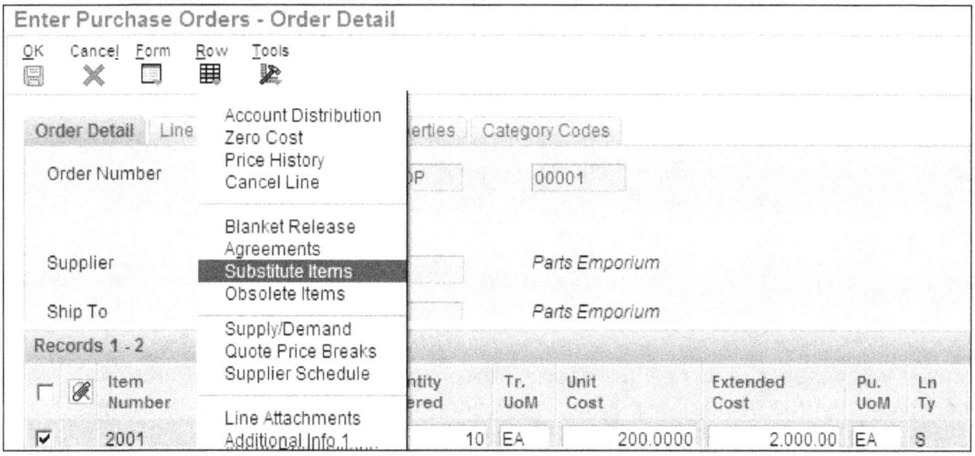

4. From the **Purchase Order form**, select the **Item Number** from the **Order Detail** tab, and then click on **Substitute Items** from the **Row** menu.

How it works...

When you activate the replacement process, the system verifies that the item cross reference has been set up, and that the purchase order application processing option has been properly tuned. The item being replaced must have a stocking type of *O* (obsolete) in the **F4101** table. The code that you enter must be a value in the **UDC table (41/DT)** for **Cross-Reference** codes. To retrieve the substitute item, the system retrieves an item's cross-reference code from the **F4104** table. If more than one substitute item exists, the system displays a check mark in the row header that is located in the detail area, and in the **Substitute Exists** column.

There's more...

The substitutes or replacements that the system displays are based on the cross-reference types from the **Inventory Management** system that you specify in the processing options for the **Purchase Order** program. You can specify whether you want to review substitute or replacement items after you enter a detail line. You can have the system replace the item number, the item description, and the cost on a detail line with that of a substitute or replacement item.

See also

- *Setting up purchase orders* in *Chapter 4, Understanding and Setting up Procurement*

Creating kits orders

Kits are comprised of component items that are associated to a parent item. Kits are useful if the company sells combinations of products. For example, if the company sells stereo systems, you can set up a kit with a parent name of "stereo". The stereo kit can contain components such as speakers and a compact disc player, which you typically want to sell together.

Getting ready

You must verify that you have set the appropriate processing option in the **Purchase Orders** program (**P4310**) that displays kit component lines. Also, verify that **Kit Items** have been set up.

How to do it...

1. Access the **Purchase Order** detail application (**P4310**) from the **G43A11** menu **Enter Purchase Order**.
2. On the **Purchase Order** detail (**P4310**) form enter Kit Configured Item and click on the **Row** menu and then click on **Kits**. The system will show the **Kits** components details. Click **OK** to save the record.

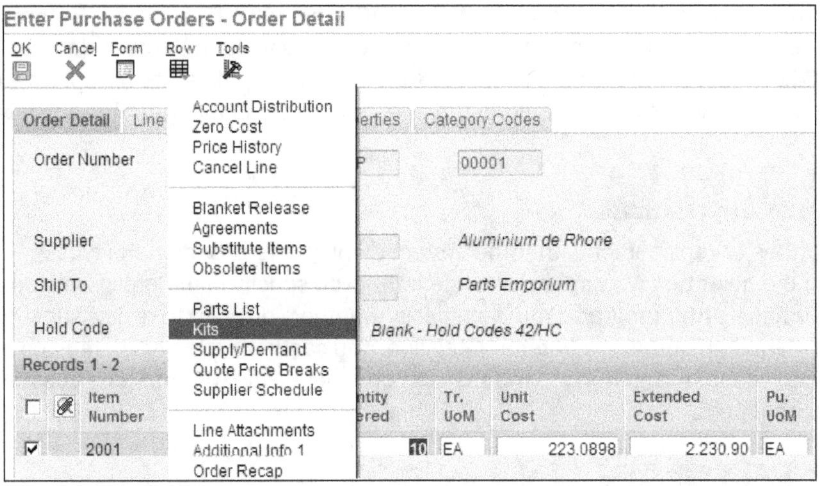

How it works...

When you enter an item number for a kit, the preselected components and the quantities that comprise the kit are displayed. If you change the quantity information for the kit, you must manually adjust the corresponding cost information. If you need to cancel component lines, you must cancel each line individually.

> You can also select any optional items that you want to include on the purchase order.

There's more...

You can have an item number for the kit that you enter on a purchase order, but the parent item, stereo, is not stocked as an inventory item.

See also

- *Creating stock/non stock-based purchase orders*

Change orders

You can change commitment details after you enter them by creating a change order, which updates the commitment information and creates a record of changes to the order. For example, to increase the committed amount for an order by 100, you enter a change order for 100.

Getting ready

In the processing options for the **Purchase Orders** program (**P4310**), ensure that the **Processing Option** in the **Defaults** section for line sequencing is set to *0*. If this **Processing Option** is set to *1*, you will have difficulty receiving change orders.

How to do it...

1. Access the **PO detail** application, search your **PO**, and click on **Find**. Then, **select** the purchase order and click on select from the menu option.
2. Select the line item for which you want to review the change order, and then click on **Chg Order Summary** from the Row menu.
3. Review the **Quantity Ordered** field to ensure it displays either a transacted quantity or units.
4. **Unit Cost** displays the price charged for the unit of measure in the adjoining field. Use these fields, for example, if the primary unit of measure is *EA* (each), but you typically use a list price per box.

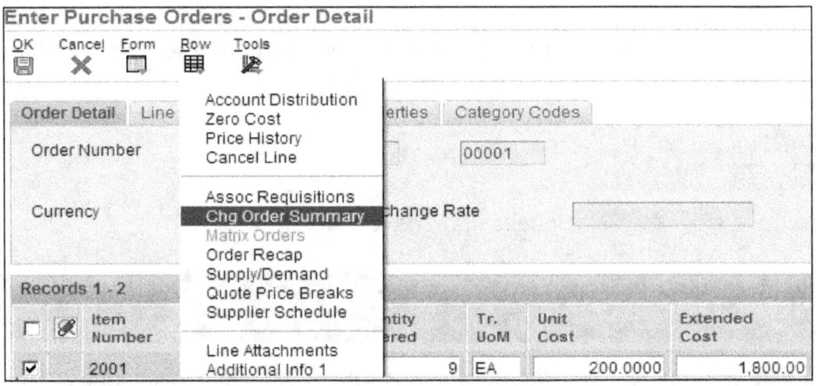

5. **Extended Cost** displays a value that is equal to the number of units multiplied by the unit price. If you want to add a new line to the order, you must first scroll through all existing detail lines to the first blank line, to ensure that the system assigns the correct number to each detail line.

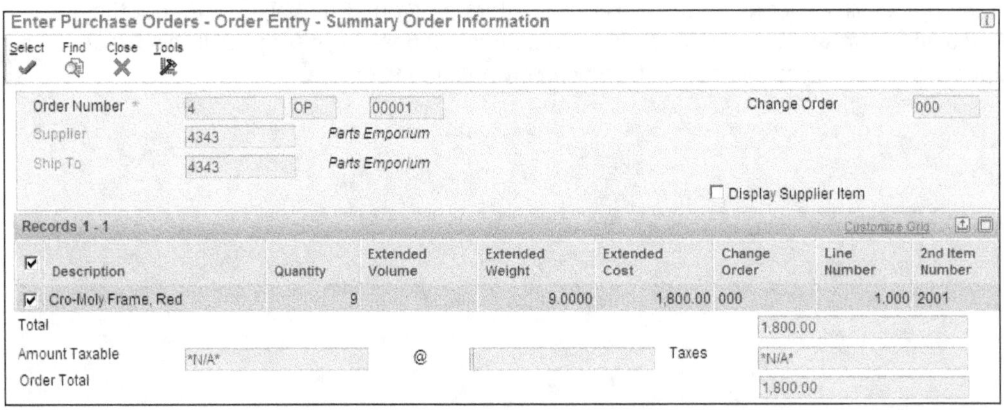

How it works...

You can set the display and processing options for order entry to determine whether you can change original commitment information by line item or if you must enter a change order. The system maintains a record after you make a change. After you enter the change order information, you can enter a descriptive text for each line item of the contract. After you enter a change order, you might need to review all of the changes. You can specify criteria such as the order number, supplier, item, and account number for the change order that you want to review. You can review additional information for each change order that appears, including the quantity ordered, the quantity open, the quantity received, and the quantity for which vouchers have been created. You can also access address numbers, dates, and tax information.

> You can copy a change order and then modify it. This feature saves you time when you have similar change orders for many purchase orders.

There's more...

Note that if you are using the EnterpriseOne Advanced Pricing system for EnterpriseOne Procurement, change orders are not priced with adjustment schedules.

See also

- *Creating stock/non stock-based purchase orders*

Printing orders

The **Printing Order** processing options enable you to specify the range of status codes that you want the system to update when you print purchase orders, and whether you want the system to update the status codes.

Getting ready

You should set up the **Processing Options** for the **Purchase Order Print Print (R43500)** batch application in order to print the order details.

How to do it...

1. Select **Procurement and Subcontract Management** | **Daily Processing** | **Stock Based Purchasing**, click the arrow on **Print Purchase Order,** and then click on **Version**.
2. Select the **XJDE0001** version, and copy the version via the menu option.

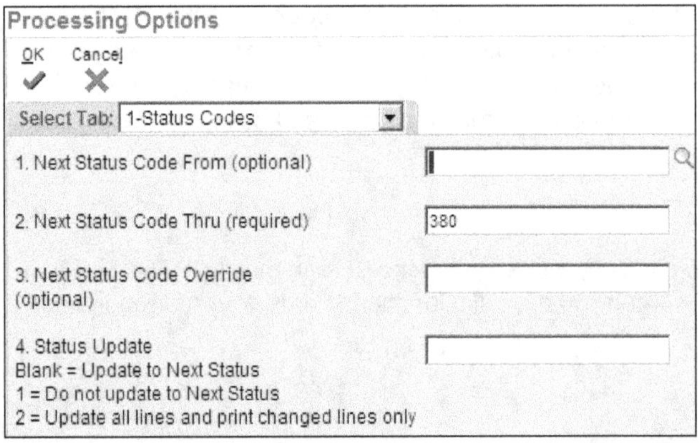

3. On the **Status Codes** tab, specify the start of the status code range that you want the system to update in the **Next Status Code From field**. You must use a **UDC (40/AT)** that has been set up on the **Order Activity Rules** form for the order type and line type that you are using.
4. Specify the end of the status code range that you want the system to update range in the **Next Status Code Thru** field. You must use a **UDC (40/AT)** that has been set up on the **Order Activity Rules** form for the order type and line type that you are using.
5. Specify the **Next Status Code Override** that you want the system to update. The override status is another allowed step in updating status codes. You must enter a **UDC (40/AT)** that has been set up on the **Order Activity Rules** form for the order type and line type that you are using.
6. **Status Update** specifies whether the system updates the status on an order. Normally, it is used to re-print purchase orders. If you don't want to update the next status, entering *1* will update the **Purchase Order** to next status as per the **Order Activity Rule**.
7. On the **Report Display** tab, processing options enable you to select the information that the system includes in the report, such as quantities and amounts, exchange rates, global messages, and notes. All of these are optional and can be set up as per business needs.
8. Specify whether the system prints the original quantity and amount or the open quantity and amount. If you leave this field blank, the system will print the original quantity and amount, and if you enter *1*, the system will print only the open quantity.

9. **Exchange Rate Display** specifies whether the system prints the exchange rate. Select *1* to print the exchange rate, or leave this field blank if you don't want to print the exchange rate.
10. The **Item Number Display** processing option enables you to specify how the system displays item numbers. Enter *1* to print only the item number and enter *2* to print both the item number and the supplier's item number.
11. Specify the **Cross Reference Type** that the system uses when printing a supplier's item number. The system stores the cross-reference information in the **F4013** table. Cross-reference information is defined via UDCs that are set up in **41/DT**.
12. The **Currency Processing** option enables you to specify whether the system prints amounts in the domestic or foreign currency. If you select *1*, the system prints amounts in the foreign currency, and if you leave this field blank then the system print amounts in the domestic currency.

How it works...

After you enter orders, you can print them to review the orders and then send them to the appropriate suppliers. The system prints the orders in the language that is specified for the supplier in the supplier master table. You can also print orders to a work file, which enables you to customize the report. Before you customize a report, you must retrieve the appropriate address information and attachments or notes. You can print orders by batch so that you can review the orders and then send them to the appropriate suppliers. Use the processing options to specify which information prints on orders. You can print orders individually so you can review those orders before sending it to the appropriate suppliers. You can create print messages by using the **Purchase Orders** program (**P4310**). After you create a print message, you can assign it to an order or detail line during order entry. You use processing options in **Order Entry** to specify whether attachments should be printed. You can assign an attachment to an order or to detail lines during order entry. Printing orders is usually a step in the sequence of processing orders. You set up these steps in **Order Activity Rules (P40204)** application. Once you print an order, you can have the system move the order to the next step in the process, or you can leave the order where it is so that you can print it again. You use processing options in **Order Entry** to specify whether the system updates status codes for orders after they print. You might want to print orders twice—once to review the orders and again to update the status codes. You can access these two versions of the print program through the processing options for **Order Entry**.

There's more...

If you have set the processing options in **Order Entry** for the system to store purchase order information for **Electronic Data Interchange (EDI)**, you can send the orders to the suppliers by using the EnterpriseOne **Electronic Data Interchange** system.

[If you print an order that is on hold, the system prints a blank page.]

See also

- *Setting up purchase orders* in *Chapter 4, Understanding and Setting up Procurement*

Creating orders for multiple suppliers

You can enter orders for multiple suppliers simultaneously, instead of entering a separate order for each supplier.

Getting ready

You should set up the **Purchase Order Workbench** application (**P43101**) processing options.

How to do it...

1. Select **Procurement and Subcontract Management** | **Daily Processing** | **Stock Based Purchasing,** and then click on **Purchase Order Workbench**.
2. On **Purchase Order Workbench**, enter the **Branch/Plant**.

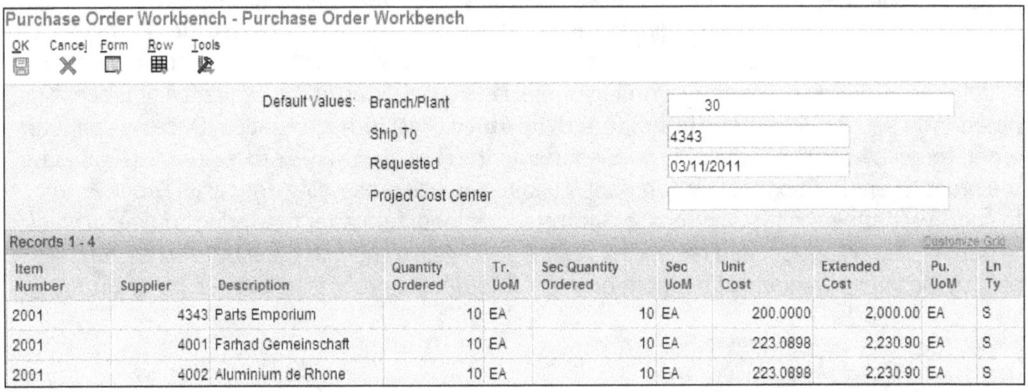

3. Enter the **Ship To** information.
4. Enter the **Requested Date**.
5. Enter the **Item Number**.

6. Enter the **Supplier** (you can see in the previous screenshot that each line has a different supplier number).
7. Enter the **Quantity Ordered**.
8. On the **Order Detail** tab, click the **Line Defaults** tab, and then enter the **G/L Date**.
9. Enter the **Item Number** on the detail line.
10. Enter the **Quantity Ordered**, and the **Unit Cost the Extended Cost** will be calculated automatically.
11. Click **OK** to generate the **Purchase Order** review, as shown in the following screenshot.

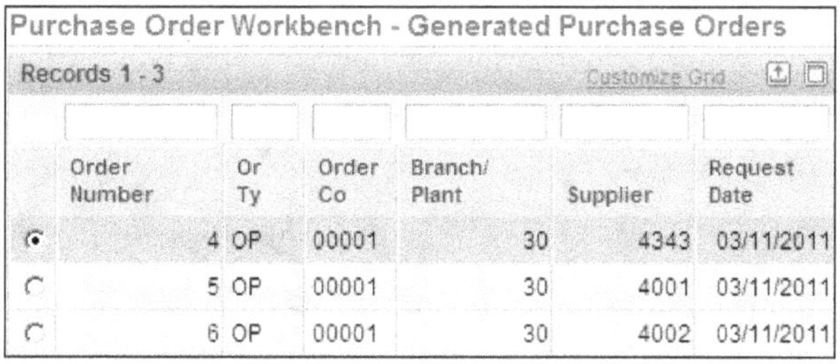
Purchase Order Workbench - Generated Purchase Orders

Records 1 - 3

	Order Number	Or Ty	Order Co	Branch/ Plant	Supplier	Request Date
(•)	4	OP	00001	30	4343	03/11/2011
( )	5	OP	00001	30	4001	03/11/2011
( )	6	OP	00001	30	4002	03/11/2011

How it works...

When you specify the items that you want to purchase, and the supplier from whom you want to purchase them on the **Purchase Order Workbench** form, the system combines items for each supplier on a separate purchase order. The information for each detail line comes from master information for the item, or from procurement instructions for the supplier, if these have been defined. You can review the orders that the system generates by using the **Order Detail** form.

There's more...

If the supplier has an Internet home page set up featuring the items that they offer, you can preview supplier and item information in the electronic catalog before entering the order.

See also

- *Setting up purchase orders* in *Chapter 4, Understanding and Setting up Procurement*

Creating supplier catalogs

Suppliers might organize their products into different catalogs due to seasonal changes in products, different product lines, and so forth. If you maintain items in catalogs in the system, you can use the catalogs to locate and select items to order.

Getting ready

Set up the processing options for the **Supplier Catalog Maintenance** program (**P41061**).

How to do it...

1. Select **Procurement and Subcontract Management** | **Daily Processing** | **Stock Based Purchasing** | **Price Management**, and then click on **Supplier Catalog Maintenance** (**P41061**).
2. Click on **Add**.

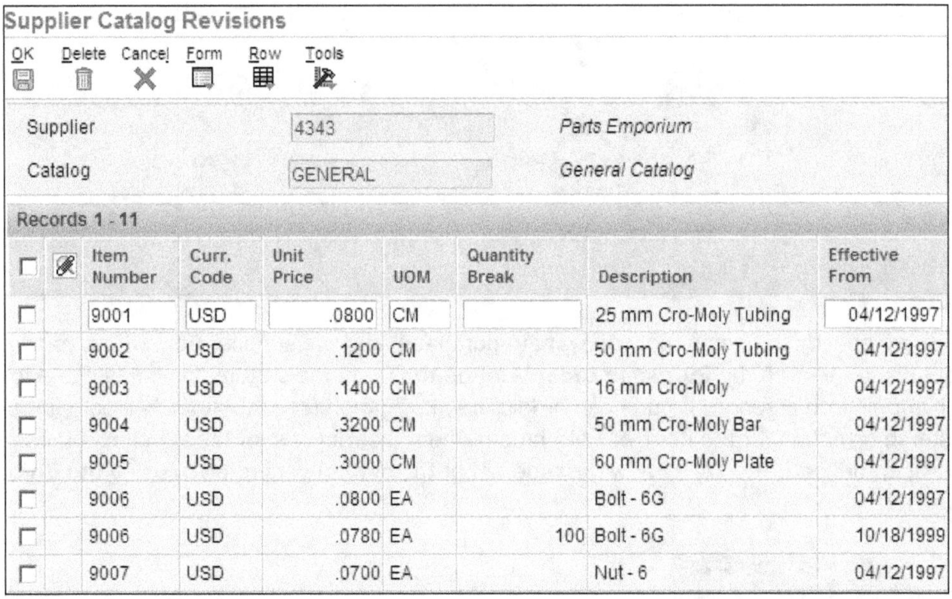

3. Enter the **Supplier**.
4. Click the visual assist button next to the **Catalog**.
5. On the **Select User Defined Code** tab, select **Revisions** from the **Form** menu.
6. On the **Supplier Catalog Revisions** tab, enter the **Item Number**, **Currency Code**, **Unit Price**, **UOM**, and **Quantity Break**.

How it works...

After you locate a catalog, you can select the items that you want to order. The system enters each item that you select on an order detail line, along with the unit price for the item as specified in the catalog. On the **Catalogs - Item Selection** form, you can use a **Form** exit to preview item information. Note that an item can have different prices, depending upon the amount that you purchase. You can review all item prices for the items in a catalog on the **Catalogs - Item Selection** form. An item that has multiple prices will appear several times, and each instance represents a different purchase quantity and the price that applies to that quantity.

There's more...

If the supplier has an internet home page set up with items that it offers, you can preview item information in the electronic catalog.

See also

- *Setting up pricing in procurement*

Entering order using order templates

You can use order templates to locate and select items that you frequently order.

Getting ready

You must verify that you have set the appropriate processing option in the **Purchase Orders** program (**P4310**) that displays the **Order Template** automatically. Also, verify that the **Order Template** has been set up.

How to do it...

1. Select a catalog on the **Supplier Catalog Search & Select** form, and click the **Select** button.
2. View each items on detail lines of the purchase order. Click on **OK** for the system to automatically generate a separate purchase order for each supplier from whom you are ordering items. If you do not want the system to automatically generate separate purchase orders, you must first cancel the orders before exiting the **Purchase Order Workbench**.

3. On the **Purchase Order Workbench** form, select **Order Templates** from the **Form** menu.

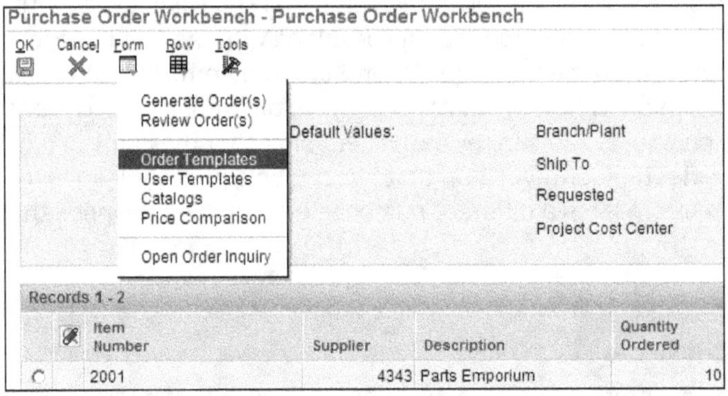

4. Select a template on the **Work With Available Order Templates** form, and then click the **Select** button.

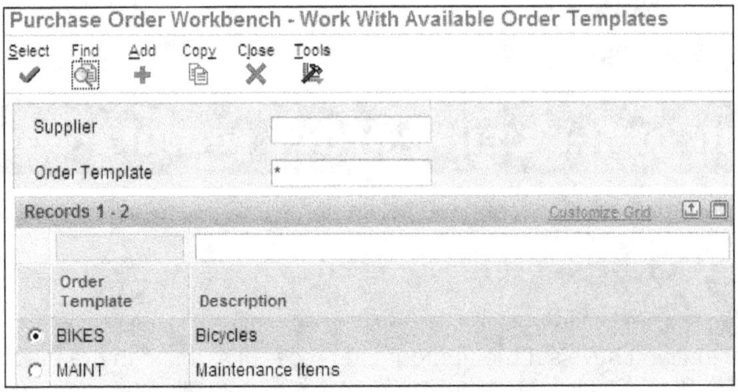

5. On the **Order Items Template**, you can order all of the items on the template in their usual quantities by selecting **Preload With Usual** from the **Form** menu.
6. Click **OK** to generate the **Purchase Order**.

How it works...

Each order template contains a specific group of items. When you enter a purchase order, you can choose to review a certain template. From the template, you select the items you want to order, and the system copies these items to the purchase order. If you access order templates before entering a supplier on the purchase order, you can review a list of generic templates. You can avoid manually entering purchase orders by having the system create new purchase orders based on existing detail line information. If the detail lines that you are working with are applicable to several different suppliers, the system creates a separate purchase order for each supplier. If there are multiple detail lines for a supplier, it is because each line pertains to a different branch/plant. The system uses the **Next Numbers Revisions (P0002)** program to assign a separate purchase order number to each supplier. You can also assign the order numbers manually. You can use **Processing Options** to specify default values for the orders that the system creates. These values include the **Order Type** and the **Beginning Status** code. You can also indicate special processing for the new orders, such as approval routes and budget checking.

There's more...

The order templates can be specific to a supplier or they can be generic, in which case you do not usually purchase the items on the template from any specific supplier.

See also

- *Setting up purchase orders* in *Chapter 4, Understanding and Setting up Procurement*

Creating order from quote order

This recipe demonstrates how, after you enter supplier price quote, you compare price quotes to identify the supplier with the best price and select a price quote for creating the purchase order.

Getting ready

Set up the **Processing Options** for the **Release Open Quotations (P43360)** program to generate the purchase order from **Quote Order**.

How to do it...

1. Access the **Release Open Quotations (P43360)** program from the **G43A13** menu.

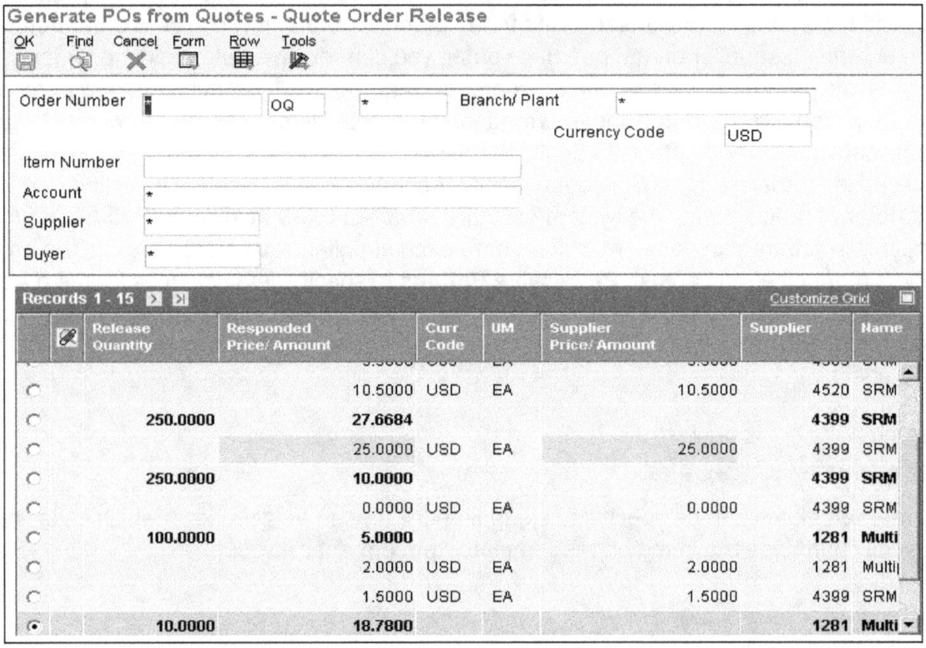

2. Enter the **Supplier** purchasing agent that is assigned to the quote order. This field is not used to enter suppliers responding with price quotes.
3. On the **Quote Order Release** form, locate the line that you want to release.
4. Enter the **Release Quantity** that indicates the price quote that the system is to use for the order, if the supplier provided price quotes for multiple item quantities. You are now ready to generate orders for the price quotes you have chosen. The system warns you if you attempt to exit at this stage.
5. The **Respond Price Amount** displays the price quote, if the supplier has provided price quotes for multiple quantities of an item. If a supplier did not return a price quote by the date that you required, you cannot use the price quote. The system does not display a release line for late quotes. To activate the line, you must change the response date for the supplier by using the **Quote Supplier Entry** (**P4330**) program.
6. Click on **OK** to generate the purchase order, or select **Generate Order** from the **Form** menu.

How it works...

When you enter the price in the **Quote Response** program, you can compare price quotes for an item by locating the quote order detail line that contains the item. You can review the item description for the detail line, and see all of the suppliers who have provided price quotes for the item. After you select a price quote for which to create an order, you can close the quote order detail line (if fully released), so that you can no longer create orders from the line, or you can leave the quote order detail line open, so that you can create recurring orders from the line. Use the processing options to specify which of the methods you want to use. Closed detail lines do not appear on the **Quote Order Release** form.

There's more...

You can record a price quote for each item, as well as the dates through which each price quote is effective. You can then use the form to enter the price quote information into the system.

> You run the **Print Quote Request** program to select the quote orders for which to print request forms. After you enter the price quote information in the system, you can print these forms to review existing price quotes for a supplier.

See also

- *Creating stock/non stock-based purchase orders*

Setting an order on hold

This recipe demonstrates order hold information, and discusses how to enter order hold information.

Getting ready

Verify that you have set up hold codes in the **Hold Codes (42/HC) UDC** table.

How to do it...

1. Enter a **Hold Code** from the **Hold Codes (40/HC) UDC** table to specify why an order is placed on hold.

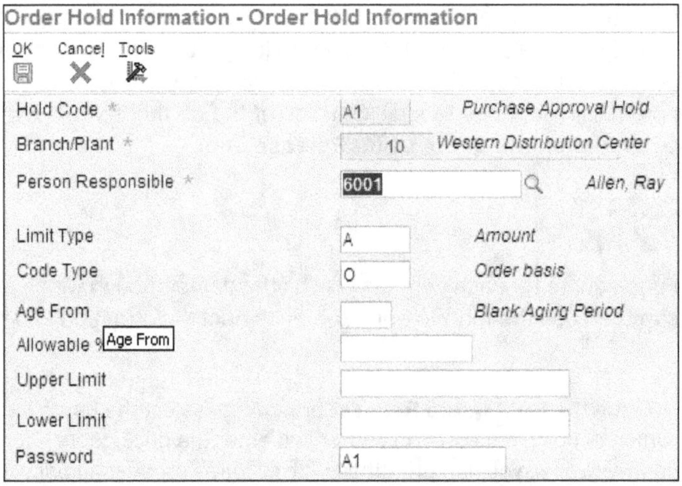

2. In the **Person Responsible** field, enter the address book number of the person who is responsible for reviewing and releasing orders placed on hold.
3. Enter a **Limit Type** value from the **Limit Type (42/LM) UDC** table to specify the type of value the system validates. For example, you might enter a value to specify an amount or a percentage.
4. Enter a **Code Type** from the **Code Type (42/TC) UDC** table to specify the hold code that applies at the order level. For credit holds, the hold code applies to the whole order. Procurement holds do not support line level-holds.
5. Enter a value from the **Aging Period (H40/AP) UDC** table to specify the aging period that the system uses when you specify a credit check based on the aging of the customer's accounts receivable.
6. Enter the allowable percentage in the **Allowable %** field that informs the system of the percentage of total receivables to accept in the column specified in the **Age From** field. You must complete the **Allowable %** field when aging credit checking is used. For example, if the customer has a total accounts receivable balance of $10,000 with $2,500 of that in the 31-60 day column, the age from value is 3 (31-60 days) and the acceptable percent value is 10 (10%). Therefore, this customer could have as much as $1,000 (10,000 x 10%) in columns 3 through 6 and still pass this credit checks. If the customer has more, the system will place the customer's orders on hold.

7. Enter the **Upper Limit** amount that the system uses as the high end of the range of acceptable margin percentages or amounts. Complete this field when you want to establish a maximum gross margin percentage, or an amount for an order or individual order line.
8. Enter the **Lower Limit** amount that the system uses as the low end of the range of acceptable margin percentages or amounts. Complete this field when you want to establish a maximum gross margin percentage, or an amount for an order or individual order line.
9. Enter the **Password** that the system requires before it releases a held order. Only users with access to the password can release the order. Do not enter blanks anywhere in the password.

How it works...

You can put an order on hold to prevent it from being processed. When you assign a hold code to an order, the system does not allow the order to be processed until you release the hold. You must set up the individual hold codes that you intend to assign to orders. Each hold code can identify a certain type of hold. For example, you might set up a hold code to identify orders that exceed budget. There are also administrative holds and approval holds. You might set up another hold code to identify orders that exceed the maximum order amount. There are also predefined system-assigned hold codes. The system will automatically assign budget holds to orders if you set the processing options for the **Purchase Orders** program (**P4310**) accordingly. The system automatically assigns approval holds after you have set the processing options for the **Purchase Orders** program (**P4310**) accordingly and the order is awaiting approval. The system also assigns a hold code to an order if you have entered a hold code for the supplier. You can specify the person who is responsible for reviewing and releasing a certain type of order hold. You must specify a password for each hold code. Only those individuals who know the password can release an order to which the hold code is assigned.

There's more...

Procurement holds must be set up at the order level. Procurement does not support line-level holds.

See also

- *Setting up purchase orders* in *Chapter 4, Understanding and Setting up Procurement*

Entering and releasing order holds

You can place an order on hold to prevent it from being processed. You might place an order on hold for reasons such as:

- You have yet to settle prices and terms with the supplier
- You are not sure whether you want to use the supplier
- The supplier's minimum order amount is not being met
- The order exceeds the budget

Getting ready

- You should set up processing options for the **Held Order Release** program (**P43070**) in order to release the order hold.

How to do it...

1. Access the **G43A13** menu from the **Fast Path**, click on the arrow for **Release Held Order**, and then click on **Values**.

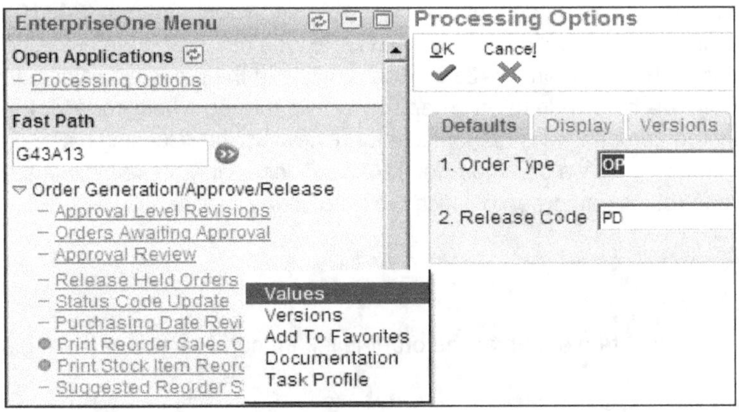

2. On the **Default** tab, enter the **Order Type** from **UDC 00/DT** that identifies the type of document.
3. On the **Default** tab, enter the appropriate **Release Code** to specify the release code at the time the held order was released.

4. On the **Display** tab, enter *1* to display SOs, or leave the field blank to display POs.
5. On the **Display** tab, enter *Y* to display previously-released orders.
6. The processing options on the **Versions** tab control which version the system uses when you call other programs from the **Held Order Release** program. You can define different versions in accordance with the business processes. If left blank, **ZJDE0001** will be used.

How it works...

When you place an order on hold, you prevent it from being processed. You might want to put an order on hold if you have yet to reach price negotiations with the supplier or if the order exceeds budget. To have the system process an order that has been put on hold, you must release the hold. You can review all holds on a certain order and select the holds that you want to release. For budget holds, you can review the budget before releasing budget hold orders by accessing **Trial Balance/Ledger Comparison** from the **Release Held Orders** (Budget) program. Note that you cannot use **Release Held Orders** (Budget) to release an order on budget hold if the order is assigned an approval route. In that case, you must use the **Approval Review** program to approve and release the order.

> There are two types of order holds: budget holds and regular holds. Budget holds are for orders that exceed the budget. Regular holds are for all other holds.

There's more...

You cannot print or receive orders that are on hold. You must release the hold to continue processing the order. To release an order on hold, you must have the correct password.

See also

- *Setting up purchase orders* in *Chapter 4, Understanding and Setting up Procurement*

6

Receipt Processing

In this chapter, we will cover:

- Setting up purchase receivers
- Printing purchase receivers
- Processing receipt information
- Entering/reversing receipts
- Reviewing journal entry for receipt transaction
- Journal entry creation for items in receipt routes
- Defining payment eligibility for item removal
- Creating and assigning receipt routes
- Working with items in receipt routes
- Transferring items to operations
- Removing items from a receipt route
- Reviewing item history
- Purchase order template

Introduction

Receipt is a process during procurement. After creating the purchase order, it is the next document that will be entered in the system. The receipt document is used for receiving the goods into your store. There are two types of receipt process to acquire the goods and services that you request on a purchase order. You must use the formal receiving process if you purchase items to inventory; and you can use either the informal or the formal receipt process when you purchase items or services and update the general ledger. The **Two Way Voucher** match uses an informal receipt, while the **Three-Way Voucher Match** uses a formal receipt where you can match the supplier invoice with receipt and the **Purchaser Order**.

Setting up purchase receivers

This recipe explains purchase receivers and how to set up the purchase receiver document that is used to manually record the receipt of goods upon delivery. A purchase receiver provides you the following information:

- Original purchase order information
- Goods that you are yet to receive
- A column for recording receipt quantities or amounts

You might need a purchase receiver to:

- Review purchase order information for incoming goods
- Confirm information about the items that you receive
- Record receipt information in the system

Getting ready

You should set up the processing option for the **Purchase Order** activity rule in order to activate and print the **Purchase Receiver document**.

How to do it...

1. Select **Procurement and Subcontract Management** | **Daily Processing** | **Stock Based Purchasing** | **Purchase Order Processing**, and then click on **Print Purchase Receiver**.
2. Select the **XJDE0001 Version**, then click **Copy** and give the user defined name, and then click **OK** and select the **Values Processing Option**.
3. On the **Edit** tab, specify whether the system should update the next status code, in the field **Enter a** *1* **to prevent updating the Next Status**.

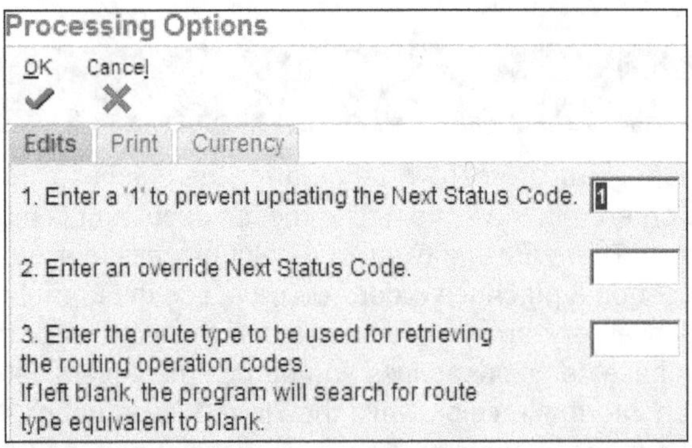

4. Specify a user-defined code (**UDC**) (**40/AT**) that indicates the next step in the order flow of the line type, in the field **Enter an override Next Status Code**.
5. Specify a code that qualifies the routing for an item and supplier combination. Examples include specific routing types for **Advance Ship Notices (ASNs)** (EDI 856 Ship Notice/Manifest transactions) and for transfers.
6. Enter the route type to be used for retrieving the routing operation codes. If left blank, the program will search for a route type equivalent to a blank code.
7. Specify whether the system prints cost information, in the field **Enter a 1 to inhibit printing of Cost Information**.

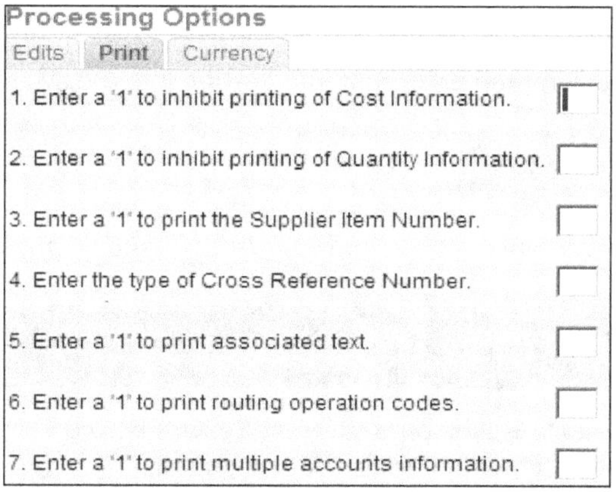

8. Specify whether the system should print quantity information, in the field **Enter a 1 to inhibit printing of Quantity Information**. If left blank, the system will print the Quantity Information.
9. Specify whether the system should print the supplier item number, in the field **Entering a 1 to print the Supplier Item Number**. If left blank, the system will not print the **Supplier Item Number**.
10. Specify a code from **UDC 41/DT** that identifies the type of cross-reference that is set up for this customer, in the field **Enter the type of Cross Reference Number**.
11. Specify whether the system prints associated text, in the field **Enter a 1 to print associated text.**
12. Specify whether the system prints routing operation codes, in the field **Enter a 1 to print routing operation codes.**
13. Specify whether the system prints information about multiple accounts, in the field **Enter a 1 to print multiple accounts information.**
14. On the **Currency** tab, specify whether the system prints amounts in a foreign currency, in the field **Enter a 1 to Print Amounts in Foreign Currency**.

How it works....

When you print a purchase receiver as per the order activity rule set-up, the system automatically advances the purchase order to the next status. The system updates the purchase order status in the **Purchase Order Detail File** (**F4311**).

If you set up the processing option of **R43510 Prevent Updating the Next Status**, the system will not advance the purchase order to the next status.

There's more...

You can use purchase receivers in the formal receipt process to manually record the receipt of goods upon delivery. You can then enter that information into the system.

See also

- *Setting up order activity rules* in *Chapter 4, Understanding and Setting up Procurement*

Printing purchase receivers

Purchase receiver documents will be printed by the system before item receipt. You can print **Purchase Receivers** in batch mode or for an individual order.

Getting ready

You should set up the **Processing Options** for the **Purchase Receiver Print program** (**R43510**) in order to print the **Purchase Receiver** document properly.

How to do it...

1. Select **Procurement and Subcontract Management** | **Daily Processing** | **Stock Based Purchasing** | **Purchase Order Processing**, and then click on **Print Purchase Receiver**.
2. Select the **XJDE0001** Version.
3. Then, select and click on **Data Selection** and then click on **Submit**.

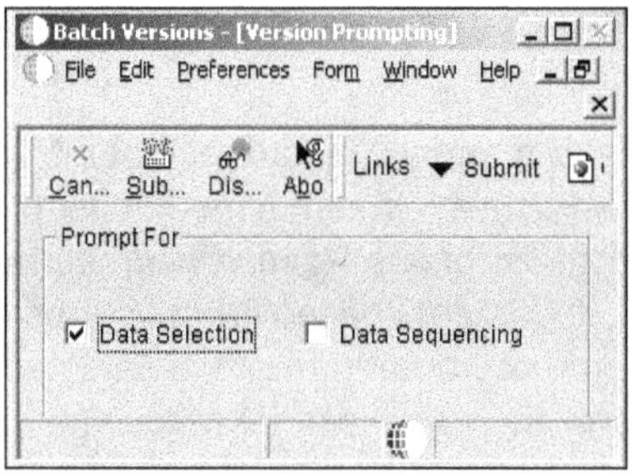

4. For **Print Batch Purchase Receipt**, enter the following values in the **Data Selection** window:
    - **Operator**: Where
    - **Left Operand**: BC Status Code - Next (F4311) (NXTR)
    - **Comparison**: is Not Equal To
    - **Right Operator**: "999"

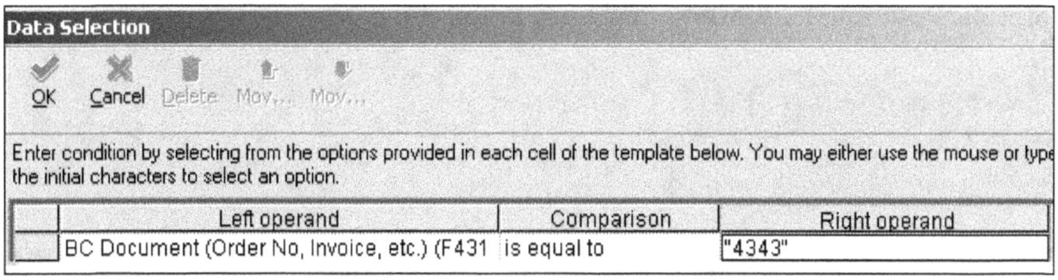

5. For **Print Purchase Receipt**, individually enter data into the **Data Selection window**. Enter the following values:
    - **Operator**: Where
    - **Left Operand**: BC Document (Order No, Invoice, etc) (F4311)
    - **Comparison**: Is Equal To
    - **Right Operator**: The order number that you want to print

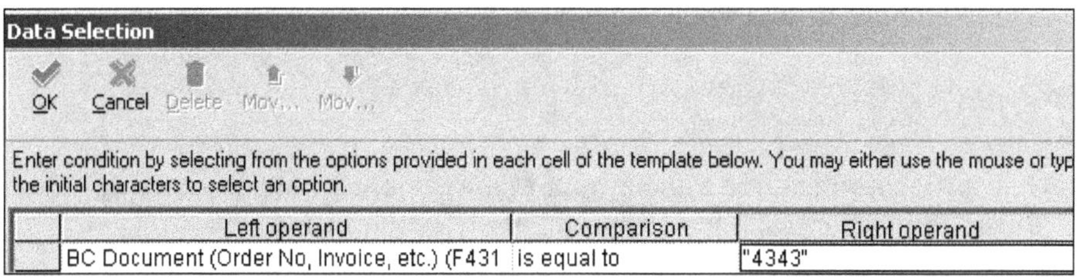

6. Click **Ok** to print the receiver document.

How it works...

You can use purchase receivers to manually record receipt information for goods upon delivery. You can print purchase receivers in batch mode based on the criteria that you specify when performing the **Print Purchase Receivers** procedure. Batch mode print gives a sequence of purchase receiver documents based on the status code of the purchase order. When you enter the purchase order number in the data selection of the purchase order receiver, the system will print only the specific order receiver.

> You can print in batch mode in order to print multiple purchase orders and purchase receivers.

There's more...

You can specify the information that is printed on the purchase receivers though processing options that enable you to specify whether to print **Price information**, **Order Quantities**, **Cross-reference numbers**, or **foreign currency amounts**.

See also

- *Setting up purchase receivers*

Processing receipt information

After you receive the goods for a purchase order, you must record the details of the receipt. The system uses the receipt information to update the item quantities and costs in the make non-breaking Edwards EnterpriseOne Inventory Management system.

Getting ready

You should set up the **Processing Options** for the **PO Receipts program** (**P4312**) in order to receive the **Purchase Order** through item receipt.

How to do it...

1. Select **Procurement and Subcontract Management** | **Daily Processing** | **Stock Based Purchasing**, and then click on **Enter Receipt by PO**.

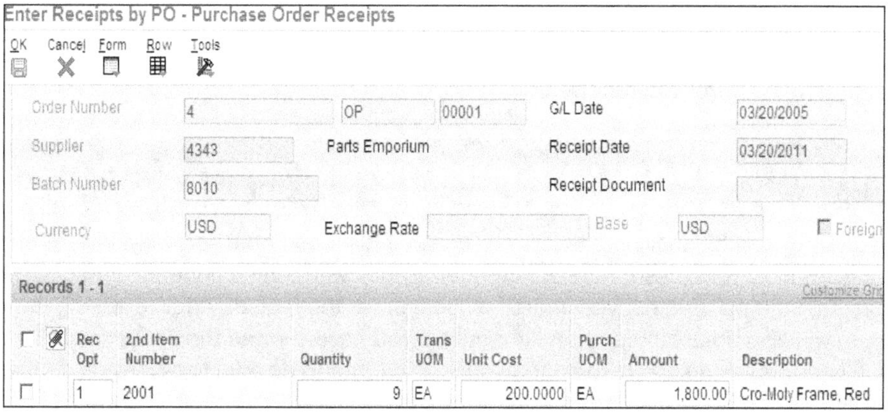

2. Enter 1 in the **Rec Opt** field for the items.
3. Enter the **Quantity** to receive.
4. Enter the **Location/Lot** information (if Location/Lot has been activated).
5. Enter the **Landed Cost Rule** (if it's a Foreign Purchase).

How it works...

During the receiving process, you should review the details of the purchase order for reconciliation with the received goods. If required, adjust the purchase order details. The system also enables the pricing and repricing of purchase order items at the time of receipt. Pricing and repricing at receipt for matrix items and quality attributes enables you to account for price changes that must be reflected when an item is received. When you enter receipts for purchase order lines, you can use the **Account Distribution Inquiry** program (**P43126**) to review multiple account distribution records that the system stores in the **F4316** table.

There's more...

After you enter a receipt for a purchase order for which lines are distributed among multiple accounts (only for inventory interfaces of A or B), the system updates item quantities and costs, and then writes and updates records to these tables:

- **F4311** (updates records)
- **F4316** (updates records)
- **F43121** (writes records)
- **F43126** (writes records)
- **F43199** (writes records only if you are using audit history)
- **F0911** (writes records)

See also

- *Setting up purchase receivers*

Entering/reversing receipts

JDE system provides the facility to reverse a receipt if it's recorded incorrectly. When you receive the goods through item receipt, the quantity on hand will be updated. You can reverse a receipt as long as you have not yet created a voucher for the receipt. After reversing the receipt, the system will also adjust the on hand quantity. If you have created the voucher after matching system, it is necessary to first reverse the voucher in order to be able to reverse the receipt.

Getting ready

You should set up the **Processing Options** for the **Purchase Receipts Inquiry (P43214)** program in order to reverse the receipt.

How to do it...

1. Select **Procurement and Subcontract Management** | **Daily Processing** | **Stock Based Purchasing** | **Purchase Order Processing** | **Receipts Matching and Posting**, and then select **Open Receipts by Supplier** (**P43214**).
2. On the **Work with Purchase Receipts** dialog box, locate your first purchase order receipt and enter the G/L Date, and then select the row that you want to receive.
3. Select **Reverse Receipt** from the **Row** menu. Notice the *Y* populated in the **Rev** column.

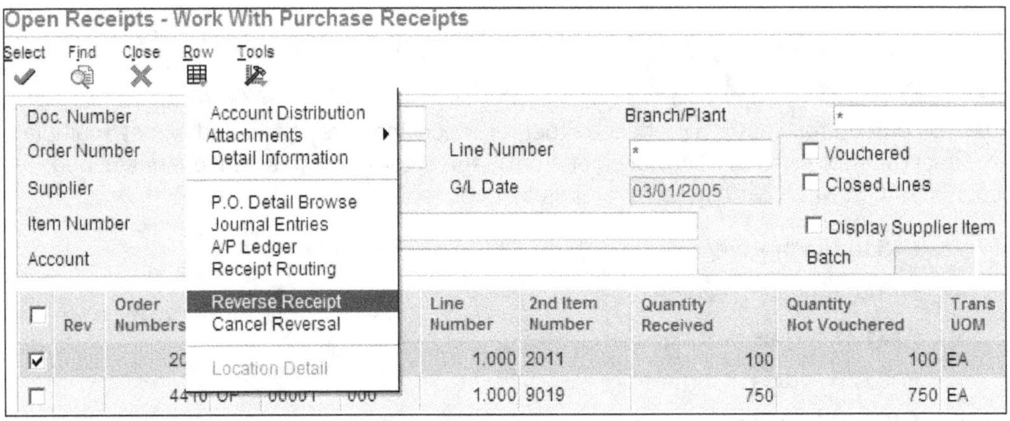

How it works...

When you reverse the receipt, system will update the **On Hand** quantity. The system will also create a journal entry that updates the general ledger. You might need to do this if you recorded a receipt by mistake, or if you recorded the wrong receipt. If the order has been vouchered, the voucher must be reversed first, in order to reverse the receipt. Items that have receipt routing activated should move back to previous operations, and then you can reverse the receipt.

There's more...

When you enter a formal receipt, the system creates journal entries that:

- Debit an inventory account if it is a stocked line, and otherwise debit the general ledger account
- Credit a received not vouchered account

See also

- *Setting up receipt routing* in *Chapter 4, Understanding and Setting up Procurement*

Review journal entry for receipt transaction

This recipe demonstrates the journal entry review for receipt transactions, and discusses how to:

- Review journal entries for receipt transactions
- Post receipts

Getting ready

You should set up the processing options for the **PO Receipt (P4312)** program in order to set up the Journal entry summarization on the **Process** tab.

How to do it...

1. To post receipts, select **Receipts Matching and Posting** (**G43A15**), G/L Receipt Post.

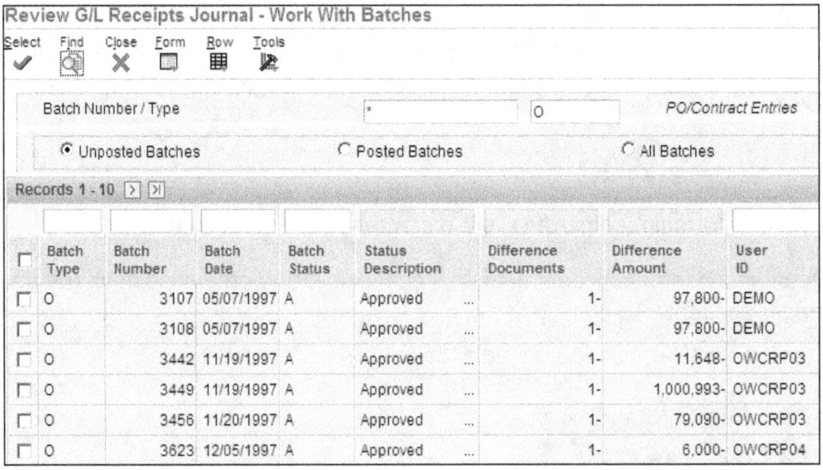

2. After you review the journal entries, you can post them to the general ledger by using the **General Ledger Post**.
3. Report program (**R09801**).

How it works...

When you enter a formal receipt, the system creates journal entries. That is, it debits an inventory account if it is a stocked line, and otherwise debits the general ledger account and credits a received not vouchered account. The system retrieves the account numbers for which it should create journal entries from AAIs. A separate AAI table exists for inventory accounts and received not voucher accounts. The account number will be obtained based on the company, business unit, and general ledger category. The system will retrieve the receipt not vouchered account from AAI table **4320**, and will obtain the tax related **General Ledger** integration information from AAI tables **4350** and **4355**.

The standard cost for an item remains consistent unless you manually change it. If a variance exists between the standard cost and the price at which you purchase an item, the system creates journal entries to account for the variance. You specify variance accounts in AAIs.

There's more...

You can set up the **Processing Option** of **P4312** in order the set up the Journal rule for receipts, and to specify whether you require detail journals or summarize journals.

See also

- *Setting up receipt routing* in *Chapter 4, Understanding and Setting up Procurement*

Journal entry creation for items in receipt routes

You need to determine when the system creates journal entries for items in a receipt route so that the value of the item is reflected in the general ledger.

You should set up the **Receipt Route** codes in user-defined code (UDC) table **43/RC**, and also set up operation codes in UDC table **43/OC**.

Getting ready

You should set up the **Branch/Plant Constant** application to activate the **Interface GL** option in order to integrate the procurement system with the general ledger system.

How to do it...

1. The system automatically creates journal entries when you enter items in the operation for which they are eligible for payment, and also at the last operation in the route.
2. Enter **P0004A** in the fast path, and then add the following **Routes Codes**:

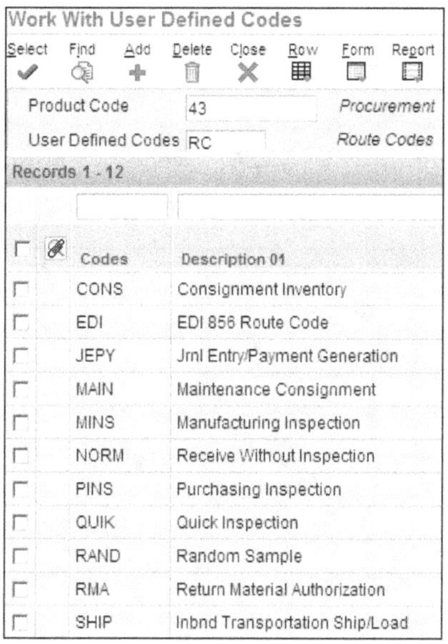

Work With User Defined Codes

Select Find Add Delete Close Row Form Report

Product Code 43 Procurement

User Defined Codes RC Route Codes

Records 1 - 12

Codes	Description 01
CONS	Consignment Inventory
EDI	EDI 856 Route Code
JEPY	Jrnl Entry/Payment Generation
MAIN	Maintenance Consignment
MINS	Manufacturing Inspection
NORM	Receive Without Inspection
PINS	Purchasing Inspection
QUIK	Quick Inspection
RAND	Random Sample
RMA	Return Material Authorization
SHIP	Inbnd Transportation Ship/Load

How it works...

When you transfer the item from one stage to another stage during receipt routing, the system creates journal entries for each operation, and the receipt will go to the payment operation. During receipt for route payment eligible operations, JDE creates a credit entry for the received not voucher account and creates a debit entry for the inventory account. The system creates the credit entry for the receipt note voucher on the first operation, and creates the debit entry for the inventory account at the last operation.

There's more...

Once you've entered the goods in operation, the suppliers are eligible for payment. You can make a payment to the supplier after voucher matching.

See also

- *The voucher creation process* in *Chapter 7*, *Creating Vouchers and Landed Costs*

Defining payment eligibility for item removal

This recipe demonstrates item removal and discusses how to define payment eligibility for item removal.

Getting ready

You should set up **Routing Disposition** in order to define payment eligibility.

How to do it...

1. Access the **Receipt Routing** (**G43A14**) | **Receipt Routing Definition** | **Work With Receipts Routing Codes**.

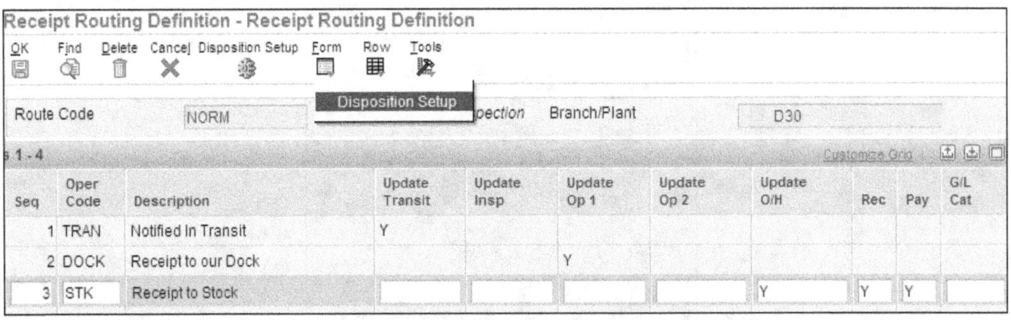

2. Select a **Receipt Route** on the **Work With Receipts Routing Codes** form, and then click the **Select** button.
3. Enter *Y* in the **Pay** field to define payment eligibility for item removal.
4. Select **Disposition Setup** from the **Form** menu on the **Receipt Routing Definition** form.
5. Define payment eligibility for item removal.

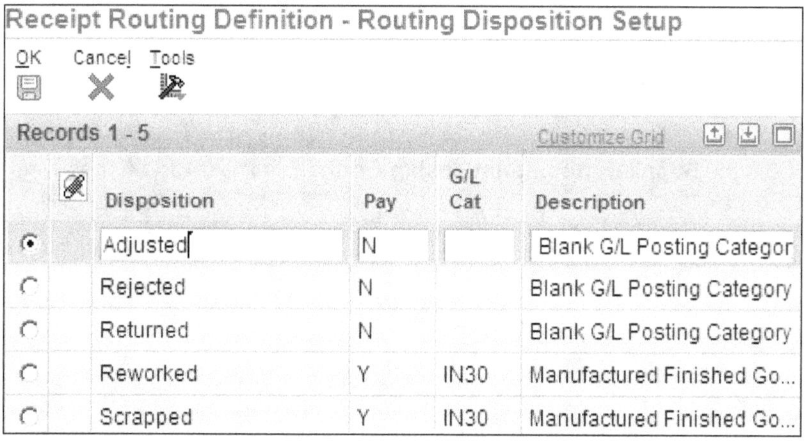

Receipt Routing Definition - Routing Disposition Setup

OK Cancel Tools

Records 1 - 5 Customize Grid

Disposition	Pay	G/L Cat	Description
Adjusted	N		Blank G/L Posting Categor
Rejected	N		Blank G/L Posting Category
Returned	N		Blank G/L Posting Category
Reworked	Y	IN30	Manufactured Finished Go...
Scrapped	Y	IN30	Manufactured Finished Go...

How it works...

When a receipt route has been activated and the item has been processed through the receipt route, you may have to rework, scrap, return, or reject items. After creating the receipt route you should pay for items that you remove from disposition, based on the route reason - for example, you want to pay for those items that you rework but you don't want to pay for those items that you have returned. You should define the removal categories for which items are payable in the **Receipt Routing Disposition Setup** mentioned above. If you specify that the rework category is payable, you should pay for those items that you classify as relevant for rework. When you remove the item from a receipt route, the system will automatically create a journal entry to update the general ledger.

There's more...

The system creates a credit entry for the received not vouchered account and a debit entry for the disposition account, based on the general ledger category set-up.

See also

Setting up receipt routing in *Chapter 4, Understanding and Setting up Procurement*

Creating and assigning receipt routes

This recipe demonstrates receipt routing activation, lists the prerequisites, and discusses how to assign receipt routes to items.

Getting ready

You should create receipt routes.

How to do it...

1. Access the **Supplier/Item Relationships** form from the **G43A14** menu.

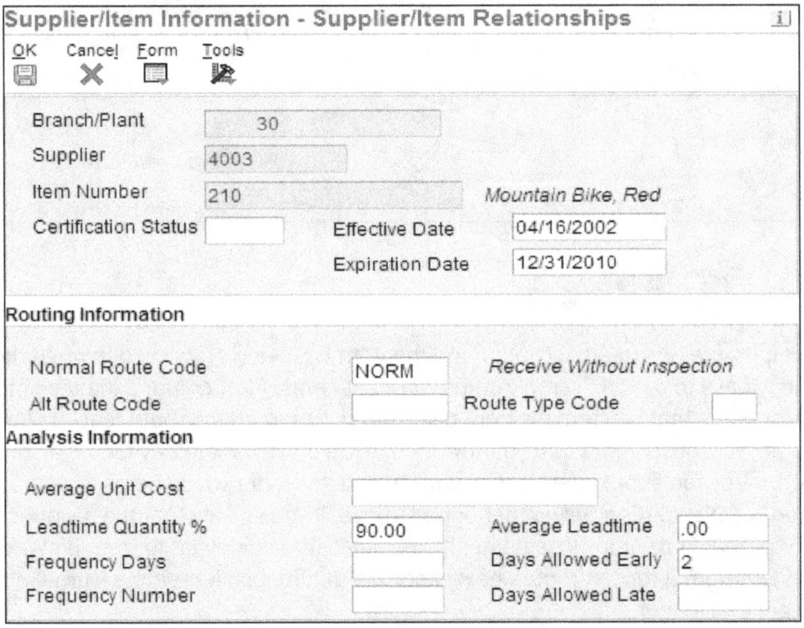

2. Enter a **Normal Route Code** from **UDC 43/RC** that identifies a receipt route. Each receipt route consists of a series of operations through which the system directs items upon receipt.
3. Enter the alternate route code in the **Alt Route Code** field from **UDC 43/RC** that identifies an alternate receipt route. Each receipt route consists of a series of operations through which the system directs items upon receipt. An item can have a normal receipt route and an alternate receipt route. The system directs an item through the alternate receipt route intermittently based on the number of days or number of receipts that you specify.

4. Enter the **Route Type Code** that qualifies the routing for an item and supplier combination.
5. Enter the frequency days in the **Frequency Days** field to determine how often the system directs an item to the alternate receipt route, based on days. For example, suppose you enter 3 in this field. If January 1, 1998 was the last date for the alternate receipt route, the system directs the next receipt performed on or after January 4, 1998 to the alternate receipt route.
6. Enter the frequency number in the **Frequency Number** field, which determines how often the system directs an item to the alternate receipt route, based on receipts. For example, if you enter 5 in this field, the system directs every fifth receipt of the item to the alternate receipt route.

How it works...

When you set up the processing options of the receipts entry program, the system initiates the receipt routing process. When you receive the item, the system enters an item in its standard receipt route, unless you have also specified an alternate receipt route, in which case it enters some items into the alternate route. For example, an alternate route can be assigned to every fifth shipment that you receive, so that a sample of received items (one in five) is inspected. The alternate route code needs to be assigned; the system process assigns a different series of function on receipt days.

There's more...

Receipt routing process is used to screen the status of items that are received during the purchase receiving process when the item is available to stock. Receipt routing can be activated by assigning the receipt routes to the items. Receipt routing can be through a standard receipt route or through an alternate receipt route.

See also

Setting up receipt routing in *Chapter 4, Understanding and Setting up Procurement*

Working with items in receipt routes

A receipt route is a process that the system provides; during item receipt there are many different stages, and each stage will take some time for review, inspection, and so on , before moving on to the next stage. For example, you purchase an item from a foreign supplier, then the supplier ships the item that is currently on the supplier dock, then it is in transit, and then it's received on customer dock, and so on.

Getting ready

You should set up the processing options for the **Receipt Routing Movement and Disposition** program (**P43250**).

How to do it...

1. On the **Movement and Disposition** application (**P43250**), click on the arrow and then click on **Values** to access the **Processing Options.**
2. On the **Default** tab, enter an **Order Type** to specify the type of document. This **UDC** (**00/DT**) also indicates the origin of the transaction. Reserved document type codes create automatic offset entries during the post program that exist for vouchers, invoices, receipts, and time sheets (these entries are not self-balancing when you originally enter them). These prefixes for document types are predefined; do not change them. If you enter a document type, the system displays only the orders with the document type that you specify. If you leave this processing option blank, the system displays all orders. You can create different versions that correspond to the different document types that you use.

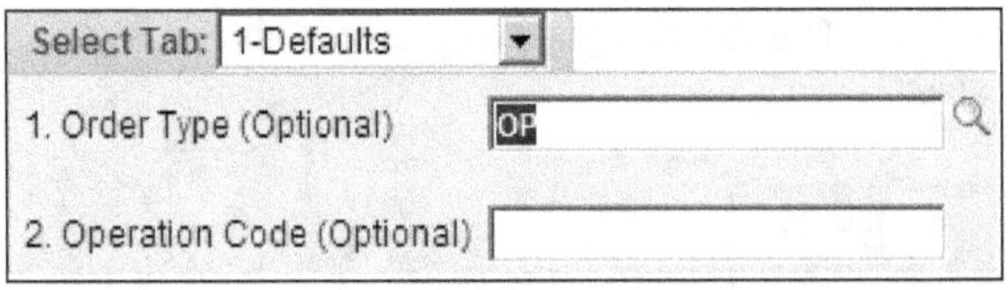

3. On the **Default** tab, enter an **Operation Code** and specify the **From Operation Code**. The system displays only the orders that contain the **From Operation Code** that you specify. This **UDC (43/OC)** represents an operation, or step, within the receipt route.
4. On the **Display** tab, specify whether the program should display operations that move quantity to inventory in the field **Move Quantity to Inventory**. If you leave this **Processing Option** blank, the system will not display operations that move quantity to inventory of, if you enter *1* the system will display operations that move quantity to inventory.
5. On the **Process** tab, specify the operation in the receipt route that the system uses as the **To Operation**. If you enter *1* the system allows only the next operation in the receipt route to be selected. If you enter *2*, the system allows the current operation or any subsequent operation in the receipt route to be selected. If you enter *3*, then the system allows any operation in the receipt route to be selected. If you leave this **Processing Option** blank, the system allows only the next operation in the receipt route to be selected.

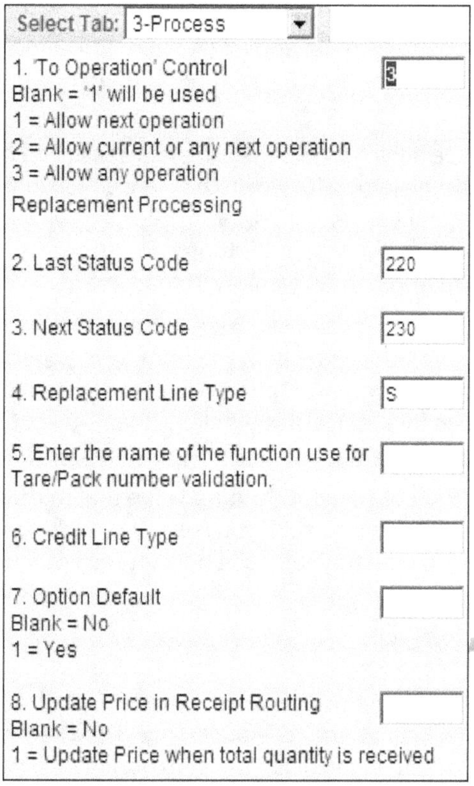

6. For the **Last Status Code**, specify a last status code for replacement processing. If you are adding an order line for a replacement item in the purchase order, you can enter a last status code for the new order line. Before you complete this processing option, review the order activity rules that you have set up, and also ensure that you have activated replacement processing.
7. For the **Next Status Code**, specify a next status code for replacement processing. If you are adding an order line for a replacement item in the purchase order, you can enter a next status code for the new order line. Before you complete this processing option, review the order activity rules that you have set up, and also ensure that you have activated replacement processing.
8. **Replacement Line Type** specifies the system processes lines on a transaction. It is mentioned *S* for Stock item and normally we activated receipt routing for stock-based items.
9. Enter the name of the function to use for **Tare/Pack Number Validation.** Specify whether the system validates the tare number or the pack number.
10. On the **Workflow** tab, specify the **Disposition Email** recipient of the e-mail that the system automatically sends when each disposition of an item is complete.

11. **Disposition Email** specifies the recipient of the e-mail that the system automatically sends after the disposition of an item. If you leave this processing option blank, the system does not send an e-mail. If you enter *1*, then an email will be sent to the project manager.
12. **Credit Line Type** specifies how the system processes lines on a transaction. The line type affects the systems with which the transaction interacts (JD Edwards EnterpriseOne General Ledger, JD Edwards EnterpriseOne Job Cost, JD Edwards EnterpriseOne Accounts Payable, JD Edwards EnterpriseOne Accounts Receivable, and JD Edwards EnterpriseOne Inventory Management).
13. **Option Default** specifies whether you want the system to automatically select all detail lines for receipt, which prevents you from having to manually select each detail line. If you leave this **Processing Option** blank, the system does not automatically select all detail lines for receipt. If you enter *1* then the system automatically selects all detail lines for receipt.
14. Enter an **Update Price in Receipt Routing** value that indicates whether the system will price the order at receipt time. If you leave this **Processing Option** blank, the system will not recalculate the purchase price at receipt time.

How it works...

After activating the receipt route that you have set up, the JDE will eliminate (disposition) items from the receipt route. That is, the receipt can reject the item that does not pass the examination phase. If the system disqualifies the item during inspection phase, the quantity will also be removed from the receipt route. When you are returning the item it can be generated as an order for exchanging the goods. This information can be reviewed for transfer and removal of items in a receipt route - that is, the amount and quantity can be established for the shipment of an item that was at the dock before it was transferred to stock. The information can also be reviewed for shipment of goods that do not pass the inspection. The system depends on the line type which involve the system that which transactions are interacting with various EnterpriseOne modules.

There's more...

The quantity can be retrieved, which transfers to inventory from the **Receipt Routing Master File (F43091)**. The operations information that moves the quantity to inventory on the **Receipt Routing Definition** form can also be reviewed.

See also

Setting up receipt routing in *Chapter 4, Understanding and Setting up Procurement*

Transferring items to operations

After activating the receipt, once you receive the item quantity, the system transfers the item quantity through many different stages.

Getting ready

You should activate the receipt route in the **PO Receipt (P4312)** program.

How to do it...

1. Access the **Work With Routing Statuses** (**P43250**) form from the **G43A14** menu.

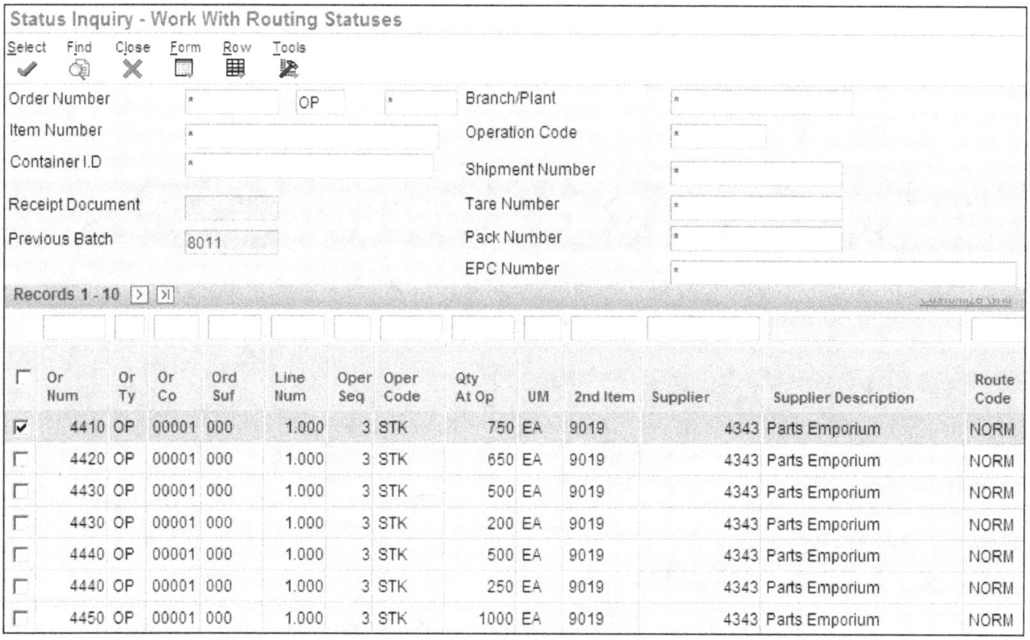

2. Enter the quantity at operation in the **Qty At Op** field; this is the number of units currently at this operation.
3. Enter a Receipt Line Number that represents the number of lines on a sales order or purchase order, or the number of receivers recorded during the receipt process. This field is used in voucher matching.

How it works...

When you transfer items to the last operation in a receipt route, the system updates the items to a received (on-hand) status. The receipt route is a sequence of operations performed when processing the receipt. The receipt route works based on the stages that you have set up. When you receive the item through receipt route it is transferred to one stage, and after confirmation of completion of this stage it maybe transferred to another stage, such as transit, staging, inspection, dock, stock, and so on.

There's more...

The remaining operations that you can set up are, for example, staging to inspection and inspection to stock. These are the standard stages in receipt routing and you can define your own stages as per business needs.

See also

Setting up receipt routing in *Chapter 4, Understanding and Setting up Procurement*

Removing items from a receipt route

This recipe provides an overview of the removal and reversal of items, and discusses how to remove an item from a receipt route.

Getting ready

You should set up the **Processing Option** for the **Receipt Routing Movement and Disposition (P43250)** program.

How to do it...

1. Access the **Routing Disposition** form from the **G43A14** menu.

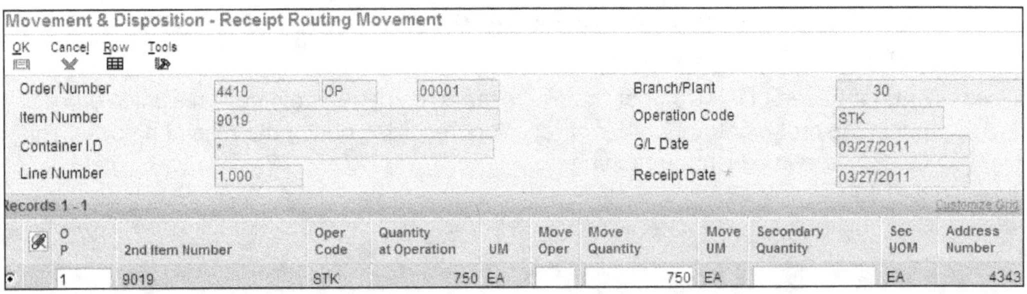

2. Enter the quantity returned **Qty Returned** field; this is the number of units that were returned to the supplier through receipt routing. You can return goods for credit or for replacement. The system writes these transactions as new lines on the original purchase order.
3. Enter the quantity reworked **Qty Reworked** field; this is the number of units that will be reworked as a result of receipt routing.
4. Enter a **Reason** from **UDC 42/RC** that explains the purpose for the transaction. For example, you can indicate the reason why you are returning items.
5. Enter the quantity scrapped **Qty Scrapped** field; this is the number of units that were scrapped through receipt routing.
6. Enter the quantity rejected **Qty Rejected** field; this is the number of units that were rejected during receipt routing.
7. Enter the quantity adjusted **Qty Adjusted** field; this is the number of units that were adjusted during receipt routing.

How it works...

Prior to removing items from the receipt route, you may review the test supplies that have been set up for a receipt route can also be reviewed. The goods' specifications that are set up for a receipt route. After you take out items from a receipt route, the system deducts the quantities that you enter from the quantity during the current operation. If it is necessary to reverse the removal, you should use the **Routing Ledger Inquiry (P43252)** program. For example, if you scrap the item and later decide to use the item, then you can reverse the item from the receipt route. The journal entries will also be created as per the receipt route status. For example, if your particular scrap category is payable, the system will create the Journal Entries for those items that you eliminate as scrap. When you move an item to the last operation in receipt route, the system updates the item to an on-hand status. If you unintentionally move the item to the last operation, you can reverse the update to on-hand status by moving the item back to a previous operation in the receipt route.

There's more...

The following categories can be used to indicate the quantity of items that you want to remove from the receipt route:

- **Returns**
- **Reworks**
- **Scrap**
- **Rejects**
- **Adjustments**

See also

Setting up receipt routing in *Chapter 4, Understanding and Setting up Procurement*

Reviewing item history

This recipe demonstrates the item history, and discusses how to set up the **P43252 Routing Ledger Inquiry**.

Getting ready

You should set up **Processing Option** for **Routing Ledger Inquiry** (**P43252**).

How to do it...

1. Enter **G43A14** on the fast path in order to access the **Receipt Routing Ledger** application.

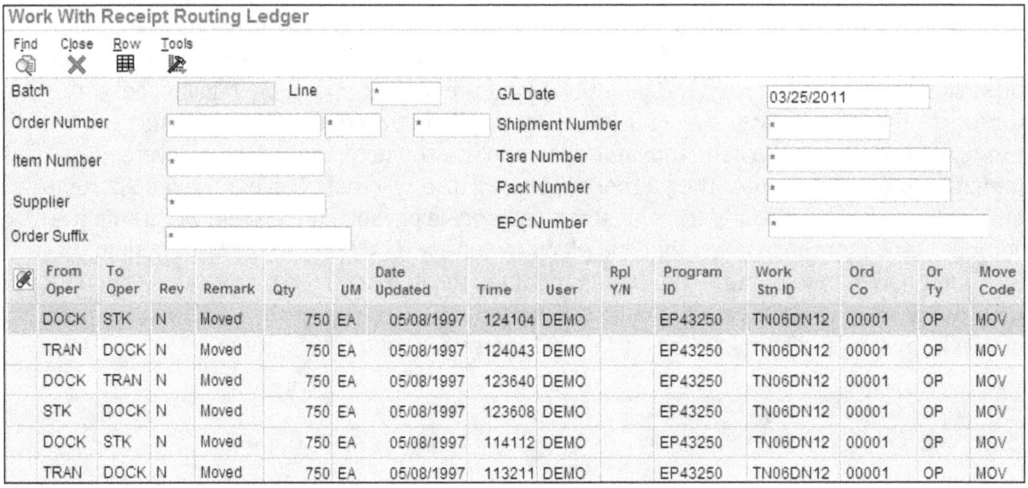

From Oper	To Oper	Rev	Remark	Qty	UM	Date Updated	Time	User	Rpl Y/N	Program ID	Work Stn ID	Ord Co	Or Ty	Move Code
DOCK	STK	N	Moved	750	EA	05/08/1997	124104	DEMO		EP43250	TN06DN12	00001	OP	MOV
TRAN	DOCK	N	Moved	750	EA	05/08/1997	124043	DEMO		EP43250	TN06DN12	00001	OP	MOV
DOCK	TRAN	N	Moved	750	EA	05/08/1997	123640	DEMO		EP43250	TN06DN12	00001	OP	MOV
STK	DOCK	N	Moved	750	EA	05/08/1997	123608	DEMO		EP43250	TN06DN12	00001	OP	MOV
DOCK	STK	N	Moved	750	EA	05/08/1997	114112	DEMO		EP43250	TN06DN12	00001	OP	MOV
TRAN	DOCK	N	Moved	750	EA	05/08/1997	113211	DEMO		EP43250	TN06DN12	00001	OP	MOV

2. Enter a **From Oper** (from operation) value from **UDC 43/OC** that indicates the routing operation or step from which the items were moved.
3. Enter a **To Oper** (to operation) value from **UDC 43/OC**, which indicates the routing operation or step to which items were moved.
4. Enter a **Rev** (reversal) code that indicates whether the transaction is eligible for reversal or has already been reversed.

5. Enter a **Move Code** from **UDC 43/MC** that indicates the movement of the quantity.
6. You can move a quantity from one operation to another, or you can disposition a quantity out of the routing process.

How it works...

When you set up the **Receipt Route** definition, the system will provide you with the information about the transfer of items from one operation to another in a receipt route. For example, when a group of items has been moved from inspection to stock, you can review who moved the items, and the date on which this happened. You can also be determine how long the goods were at a certain operation. For example, the quantity of items in a shipment that did not pass inspection and the quantity of items that were returned to the supplier can be reviewed.

There's more...

- You should specify whether the system displays shipment and pack information.
- You should also specify a business function name that the system uses when validating the Serial Shipping Container Code number.

See also

Setting up receipt routing in *Chapter 4, Understanding and Setting up Procurement*

Purchase order template

A purchase order template can be set up to streamline the purchase order entry process. Purchase order templates contain the items that are used frequently. These templates can be accessed during purchase order entry.

Getting ready

You should set up the names of order templates in the **Order Template** (**40/OT**) **UDC** table.

How to do it ...

1. Access the **Order Template** revision form from **EnterpriseOne menu | Logistic Management | Procurement and Subcontract Management | Procurement Advance and Technical Ops**, and then click on **Supplier Template Revision**.
2. On the **Supplier Template Revision** form, specify the Supplier, and locate and select the template code.
3. Enter the **Item Number**.

4. Enter the **Usual Quantity**.
5. Enter the **Unit of Measure**.
6. Enter the **Effective Date From** and **Effective Date To**, and then click on **OK** to save.

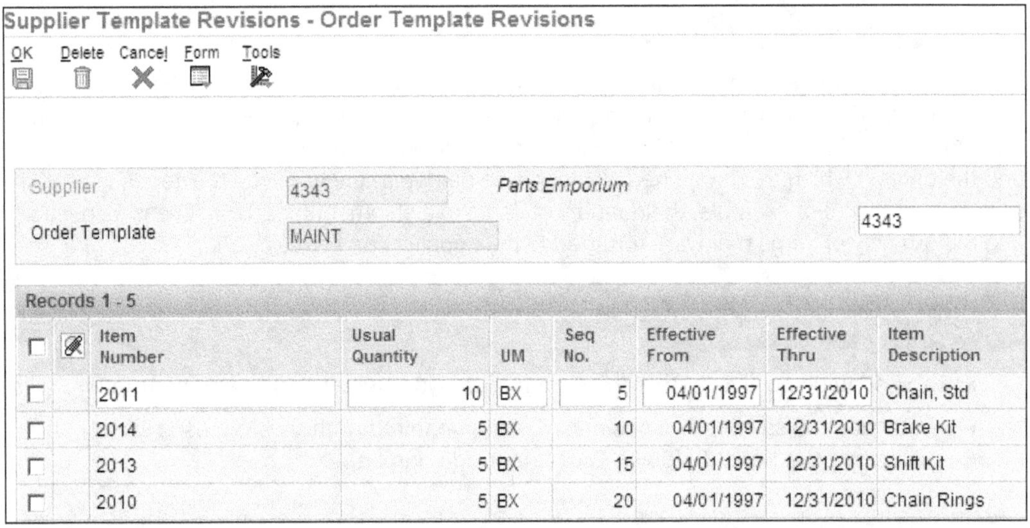

How it works...

A purchase order template is a group of items that is ordered frequently. The order templates can be selected during purchase order entry to select items to order. The order templates are created for a certain supplier. The purchase order will be created quickly after creating a supplier template and use the existing template based on items and item quantities , and an effective date range for the template.

There's more...

You can create standard templates that are not specific to a supplier—those items that are ordered frequently from different suppliers. The template can also be set up based on a specific user and the items most commonly ordered by that user.

7

Creating Vouchers and Landed Costs

In this chapter, we will cover:

- The voucher creation process
- Reviewing open receipts
- Setting up retainage
- Working with retainage
- Setting up landed costs
- Entering landed costs
- Landed cost entry during the receipt process
- Landed cost entry as a standalone process

Introduction

A voucher can be created based on an invoice and the receipt for the purchase order. There are two types of voucher matching—a two-way voucher match and a three-way voucher match. This chapter will cover the voucher matching process and retainage in procurement. It will also cover the landed cost (the additional cost incurred during purchasing) during the receipt process, as well as stand-alone landed costs.

The voucher creation process

You can create a voucher based on an invoice and receipt. There are two types of voucher matching:

- **Two-way voucher match**: This is used normally for non-stock materials, and services. The two-way voucher match is based on matching the purchase order with the supplier invoice.
- **Three-way voucher match**: This is used for stock-based purchases. The three way voucher match is based on matching the purchase order with both the receipt and the supplier invoice.

Getting ready

You should set up the processing option of the voucher matching program **Match Voucher to Open Receipt** (**P0411**).

How to do it....

1. Select **Procurement and Subcontract Management** | **Daily Processing** | **Stock Based Purchasing** | **Purchase Order Processing** | **Receipts Matching and Posting,** and then select **Match Voucher to Open Receipt** (select **P0411**, click on the arrow and then select **Values**).
2. On the **Display** tab, leave all of the options blank. On the **Purchasing** tab, set the **Voucher Delete** option to **1** in order to issue a warning message if a user attempts to delete the voucher the voucher.
3. On the **Voucher Match** tab, enter `1` for the **Match Processing** option, and then click on **OK** to save the **Processing Option** set-up.
4. On the **Supplier Ledger Inquiry** form, click **Add.**

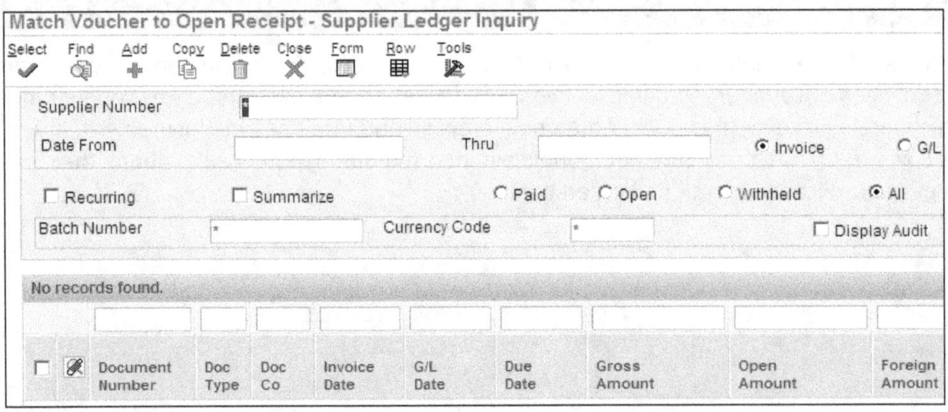

5. On the **Voucher Match** form, enter the **Supplier Number**.
6. Enter the **Invoice Number**.
7. Enter the **G/L Date**.
8. Enter the **Branch/Plant**.
9. Select **Receipts To Match** from the **Form** menu.

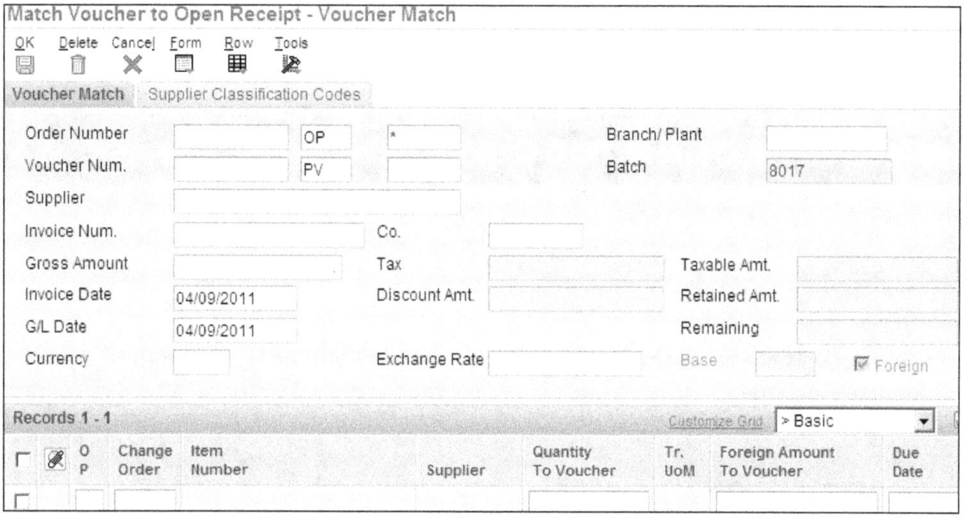

10. On this page, click **Find**.
11. Select all of the purchase order lines for your first stock order worksheet for procurement orders.
12. Click **OK**.
13. On **Voucher Match**, verify that the system loaded your order lines into the grid area.

How it works...

Voucher Match in procurement is a process of integrating the procurement system with the payable system and making payment to the supplier through the payable system; this process is also known as **Procure to Pay**. When you create the voucher without receipt information, the system treats it as a two-way voucher match and the payment invoice will be matched with the purchase order. This method is used to verify that the invoice information corresponds to the purchase order detail lines before you create the vouchers. This method does not verify the receipt; it is normally used for services and non-stock items. For stock-based orders, the payments will be based on the number of units received. When you enter the number of units that you want to pay for, the system calculates the extended value based on the unit price. The system searches this information to add the landed costs (additional cost incurred for item receiving).

There's more...

You can make a payment to a supplier before receiving the items, by creating a preliminary voucher. After that, you can receive the goods specified on the invoice, and transfer the amounts to the appropriate general ledger accounts.

See also

- *Reviewing open receipts*

Reviewing open receipts

This recipe discusses how to review open receipts.

Getting ready

You should set up the **Processing Options** for the **xxx** program **(P43214)** in order to review the **Purchase Receipts**.

How to do it....

1. Access the **Open Receipts by Supplier** form from the **G43A15** menu.

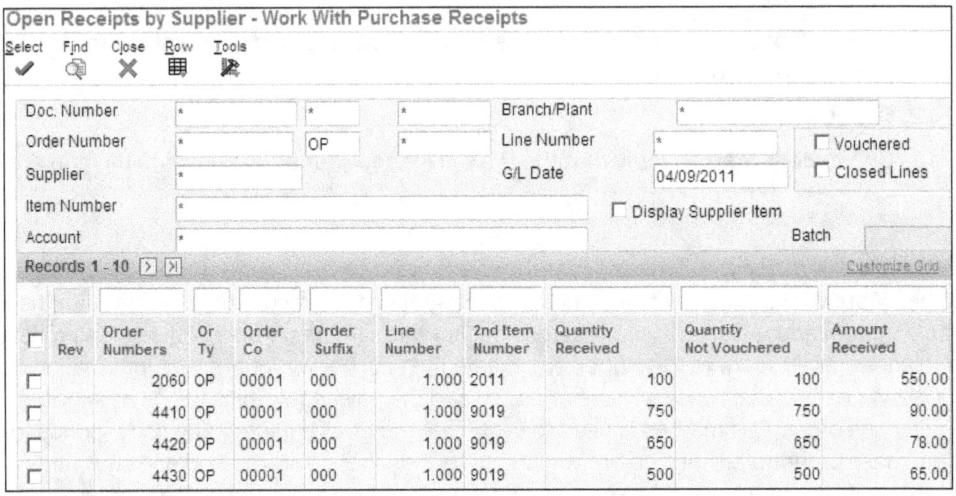

2. **Quantity Not Vouchered** displays the original quantity for the order detail line, plus or minus any changes to that quantity, minus all quantities shipped, received, and vouchered to date.
3. **Amount Not Vouchered** displays the amount of the order, invoice, or voucher that is still unpaid or open.

How it works...

When you enter the document number for enquiry, the document number can be an order number, invoice number, and so on. Any change in the original amount will also change the open amount and also reduce the net change. The **Open Receipt by Supplier** application provides information on open receipts that have been vouchered but not yet been created. This may provide you with details as to which vouchers have not been created. You can also review the already-created vouchers by using the voucher option. The system shows the order detail lines with the quantity and amount that you entered in the voucher.

There's more...

The **Open Receipt** application provides you with verification of the value that is open and how much quantity is open for each receipt.

See also

- *Entering and reversing Receipts in Chapter 6, Receipt Processing*

Setting up retainage

Retainage is the percentage of the committed payment for the purchase order that is withheld for a specified period (usually until the transaction completes). For example, if you create a voucher for 100 dollars with a retainage of 5 percent, the actual payment will be 95 USD, with 5 held as retainage. You should set up the processing options of **Match Voucher to Open Receipt** to be able to specify the retainage percentage or the retainage amount as a default value in the **Voucher Match** program (**P4314**).

Getting ready

Set up the processing options to apply taxes to retainage.

How to do it....

1. Access the **Voucher Match** program (**P4314**) from the **G43A15** menu.
2. The **Display Retainage Indicator** processing option specifies whether the system displays the **Retainage Indicator** column in the Voucher Match grid.

3. **Default** specifies whether to automatically load the **Retainage Percentage** or amount from the order header. Do not load the retainage percentage or amount from the order header.
4. In the Taxes field, specify whether the system applies taxes to the retained or voucher amount.

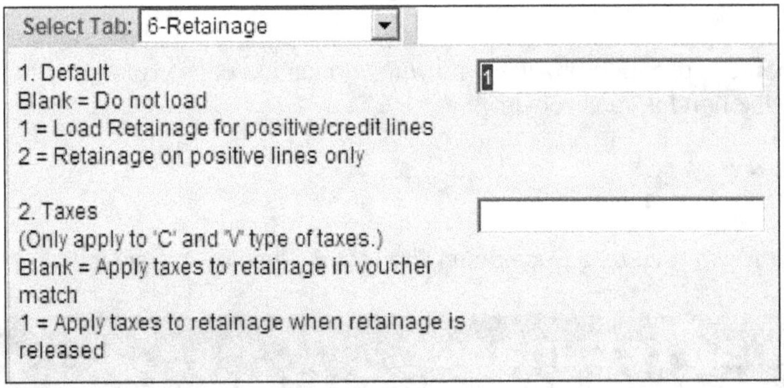

How it works....

Setting up retainage will allow the system to retain a percentage of the total bid, which a contractor (or subcontractor) pays upon submitting a bid for work. It is considered insurance, and a "good faith" tool. It is a way for public institutions and general contractors to ensure that a company they are entering into an agreement with is solvent, insured, and will be around for the duration of the project. When you activate retainage, the system will start holding a certain amount or percentage from payment as a retainage amount.

There is more....

The **Withholding Percentage** can also be set up in the supplier master information, on the tax information tab.

See also

- *Working with retainage*

Working with retainage

This recipe provides you with the details of retainage, and discusses how retainage works. It covers the following topics:

- Enter a voucher with retainage
- Enter a voucher to release retainage

Getting ready

Set up the processing options of the **Match Voucher to Open Receipt** program.

How to do it....

1. Access the **Receipts Matching and Posting** (**G43A15**) menu, and select **Match Voucher to Open Receipt- Supplier Ledger Inquiry**.
2. Click on **Add** to access **Match Voucher to Open Receipt** – **Voucher Match**.
3. Enter a voucher with retainage by entering the voucher details and then specifying either the **Retained Amount For** or the **Percentage Retained**.

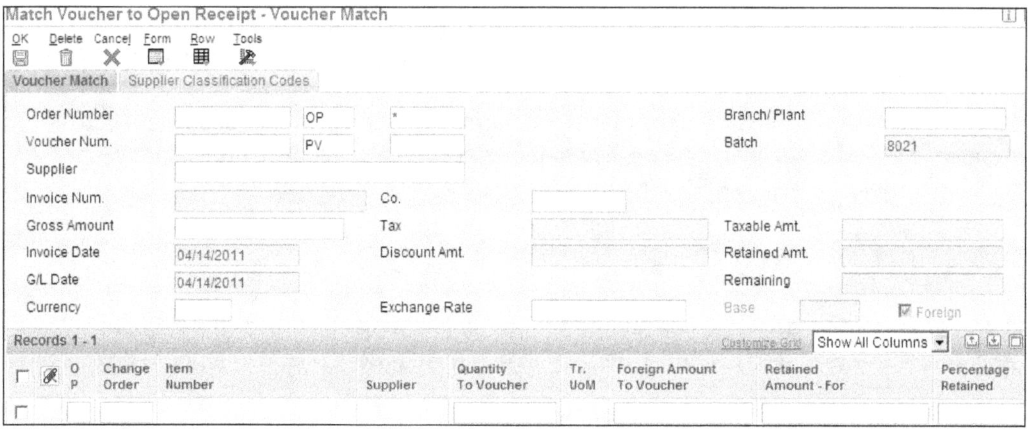

4. Enter a voucher with **Release Retainage** and enter the **Retainage Release** amount.

How it works....

Retainage is a process to hold a part of the payment from the supplier. When you create a voucher you can enter the retainage amount / percentage. Retainage is the percentage of a committed amount that is held until a specified date. The retainage can be entered during purchase order entry by specifying the retainage percentage, with the balance amount being specified or confirmed during payment voucher creation. For example if you create a payment for 1000 USD and the retainage percentage is 15%, then the system will hold 150 USD and the actual payment will be 850 USD. You should release the retainage by entering a payment voucher for the amount that you want to release. You can also use the **Tax With Retainage** processing option to reschedule tax on retainage. When you activate the processing option for **Tax With Retainage** and if you use a tax type C or V, then the system will compute the amounts through a different method. It deducts the retainage from the actual taxable amount and recalculates fresh amounts. You can release retainage either through a partial release that still leaves an unpaid balance or through a full release, which means that there will be no outstanding balance.

There's more...

During voucher creation, you can release retainage and create a voucher at the same time. The retainage can be applied to the entire voucher, or can be applied by line item of the voucher.

See also

- *Setting up Retainage*

Setting up landed costs

Landed costs are additional charges that are incurred in delivering an individual item into inventory. Landed costs cannot be applied to the total cost of a purchase order, and are also non taxable.

Getting ready

In order to set up landed cost, you should set up the following options for the **Purchase Order** program **P4310** (see the *Chapter 4, Setting up purchase orders* recipe in order to do this):

- **Cost field display** should be activated
- **Display header** is set to display in the processing option
- **Revision tracking** should be de activated

How to do it....

1. Select **Procurement and Subcontract Management** | **Procurement Setup** | **Procurement System Setup**, and then click on **Landed Costs Revisions**.

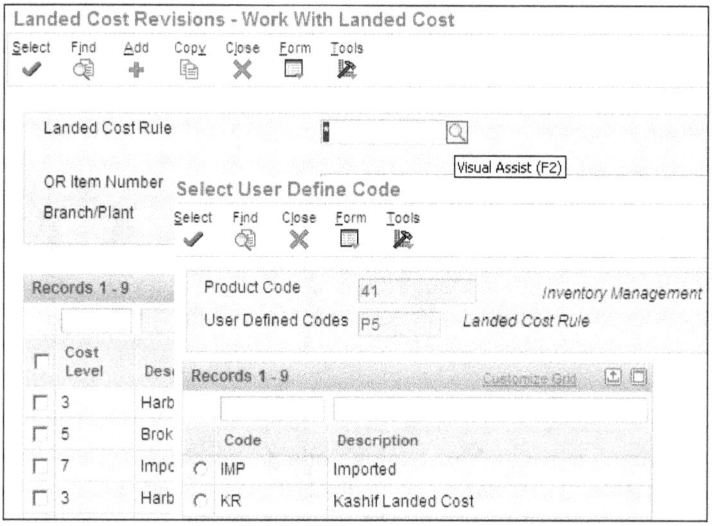

2. On the **Work With Landed Cost** form, click on the **Landed Cost Rule** visual assist button to access the UDC code **41/P5**.
3. Select **Revisions** from the **Form** menu.
4. Click **Add**.
5. Add the landed cost rule code and description.
6. Click **OK** to save the information.

How it works....

When you set up the cost rule, you can allocate the landed cost for a specific item and branch/plant. After you create a cost rule, you can link it to an inventory item, vendor, and purchase order. You can also track the actual cost of purchasing an item. When you assign landed costs to an item or cost rule, you classify the calculation for each landed cost. The landed costs can be added based on a percentage of the unit price, the amount of the items, and also based on a specific rate.

There's more...

You can use GL class code to verify the general ledger accounts—to see which system created journal entries for landed costs. The AAI tables **4385** and **4390** are used to create landed cost journals.

See also

- *Entering landed costs*

Entering landed costs

Landed costs are expenses that are incurred during purchase of an item. These expenses can be delivery charges for an order, broker fees, commission, shipment charges, and so on.

Getting ready

You should verify that the **Override Next Status Code** is blank and that the landed cost rule is not populated in the **Purchase Order** program (**P4310**) processing option.

How to do it....

1. Access the **Landed Cost Revision** program from the **G43A14** menu.
2. On the **Work With Landed Cost** form, click **Add.**

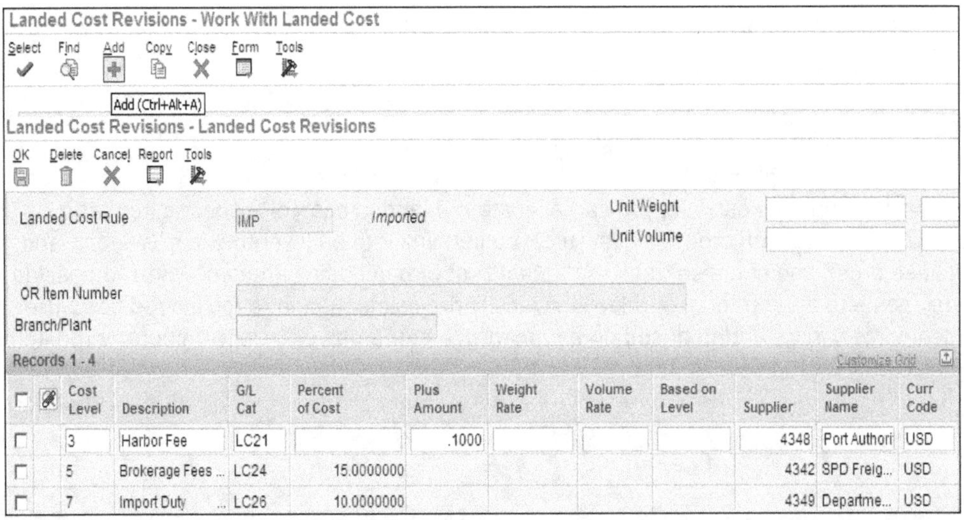

3. Enter the **Cost Rule** name in the **Land Cost Rule** field.
4. Enter a **Cost Level** of *3*.
5. Enter a **G/L Cat** of *LC21*.
6. Enter a **Percent of Cost** of *10* (as an example) or enter **Plus Amount**.
7. Enter a value for **Based on Level**.
8. Enter the **Supplier Number**.
9. Click **OK** to save the record.

How it works....

During purchasing, it is logical to pay additional amount as shipment charges, harbor fees, broker fees, import taxes, and so on. You can enter landed costs for items during the receipt process or as a stand-alone process. Once you link a **Landed Cost** with an item during the **Receipt** process or as a **Stand-Alone Landed Cost**, then the system will update the item cost automatically. You can review the item cost via the **Item Master Cost Revision** program (**P4105**). You should verify the **Update Item Cost Online** in the **Branch Plant System Constants**.

See also

- *Setting up landed costs*

Landed cost entry during the receipt process

This recipe provides details of landed cost entry during receipt.

Getting ready

You should set the **Update Item Cost Online** option in the **Branch Plant System Constants**, in order to automatically update item costs with the landed cost.

How to do it....

1. Select **Procurement and Subcontract Management** | **Daily Processing** | **Stock Based Processing** | **Purchase Order Processing**, click the arrow to the right of **Enter Receipts by PO**, and then choose **Values**.
2. On the **Status Default** tab, verify that the **Incoming 1** status is set to *230*, and also verify that the on the **Process** tab, the **Option default** is set to `1`, **Landed Cost** is set to *1*, and **Receipt Routing** is left as blank.

3. On **Work With Purchase Orders to Receive**, look for your **Order Number** and then click **Select** from the menu option and select your landed cost. Enter the **G/L Date** and **Receipt Dates**.

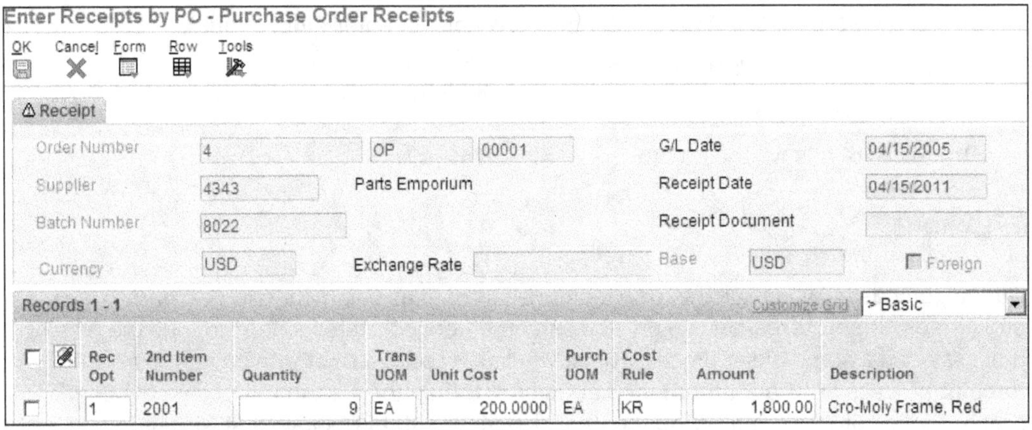

4. Click **OK** to receive your purchase receipt.
5. For the **Cost Rule** selection, select your created landed cost rule.
6. Click **OK**.

How it works....

When you enter a receipt, the system displays the landed costs that apply to the items so that you can review or change the landed costs during receipt entry. The landed costs can also be set via the processing option of **Purchase Order Receipts** (**P4312**) to automatically apply the landed cost rule without displaying the **Landed Cost Selection** form. After applying the landed cost, the item cost will update the item cost table with the item cost, along with the landed costs. After applying the landed costs, the sales department can start creating sales orders for related items.

There's more...

A landed cost rule will search for the following options in the procurement system:

- Landed costs can be assigned to the **Item/Branch**
- Cost rules can be assigned to the detail line of a **Purchase Order**
- Cost rules can be assigned to the item on the **Item Master Revisions** form

See also

- *Entering landed costs*

Landed cost entry as a standalone process

Standalone entry of landed cost can be done as per business requirement - that is, if the procurement department receives the shipment charges, agency fees, broker fees, custom charges, and many other expenses that are related to procurement late, and the item has already been received in the system through receipt processing, or the company is using receipt routing during item receipt. The **Standalone Landed Cost** process is a recommended feature in such cases.

Getting ready

You should enter landed costs in the following applications in order to activate the **Standalone Landed Cost** process:

- Landed costs definition in **Landed Cost Revisions**
- Assign landed cost rules to items or purchase orders
- Verify in the processing options of Stand-Alone Landed Cost program that you enter the landed costs

How to do it...

1. Access the **Stand-Alone Landed Cost** program from the **G43A15** menu.

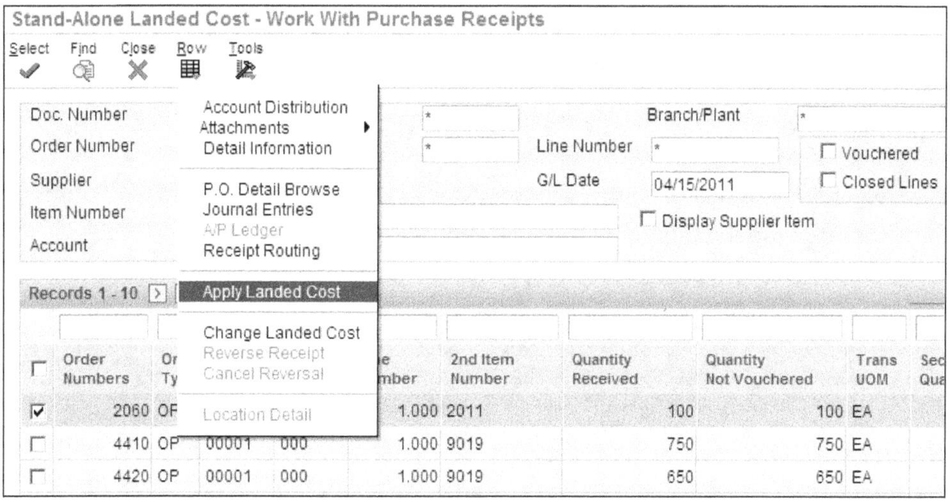

2. Select the **Purchase Order** to which you want to apply the landed cost.
3. Select the PO line from the detail grid, and then from the **Row** menu click on **Apply Landed Cost**.

4. The next screen will show the landed cost component; you should click **OK** to confirm the **Landed Cost Rule**.
5. After clicking **OK**, the general entries will be created automatically and the item cost will be updated.

How it works....

The landed costs can be entered as a stand-alone process if the landed cost information is not available at the time of receipt. Standalone landed costs are only applied to items for which you record receipt information. When you enter landed costs, the system will only allow you to work with the landed costs that have been set up and assigned to the item. When you receive each item you can review, change, and enter the landed costs for the item. Once the landed costs have been applied, the system may create a separate landed cost detail line voucher. The additional voucher will depend on how you set up each landed cost. The landed cost can be reviewed via the detail lines on the **Voucher Match** form.

> Tolerance rules can be set up during purchase receipt, match voucher, blanket release, and acknowledgment tolerance. Tolerance setup can be based on a percentage or a unit cost or extended cost, in the **Purchasing Tolerance Rules (P4322)** program.

There's more...

After entering the landed costs, you can also run the **Copy Cost Components** (**R41891**) batch application, which copies simulated or frozen cost information from the **F30026** table to the **F41291** table.

See also

- *Entering landed costs*

8

Processing Special Orders and Approvals

In this chapter, we will cover:

- Creating a purchase requisition
- Generating a quote from a requisition
- Creating an RFQ from a requisition
- Creating a supplier price quote
- Generating a purchase order from an RFQ
- Reviewing order revisions
- Entering order revisions
- Stocked item reorder point
- Creating an approval route
- Approval delegation
- Setting up the Order Awaiting for Approvals application
- Working with Orders Awaiting for Approval

Introduction

Oracle JD Edwards EnterpriseOne provides a variety of special orders that may be required, depending upon the company's business processes. For example, some companies require a quotation process and some may have a long term purchase contract called a blanket order, with their vendors . In this chapter, you will see the processing of special orders such as requisition orders, quote orders, long term contracts or blanket orders, and creating supplier prices. This chapter will also cover generating purchase orders and purchase order approval, including approval route set-up.

Creating a purchase requisition

A purchase requisition is an internal document that is requested by the store for stocking, the sales department for customer orders, and the production plant for the manufacture of goods. It contains the required items, along with quantity and cost information.

Getting ready

Set the processing option of the **Purchase Orders (P4310)** program, to create a purchase requisition.

How to do it....

1. Select **Procurement and Subcontract Management** | **Daily Processing** | **Stock Based Purchasing** | **Requisition and Quote Management**.
2. On the **Enter Requisition – Work with Order Header** form, click **Add**.

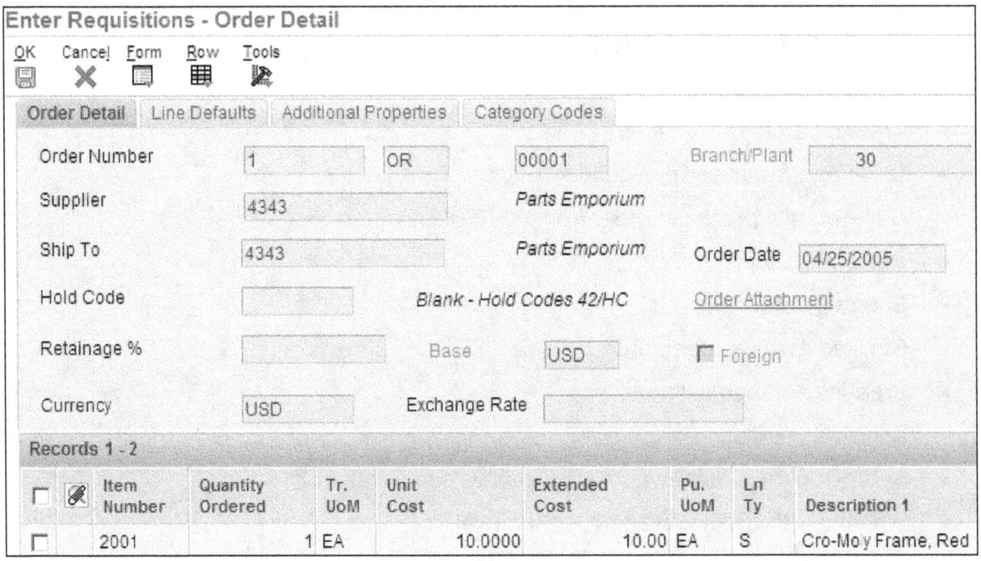

3. Enter the **Branch/Plant**.
4. Enter the **Supplier** address number.
5. Enter the **Ship To** number.
6. Enter the **Requisition Date**.

7. On the **Order Detail tab,** on the grid on the first row in the item table, enter the **Item Number**, **Quantity Order**, and **Unit Price**; the **Extended Price** will automatically be calculated by the system.

How it works....

Requisition is the first step, and the first official document that is created, for the purchase of items, goods, and services. Companies normally create a purchase request before creating a purchase order. The process of requisition entry is the same as that of purchase order entry. When you enter the purchase requisition, you will enter the address book number as the ship-to address, so that you can track who has requested the requisition. In general, the purchase department manages the purchase request, and you can enter the purchase manager, address number instead of the supplier's. Requisition printing uses the same procedure as that used for purchase order printing.

There's more...

The requisition can be duplicated in order to create recurring orders. For example, say that every month you create the same request for office supplies. You can duplicate the requisition to create recurring orders, so that the requisition will remain open and the system does not close it.

See also

- *Creating stock/non stock-based purchase order in Chapter 5, Understanding Pricing In Procurement and Purchase Orders*

Generating a quote from a requisition

In this recipe, you will learn how to generate **RFQ** and Blanket Order from a **Requisition**. The RFQ (Request for quote) is an official document that must be sent to the supplier in order to receive the quotation from supplier.

Getting ready

In order to generate an **RFQ** and Blanket Order, you should create a **Purchase Requisition**.

How to do it....

1. Select **Procurement and Subcontract Management | Daily Processing |Stock Based Purchasing | Requisition and Quote Management**. Click on the arrow next to **Generate Quotes from Reqs.** (**P43060**), and then select **Values**.
2. On the **Defaults** tab, enter a **Default Order Type** of **OR**.

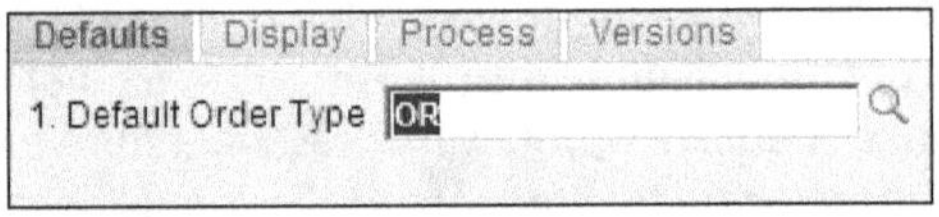

3. On the **Display** tab, enter an **Incoming Status Code 1 of 110,** and an **Incoming Status Code 2** of **120**.

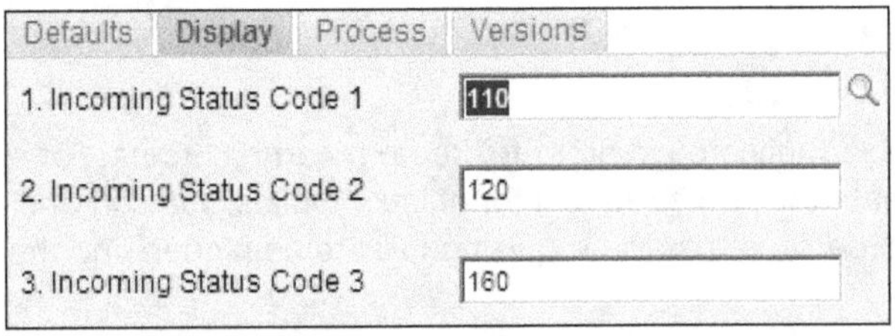

4. Enter the **Purchase Order Entry** (**P4310**) application version as **ZJDE0002**.

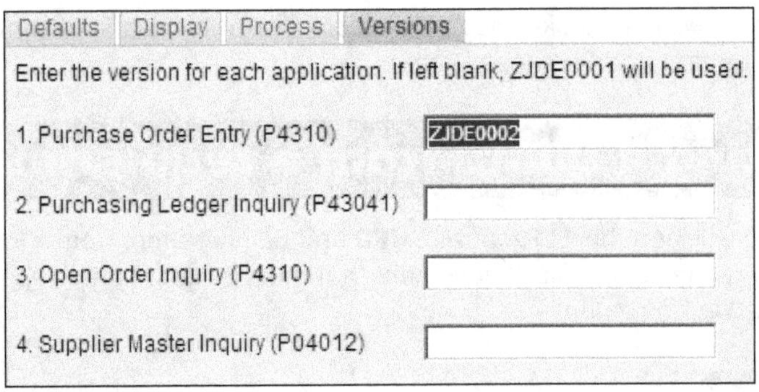

How it works....

When you set up the **Processing Option** of (**P43060**), the system activates the quote generation from requisition functionality. To set up the **Generate Quote Order activity**, you should set up the **Order Activity Rule** in order to set up the quote order. You can create quote orders using detail lines from requisitions, if the detail line on a quote order was created from multiple requisitions.

There's more...

The **Versions** tab provides the option to use your already-configured versions for reviewing the **Purchase Ledger Inquiry**, **Open Order Inquiry,** and **Supplier Master Inquiry**.

See also

Creating an RFQ from a requisition

Creating an RFQ from a requisition

You can generate the **RFQ** by using the requisition that you created in the previous recipe, and releasing all of the line items for which you want to generate the the **RFQ**.

Getting ready

You should verify that the required processing options for **Generate Quotes from Reqs** (**P43060**) has been set.

How to do it....

1. Select **Procurement and Subcontract Management** | **Daily Processing** | **Stock Based Purchasing** | **Order Generation/Approval/Release,** and then click on **Generate Quote from Reqs**.
2. On **Work with Order Release**, locate the **Purchase Requisition** that you created in the previous activity.

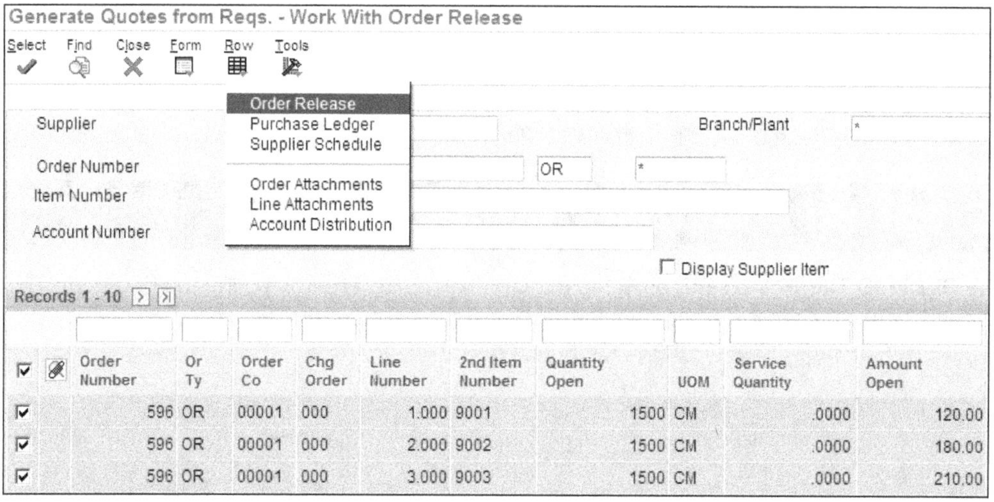

3. Select all of the rows of the order.
4. Select **Order Release** from the **Row** menu.
5. On the **Release Information** tab, do not change any of the default information.
6. Select the **Dates** tab, and enter a **G/L Date**.
7. Click **OK**.
8. On the **Work With Order Release form**, select **Generate Order** from the **Form** menu.

How it works...

When the purchase requisition has been approved for the items or services, the next step is to generate a quotation in order to obtain the price from the supplier. The quote order can be created by using the detail lines of purchase requisitions. When you generate the quote from the requisition, you can generate it from multiple requisitions, and it can be reviewed with the list of all requisitions showing which line was created and who requested the items and quantities. The system maintains this information about the consolidated requisitions that it creates for quote orders in the **F4332** table.

There's more...

After entering the price quote information, you can print the **Request for Quote Report (R43530)** report to review existing price quotes for supplier.

> You can generate a customized price comparison report based on the price received from the supplier. This report will also cover the delivery time warranty details and payment terms, for comparison.

See also

- *Generating a quote from a requisition*

Creating a supplier price quote

The Oracle JD Edwards system provides the capability that, after receiving the quotation from supplier, you can enter the supplier quote price in the system and make an online comparison, in order to generate a purchase order.

Getting ready

To enter the response for the quote, you should create the quote order first, with complete details.

How to do it....

1. Select **Procurement and Subcontract Management** | **Daily Processing** | **Stock Based Purchasing** | **Requisition and Quote Management,** and then select **Enter Quote Response**.

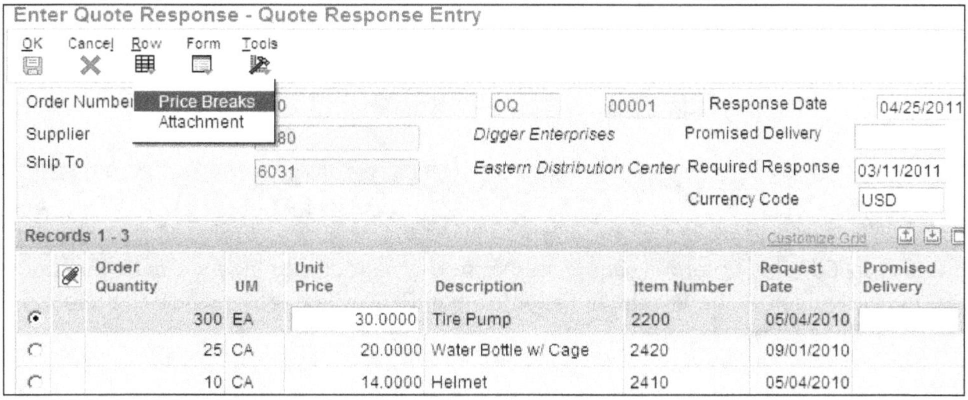

2. On **Work With Suppliers**, locate your quote order.
3. Select the **Quote for Supplier**.
4. On the **Quote Response Entry form**, enter the **Response Date** and the **Promised Delivery** date.
5. In the list of item records, select the item, and enter a **Unit Price**.
6. Click **OK,** and then click **Close**.

How it works....

After you've entered supplier price quotes for an item or service, you can compare price quotes from multiple suppliers, in order to identify the supplier with the best price and select the price quote for which to create an order. After you select a price quote, you can close the quote order detail line (if fully released), so that you no longer create orders from the line. Leave the quote order detail line open if you want to create recurring orders from the line. Utilize the processing options to specify which of the methods you want to use. Closed detail lines do not appear on the **Quote Order Release** form. You can compare price quotes for an item by locating the quote order detail line that contains the item. You can review the item description from the detail line, along with details of all of the suppliers who have provided price quotes for the item.

There's more...

You can add the supplier prices through the price break option if supplier quote prices vary based on quantity. To enter supplier prices break, perform following steps:

1. Access **Quote Order Release**, locate your quote order, and select the row for the item and supplier for which you want to enter the price
2. Select **Price Breaks** from the **Row** menu.
3. Enter the price and quantity.
4. Click on **Cancel**.

See also

- *Creating an RFQ from a requisition*

Generating a purchase order from an RFQ

The Oracle JD Edwards EnterpriseOne system provides various options for creating a purchase order. You can generate the **Purchase Order** from an RFQ, which provides you the relation between purchase order and **RFQ**.

Getting ready

You should set up the processing options for the **Generate POs from Quotes** (**P43360**) application in order to generate the purchase order from a quote.

How to do it....

1. Select **Procurement and Subcontract Management** | **Daily Processing** | **Stock BasedPurchasing** | **Requisition and Quote Management**, and then click on **Generate POs from Quotes** (**P43360**).

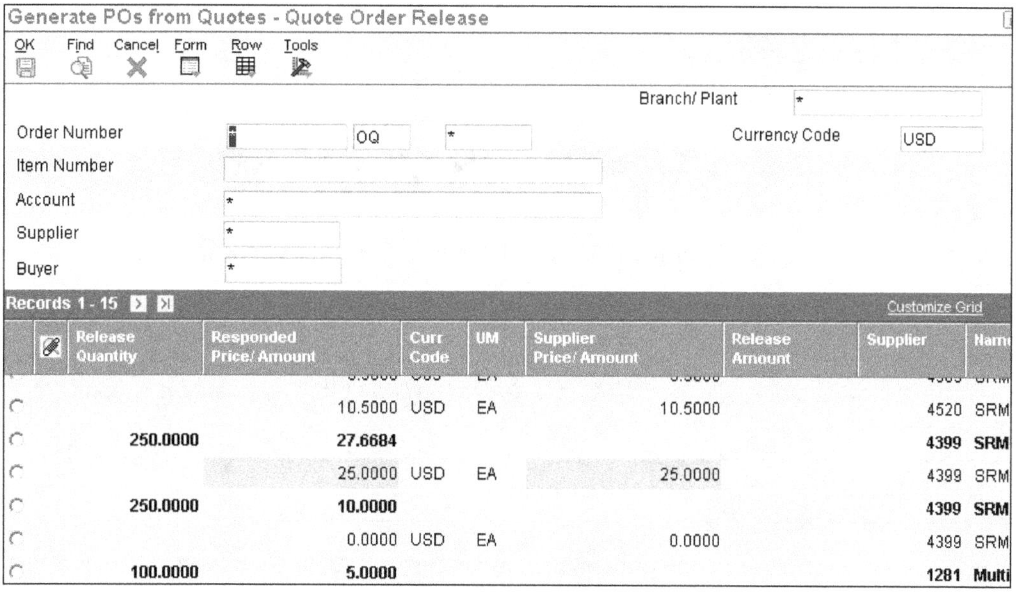

2. On the **Generate Pos from Quote – Quote Order Release form**, locate the quote order that you want to release.
3. Enter a **Release Quantity** based on the **Item Number and Supplier.**
4. Click **OK** to generate the purchase order, or select **Generate Order** from the **Form** menu.

How it works...

When you enter the supplier price quotes, you can compare the price quotes in order to identify the supplier with the best price and select a price quote to create a purchase order. Select the price quote for which you want to create an order. When you release the item quantity from quote order, the system generates the purchase order, and the quote order will be completely closed after releasing the full quantity. The processing option set-up specifies which methods you want to use to close the quote order. The closed quote order detail lines do not appear on the **Quote Order Release** program.

There's more...

If you want to create a recurring purchase order, leave the quote order detail line open.

See also

- *Generating a quote from a requisition.*

Reviewing order revisions

The order revision review allows you to review changes in the order's information.

Getting ready

Verify the following processing options on the **Order Revision** tab: The **Revision Tracking** value should be *2*.

How to do it....

1. Select **Procurement and Subcontract Management** | **Daily Processing** | **StockBased Purchasing** | **Stock Based PO Processing, and then** click on **Purchase Order**.

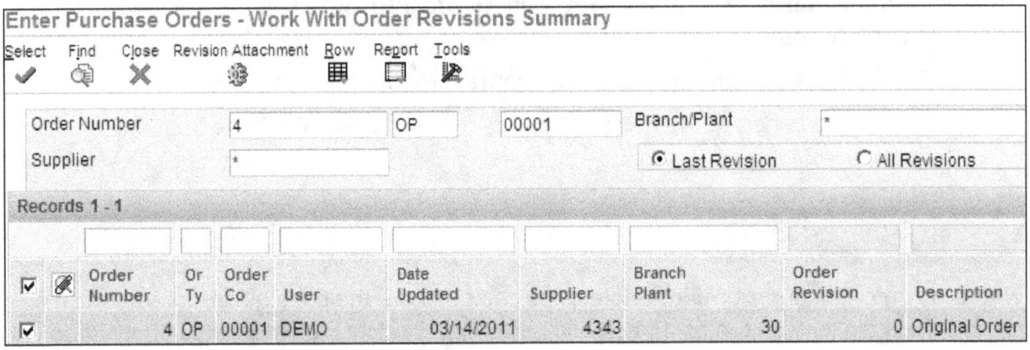

2. On the **Work With Order Headers form** locate the purchase order that you created, and then select the row for your order.
3. Select **Order Revisions** from the **Row** menu.
4. Select the row for your order, and then select **Revision Details** from the **Row** menu.
5. On **Order Revision Detail**, notice that the **Order Revision** field is set to *0*.
6. In the grid area, locate the **Line Number** and **Order Revision** columns.
7. Record the order revision number for each line in the **Original Order** Revision column of the **Order Revision Tracking** table in the **Activity Overview**.

How it works....

When you activate order revisions, the system tracks the changes that you make to your purchase order. For example, if you entered an order with 10 as the quantity irrelevant and after that you change the item quantity to 20, you can review the changed information that was entered for that purchase order. When you review an order, the last order revision that was created appears at the top. All of the revisions for each detail line will also be displayed. The order revision value shows how many times the order has been modified. The purchase order revision is stored in **F4311** table, and the **Change Order** column get incremented with each revision.

There's more...

You will see the following information in the order revision details:

- The number of times the order has been revised
- The information that has revised - such as item number, the costs, and other details
- The reason for each revisions
- The person who made the revisions
- The dates that the revisions came into effect

See also

- *Creating stock/non stock-based purchase orders in Chapter 5, Understanding Pricing In Procurement and Purchase Orders*

Entering order revisions

The order revision entry allows you to enter changes to order information.

Getting ready

Set up the processing options for the **Purchase Orders** (**P4310**) application, in order to activate the tracking of information that has been changed.

How to do it....

1. Select **Procurement and Subcontract Management** | **Daily Processing | Stock Based Purchasing** | **Stock Based PO Processing,** and then click on **Enter Purchase Orders**.

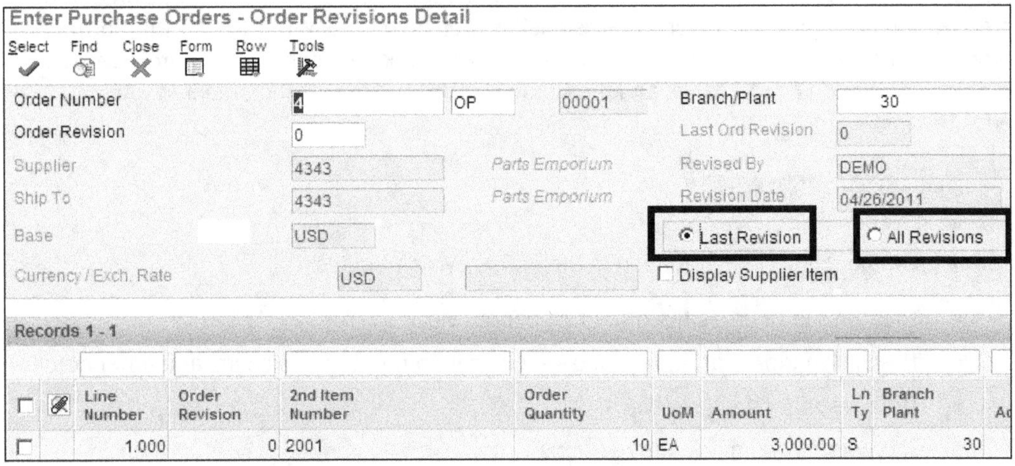

2. On the **Work With Order Headers form**, locate your order, and then select **Detail Revision** from the **Row** menu.
3. Change the **Quantity Ordered** for an item, and then click **OK**.
4. On the **Media Objects form**, enter the message **Quantity Revised**.
5. Click **OK**.
6. On the **Work With Order Headers form**, select the row for your order.
7. Select **Order Revisions** from the **Row** menu.
8. Select the **Row** with the **Order Revision** of *1*, and then select **Revision Details** from the **Row** menu.
9. Record the revision levels for each of your detail lines in the Order Revision *1* column of the Order Revision Tracking table, and then click **Close**.

[Media Objects are attached to documents, and can be messages, pictures, and so on.]

How it works...

When you revise detail lines, the system creates order revisions at that time. If you revise the header information, the system does not create any order revisions. The system creates an order revision each time that you enter or modify the purchase order. For example, if you enter the purchase order with five as the quantity, the system creates purchase order revision 000 in the order revision table. After that, if you modify the order quantity to 10, the system creates order revision 001. Any revision can be reviewed; order revision 000 being is the original order including tailored fields. Order revision notes also can be entered each time that you create an order revision.

There's more...

Order revision tracking can be activated through the **P4310** application processing option, and you can specify which options you want to enable.

You can activate only the existing order revision or new order entry with the existing order can also be activated.

See also

- *Creating stock/non stock-based purchase orders in Chapter 5, Understanding Pricing In Procurement and Purchase Orders*

Stocked item reorder point

You can generate purchase orders for stock based on a stock reorder point. The system suggests the items and quantities that need to be ordered. The system is based on the order suggestions through backorders or the sales history.

Getting ready

You should set up **Item Branch Quantities** in order to generate the purchase order by using stock reorder points.

How to do it....

1. Access the **Purchase Order Generator (P43011)** application from the **G43A13** menu.
2. On the **Purchase Order Generator** form, enter **Supplier/ Buyer** number and click find, and then the system will show those items that need to be ordered, based on the quantity that you have set up in the **Item Branch Quantities**.
3. Select the item that you want to order, and then click **Select** from the menu bar.
4. Click on **Generate Order** from the **Form** menu to generate the purchase order.

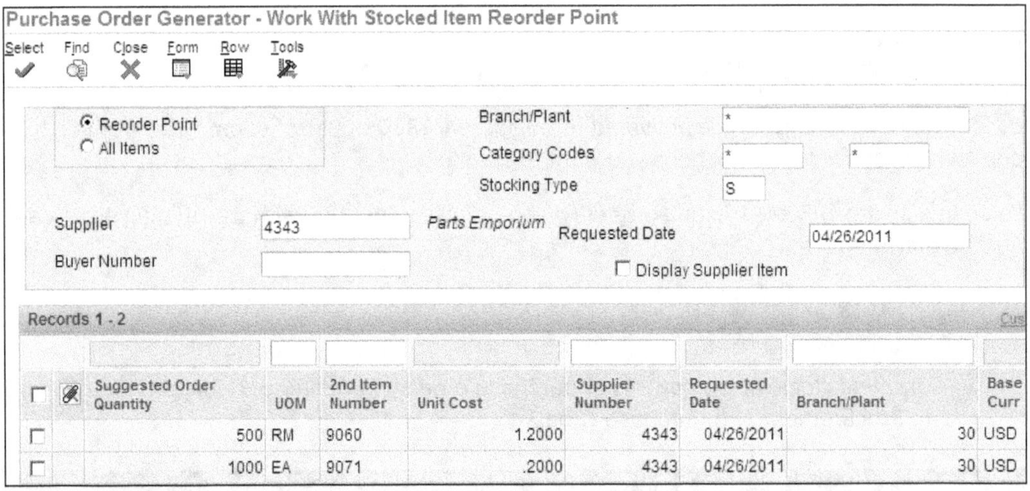

How it works....

The order generation suggestions can also be changed before generating the purchase order. The **Purchase Order Generator** program (**P43011**) has a zero reorder point feature: when the item's inventory level is equal to zero, the system calculates the reorder point for that item. For example, the item can also be reordered if it's not in stock. The zero reorder feature can be enabled by selecting the appropriate options for system's additional information in the **Item Branch** (**P41026)** application. For instance, if you enter *0* in the **Order Policy Code** field, the system generates purchase orders. When the **Value Order Policy** field has a value of *1*, it overrides the value in the **Reorder Point Input** field with *0*.

There's more...

The purchase order generator works based on the stock order point that is set up in the Item Branch quantities, which is a program in the Inventory Management System. In the item branch quantities set-up, there are multiple quantity options that can be set up.

See also

- *Item branch/plant setup in Chapter 1, Inventory Management*

Creating an approval route

You set up approval routes to specify the persons who are responsible for approving an order. The approval route code needs to be defined in the **Branch/Plant Constants** set-up.

Getting ready

You should identify the approval route codes that need to be assigned, in the application processing option for each version.

How to do it....

1. Select **Procurement and Subcontract Management** | **Daily Processing** | **Stock Based Purchasing** | **Order Generation/Approve/Release** | **Approval Level Revisions** (**P43008**).

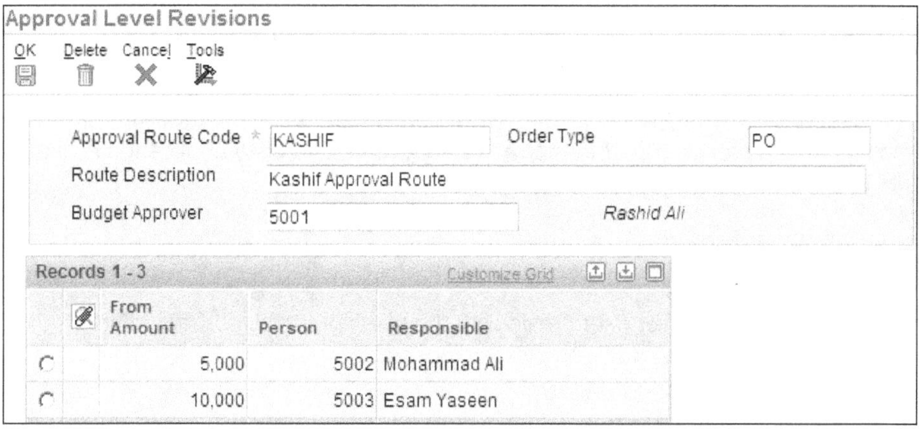

2. Click on **Add**.
3. On the **Approval Level Revisions form**, enter the **Approval Route Code**.
4. Enter the **Order Type**.
5. Enter the **Route Description**.
6. Enter the **Budget Approver**.
7. Enter the **From Amount and Person**.

How it works....

When you activate the approval route, and after assigning an approval route, the system does not process the order until the approver approves the order, the authorized person's user ID should be linked to the employee address book number by using the **User Profile Revisions (P0092)** application. The approver who is responsible for approving an order may depend upon the department or location, and also based on items that you want to purchase. Multiple approval routes can also be created that contain different groups, different persons, and different levels of approval. It also depends on the cost of the items or services that you want to purchase, and you may need to obtain approval for an order from more than one approver.

There's more...

You should specify the value of purchase orders that require order approval in the approval route. If the amount exceeds from one approver's limit, then the succeeding approver should approve the order, based on their approval level.

See also

- *Approval delegation*

Approval delegation

In some cases when the original approver may be absent, for example they may have gone on a vacation or a business trip, the **Approval Delegation (P43280)** application is used to delegate the order approval.

Getting ready

You should set up the approver user profile with the user's address number in order to receive the order approval messages in the employee work center.

How to do it....

1. Access the **Approval Delegation** program from the **G43A13** menu.
2. Enter the **Approver** address number for the delegate.
3. You will find some order types with an approval route code. Select the required row, and then click **Select** from the menu bar.

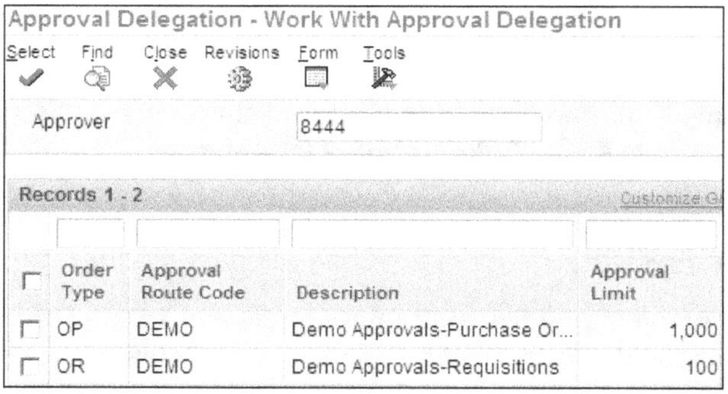

4. In the **Approval Delegation** application, enter the new approver address as the **Delegate To** number, and then click **OK**.

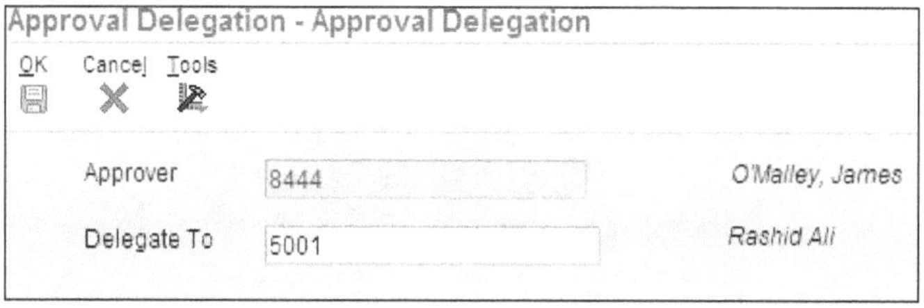

How it works....

1. On the **Approval Delegation form**, specify the individual to whom you are now delegating authority.
2. You can review the approval routes to which you transfer authority (approver), and then select a route for which you delegate the authority.
3. When you enter the delegate address number, the system will start sending the order approval messages to the new approver that you have set up.

See also

- *Creating an approval route*

Setting up the Order Awaiting for Approvals application

You can set up the **Order Awaiting for Approvals** application in order to access the orders awaiting approval. You can use it for approving, reviewing, and rejecting the purchase order.

Getting ready

Set up the **Order Activity** for **Purchase Order Approval** status, and adjust the **User Profile** address number in order to set up **Order Awaiting for Approval**.

How to do it...

1. Select **Procurement and Subcontract Management** | **Daily Processing** |**Stock Based Purchasing** | **Order Generation/Approval/Release**, click the arrow to the right of **Orders Awaiting Approval** (**P43081**), and then select **Values**.

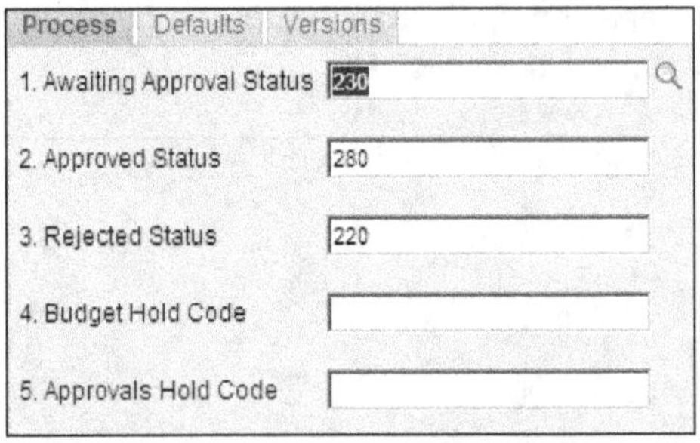

2. Enter the **Awaiting Approval Status** on the **Process** tab.
3. Enter the **Approved Status**.
4. Enter the **Rejected Status**.
5. On the **Defaults** tab, verify that the **Order Type** is **OP**.

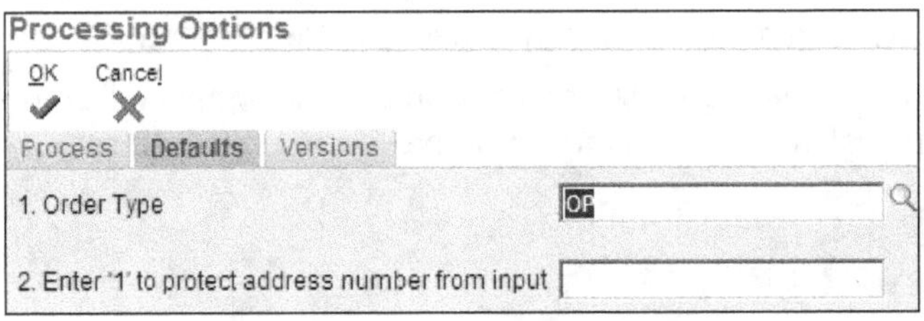

6. Click **OK**.

How it works...

When you set up the **Purchase Order Approvals (P43081)** application processing option, the system activates purchase order approval. The purchase order will advance in order status based on the processing option's approved and rejected status. Specify the order type that you want to use for the approval route. The purchase order can be located based on the address book number; it can also be located based on the age of the order, so that orders requiring urgent concentration can easily be identified.

> OP is the document type for Purchase Orders. You can also set up your own user-defined document type for Purchase Orders.

There's more...

You should set up separate versions for each order type, in order to activate the order approval for that order type.

> The application Processing Option versions can also be set up by accessing the **Interactive Versions (P983051)** application (**IV**) from the Fast Path and locating your application and the version.

See also

- *Working with Orders Awaiting for Approval*
- *Setting up order activity rules in Chapter 4, Understanding and Setting up Procurement,*

Working with Orders Awaiting for Approval

Pending orders can be located via the **Purchase Order Approvals (P43081)** application. You can select individual orders in order to review the order status while it's approved or rejected. The order can also be located by the originator's user ID in order to review the status of the order, that is, whether the order is approved, rejected, or pending.

Getting ready

You should set up the **Purchase Order Approvals** application in order to activate the **Order Approval**.

How to do it...

1. Access the **G43A13** menu from the Fast Path.
2. Click on **Work With Orders Awaiting Approval**.
3. Select the purchase order, click **Select,** and the from the **Form** menu, click **Approve/ Reject** in order to approve or reject the purchase order.
4. After approval, the purchase order will disappear from **Order Awaiting for Approval** application, and the **Originator** can review the **Order Status**.

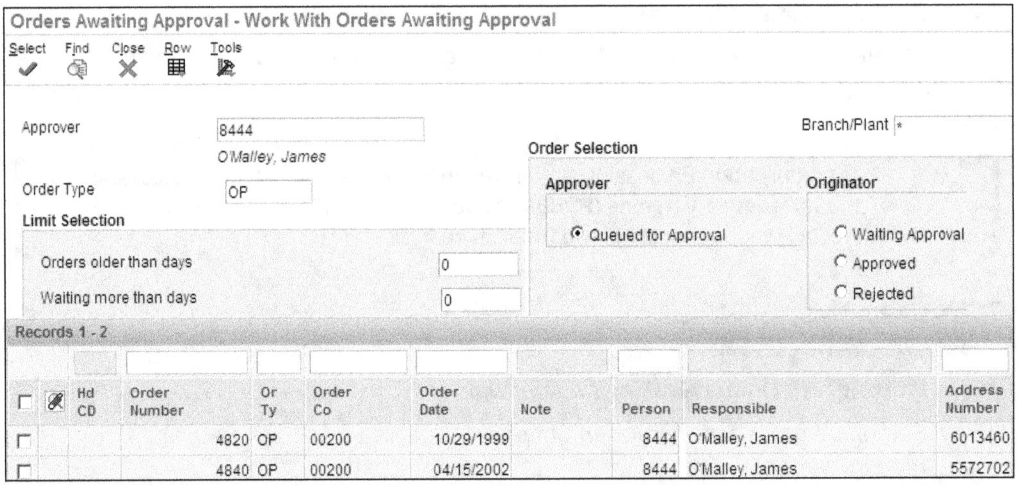

How it works....

You can review, approve, and reject an order via the **Order Awaiting for approval** program. The authorized approver should approve the order that you have created. The order can also be rejected if you want to reject the purchase. When you approve the order, the system updates the order status based on the order activity set-up, or it can send the order to the next authorized approver based on the approval route. If the order was rejected, the system returns the rejected order, along with a rejection message to the originator, and purchase order processing will stop. The user will receive the message via the system work center. The originator can review the status of all of the orders , to see if they are approved, rejected, or pending. Rejected orders can be amended and resubmitted again for approval. You can check a pending order to see who is the next responsible approver for approving the order. The system sends a notification e-mail when a particular order requires approval. The system also notifies the originator that the order has been either approved or rejected, in the employee workstation.

There's more...

You can review a summary of orders on budget hold; you should set up the **Budget Hold Code** processing options for the **Purchase Order Approvals** program (**P43081**).

> You can redirect the approval message directly to an approver's mail box by entering the approver email address in the **Revise Who's Who (P0111)** application.

See also

- *Setting up the Order Awaiting for Approvals application*

9

Sales Order Management and Additional Orders

In this chapter, we will cover:

- Setting up Order Activity Rules
- Setting up AAI
- Setting up a Credit Sales Order
- Setting up a Return Order
- Creating a Sales Order
- Updating and copying Sales Order Information
- Creating a Sales Order with Templates
- Reviewing an Order Revision History
- Ordering for Kits and Configured items
- Processing Recurring Sales Orders
- Sales Order for Matrix Items
- Reviewing Sales Ledger Inquiry
- Processing a Sales Transfer
- Creating Direct Ship Sales Orders
- Creating a Blanket Order
- Creating Quote Order

Introduction

The Sales Order Management system allows you to review and examine Sales Order information and follow up a Sales Order's status, such as customer payments and sales invoice standings, as well as plan future requirements. You can quickly receive information about the item number, availability, quantity, cost, and so on. Through this chapter, you will get to know the details of a Sales Order system, including the setting up of Order Activity Rules, AAI, Credit Sales Orders, and a Return Orders.

Setting up Order Activity Rules

To push the order status through to the order process, you should set up the Order Activity Rules. The Sales Order Management system uses Order Activity Rules to establish a series of steps for processing order information; the Order Activity is the base of the system and order line processes based on **Order Type** and **Line Type**.

Getting ready

Set up the **Order Type** in **UDC 00/DT** and the **Activity Status** in **UDC 40/AT**.

How to do it...

1. Access the **Order Activity Rules (P40204)** application for **Sales Order Management Setup** from the **G4241** menu.

Order Activity Rules - Work With Order Activity Rules

Select Find Add Copy Close Form Row Tools

Records 1 - 6 Customize Grid

Order Type	Line Type	Last Status	Description	Next Status	Other 1	Other 2	Other 3	Other 4	Other 5	Ledger (Y/N)
SG	S									
SG	**S**	**520**	**Enter Sales Order**	**560**						**Y**
SG	S	560	Shipment Confirmation	565	580	620	560			Y
SG	S	565	Print Delivery Documents	580	620					N
SG	S	580	Print Invoices	620	580					Y
SG	S	620	Sales Journal/Update	999						Y
SG	S	999	Complete - Ready to Purge							N

2. Click on **Add** to enter the **Order Activity Rules** application.
3. Enter the **Order Type** that you have set up in **UDC 00/DT** in the first column.

4. Enter **S** as the **Line Type** for the stock item.
5. Enter the **Last Status** code as **520** and the **Next Status** code as **560**, if you want to activate the **Confirm Shipment**.
6. On the next row, enter the **Last Status** code as **560** and the **Next Status** code as **565**, if you want to print the **Delivery Note**.
7. On the next row, enter the **Last Status** code as **565** and the **Next Status** code as **580** for printing the **Delivery Note**.
8. On the next row, enter the **Last Status** code as **580** and the **Next Status** code as **620** for printing the **Invoice**.
9. On the next row, enter the **Last Status** code as **620** and the **Next Status** code as **999** for **Sales Update**.
10. On the **Ledger** column, select **Y/N** for the activities that you want to see in the **Sales Ledger Inquiry**. If you select **Y**, then the system will write the information to the **Sales Ledger** table.

> **S** is used for stock items and **N** is used for non-stock items in the the Sales Order detail line.

How it works...

When you set up the **Order Activity** rule, the system processes the **Sales Order** as per the order activity set up. A status code is a number that the system uses to identify the current status of an order line. The **Next Status** and **Last Status** that you have set up for the specific order type and line type, cause the system to advance the Sales Order status as per the order activity rule. You should allocate a status code for each and every step of the order process. The status codes should be arranged in ascending order to allow the system to establish the sequence of steps. The progression of steps can be changed in the Order Activity Rules to include alternate steps. That is, the Order Activity Rule can be set up for **Direct Ship** Sales Order in such a way that you can bypass the step of **Confirm Shipment** and **Delivery Note** and directly advance the order line to **Print Invoice**.

There's more...

You can set up **Other allowed** status codes for bypass processing steps. These codes are normally set up in the **Processing Options** such as **Override Next Status** codes in the **Sales Order Entry** (**P4210**) application.

See also

- *Setting up a Credit Sales Order*

Setting up AAI

This recipe provides details of AAIs for Sales Order Management and describes the steps for setting up AAIs for Sales Order Management.

Getting ready

You should set up the document type for Sales Order in order to activate the Order Management financial integration.

How to do it...

1. Access the **Automatic Accounting Instructions** program from the **G4241** menu.
2. Enter the **Revenue** account as **4230,** and then click on **Find** to review the **Revenue** account.

3. Enter the company number in the **Co** column.
4. Enter the document type that you want to integrate in the column **Do Ty**.

5. Enter the **G/L Cat**—if you have setup the G/L Category Codes—that is used for General Ledger entries.
6. Enter the **Obj Acct** and **Sub** account that you have set up in the financial system.
7. Enter the **Cost of Goods Sold** account **4220,** and then repeat steps 3 to 6 in order to set up the **Cost of Goods Sold** account.
8. Enter **4240** into the **Inventory** account, and repeat steps 3 to 6 in order to set up the **Inventory** account.

How it works...

When you set up AAIs for Sales Order Management, the system integrates the order management system with the general ledger object accounts that determine how to allocate amounts that are linked to general ledger entries that the system generates. The financial system creates journal entries based on the AAI setup. The AAIs that you set up should have distinctive grouping of the company, document type, GL category, and transactions that you want to use. The AAIs that have been linked with precise general ledger object accounts, which consist of business unit, object, and subsidiary. If taxation is enabled on customer invoices, then you should allocate the tax amounts to the correct GL accounts. When you set up AAIs for a precise kind of tax, such as Value Added Tax or Sales Tax, you should specify which accounts you want to debit and credit for an invoice tax amount.

There's more...

The system stores AAIs in the **Distribution/Manufacturing – AAI** table (**F4095**). The AAI set-up is used for accounting/general ledger integration.

See also

- *Setting up Order Activity Rules*

Setting up a Credit Sales Order

This recipe provides you will details of setting up the **Sales Order Entry (P4210)** application.

Getting ready

You should set up the **Order Activity Rules** for **Sales Order** document type **SO** in order to set up the **Sales Order Entry** application.

How to do it...

1. Select **EnterpriseOne Menus | Logistics Management Sales Order Management | Daily Sales Order Management Processing | Sales Order Processing | Update Sales Order**, then click on the arrow and select on **Values**.

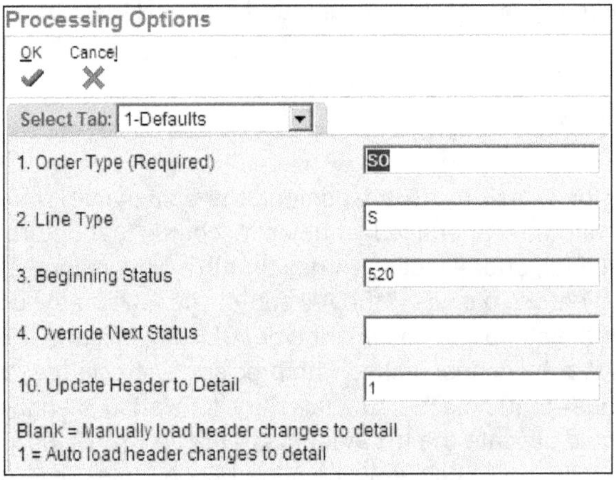

2. Enter the type of document as **SO** for Credit Sales Order.
3. Enter a line type code **S** for stock Sales Orders or **N** for non-stock Sales Orders.
4. Enter the **Beginning Status** for the Sales Order; you have set up this status in the **Order Activity Rules** application.
5. Leave the **Override Next Status** blank.
6. Enter **1** in the **Update Header to Detail** field. The system will automatically update the detail information when the header information has changed.

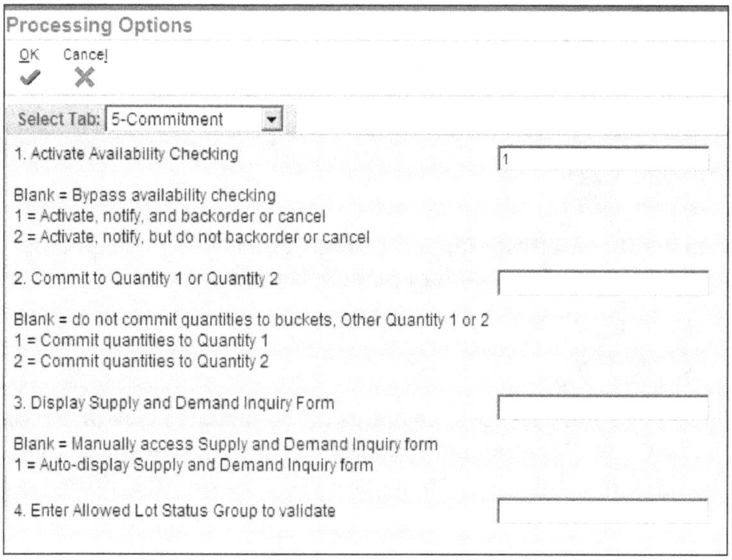
Processing Options

OK Cancel

Select Tab: 5-Commitment

1. Activate Availability Checking — 1

Blank = Bypass availability checking
1 = Activate, notify, and backorder or cancel
2 = Activate, notify, but do not backorder or cancel

2. Commit to Quantity 1 or Quantity 2

Blank = do not commit quantities to buckets, Other Quantity 1 or 2
1 = Commit quantities to Quantity 1
2 = Commit quantities to Quantity 2

3. Display Supply and Demand Inquiry Form

Blank = Manually access Supply and Demand Inquiry form
1 = Auto-display Supply and Demand Inquiry form

4. Enter Allowed Lot Status Group to validate

7. Enter **1** in the **Activate Availability Checking** field in order to activate availability checking. The system will check the item quantity availability from the **F41021** table.

How it works...

When you set up the Credit Sales Order, the system validates the **Order Type** in the user-defined code **00/DT** and the **Line Type**, which you have set up in the **Order Line Type** application **P40205**. The system also verifies the **Beginning Status** of the order activity from the **Order Activity** table **F40203**. Each combination will be validated based on the **Order Activity** rule, **Order Type**, and **Line Type** combination. The system will also validate the **Override Next Status**, if you enabled it in the **P4210** application processing option. The combination of the beginning status and the override next status must be a valid **Last Status** and **Next Status** combination specified in the **F40203** table.

There's more...

If you want to activate availability checking, then you should activate it in the **P4210** application, via the **Commitment** tab.

See also

- *Setting up Order Activity Rules*

Setting up a Return Order

This recipe provides you with the details of setting up the **Return Order** (**P4210**) application.

Getting ready

You should set up the **Order Activity Rules** for **Credit Order** (Return Sales Order) document type **CO** in order to set up the **Sales Order Entry** application.

How to do it...

1. Select **EnterpriseOne Menus** | **Logistics Management Sales Order Management** | **Daily Sales Order Management Processing** | **Sales Order Processing**, and click on the arrow on **Sales Order,** in order to access the **Sales Order Processing Option**.

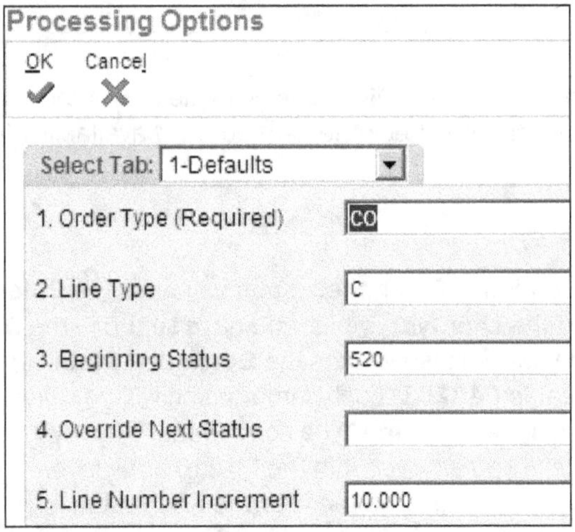

2. Enter the document type **CO** for **Credit Sales Order**.
3. Enter a **Line Type** code **S** for stock Sales Order or **N** for non-stock Sales Order.
4. Enter a **Beginning Status** for the **Sales Order**; you set the status up in the **Order Activity Rules** program.
5. Leave the **Override Next Status** field blank.

How it works...

When you set up the Return Sales Order, the system validates the **Order Type** (Return Order) from the user-defined code **00/DT** and **Line Type**, which you have set up in the **Order Line Type** application **P40205**. The **Beginning Status** should look similar to the Credit Sales Order, which you have set up in the order activity in the **Order Activity** table **F40203**. The system validates the Return Order Activity Rule combination from the **Order Activity** rule, **Order Type**, and **Line Type**. The Return Order is working based on line type **C**, which has been set up in the **Line Type** application. In the line type **C** set-up, the **Reverse Sign** checkbox has been selected, so the system creates the Sales Return based on **C** line type.

There's more...

You should set up the **Line Type** for Return Sales Orders in the **Order Line Type** application **P40205** and select the checkbox.

See also

- *Setting up Order Activity Rules*

Creating a Sales Order

The **Sales Order Entry** (**P4210**) application provides you details of Sales Orders to follow all of the related information for each sale. This recipe provides you the details of entering **Credit Sales Order** in the **Sales Order** application (**P4210**).

Getting ready

You should set up the **Processing Option** for the **Sales Order** program (**P4210**) in order to create Sales Orders.

How to do it...

1. Select **EnterpriseOne Menus | Logistics Management | Sales Order Management | Daily Sales Order Management Processing | Sales Order Processing**, and then click on **Sales Order**.

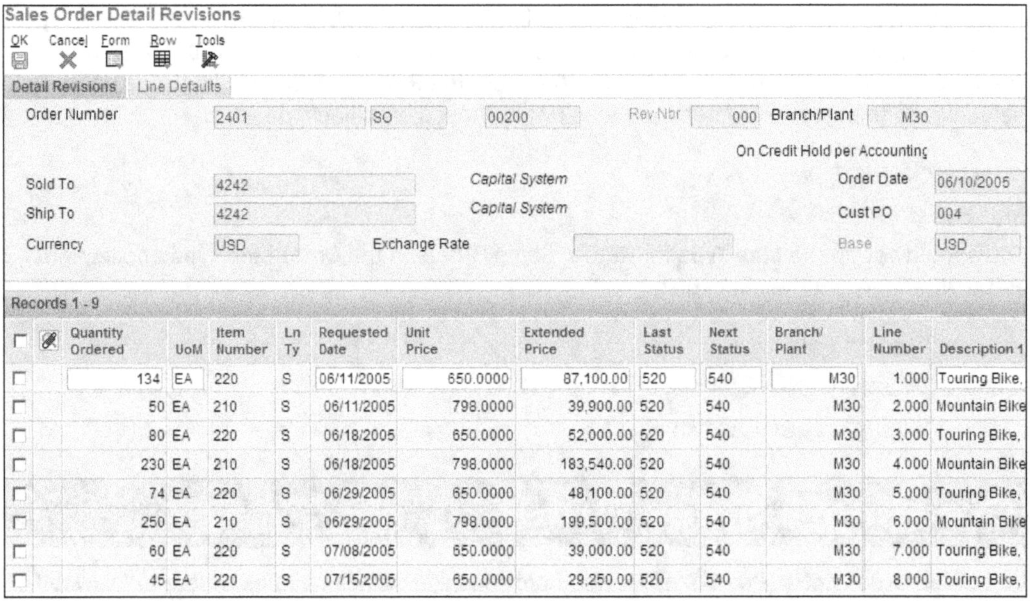

Sales Order Detail Revisions

OK Cancel Form Row Tools

Detail Revisions | Line Defaults

Order Number 2401 SO 00200 Rev Nbr 000 Branch/Plant M30

On Credit Hold per Accounting

Sold To 4242 Capital System Order Date 06/10/2005

Ship To 4242 Capital System Cust PO 004

Currency USD Exchange Rate Base USD

Records 1 - 9

Quantity Ordered	UoM	Item Number	Ln Ty	Requested Date	Unit Price	Extended Price	Last Status	Next Status	Branch/ Plant	Line Number	Description 1
134	EA	220	S	06/11/2005	650.0000	87,100.00	520	540	M30	1.000	Touring Bike,
50	EA	210	S	06/11/2005	798.0000	39,900.00	520	540	M30	2.000	Mountain Bike
80	EA	220	S	06/18/2005	650.0000	52,000.00	520	540	M30	3.000	Touring Bike,
230	EA	210	S	06/18/2005	798.0000	183,540.00	520	540	M30	4.000	Mountain Bike
74	EA	220	S	06/29/2005	650.0000	48,100.00	520	540	M30	5.000	Touring Bike,
250	EA	210	S	06/29/2005	798.0000	199,500.00	520	540	M30	6.000	Mountain Bike
60	EA	220	S	07/08/2005	650.0000	39,000.00	520	540	M30	7.000	Touring Bike,
45	EA	220	S	07/15/2005	650.0000	29,250.00	520	540	M30	8.000	Touring Bike,

2. On the **Sales Order Detail Revisions** form, click on **Add**.
3. Enter the **Sold To** address number.
4. Enter the **Ship To** address number.
5. Enter the **Order Date**.
6. Enter the **Customer PO**.
7. Enter the **Currency**.
8. Enter the **Quantity Ordered** information in the grid area.
9. Enter the **UoM**.
10. Enter the **Item Number**.
11. Enter the **Requested Date**.
12. Enter the **Unit Price**; the **Extended Price** will be calculated automatically.

How it works...

When you enter the Sales Order on the **Sales Order Entry** form, it contains fields that may be mandatory or voluntary, depending on the Sales Order complexity. It is necessary to determine which fields need to be entered. When you enter the required field, the system retrieves the default value from the customer master, item master, along with preference information from a variety of tables. The Sales Order retrieves the item base price information when you enter the item. If it's required, you can override the default information. When you override the default information, this only overrides the values copied from the **Sales Order** table **F4211**; the master tables remain unchanged. The system stores the **Sales Order** header information in the **F4201** table, and the **Sales Order** detail in the **F4211** table.

There's more...

The system retrieves customer information from the **Address Book Master** table (**F0101**). and billing instructions details from the **F03012** table. in order to complete the order information.

See also

- *Setting up a Credit Sales Order*

Updating and copying Sales Order Information

This recipe provides details of the prerequisites for updating and copying Sales Order Information details.

Getting ready

Verify that you have activated the duplication processing options for **Sales Order Entry** for the new document types or statuses.

How to do it...

1. Select **EnterpriseOne Menus** | **Logistics Management** | **Sales Order Management** | **Daily Sales Order Management Processing** | **Sales Order Processing**, and then click on **Sales Order Header** and access the **Work with Sales Order Headers** form.
2. Select an order, and then click on **Select**.

3. On the **Sales Order Header** form, click on **Header to Detail** and then **Define** on the **Form** menu to review and revise which header fields are selected for update, as shown in the following screenshot:

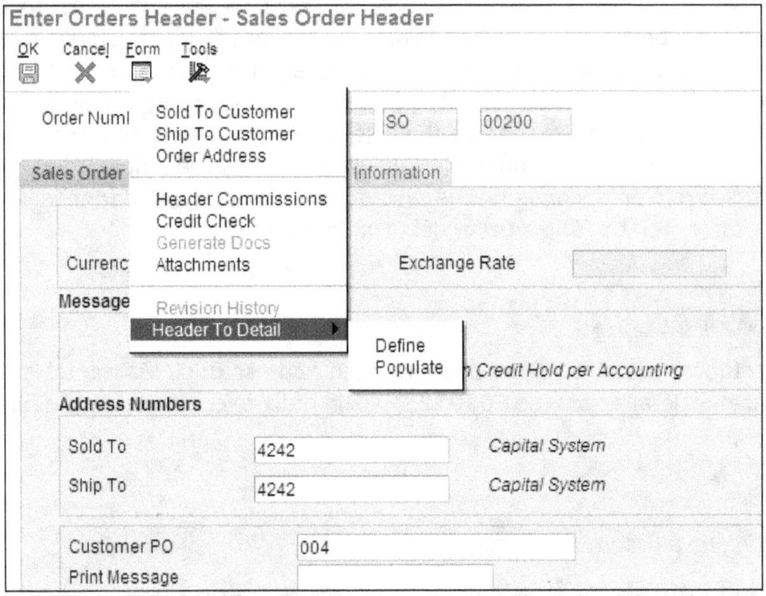

4. On the **Define Header Columns to Detail Table** form, select the fields that you want to update, and then click on **OK**.
5. On the **Sales Order Header** form, if the **Sales Order Entry Processing Option** is set for **Automatic Header to Detail**, click on **OK**. If the **Processing Option** is set for manual update, click on **Populate to Manually** update the detail lines with the header changes.

How it works...

Sometimes a customer orders the same or similar items and quantities on a frequent basis. To avoid the repetition of manual entry every time the customer places a similar order, you can restructure the **Sales Order Entry** by copying the header and detail information and adding the new Sales Order. If the order information is the same, you can copy only the detail information and change the **Ship-to** or **Sold-to** information, which can be based on the set up of processing options. The information may be different between the original and the copied Sales Order as per the document type and beginning status code. The copied Sales Order number will be different from the original order.

There's more...

The item information can be copied from any Sales Order application—that is, the duplication processing options can be set up for the **Blanket Order** version of the **P4210** application so that when you copy the order information from the **Blanket Order** version, the system creates a new Sales Order.

See also

- *Setting up a Credit Sales Order*

Creating a Sales Order with Templates

The **Order Templates** can be set up to accelerate order processing for the most frequently sold items. A **Template** is the system-generated forecast about what the customer will order.

Getting ready

You should verify the **Processing Options** of **Sales Order** application to authorize order template processing.

How to do it...

1. Select the **Sales Order** that you want to copy, and then click on **Copy**.

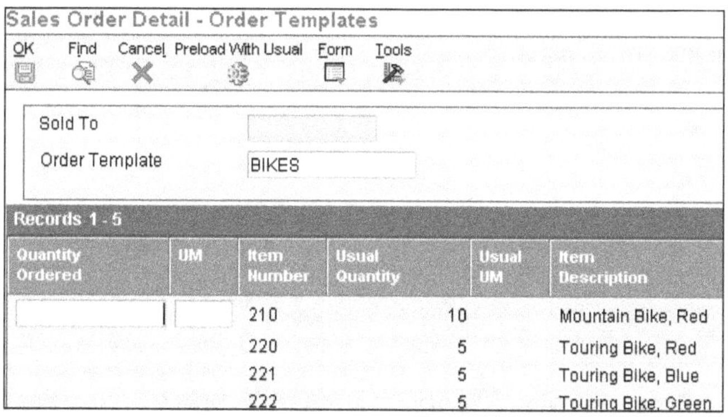

2. On **Sales Order Detail Revisions form**, review the field information that is automatically calculated, and make any necessary changes.
3. Enter additional information for the order, and then click on **OK**. The system saves the order when you click on **OK**.

How it works...

When you set up the default template it can be used for every customer. Customer-specific templates can also be set up; you can select any specific template that has been created already. Using order templates can also reduce errors and eliminate duplicate data entry, saving time and data entry cost. The **Sales Order Entry** processing option enables you to specify the **Default Template**, which is based on the **Sold-to** or **Ship-to** address from the **Customer's billing instructions**. The order template form will be displayed when you enter the **Sales Order Detail** in **P4210** application. If you have set up a customer-based template, the system will retrieve and display the template during **Sales Order Entry**. The default template will be displayed if a customer-based template has not been set up.

There's more...

When you set up the templates, each template will consist of sets of information automatically retrieved from the JDE tables. This allows you to rapidly produce configured credentials for customers.

See also

- *Setting up a Credit Sales Order*

Reviewing an Order Revision History

The Sales Order Management system gives you a way of tracking manual adjustments and reviewing the manual changes that have been made to that order. This recipe gives you the details of the audit log and revisions.

Getting ready

You can activate the **Order Revision History** from the **Sales Order** program (**P4210**) in order to capture the order revision history.

How to do it...

1. Access the **Order Revision History** program (**P42420**) from the **Fast Path**.
2. Enter the **Order Number**, **Order Type**, and **Order Company**, then click on **Find**.
3. Review the **Order Revision**.

4. Select the statuses that you want to review—that is, **Approved**, **Pending**, **Rejected**, and **No Approval Req**, as shown in the following screenshot:

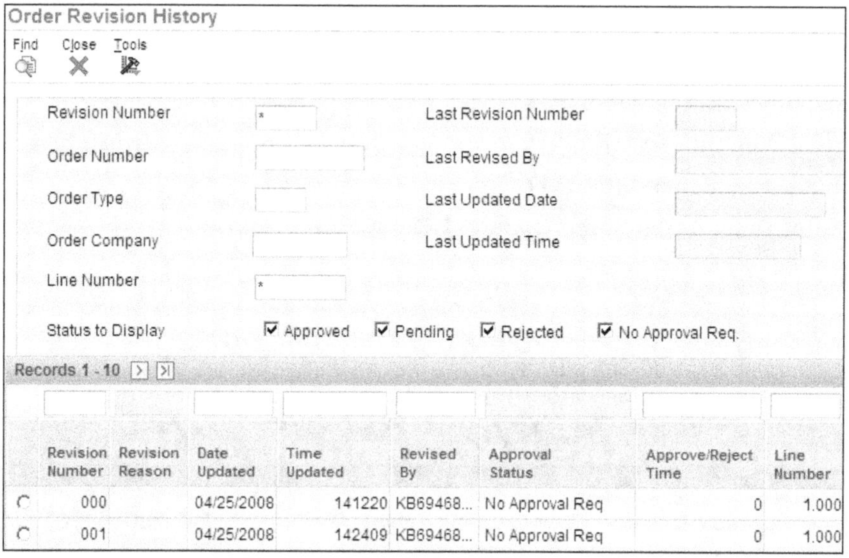

How it works...

When you activate the appropriate processing options in the **P4210** application, the system starts to track every manual change that the users make to Sales Orders. You can review the revision information for the changes that have been made. When you enter the changes, the system creates a new revision number every time and also creates an **Audit Log** for every change. The Revision Information is stored in the **Audit Log Transaction** table (**F42420**). The Audit Log Information will consist of the user ID of the person who made the changes, and the reason code (purpose of change), which you have set up in the processing option.

> You can bypass the audit log generation by setting up the specific customer on the **Customer Billing Instruction Application**.

There's more...

The **Order Revision History** program can track the changes from the following programs:

- **Sales Order Entry** (**P4210**)
- **Shipment Confirmation** (**P4205**)
- **Held Order Release** (**P43070**)
- **Backorder Release** (**P42117**)
- **Sales Order Speed Status Update** (**P42040**)

See also

- *Setting up a Credit Sales Order*

Ordering for Kits and Configured items

Kits and **Configured** items are the collection of inventory items called components, which are linked with a description called a parent item. This recipe provides details of **Kits** and **Configured** items.

Getting ready

You should set up the **Kits** and **Configured** items in order to create the kit order. Refer to *Chapter 3, Updating Costs, Using Kits and Lot Processing*.

How to do it...

1. Select **EnterpriseOne Menus** | **Order Management** | **Sales Order Management** | **Sales Order Management** | **Daily Sales Order Processing** | **Sales Order Processing**, and then click on **Sales Order Detail**, as shown in the following screenshot:

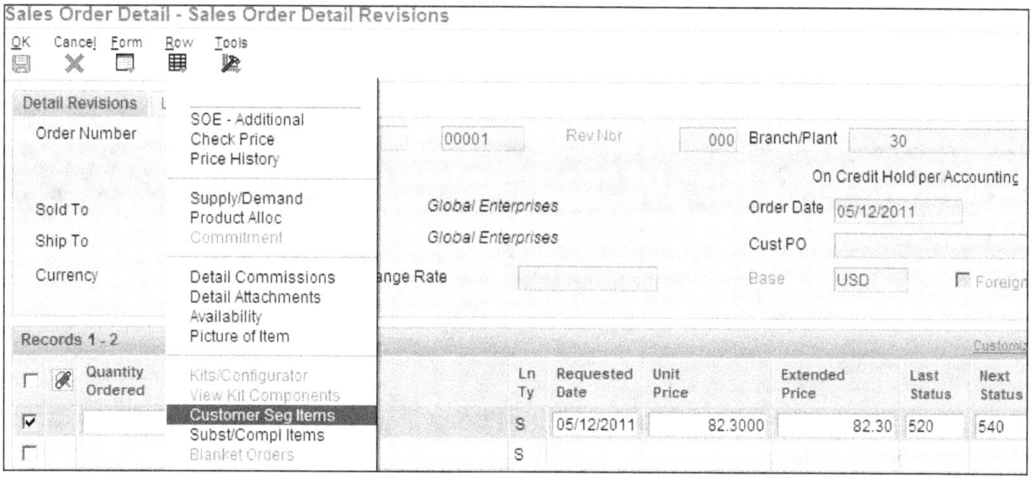

2. On the **Detail First – Manage Existing Order** form, click on **Add**.
3. Enter **Sold To**.
4. Enter the **Order Date**.
5. Enter the **Quantity Ordered**.
6. Enter the **Unit of Measure**.
7. Enter the **Item Number** (should be kit-configured).
8. Enter the **Requested Date**.

How it works...

When you enter the Sales Order for a **Kit** and **Configured** item, the system automatically alerts you to enter the values of **Kit** and **Configured** items. A segment is a feature of a configured item, such as brand, model, size, and so on; the system validates each segment value aligned with the user-defined information. The system processes the order for only valid combinations of items. That is, various computer components such as monitor, hard drive, keyboard, and mouse can be one **Kit** and **Configured** item. When you sell the items, you may sell the complete system. When you set up a **Configured** item, you define the segments to represent the uniqueness of a configured item. A sub-assembly can also be set up for **Configured** items.

> **Configured** items include special features that are requested by the customer.

For example, if you manufacture and sell automobile components, you could present the same parts category, but with a range of features and selections.

See also

- *Setting up a Credit Sales Order*

Processing Recurring Sales Orders

Recurring Sales Orders can streamline the order entry process. This recipe will provide you the details of how to create the **Recurring Sales Order**.

Getting ready

You should set up the **Processing Option** of the **P004Z** application in order to create a **Recurring Sales Order**.

How to do it...

1. Access the **Recurring Sales Order Entry** application from the **G4212** menu.
2. Enter the **Quantity Ordered**, **Unit of Measure**, **Item Number**, and **Unit Price**.
3. Click on **OK** to save the **Recurring Sales Order**.

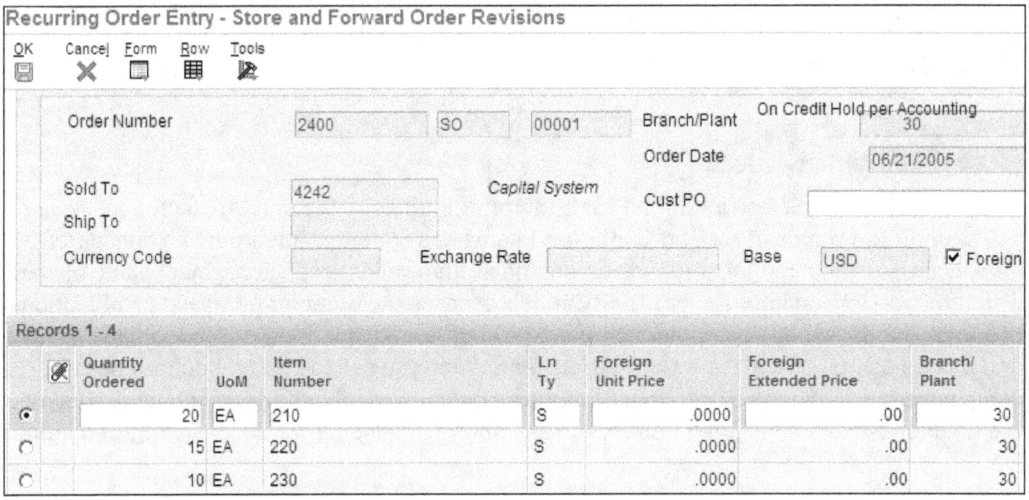

4. Access the **Recurring Order Information** from the **Form** menu.
5. Enter the **Order Frequency**.
6. Enter the **Next Order Date** for generating the order.
7. Enter the **Suspended Date** (the date on which you want to stop generation).

8. Enter the **Days of Week** (if **Order Frequency** is **W**).

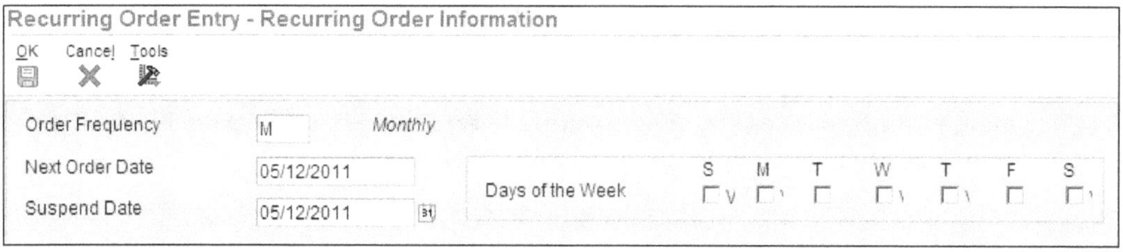

How it works...

Recurring Sales Orders eliminates the manual re-entering of information that always remains the same into the Sales Order. The system creates the order automatically based on the frequency set up—that is, weekly, monthly, or yearly. When you set up a Daily frequency (**D**), you can indicate on which days of the week the system will create the Sales Order. When you define a Weekly (**W**) or Monthly (**M**) frequency, the system will work out the future dates to create the orders based on the next order date that you entered. When you complete the recurring **Sales Order Entry**, you should run the recurring order generation through the **Recurring Orders Edit and Creation** (**R40211Z**) program. The system modifies the information that you have entered, and creates orders on the selected date.

There's more...

Those orders that contain errors remain unprocessed in the batch receiver tables. It is required to correct this related information and re-run the **Recurring Orders Edit and Creation** batch program.

See also

- *Setting up a Credit Sales Order*

Sales Order for Matrix Items

A group of products may have the same basic properties, with a number of specific variations. This recipe provides details of Sales Orders for **Matrix Items**, including the steps of how to enter a **Sales Order** for **Matrix Items**.

Getting ready

You should set up the **Matrix Items** in the Inventory Management system in order to enter the **Sales Order** for **Matrix Items**.

How to do it...

1. Access the Sales Order from the **Sales Order Detail** (**G4211**) menu.
2. On the **Customer Service Inquiry** page, click on **Add** and add a line for the **Matrix Item**, and then click on **OK**. On the **Matrix Order Entry** form, select the row for each item, and enter the quantity for each product variation.

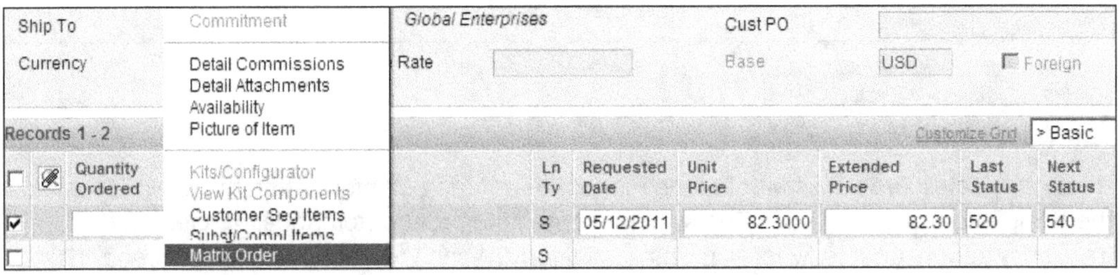

3. Enter an order for a product with the required variations.

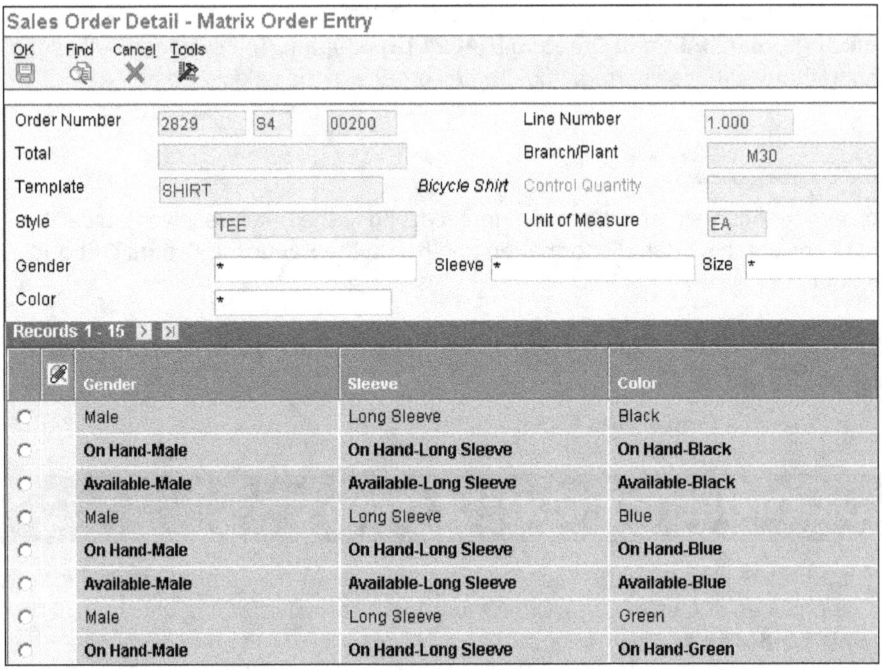

How it works...

Matrix Items are those items that have the same basic properties but with some specific variations for each item. For instance, Inventory Management may comprise cars and trucks, but customers may demand a number of variations in the attributes of these such as requirements for alloy rim, sun roof, air conditioner, camera, and so on. Each car may arrive with various options; additionally, each car with five different colors. However, the car remains the same in its basic properties.

See also

- *Setting up a Credit Sales Order*

Reviewing Sales Ledger Inquiry

Sales Ledger Inquiry provides you with detailed information for each **Sales Order** that has been processed through the Sales Order Management system.

Getting ready

You should activate the **A/R Line** of business processing in the order **Credit Check** form, which will process the **Enhanced A/R Constants**.

How to do it...

1. Select **EnterpriseOne Menus** | **Logistics Management** | **Order Management** | **Sales Order Management** | **Daily Sales Order Management Processing** | **Sales Order Inquiries**, and then click on **Sales Ledger History Inquiry**.
2. Enter the **Customer PO** and then click on **Find**.

3. Review the **Last Status Code** and **Next Status Code** column and determine whether the order was invoiced or not.

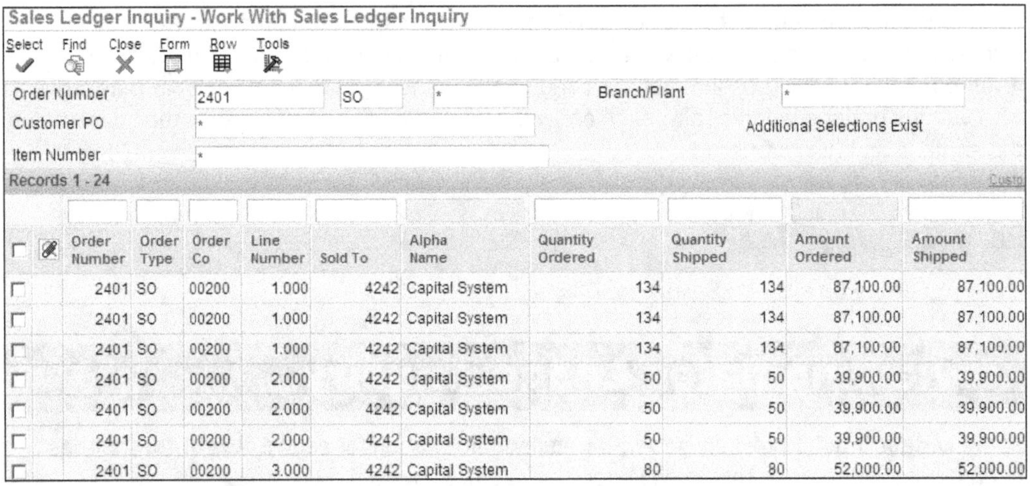

How it works...

A **Sales Ledger Inquiry** can be performed for any orders that have been processed through Sales Order Management. A **Sales Ledger Inquiry** can be used to track Sales Orders to verify when the order was entered; it's printed or not printed. When you process a Sales Order, the system writes the order information the the **Sales Order Detail Ledger** table (**F42199**) based on the Order Activity Rules program set up. When you set up the Order Activity Rule, you can determine at which point the system writes the order information to the **F42199** table through status codes. When you create a **Return Sales Order** (Sale Return) from the history, the system retrieves the original order detail from the **Sales Order Detail Ledger File**. It is required to specify the correct version of **Sales Order Entry** (**P4210**) in the **Sales Ledger Inquiry** processing options.

There's more...

Sales Ledger Inquiry information can also be used for the internal audit process.

See also

- *Setting up Order Activity Rules*

Processing a Sales Transfer

Transfer Order functionality provides you with the ability to ship inventory between Branches/Plants inside the corporation in order to maintain accuracy of the on-hand inventory amount and quantity. In the Sales Transfer, you need to set up each branch as a customer in the Customer Master Revision Table and also need to set up the customer billing instructions of that branch.

Getting ready

You should create a new version of the **Sales Order Entry** program (**P4210**) by copying the **Transfer Sales** version **ZJDE0007** to use for **Sales Transfer Orders**, and then set up the processing options.

How to do it...

1. Select **EnterpriseOne Menus** | **Order Management** | **Sales Order Management** | **Daily Sales Order Management Processing** |**S ales Order Processing**, and then click on **Transfers** (**P4210**).

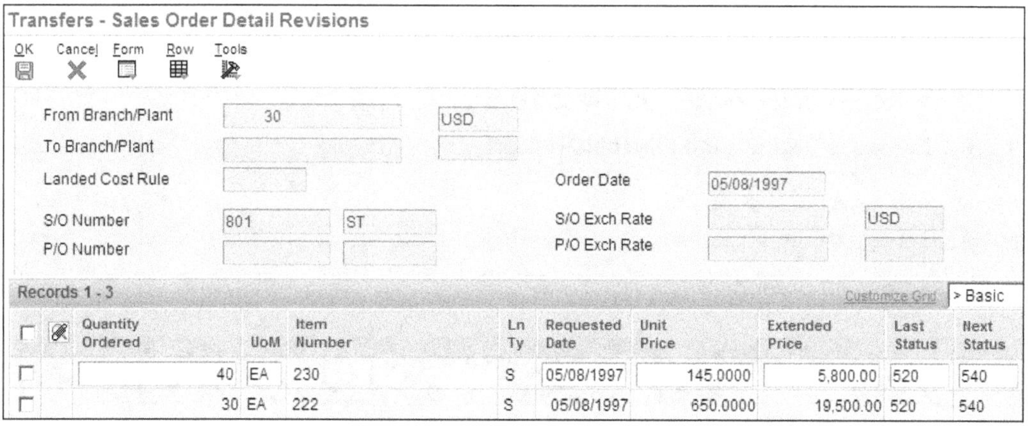

2. On the **Customer Service Inquiry** form, click on **Add**.
3. Enter the **From Branch/Plant** and **To Branch/Plant**.
4. Enter the **Order Date**.
5. Enter the **Ordered Quantity**.
6. Enter the **Unit of Measure**.
7. Enter the **Item Number**.
8. Enter the **Line Type**.
9. Enter the **Requested Date**.

How it works...

When you create a **Transfer Order**, the system creates a purchase transfer, which includes the supplier in the **To Branch/Plant**, and which Branch/Plant ships the items. It creates a Sales Transfer for supplying Branch/Plant to the customer and creates the purchase transfer for the receiving branch/plant. You can create the transfer documents–that is, pick slips, delivery notes, or transfer invoices, which are essential to complete the transfer. The transfer transaction can be recorded by using the **Inventory Transfers** program (**P4113**) or the **Sales Transfer Entry** program (**P4210**) from **Sales Order Management**. When you create a **Sales Transfer**, the system decreases the inventory after confirming shipment or printing the invoice, depending upon your transfer system set-up. The requested branch will receive the inventory quantity during inventory receipt by putting the **OT** number in the **Purchase Receipt** program. The system processes the transfer order based on the Order Activity Rules set up for the document type and line type combination.

There's more...

When you create a **Transfer Order**, the system stores the **Transfer Order** information in the following tables:

- **Sales Order Header File table** (**F4201**)
- **Sales Order Detail File table** (**F4211**)
- **Purchase Order Header table** (**F4301**)
- **Purchase Order Detail File table** (**F4311**)

See also

- *Setting up Order Activity Rules*

Creating Direct Ship Sales Orders

A direct ship order is a type of sales order where you can purchase a specific item based on the customer's requirement and ship the item directly from the supplier to the customer without affecting inventory operations.

Getting ready

You should set up the **Processing Option** for (**P42101**) in order to create the **Direct Ship Sales Order**.

How to do it...

1. Access **Sales Order Management Processing** | **Sales Order Processing**, and click on **Update Direct Ships** (**P42101**), as shown in the following screenshot:

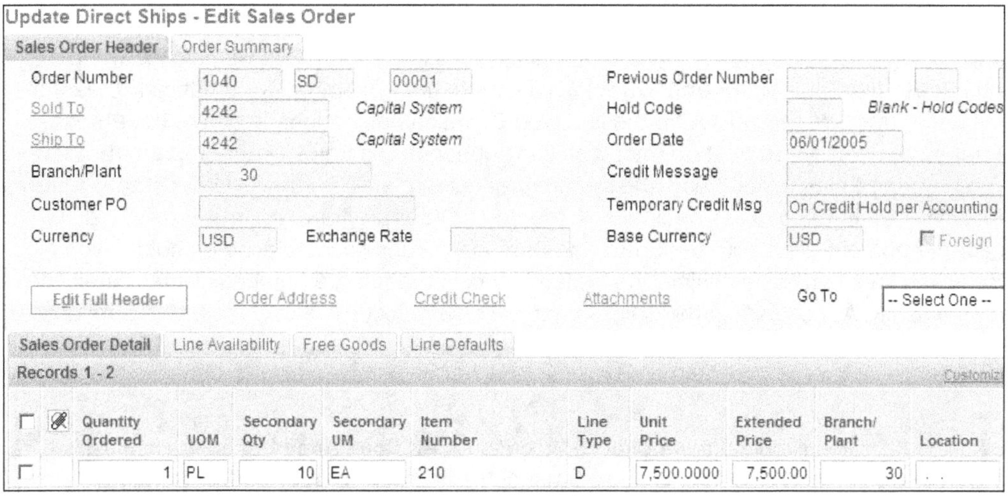

2. On the **Direct Ship Sales Order** form, click on **Add**.
3. Enter the **Sold To** party and the **Order Date**.
4. Enter the **Quantity Ordered**.
5. Enter the **Unit of Measure**.
6. Enter the **Item Number**.
7. Enter the **Requested Date**.
8. Enter the **Supplier Number**.

> **Line Type D** is an option that will **Generate a Purchase Order** when we create the Sales Order.

How it works...

When you create a **Direct Ship** order, the system creates the Sales Order and also the Purchase Order for the vendor at the same time. The Purchase Order instructs the supplier to ship the item directly to the customer. The system doesn't create the Purchase Order if you activated the **Commit to Quantity 1** or **Quantity 2** commitment in the processing option of the **Sales Order Entry** program. A Direct Ship quote can also be set up, in which case whenever you release the Sales Order from **Direct Ship Quote**, the system will automatically create the Purchase Order. When you set up the line type **D**—which has options to create the Purchase Order automatically—and set up the processing option of the Sales Order program with line type **D** during **Sales Order Entry**, the system creates a related Purchase Order. If the Order Hold is set up in the processing option of the Sales Order program and the system places the order on hold, then both the Sales and Purchase Order will be placed on hold. If you cancel the sales order detail line, the system cancels the related Purchase Order detail line automatically. Any change in the Sales Order will also reflect the Purchase Order. Similarly, if you change the Purchase Order, the system will automatically update the Sales Order.

> You cannot enter a Direct Ship order for **Kit Configured Items**. You can use regular sales or Purchase Order entry programs for **Kit Configured Items**.

There's more...

You can set up the **Direct Ship Sales Quotation** in order to create the **Direct Ship Sales** order, which does not affect inventory operation.

See also

- *Setting up Order Activity Rules*

Creating a Blanket Order

A Blanket Order is used when a customer purchases a product based on a contract for the purchase of a specific amount and quantity over a specified period of time. This recipe provides the details of Blanket Orders.

Getting ready

You should set up the **Processing Options** of the **P4210** application in order to set up the **Blanket Order** application.

How to do it...

1. Select **EnterpriseOne Menus | Order Management | Sales Order Management | Daily Sales Order Management Processing | Sales Order Processing**, and then click on **Update Blankets**, as shown in the following screenshot:

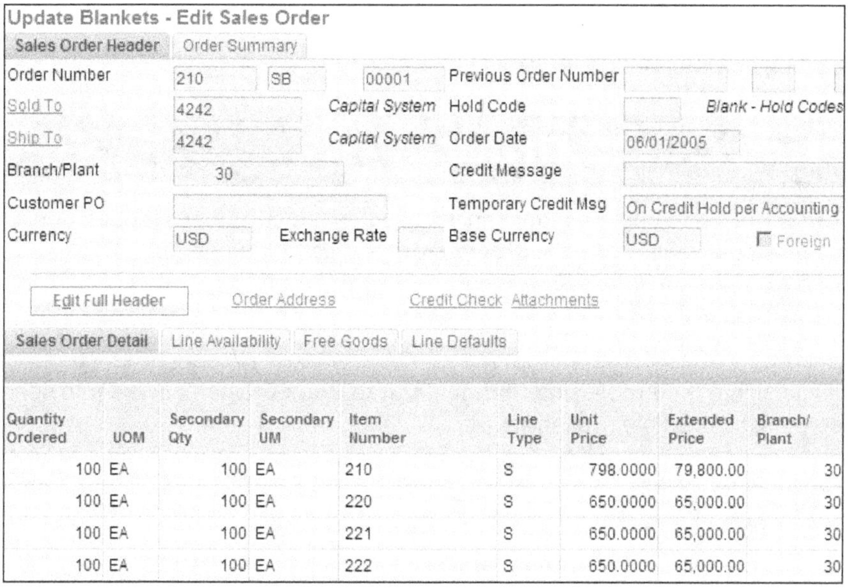

2. On the **Manage Existing Order** page, click on **Add**.
3. Enter the **Sold To** party and the **Order Date** in the order header.
4. Click on the **Order Detail** tab and enter the **Quantity Ordered**.
5. Enter the **UoM** (**Unit of Measure**).
6. Enter the **Item Number**.
7. Enter the **Unit price**.

How it works...

A **Blanket Order** can be entered with one line with a requested date, and on the basis of this agreement you can create the sales orders for limited quantities of the **Blanket Order**. The **Sales Order** can be entered directly to subtract the quantity from the **Blanket Order**, or release the quantity from the **Blanket Order**. The **Blanket Order** can be reviewed with the original quantity and released orders, along with the open quantity. If you set up the **P4210** program commitment **Processing Option** on the **Commitment** tab, the system does not commit the item quantity in the inventory program when the **Blanket Order** is created. The blanket order will be created with the same procedure as the Sales Order.

There's more...

Specify correct values in these **Processing Options** of the **P4210** program in order to create the **Blanket Order** contract.

See also

- *Setting up Order Activity Rules*

Creating Quote Order

A **Quote Order** is used to quote a formal price based on the customer's requirements. This recipe provides details of **Quote Orders Entry** and its fundamentals.

Getting ready

You should configure the **Processing Option** of **Quote Order** program, in order to specify how quote orders affect inventory availability.

How to do it...

1. Access the **Quotes Order Detail Revisions** form from the **G4211** menu, and then click on **Create Quotes** in order to enter the new **Quote Order**.

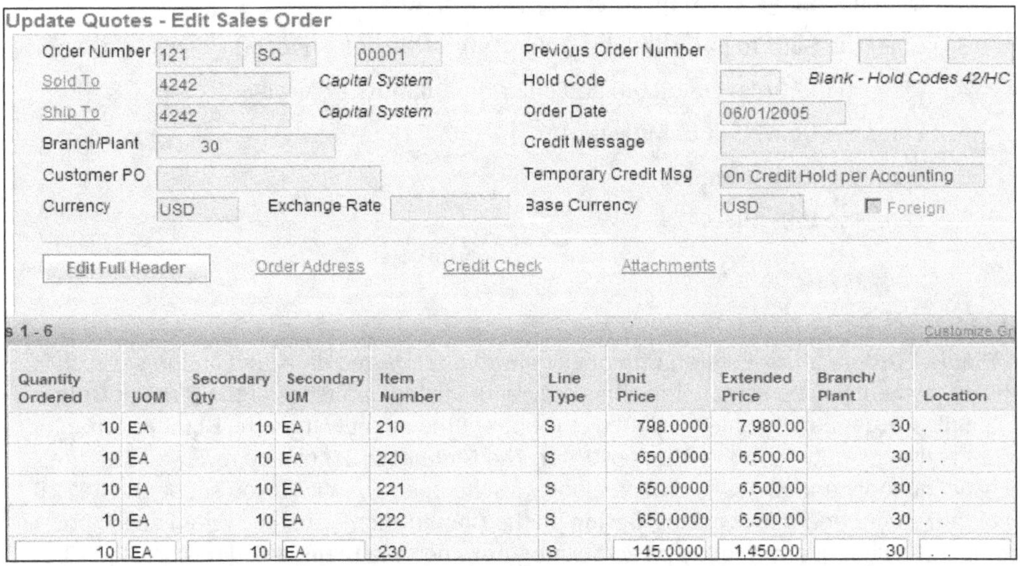

2. On the **Update Quote – Edit Sales Order** program, click on **Add**.
3. Enter **Sold To** and the **Order Date** in order header.
4. Click on the **Order Detail** tab and enter **Quantity Ordered**.
5. Enter the **UoM** (Unit of Measure).
6. Enter the **Item Number**.
7. Enter the **Unit price**.
8. Click on **OK** to save the **Quote Order**.

How it works...

The **Quote Orders** can be entered to provide the prices and availability to their customers of a bulk amount of items and quantity and documented the quoted quantity and price for future reference. When you enter the **Quote Order**, the system does not commit any quantity from the item inventory based on the setup of the **Processing Option** of **P4210** program. When the customer sends the Purchase Order, you then convert the **Quote Order** into a **Sales Order** by releasing the **Quote Order** from the **Quote Order Released** program. The **Quote Order** can be printed by creating a separate version of the **Print Invoices** program (**R42565**) to print the Quote Order. The messages can also be printed by setting up the **Processing Option** of the **Print Invoice** program. After entering the **Quote Order**, the automated proposal document can also be generated, which includes data of **Quote Orders**. The proposal can be configured to include the information related to a specific customer.

> Customers self-service can be activated through the **Processing Options** of **Sales Order Entry** (**P4210** and **P42101**), **Customer Ledger Inquiry** (**P03B2002**), and **Item Availability** (**P41202**) applications.

There's more...

Quote Orders can be configured to reduce or not reduce the quantity through **Document Type Maintenance** program (**P40040**).

See also

- *Setting up Order Activity Rules*

10

Holding, Releasing, and Reviewing

In this chapter, we will cover:

- Setting up an Order Hold
- Releasing Held Orders
- Blanket Order Release
- Releasing Quote Orders
- Customer Master Information
- Customer Billing Information
- Reviewing Sales Ledger Information
- Sales Commission Information

Introduction

This chapter will explain the details of the **Additional Sales Order Management** system processes, and will also describe the Release Hold Order that can be set up as per business needs, and the detailed procedures of Release Quote Order and Release Blanket Order created in the previous chapters. When you activate the Order Hold, it requires the release to be set up and also needs an authorized person assigned to release the Hold Order.

Setting up an Order Hold

This recipe provides the details of setting up the Order Hold information, how the Hold Codes are assigned to orders, and customer billing instructions.

Getting ready

You should define the employee address book number in the address book application (**P01012**) in order to set up the "Person Responsible" for Order Release.

How to do it...

1. Access the **Order Hold** (**P42090**) information program from the **G4211** menu:

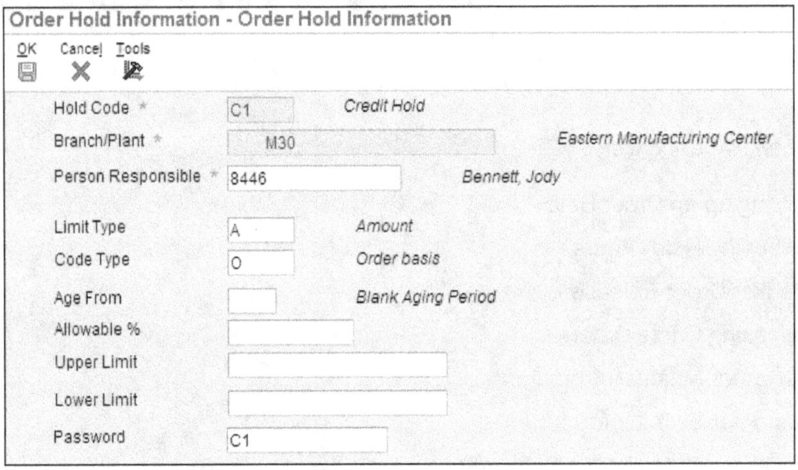

2. Specify the **Address book** number of the person who is in charge of reviewing and releasing orders that are placed **On Hold**.
3. Specify whether the **Limit Type** is based on an **Amount** or a **Percentage**. The **Limit Type** usually applies only on order or line gross margin limits.
4. Specify the appropriate **Code Type** for the hold to be based on either an individual line or the entire order.
5. Specify the aging period that the system uses if the credit check will be specified based on the aging of the customer's accounts receivables.
6. Indicate what percentage of total receivables to accept in the column specified in the **Age From** field.
7. Specify the **Upper Limit** of acceptable margin percentages or amounts.
8. Specify the **Lower Limit** of acceptable margin percentages or amounts.

How it works...

When you set up the Order Hold system on the total amount and this does not lie within the specified range, the system assigns a Hold Code to put the order on hold and stop processing from continuing. The Sales Margin and Credit Holds can also be defined in the credit hold setting. The system places the order on hold based on the credit hold setting if the entire order or order line does not meet the sales margin. It also places the order on hold when the order takes the customer's receivables above the customer's credit limit. You can set up the Order Hold information that the system uses to place orders on hold. When the processing option of **Sales Order Entry** (**P4210**) is set up, the system will put a hold on the order. When you set up the credit hold code, the system automatically compares the credit limit, which you set in the customer master, against the order, and also checks the outstanding balances in accounts receivable. That is, the customer has set up with credit limit as 10,000 USD, when you create the Sales Order, the system verifies the credit limit in the **F03B11** table for the **Customer Open Invoices** table and **Sales Order Detail** (**F4211**) table, in order to verify the customer credit limit.

> The aging period is based on the accounts receivable payment setup.

There's more...

The Order Hold can be set up based on the percentage of the outstanding balance in the accounts receivables. The credit hold code will be applied to the entire order. A **Margin Hold** can be applied to a single order line or also on to a complete order. For example, some companies may define a fixed margin for the selling price of each item and will not sell an item for less than 10 percent profit. The system gets the item cost from the **Item Cost** (**F4105**) table, which is then compared with the item price in the sales order.

See also

- *Releasing Held Orders*

Releasing Held Orders

Some business processes require the Order Hold and Hold Release processes. The system provides the Credit Hold Release, Margin Hold Release processes in order to apply the release process as per business needs.

Getting ready

You should set up the Order Hold information, which includes user IDs and passwords.

How to do it....

1. Select **EnterpriseOne Menus | Order Management | Sales Order Management | Daily Sales Order Management Processing | Additional Sales Order Processing**, and then click on **Release Hold Orders**:

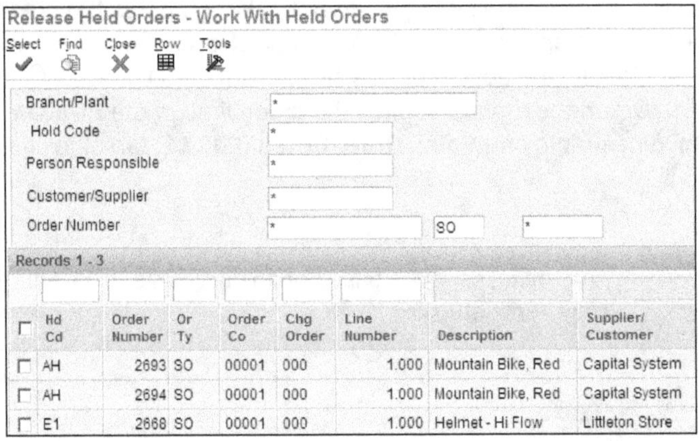

2. On the **Work With Held Orders** page, enter the **Order Number**, and then click on **Find**
3. Select the row that you want to release, and then click on **Select**.
4. On the **Password Confirmation** page, enter the **Password,** and then click on **OK**:

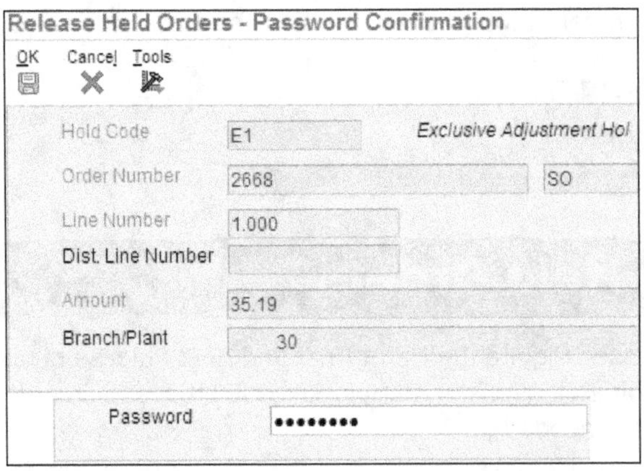

How it works...

When the order has been entered, it is necessary to release the Held Order, in order to process the Sales Order for the next operation, based on the order activity set up. When the system places the order on hold, the order is taken out from Sales Order processing. When you release the order, it's returned back to Sales Order processing. When you activate the Order Hold processing, the system calculates the order information in order to determine whether to place the order on hold or not. If the system verifies the order, it issues the warning Order Hold for further processing. The system performs the credit check when you enter the order, and places it on credit hold. Sometimes, you may need to verify the customer's credit limit against existing Sales Orders and place the orders on credit hold.

There's more...

The **Batch Release Credit Holds** (**R42550**) is used to release **Sales Orders** that are on **Credit Holds**. The **Sales Orders** are released based on the **Pick Date** and **Customer Credit Limit**. You can also print the **Held Sales Order** (**R42640**) report. You can also set up the processing options for the R42550 report before running.

See also

- *Setting up an Order Hold*

Blanket Order Release

This recipe provides the details of Blanket Order Release including the **Blanket Order Release** details from **Sales Blanket Order Release** (**P420111**), and also explains how to release a blanket order. The **Blanket Order Release** program is used to release the quantity from a **Blanket Order** in order to create a **Sales Order**.

Getting ready

You should enter a **Blanket Order** in order to have a **Blanket Order** to release into **Sales Order**.

How to do it....

1. Select **EnterpriseOne Menus** | **Order Management** | **Sales Order Management** | **Daily Sales Order Management Processing** | **Additional Order Processes**, click on the **Release Blankets** (**P420111**) arrow, and then click on **Values**.

2. Verify that the default **Order Type** is **SB,** and that the **Outgoing document type** is **SO**:

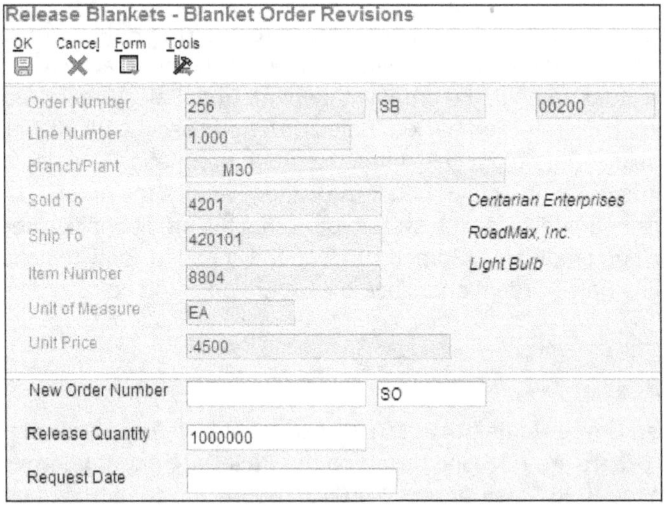

3. On the **Release Blanket - Work with Order Blanket Release** page, enter the **Order Number,** and then click on **Find**.
4. Select the order that you want to release**,** and enter the **Release Quantity**, and then click on **OK**.
5. Click on the **Form** menu, and then click on **Order Generation**.

How it works...

When you create sales orders from Blanket Orders just confuses things, the **Sales Blanket Order Release (P420111)** application will be used to manually deduct item quantities from the Blanket Order. The system will create the sales order for the specified quantity that you released from the **Blanket Order** and also give you the **Sales Order** number. The system retains the remaining balance on the Blanket Order for future sales orders. When you release the Blanket Order, it can be specified with sales order number during the verification of **Blanket Order** with release date and quantity. The system ensures that the sales order number and line type combinations is unique and if this is not the case, the system discontinues the processing of the sales order and issues an error message stating that *document number already exists*.

There's more...

The system identifies when the sales order quantity goes over the Blanket Order quantity. It also merges the order lines based on Sold To, Branch/Plant, and Currency Code information.

See also

- *Releasing Quote Orders*

Releasing Quote Orders

You can release a Quote Order in the same way that you release a Blanket Order—by using the **Sales Blanket Order Release** (**P420111**) application. This recipe explains the details of the Quote Order Release and describes the Quote Release process.

Getting ready

You need to create a **Quote Order** in order to release the **Quote** via the **Quote Release** program.

How to do it....

1. Select **EnterpriseOne Menus** | **Order Management** | **Sales Order Management** | **Daily Sales Order Management Processing** | **Additional Sales Order Processing**, and then click on **Release Quote** (**P420111**).

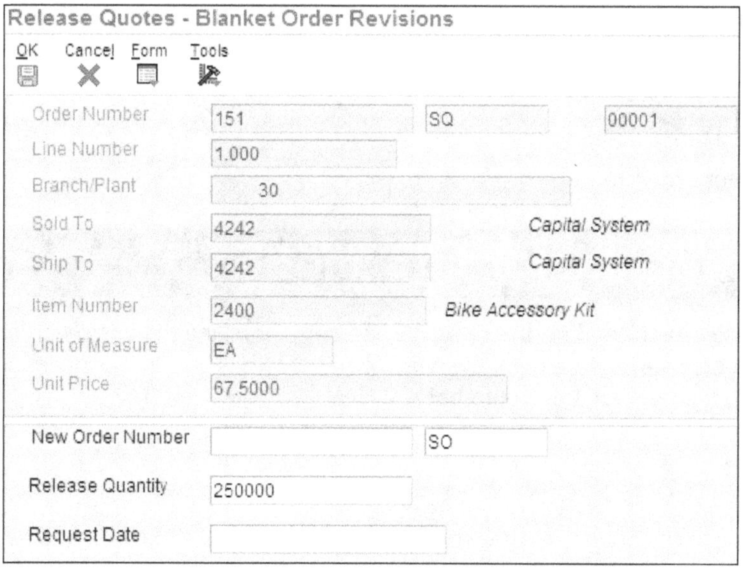

2. On the **Release Quote - Work with Order Quote Release** page, enter the **Quote Order Number**, and then click on **Find**.
3. Select the order you want to **Release** and enter the **Release Quantity**, and then click on **OK**.
4. Click on the **Form** menu, and then click on **Order Generation**.

How it works...

When you release some partial quantity from the **Quote Order**, the system keeps the remaining quantity balance with the original Quote Order. When you review the Quote Order, the system will show the adjusted quantity. When you release the Quote Order, the **Sales Order** number can be specified, along with the **Release Date** and **Release Quantity.** If the quote order has been created for the customer and the customer sends a purchase order for the quoted items, the Quote Order can be utilized to create a Sales Order. Multiple Quote Orders can be released at one time by choosing **Release Full Quantity**. When the unit of measure in the Sales Order does not match with the **Unit of Measure** in the Quote Order, the system does not initiate the Quote Order Release.

There's more...

The system verifies the order number and document type combination, in order to check for duplicate orders. The system stops the processing of the order and also displays the error message, if the document number already exists.

See also

- *Blanket Order Release*

Customer Master Information

Customer Master Information is the basic requirement for billing the customer for goods or services that you have sold to them. Every customer record is exclusively defined by a unique number called the **Address Book Number**.

Getting ready

Set up the processing options for the Address Book application (**P01012**) and the Customer Master Information program (**P03013**), in order to create a customer master with a search type of *C*.

How to do it....

1. Go to **EnterpriseOne Menus | Sales Order Management | Periodic Sales Order Management | Customer Revision**, select the **Customer Master Revision** (**P03013**) form, and then click on **Add**:

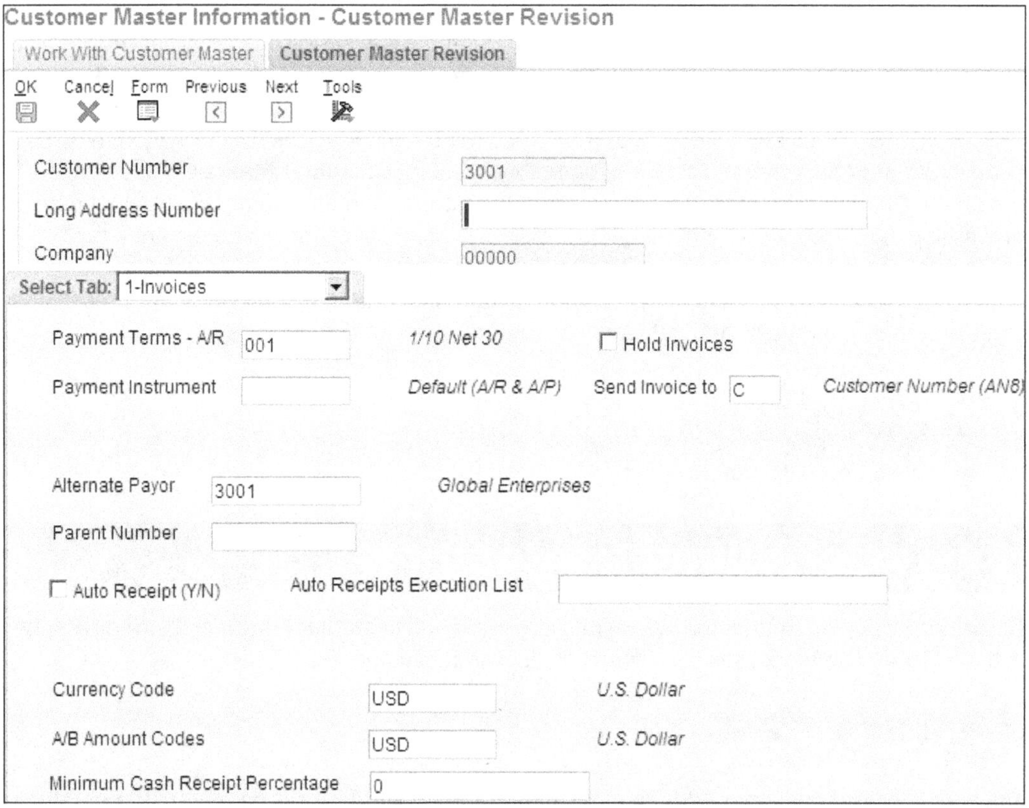

2. On the **Address Book Revision** form, enter the **Alpha Name**.
3. Enter the **Search Type** as **C**.
4. Enter the **Mailing Name** on the **Mailing** tab.
5. Enter the **Address Line 1**.
6. Enter the **City**.
7. Enter the **State**.
8. Enter the **Postal Code**.
9. On the **Customer Master Revision** form, enter the **Payment Terms – AR**.
10. Enter the **Currency Code**.

11. Enter the **Tax Exp Code**.
12. Enter the **Currency Code**.
13. Enter the **A/B Amount**.

How it works...

Customer Master Information can be entered through the **Address Book** program (**P01012**) or can be entered directly by using the **Customer Master Information** program (**P03013**). When you enter the **Customer Information** by using the **Customer Master** Information program (**P03013**), the address book record for that customer should first exist in the system or you should add the **Address Book** information before creating **Customer Master**. When you create the **Customer Master**, you should enter the information for invoice and manual receipt processing, G/L account information, information for processing automatic receipts, tax information, currency information, billing and shipping information for processing sales orders, credit and collection information, EDI (electronic data interchange) information for processing sales orders electronically, and category code information for the customer.

See also

- *Customer Billing Information*

Customer Billing Information

Customer Billing Information provides you with additional customer information—what are the exact features and processes you require for individual customers.

Getting ready

You should create Customer Address Book Information in order to set up the Customer Billing Information of individual customers.

How to do it....

1. Access the **Customer Master Revision** menu (**G4221**) from **Fast Path** and then click on **Customer Master Revision**. Next, from the **Form** menu, click on the **Customer Billing Information**:

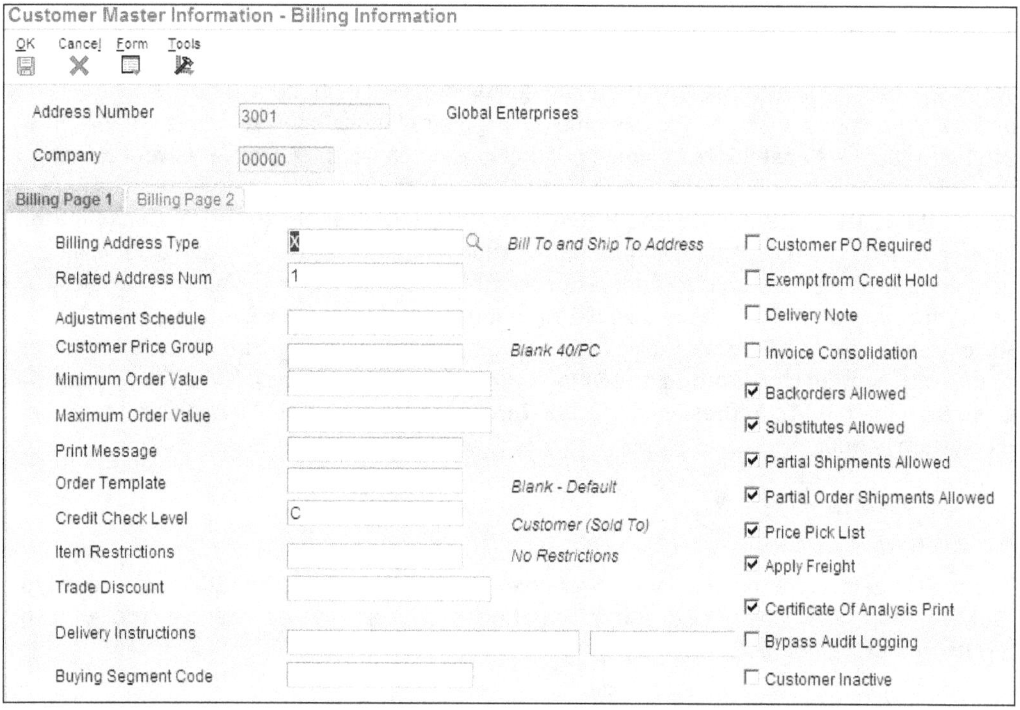

2. Select the **Backorders Allowed** checkbox, if you want to activate the **Back Order** process.
3. Select the **Substitutes Allowed** checkbox, if you want to activate the **Substitute Items**.
4. Select the **Partial Shipments Allowed** checkbox, if you want to use the partial shipment process.
5. Select the **Customer PO Required** checkbox, if a PO is necessary, as per business needs.
6. Select the **Delivery Note** checkbox, if you require the printing of a delivery note for the customer.
7. Select the **Invoice Consolidation** checkbox, if you require printing of the consolidated invoice for that customer.

How it works...

When you set up the advance options in the customer billing instructions, the system activates the option based on the customer billing instructions that were set up. That is, if you activated the **Consolidated Invoice** printing or you activated the **Delivery Order** printing, you should set up the order activity rule for that order type, and also set up the processing option of **P4210** program. Then, the system will print the **Delivery Note** and/or **Consolidated Invoice** based on the **Customer Billing Information**. The address number can also be set up for the invoice to use **Sold-To Address** or the **Ship-To Address**. When you enter a sales order, the system retrieves the receivable information—that is, the **Tax Explanation** code and **Rate Areas**—from the **F03012** table. When you enter direct shipping, transfer orders or sales orders with contradictory **Sold-To** and **Ship-To** addresses, the system gets the **Tax Explanation Code** from the **Sold-To Address** and the **Tax Rate/Area** from the **Ship-To Address,** based on the system set-up.

There's more...

The system gets additional accounts receivable information, such as the **Billing Address Type** (**Sold-To**, **Ship-To**, or together), **Credit Information**, and invoice copies, based on the set-up of the **Customer Billing Instructions**.

See also

- *Customer Master Information*

Reviewing Sales Ledger Information

You can review the Sales Ledger Information for every order that has been processed through the **Sales Order Management system**.

Getting ready

You should verify that you have set up the correct status code in the **Order Activity** program, in order to record the entry of the **Sales Order Detail** in the **Ledger File** table (**F42199**).

How to do it....

1. Select **EnterpriseOne Menus** | **Logistics Management** | **Order Management**| **Sales Order Management** | **Daily Sales Order Management Processing** | **Sales Order Inquiries** (**G42112**), and access the **Sales Ledger History Inquiry** (**P42025**):

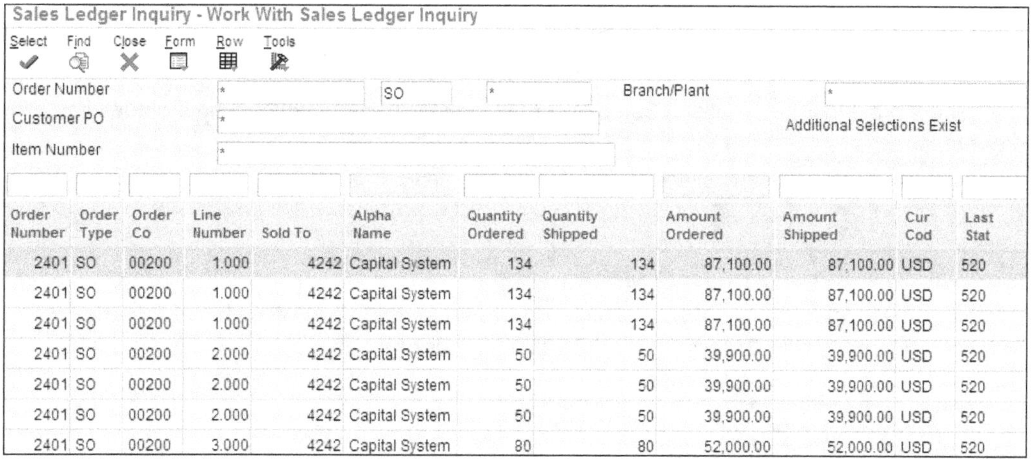

Sales Ledger Inquiry - Work With Sales Ledger Inquiry

Select Find Close Form Row Tools

Order Number * SO * Branch/Plant *

Customer PO *

Item Number *

Additional Selections Exist

Order Number	Order Type	Order Co	Line Number	Sold To	Alpha Name	Quantity Ordered	Quantity Shipped	Amount Ordered	Amount Shipped	Cur Cod	Last Stat
2401	SO	00200	1.000	4242	Capital System	134	134	87,100.00	87,100.00	USD	520
2401	SO	00200	1.000	4242	Capital System	134	134	87,100.00	87,100.00	USD	520
2401	SO	00200	1.000	4242	Capital System	134	134	87,100.00	87,100.00	USD	520
2401	SO	00200	2.000	4242	Capital System	50	50	39,900.00	39,900.00	USD	520
2401	SO	00200	2.000	4242	Capital System	50	50	39,900.00	39,900.00	USD	520
2401	SO	00200	2.000	4242	Capital System	50	50	39,900.00	39,900.00	USD	520
2401	SO	00200	3.000	4242	Capital System	80	80	52,000.00	52,000.00	USD	520

2. Enter the **Customer PO number/Sales Order Number/Item Number,** and then click on **Find**.
3. Review the **Last** and **Next** status code columns and determine if the order was invoiced, by reviewing the displayed order details.

How it works...

When you set up an **Order Activity Rule** and process the sales order through the sales **Order Management** system every single activity is recorded, based on the **Order Activity Rule** set up in the **Sales Order Detail Ledger File** table (**F42199**) for those order lines which you activated the Ledger **Y** in the **Order Activity Rule** setup. The system uses the Sales Ledger information to track the sales orders and verify when the sales order has been entered and when it has been printed. When you create a credit order (**Sales Return**) from the history, the system retrieves the original order information from the **Sales Order Detail Ledger File**. It is necessary to specify the correct version of the **Sales Ledger Inquiry** in the processing options of **Sales Order Entry** (**P4210**), which you set up for credit orders.

There's more...

The **Sales Ledger Inquiry** information can also be used for the internal audit process.

See also

- *Setting up Order Activity Rules in Chapter 9, Sales Order Management and Additional Orders*

Sales Commission Information

This recipe provides the details of Sales Commission Information, which also includes its pre-requisites.

Getting ready

You should run the **Sales Update** (**R42800**) program in order to review the Sales Commission information. You should also ensure hiding the **Commission Information** located in the **Display** tab in the **Sales Order** program (**P4210**) processing options.

How to do it....

1. Access the **Commission/Royalty Management** (**G4223**) from the **Commission/ Royalty Related Salesperson** menu.
2. Enter the **Salesperson Address Number** in the **Sales Rep Number** field.
3. Enter the **Effective Date** and **Expiration Date**.
4. Enter the commission type in **Related Salesperson**. The commission calculation is based on the **Invoice Amount**, the **Cost**, or the **Gross Margin**.
5. Enter the calculation type. This is either calculated based on the **Order** or the **Line**.
6. Enter the calculation percentage in the **Related Comm Percent field**:

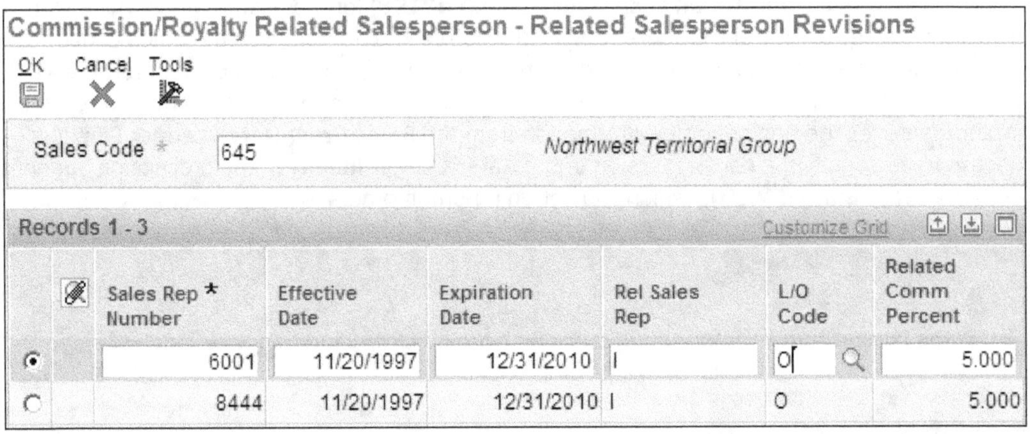

How it works...

When you set up the Commission Information, it reflects the sales environment. During set-up, multiple salespersons can be set; you can also set up the sales group for each customer. When you enter the sales order and run the **Sales Update** program (**R42800**), the system calculates the commission amount to the salesperson's address book number, or the address book number of each salesperson in the sales group. Subsequent to the sales update, the Commission Information is reviewed to make sure the salespersons receive the correct amount.

There's more...

The accrued sales commission can be reviewed in the **Commission Maintenance Revisions** program:

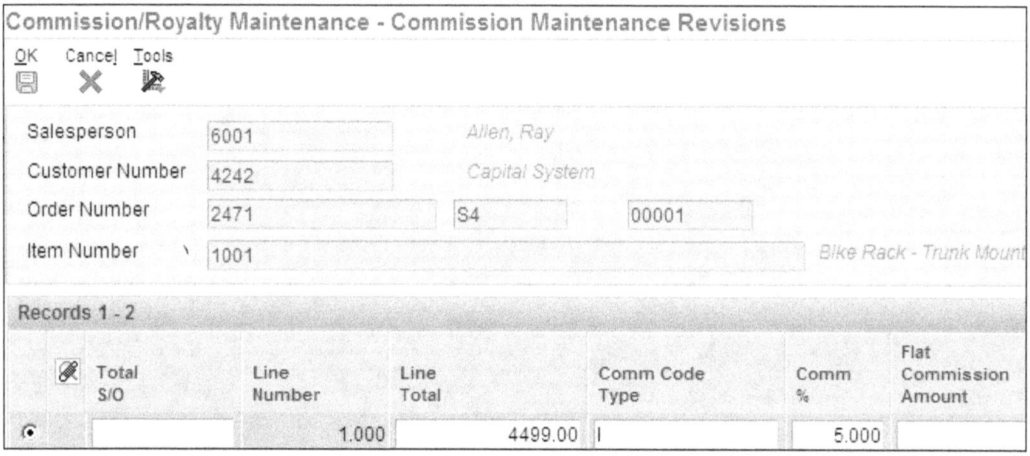

See also

- *Chapter 9, Sales Order Management and Additional Orders*

11

Order Processing, Prepayments, and Invoicing

In this chapter, we will cover:

- Printing pick slips
- Setting up serial number processing
- Running shipment confirmations
- Setting up bills of lading
- Printing delivery notes
- Setting up prepayment processing
- Setting up authorized credit card transactions
- Updating the transaction status
- Creating an invoice cycle
- Printing standard invoices

Introduction

In the previous chapters, we have seen important Sales Order Management system processes that include releasing Hold Orders and the detailed procedures for releasing Quote Orders and Blanket Orders.

In this chapter, you will learn how the system processes the sales order that you have already created. This includes everything from printing pick slips, confirming the shipment, printing delivery notes, and printing standard invoices. Towards the end of this chapter, you will learn the details of settling prepayment transactions, setting up bills of lading in the order management system for shipping the documents to their destination, setting up serial number processing, authorizing credit card transactions, and creating an invoice cycle in the Sales Order Management system.

Printing pick slips

A **Pick Slip** document can be printed by warehouse personnel to support the collection of inventory from the warehouse in order to fulfill the customer's order. The pick slip document contains location and lot information for the product that needs to be shipped to the customer. You should set up the order activity rule for printing the pick slips document.

Getting ready

You should create a sales order before printing the pick slip document.

How to do it...

1. Select **EnterpriseOne Menus** | **Order Management** | **Sales Order Management** | **Daily Processing** | **Sales Order Processing** | **Update Sales Order - Detail First**.
2. On the **Update Sales Order - Detail First** form, click on **Find** to search for your order.
3. Select the **Order** checkbox and then, from the **Row** menu, click on **Order** and then click on **Print Pick Slip**, as shown in the following screenshot:

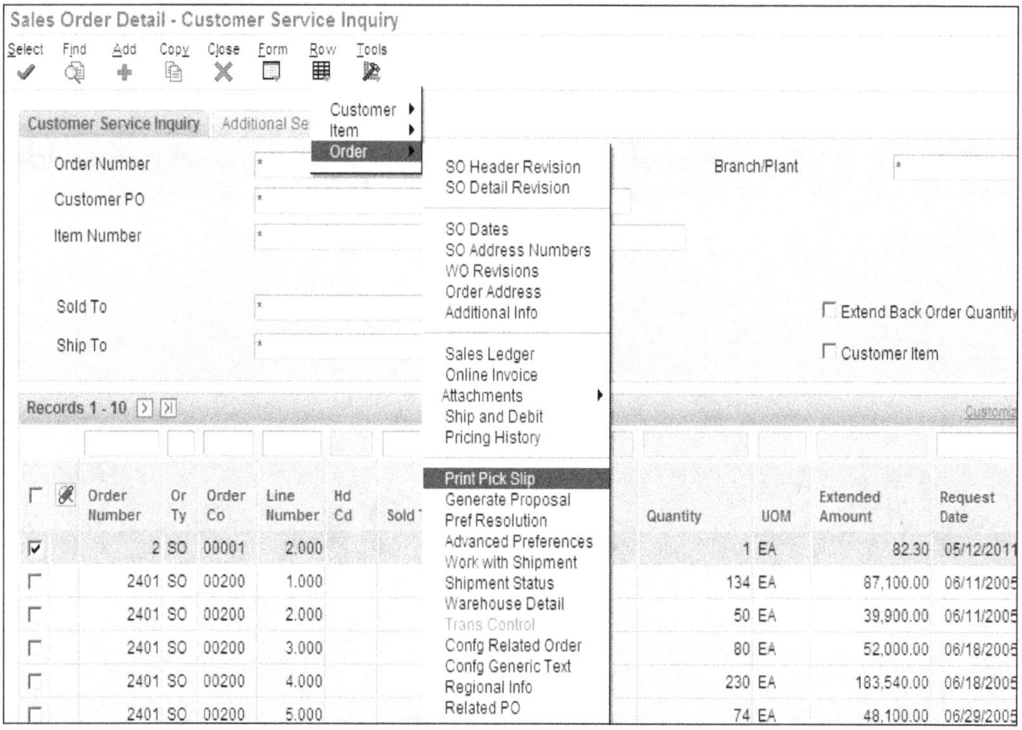

4. Get the PDF document from menu option **View Job Status** | **Submitted Job Search**.

How it works...

The pick slip document contains the item's shipping information; that is, quantity, location, and lot information, if the lot feature is activated. Pick slips are used to review prices for individual items or for an entire order. A pick slip also contains the delivery personnel's information. It can be verified by the customer during the delivery. When you print pick slips for hard-commit inventory (items issued from specified location), and includes the locations and lot information that were selected during sales order entry. When you select the item quantity from a specific location or lot, the system makes those commitments as a hard commitment. If the full item quantity is not available for a particular lot or at a particular location, the system divides the line and creates a separate line for each lot and location combination. The system assigns the pick slip number by order number and prints the total number of items for that order.

There's more...

Additionally, pick slips can be printed for multiple sales orders. A control pick slip or a pick list enables warehouse personnel to fulfill multiple sales orders efficiently. The control pick slip contains the details of more than one sales order for a shipment. The following is the control pick slip screen, which is showing the **Processing Options** of the control pick slip:

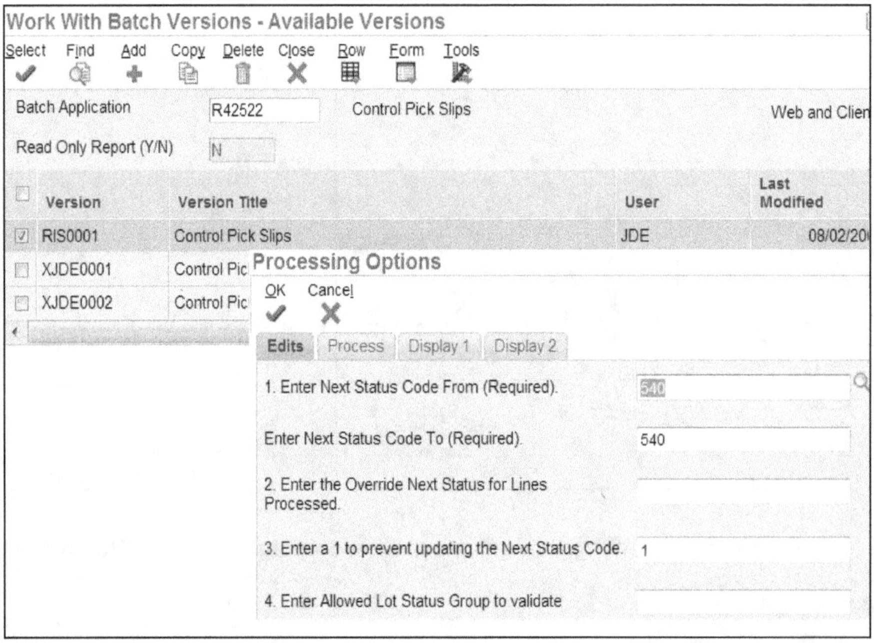

See also

- *Running shipment confirmations*

Setting up serial number processing

This recipe explains the details of serial number processing in the supply chain management system.

Getting ready

Create item branch information in order to set up the serial number processing.

How to do it...

1. Access the **Work with Serial Numbers** (**P4220**) program from the **Fast Path**.
2. Click on **Add,** and then enter the **Item Number** and **Branch/Plant**.
3. Enter **Serial Number 1** and **Serial Number 2**.

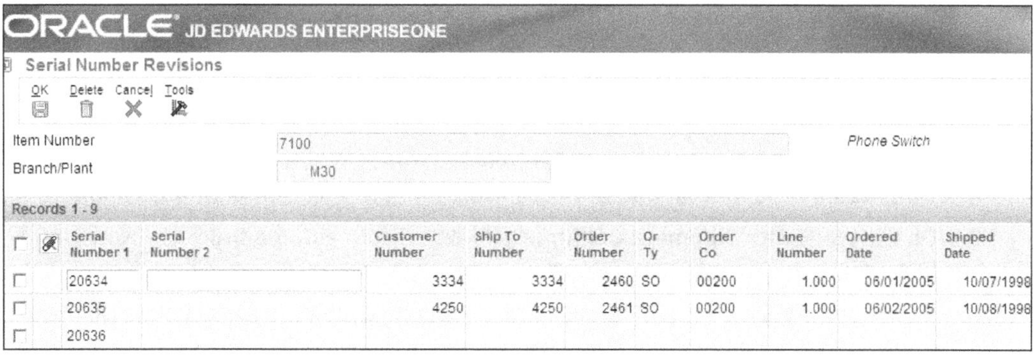

How it works...

You enter serial numbers in order to exclusively recognize a particular item and track it through the system. Serial numbers will help track information for a specific part; that is, when it arrived in the store, when it was received, when and to which customer it was sold, and when it was delivered. Based on requirements, the serial number can be added to the **Branch/Plant** when you receive the item. When you sell the item, you should enter the serial number throughout the order entry, and verify the serial number at the time of shipment confirmation. To allocate serial numbers within the branch/plant, you can access the **Basic Serial Numbers** (**P4220**) program.

There's more...

The serial number processing is an enhancement of lot processing. The system processes serial numbers for a lot, with single quantity. A single quantity lot is the lowest trackable unit.

See also

- *Chapter 3, Updating Costs, Using Kits, and Lot Processing, Creating lot processing*

Running shipment confirmations

This recipe explains the details of how to confirm order shipments.

Getting ready

You should set up the order activity rule in order to activate the **Confirm Shipment** process.

How to do it...

1. Select **EnterpriseOne Menus** | **Order Management** | **Sales Order Management** | **Daily Sales Order Management Processing**, and then click on **Confirm Shipment**.
2. On the **Work with Shipment Confirmation** form, find the **Sales Order** that you want to confirm.
3. Select **Confirm Line** from the **Row** menu to confirm a single line, or choose **Confirm Shown Rows** from the **Form** menu to confirm multiple lines.

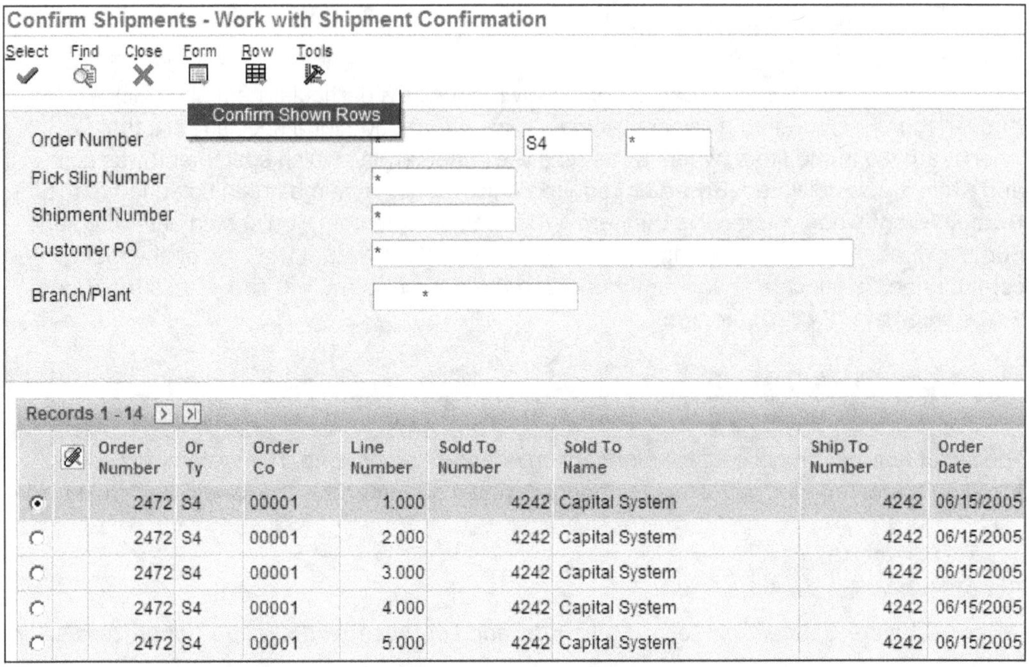

4. Select the next row, and enter the **Quantity** that you want to confirm.

How it works...

When you run the **Confirm Shipment** process, the system performs other processes for the order. During the **Confirm Shipment** process, you must update the **On-Hand** inventory as this improves the inventory correctness. The **On-Hand** quantities will relieve the item at the time of **Confirm Shipment** or **Sales Update**. When you deduct the on-hand quantity from the inventory when confirming the shipment, the system creates a record in the **Item Ledger** (**F4111**) table with the sales order as the document number and the order type as the **Document Type.** At the time of **Sales Update**, the system overwrites the record with the **Invoice Number**, **Type**, **GL Date**, and **Batch Number**.

There's more...

You can also guarantee the accuracy of the order by entering serial number information or confirming the test results for the shipped items during **Confirm Shipment**.

See also

- *Printing delivery notes*

Setting up bills of lading

The shipping documents, that is, bills of lading and delivery reports, can be printed before shipping the order.

Getting ready

You should set up the processing options to set default values and define how the system should process the data, control printing options, and also specify the default currency.

How to do it...

1. Access the **Bill of Lading (Shipping Document)** from the **G42111** menu and set up the processing option of **R42530**.
2. The **Default 1** tab indicates the next status in the order flow. Enter a **Status Code** value by selecting the **UDC** (**40/AT**) that indicates the next step in the order flow of the line.
3. On the **Defaults 2** tab, enter **Override Next Status** by selecting the **UDC** (**40/AT**) that specifies the next standard step in the processing cycle for this order type. You set up the steps for the processing cycle on the **Order Activity Rules** form.

4. **Next Status** code specifies whether the system updates the next status code from the order activity rules.
5. In the **Display future committed inventory** window, specify whether the system should display future committed inventory.
6. In the **Process** tab, specify the units of measurement that are used to calculate the volume and weight.

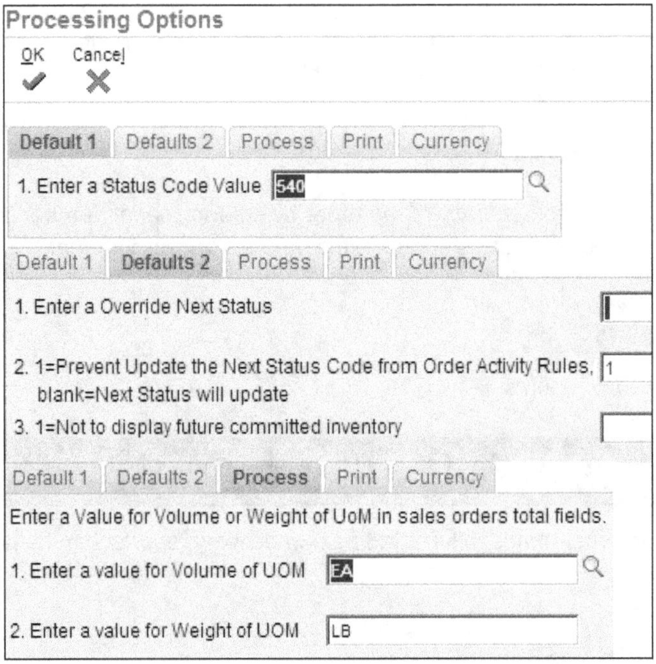

7. Specify the **Volume of UOM** as the unit of measurement that is used to calculate the volume.
8. On the **Print** tab, you will notice that the system prints kit components by default. Enter **1** against the second option if you do not want the system to print **Kit Components**.
9. On the fourth option, you need to enter the type of cross-reference to use in order to retrieve the customer item number.
10. The **Print serial numbers** option specifies whether the system prints serial numbers.
11. The **Print Additional Header Text** option specifies whether the system prints additional header text.

12. The **Currency Processing** option determines the currency to print. The **Type of Currency to Print option** specifies whether the system prints values in the domestic currency, the foreign currency, or both.

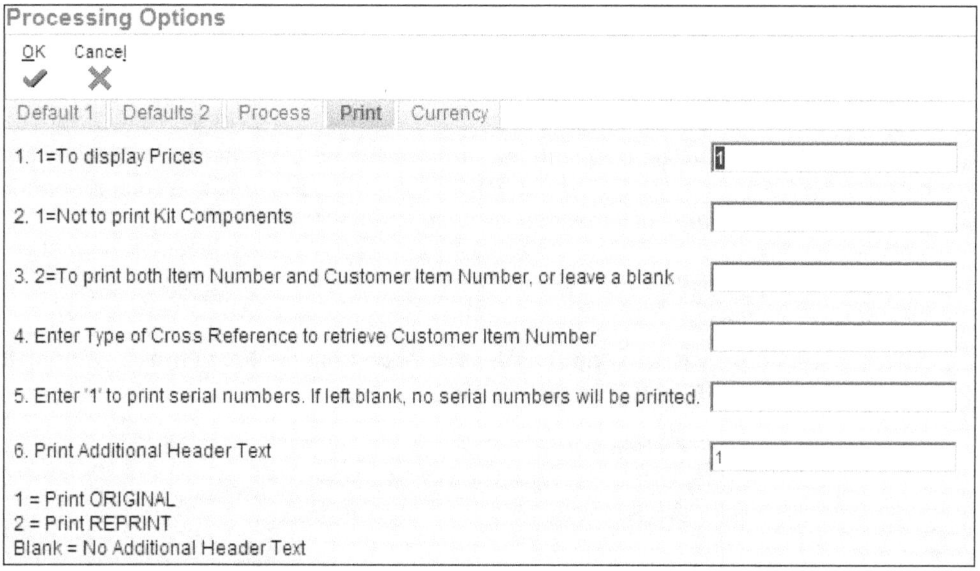

How it works...

Shipping documents accompany the order to its destination. Delivery personnel can use these documents to compare what they are supposed to deliver with what they are transporting. A bill of lading lists this information for the order. It includes the item description, quantity, weight, and volume. Billing documents include the customer address and price. Shipping documents include the shipping instructions, total weight, and total volume. Delivery documents include signature lines for the driver and the customer. You can specify the heading that prints at the top of the document, such as bill of lading, when you run the program. Because a shipping document has signature lines for the delivery person and the customer, you can also use it as a receipt.

There's more...

If you use **EnterpriseOne Demand Scheduling** (**40R**), the report displays these fields in a column labeled **Date/Time**.

See also

- *Printing delivery notes*

Printing delivery notes

A delivery note is printed in order to ensure accurate delivery of the item as per the provided PO.

Getting ready

You should verify that the **Customer Billing Instructions** for the customer allow **Delivery Note** printing. You should also verify that the order activity rules include the status code for printing delivery notes—that is, between shipment confirmation and printing invoices.

How to do it...

1. Access the **Delivery Notes Print batch** application from the **Fast Path** by entering **BV** followed by **R42535**, and then click on **Find**.

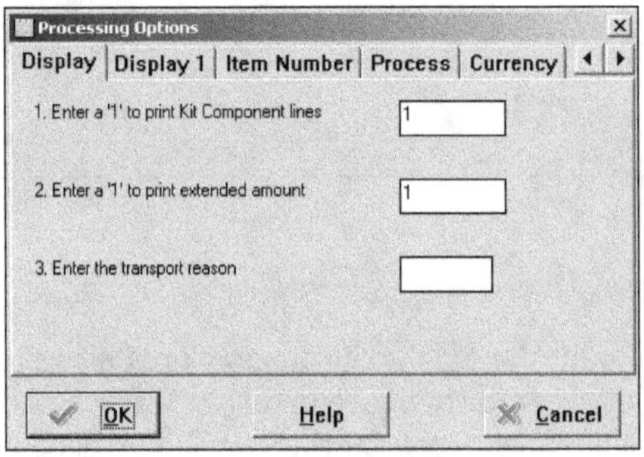

2. Set up the **Processing Option** (**R42535**) from the **Row** menu **Processing Option**.
3. Select the version and then click on **Select** from the **Menu** option. Click on the **Data Selection** checkbox and then click on **Submit**.
4. Enter the data selection—that is, **Status Code Next** (**F4211**) (**NXTR**), put **Is Equal To** in the **Comparison** clause, and then enter **560** in the **Right Operand**.
5. Click on **OK** to submit the document for printing.

How it works...

When you run the **Print Delivery Notes** program, the system prints the delivery details that the carrier will use during item delivery. The delivery people will use it to compare the items that need to be delivered with the items that are shipped on the delivery van. To ensure that the customer invoice is perfect, the delivery notes can be printed after shipment confirmation but before you generate a customer invoice for an order.

There's more...

You can provide delivery notes to a customer only if the customer's billing instructions allow delivery notes. In the **Customer Billing Instruction**, if you select the **Print Delivery Notes** checkbox, the system will allow printing of the delivery note.

See also

- *Running shipment confirmations*

Setting up prepayment processing

This recipe provides the details of settling prepayment transactions, and explains how to run the Settle Prepayment Transactions program.

Getting ready

You should set up the processing options for the **Settle Prepayment Transactions** program (**R004202**).

How to do it...

1. Access the **Authorize Prepayment Transaction** print program from the **Fast Path** by entering **BV,** and then enter the report batch application name (**R004201**) and click on **Find**.

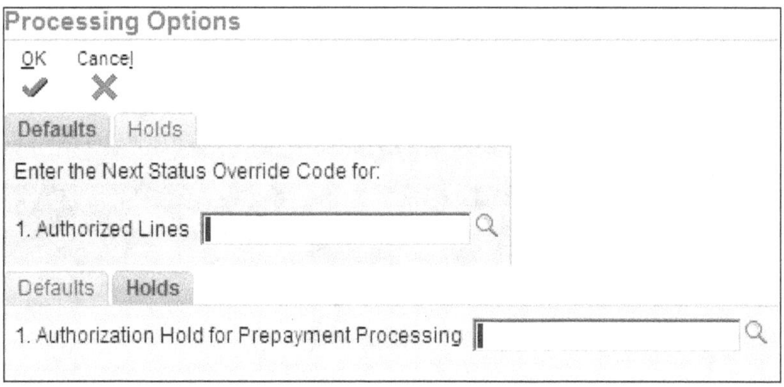

2. On the **Settle Prepayment Transaction** page, enter the version of the **Settle Prepayment Transaction** program to use. If you leave the **Processing Option** blank, the system will not run this application.

3. For the **Authorization Hold for Prepayment Processing** option, enter the hold code to display on the order if the authorization process fails.
4. For the **Settlement Hold for Prepayment Processing** option, enter the hold code to display on the order if the settlement process fails.
5. For the **Carton Detail** options, specify how the system processes the cartons.
6. For the **Reconcile Carton Detail to Shipment Detail** option, specify whether the system should reconcile the carton detail to the shipment detail.

How it works...

Prepayment of an order takes place when a vendor receives a form of payment from the customer at the time of order entry. Multiple types of prepayments are available for a customer to use, such as cash, check, and credit card. When you make any type of prepayment, the system records transaction information for each order detail line, and indicates the payment on the invoice. If the order detail line is over-shipped, or an additional order detail line is added to the order, you should receive a new authorization.

> The hold code is a user-defined code **42/HC**, which is used for putting the order processing on hold.

There's more...

The settlement phase should take place after confirmation of the shipment but before invoicing. After confirming the shipment of supplies, you can perform settlement. This way, when you print invoices, you can indicate that the customer invoice has been paid.

See also

- *Setting up authorized credit card transactions*

Setting up authorized credit card transactions

This recipe explains the credit card authorization process.

Getting ready

Run the **Authorize Prepayment Transactions** program.

How to do it...

1. Access the **Authorize Prepayment Transactions** (**R004201**) processing option, access the application from the **Fast Path**.
2. On the **Defaults** tab, enter **Authorized Lines**; enter the **Next Status Override UDC** (**40/AT**).
3. On the **Holds** tab, in **Authorization Hold for Prepayment Processing**, enter the **UDC (42/HC)** that identifies why an order is on hold, as shown in the following screenshot:

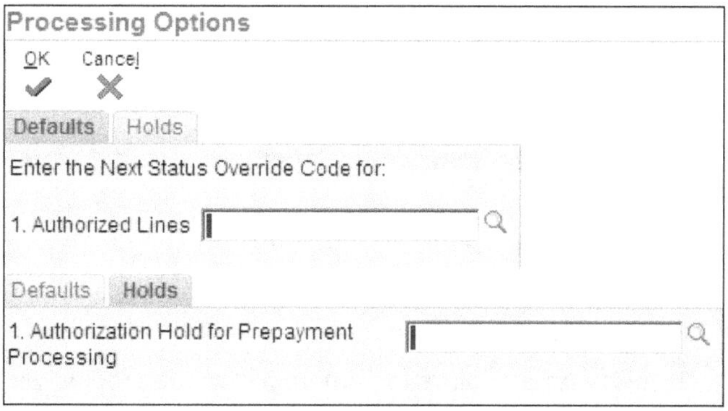

How it works...

When you enter a sales order, the customer's credit card transaction information can be captured and the order amount is transmitted through the middleware solution—a credit card processor. The cardholder's account can be checked for available funds and the order placed on hold for those orders which has equivalent order amount in excess of the customer's credit line. The authorization process varies based on **Credit Card Processor**. When the authorization is successful, the JDE system returns the authorization code, and the system revises the transaction status in the **Prepayment Transaction** table (**F004201**).

See also

- *Updating the transaction status*

Updating the transaction status

This recipe explains the details of updates to the transaction status, and describes how to update the transaction status code.

Getting ready

Set up the processing option of the **Work with Prepayment Processing Information** program (**P004201**).

How to do it...

1. Access the **Pre Payment** information from the **Work with Prepayment Processing Information** program (**P004201**).
2. The **Prepayment Origination Flag** displays a **UDC (00/PO)** that specifies the system from which the prepayment originated.
3. **Sequence Number** displays a number that specifies the sequence of information.
4. The **Prepayment Transaction Status** displays the status of the prepayment transaction.
5. The **Authorize Transaction Amount** displays the amount of the prepayment credit card authorization.
6. The **Cash Payment Amt** displays the amount that was paid in cash.
7. The **Check Payment Amt** displays the amount that was prepaid with check.
8. In the **Settle Transaction Amount** option, review the amount of the prepayment settlement.

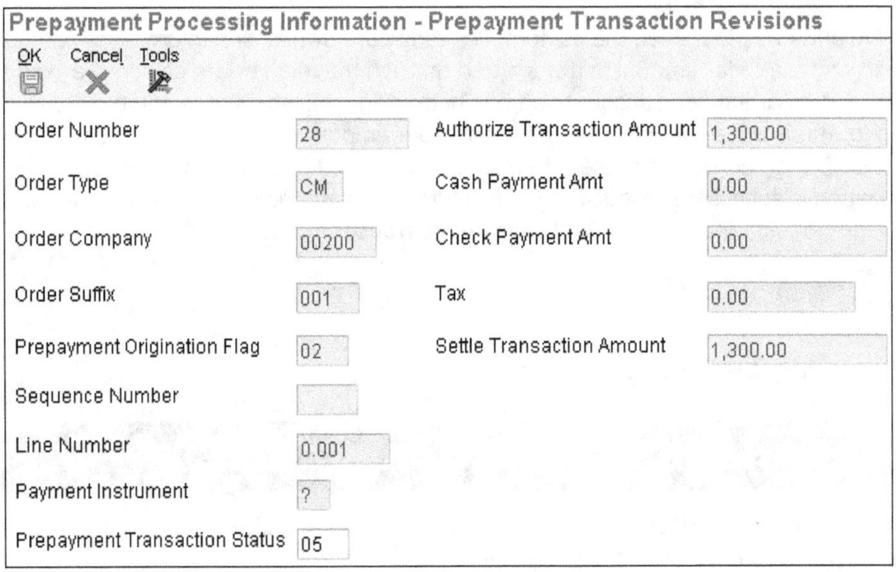

How it works...

Prepayment can be entered or updated during order entry if the prepayment processing options for **Sales Order** Entry (**P4210**) have been defined for **Prepayment Processing**. When you enter **Sales Order**, the **Prepayment Transaction Revisions** can be entered to check the number or credit card information. The system retrieves the order amount and the calculated taxes as the total prepayment amount. When you enter prepayment information, the system writes a record to the **F004201** table, which you can review. The prepayment status for a particular customer or status can also be reviewed.

There's more...

You can modify the prepayment status of a transaction by using the **Work with Prepayment Processing Information** program (**P004201**).

See also

- *Creating an invoice cycle*

Creating an invoice cycle

This recipe explains the details of invoice cycle setup and describes how to create an invoice cycle preference.

Getting ready

You should set up the **Invoice Cycle Calculation Rule** in order to set up the **Invoice Cycle Preference**.

How to do it...

1. Access the **Preference Master** (**P40070**) program from the **G4231** menu.
2. Select the **Invoice Cycle,** and then click on **Select**.

3. Click on **Add,** and select a preference type of either **Item and Customer**, **Item Group and Customer Group**, or **Customer Only**. Each preference type has the priority set up such that if you select **Item and Customer**, the system will see specific items and specified customers, whereas if you select **Customer Only** the system will see only specific customers, and so on.

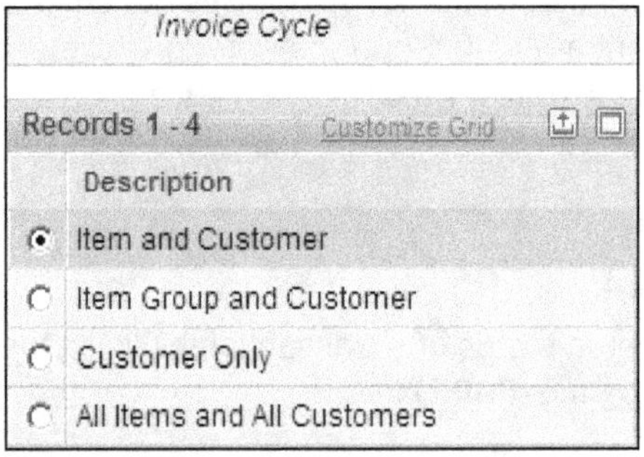

4. Enter **Customer Number**, **Customer Group**, **Item Number**, and **Item Group**.
5. Enter **Invoice Cycle**, **Branch Plant**, **Preference Status**, **Effect From**, and **Effect Thru**.
6. Click on **OK** to save the information:

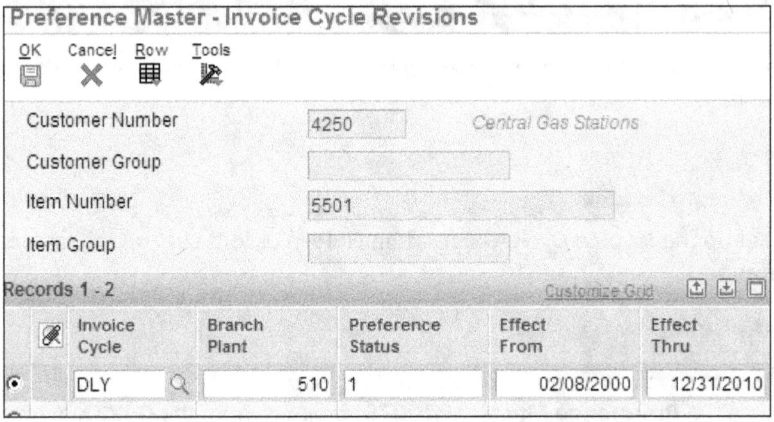

How it works...

When you set up the invoice cycles to control the **Cycle Billing** program, the system calculates the scheduled invoice date. When you set up invoice cycles, the different cycles of calculation rules and schedule can be applied to dissimilar customers and item recipes. The invoice cycle calculation rule set up should be defined in the category of computation that the system uses to work out the invoice date. When you set up invoice cycles, these can be assigned to customers and item recipes with the **Invoice Cycle Preference**.

There's more...

In some cases, one customer may prefer the invoice at the end of the month for all shipments made throughout the month, and some may want a weekly invoice for specific items. For weekly invoicing, you can enter weekly, while for monthly invoice you can enter at the end month. The invoice cycle can also be specified in the invoice cycle revision application.

See also

- *Printing standard invoices*

Printing standard invoices

This recipe explains the details of the print invoices program and shows how to print the standard invoice.

Getting ready

You should set up the **Processing Options** for the **Print Invoices (R42565) batch** application.

How to do it...

1. Select **EnterpriseOne Menus** | **Order Management** | **Sales Order Management** | **Daily Sales Order Management Processing** | **Sales Order Processing** | **Invoice Processing**, and then click on **Print Invoices** (**R42565**).
2. Click on **Find,** and select version **XJDE0001** (**Print Invoices**), and then click on **Copy**.
3. Enter your **user ID** in the **New Version** and **Version Title** fields, and then click on **OK**.

4. On the **Work with Batch Versions**—available versions form—find and select your version.
5. Select **Data Selection** from the **Row** menu and insert the query **Where** (**Order No., Invoice,** and so on).

   (**F4211**) (**DOCO**) (**BC**) is equal to enter the order numbers that are not backordered).
6. Click on **OK**.
7. On the **Available Versions** form, select **Processing Options** from the **Row** menu.
8. To **Print Invoices** on the **Work with Batch Versions** form, click on the checkbox next to your version, and then click on **Select**.
9. On the **Version Prompting** form, click on **Submit**.
10. Click on **OK** twice to return to the **Available Versions** form.

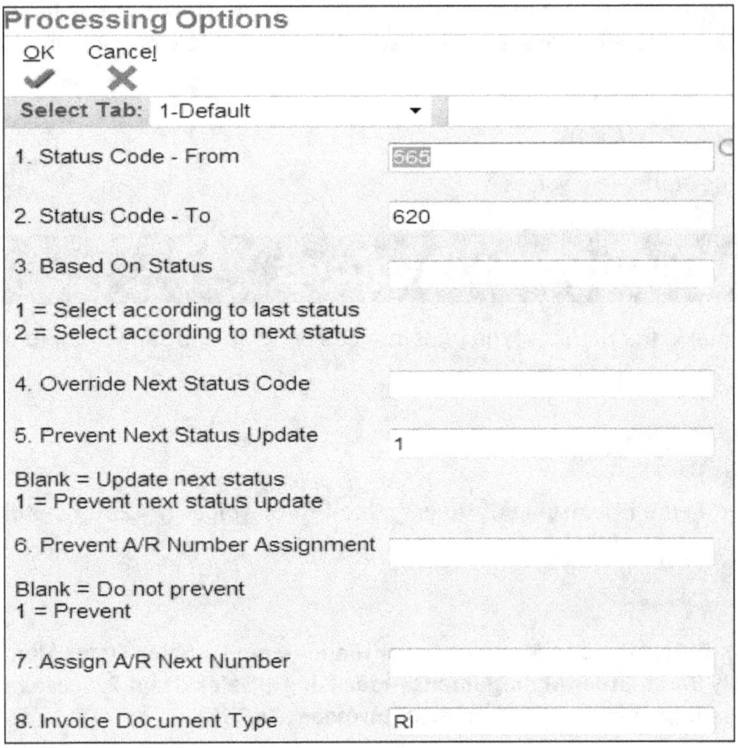

How it works...

The **Print Invoices** program (**R42565**) updates the information in the **Sales Order Detail File** table (**F4211**) having the invoice number, invoice date, and invoice document type. The status codes of the program set the next status code to run the **Sales Update** program. You must specify the **Next Status** code that the system selects for processing. You can process and print a group of invoices in a batch by using a proof or final mode. When you run **Print Invoices** in proof mode, the system does not perform updates to the status codes or any files. You can use the **Proof Version** for other functions, such as sales order acknowledgements or invoice reprints.

There's more...

To accurately process the invoice proofs, you should run the version **XJDE0005** or make a copy from this version.

See also

- *Creating an invoice cycle*

12
Updating Prices, End of Day Processes, and Sales Returns

In this chapter, we will cover:

- Updating the base prices
- Updating prices for a customer
- Setting the end of day processing
- Running the end of day processing
- Journal entry batch review and approval
- Reviewing electronic mail for messages
- Returned material authorization
- Interbranch and intercompany orders
- Reposting orders
- Setting up sales journal

Introduction

In this chapter, you will see order management pricing, which includes the base price revision (standard pricing) based on the customer, items, customer group, and item group. It also gives you the details of how to process the end of day operations, which updates the financial modules as per the financial integration setup.

Updating the base prices

This recipe provides details of the base price updates and how to run the **Base/Price Maintenance - Batch** program.

Getting ready

You should set up the **Processing Options** for **Base/Price Maintenance - Batch** (**R41830**).

How to do it...

1. Go to **EnterpriseOne Menus | Logistics Management | Order Management | Sales Order Management | Periodic Sales Order Management Processing | Price Management**, and then click on **Batch Base Price Revisions**.

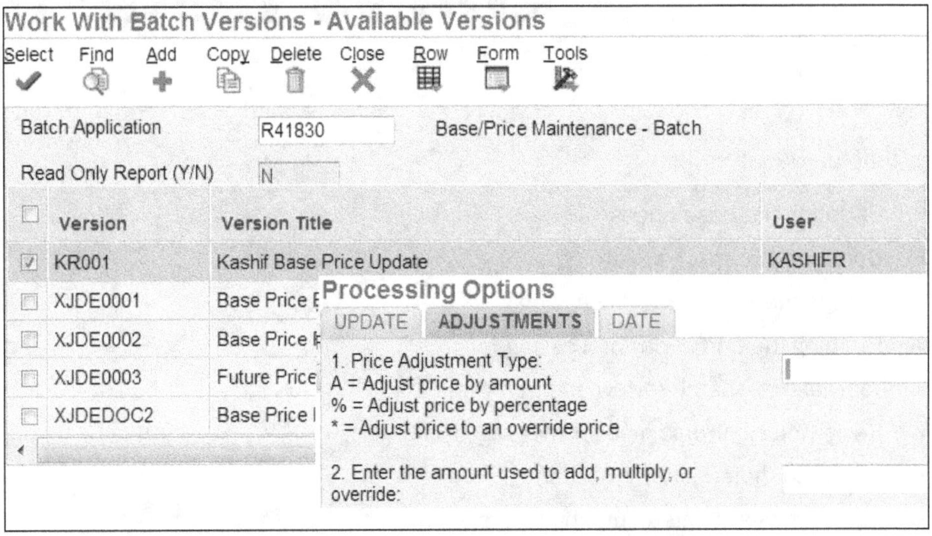

2. Select the **XJDE0001** version and then click on **Copy** to add a new version. Then select the new version. Go to **Data Selection** and enter the **2nd Item Number** in the **Data Selection**.
3. Enter the **Price Adjustments Type** on the **Adjustments** tabbed page.

4. Enter the amount that should be used to add, multiply, or override, based on the **Price Adjustment Type**. For example, if you entered an adjustment type code of amount (**A**), enter **10** to increase the price by 10 or, **-10** to decrease the price by 10. If you entered an adjustment type code of percentage (%), enter **10** to increase the price by 10 percent, or **-10** to decrease the price by 10 percent.
5. Enter the **Effective** Date and **Expiry Date**.
6. Click on **Submit**.

How it works...

When you submit the **Base/Price Maintenance - Batch** (**R41830**) program, it will change the current price or create a new price that will be effective on a future date, depending on the effective date specified. The **Base Price Maintenance - Batch** program (**R41830**) will update multiple prices at one time. When you update multiple prices in batch mode, the system likewise overrides the existing price with the latest price, or calculates the adjustment to the existing price, depending on the configuration of the processing options of the **Base/Price Maintenance - Batch** program. During the configuration of this version, you should identify the specific fields that you want to select. The new price records that the system creates are included in a change report, along with their effective dates, and the old prices that the system used as the basis for the new prices.

There's more...

When you run the **Base/Price Maintenance - Batch** version in **Proof** mode, the system generates the change report, which displays the updates that will be made, but does not actually make the updates. This program can be run in **Proof** mode multiple times by selecting this mode in the processing options. The **Base Price Maintenance** can be run from **Periodic Processing** | **Inventory Price and Cost Updates** | **Base/Price Maintenance**.

> The change report can be viewed from **EnterpriseOne menu** | **Submitted Jobs** | **Form menu** | **Submit Job Search** | **Find**, then select the report that you want to review, and then click on the **Row** menu and click on **View PDF**.

See also

- *Updating prices for a customer*

Updating prices for a customer

Sales orders use the customer price based on the most current price or price adjustment from the **Base Price Revision** program. For example, for some customers you have some special discounts, so you can set up the discount for a specific customer or customer group; and vice versa for some items for which you have some special prices or discounts offers.

Getting ready

You should define the **Customer Master** and **Item Master** in order to set up the **Base Price**.

How to do it...

1. Go to **EnterpriseOne Menus** | **Logistics Management** | **Order Management** | **Sales Order Management** | **Periodic Sales Order Management Processing** | **Price Management**, and then click on **Base Price Revisions**.

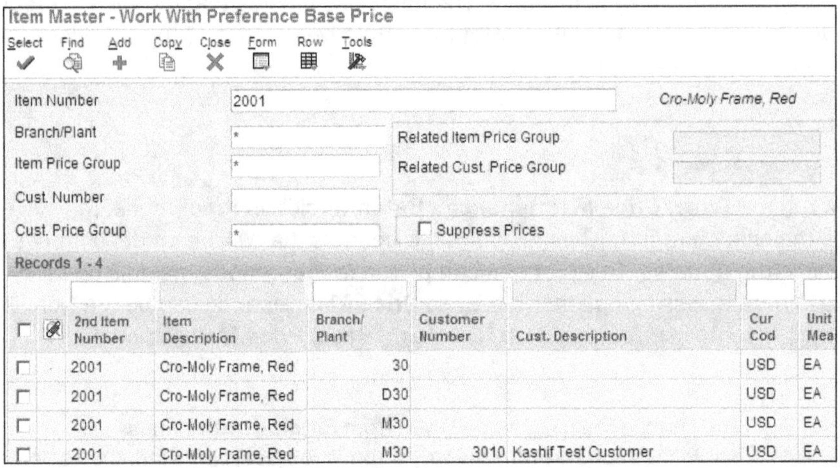

2. Click on **Add** and then select one of the options shown in the following screenshot:

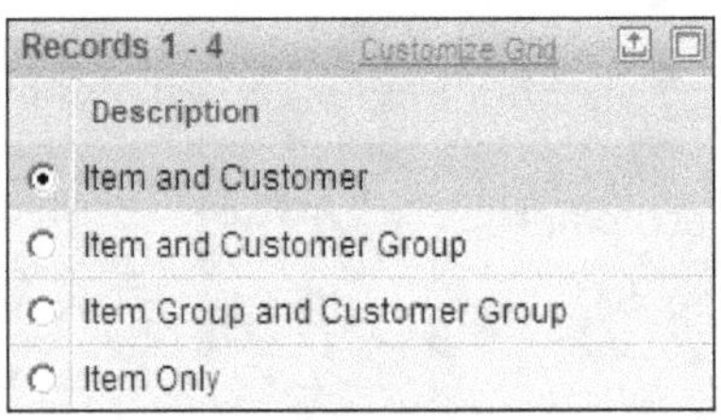

3. Enter the **Item Number**.
4. Enter the **Item Branch**.
5. Enter the **Currency Code**.
6. Enter the **Unit Price**.
7. Enter the **Effective Date** and **Expiry Date**.

How it works...

When you enter the item price by using **Base Price Revision**, the system retrieves the item price from the base price table during sales order entry. The base prices can be defined with various combinations of items, item groups, customers, and customer groups. When you enter an item in the **F4101** table, you should enter the sales price to define the base price of the item. When you define the special pricing or discounts for the item or customer, the system will calculate the discounted price based on the **Base Price Revision**. When you define the effective dates of base price for an item, item group, customer, or customer group, the system use these dates. If you leave the effective date blank, the system will assign a date of *12/31/2040* automatically.

There's more...

The system retrieves the sales price in the sales order application based on the item base price.

See also

- *Updating the base prices*

Setting the end of day processing

The **End of Day** application processing options set-up determines the default values that update the customer sales program, and also creates **General Ledger** and **Accounts Receivable** entries.

Getting ready

You should set up the **Order Activity** rule in order to set up the **End of Day** processing.

How to do it...

1. Go to **EnterpriseOne Menus** | **Order Management** | **Sales Order Management** | **Daily Sales Order Management Processing** | **End of Day Processing**, and then select **Update Customer Sales** (**R42800**). Click on the **Row** menu and then select the **Processing Option**.

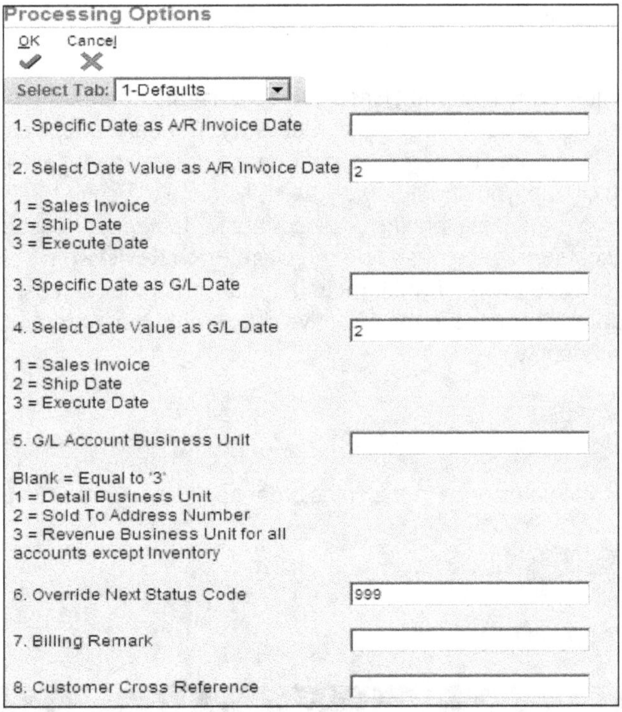

2. In the **Invoice Date** option, enter the invoice date for the accounts receivable.
3. In the **Select Date Value as A/R Invoice Date** option, specify the order processing date.
4. Enter the **Specific Date as G/L Date.**
5. For the **Date Value as G/L Date** option, specify the order processing date. If you do not specify a G/L date in this field, then you should specify a value of either **1** for **Sales Invoice**, **2** for **Ship Date**, or **3** for **Execute Date.**
6. Specify the **G/L Account Business Unit** to which the system assigns general ledger entries, if you do not specify a business unit in the AAIs.
7. For the **Override Next Status Code** option, enter the **UDC** (**40/AT**) that is the next step in the order process.

8. On the **Update** tabbed page, select the mode as either **Proof** or **Final** mode.
9. Use **Bypass Update to Accounts Receivable** (**F0311**) especially for cash sales orders, as the system does not create an AR invoice for these order types.
10. Specify **Bypass Update to Inventory** (**F41021/F4115**), if the system updates **On-Hand** inventory in the **F41021** and **F4115** tables.
11. Specify **Bypass Update to Commissions** (**F42005**), if the system updates the commission information in the **F42005** table.
12. Specify **Bypass Update to Sales History Summary** (**F4229**), if the system updates the **F4229** table.
13. Specify **Purge to Sales Detail History** (**F42119**), if the system purges detail information from the **F4211** table.
14. Specify **Purge to Sales Header History** (**F42019**), if the system copies records from the **F4201** table to the **F42019** table, and then deletes the original records.
15. Specify the **A/R Next Number** index to indicate the next number that the system uses to assign an invoice (**Account Receivable**) number.
16. Specify the **Sales Journal Version** (**R42810**) that the system uses to print the sales journal before running the **Update Customer Sales** program.
17. Specify whether the system writes **General Ledger** journal entries in **Summary** or **Detail**.

How it works...

When you set up the **Sales Update** (**R42800)** processing option, you should specify the specific date to use as the accounts receivable invoice date. You should also enter the specific date for **G/L Date** in the processing option. The **R42800** processing option provides the set up of default values that affect the cost update, interbranch orders, flexible accounting, bulk products, agreement management, and prepayment processing. Through the **R42800** processing option, you can also instruct the system to avoid updating the tables during the **Sales Update** process. You can also control the sales journal printing option, and define whether entries are written in detail or in a summarized format.

There's more...

When you run the **Customer Sales Update**, the system will move the order detail lines from the **F4211** table to the **F42119** table based on the processing option set-up, in order to improve system performance.

See also

- *Running the end of day processing*

Running the end of day processing

This recipe explains how to run **End of Day** processing in order to update the customer ledger, **AR Invoices**, and **General Ledger**.

Getting ready

You should set up the **End of Day** (**R42800**) processing option in order to run the end of the day processing.

How to do it...

1. Go to **EnterpriseOne Menus** | **Order Management** | **Sales Order Management** | **Daily Sales Order Management Processing** | **End of Day Processing**, and then select **Update Customer Sales** (**R42800**).
2. Select the **XJDE0001** version, click on **Copy** from the menu bar and give the new version a name (**Sales Update – Proof Mode**).
3. Select your new **Version**, select **Data Selection** from the **Row** menu, and enter **Where Document** (Order Number, Invoice, and so on) (**F4211**) (**DOCO**) (**BC**) equals **Sales Order Number**.
4. On the available versions form, select **Processing Options** from the **Row** menu.
5. Select your **Version** of **R42800 – Sales Update** and click on **Select**. On the **Version Prompting** form, click on **Submit**:

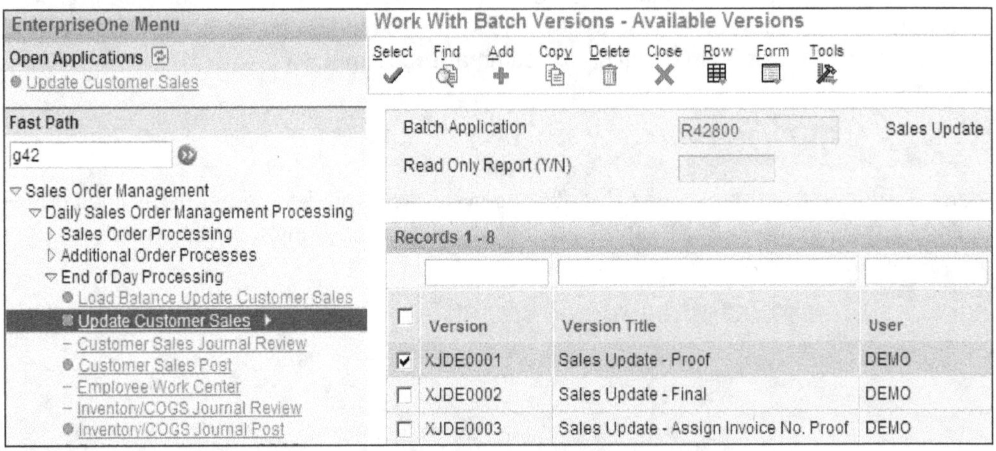

How it works...

The **End of Day** processing is the final step of **Sales Order Management**, and consists of updating, verifying, and posting the daily sales activity. The **End of Day** processing integrates the **Sales Order Management** system with the **Accounts Receivable** and **General Ledger**. It also updates the **On-Hand Inventory**, if the inventory does not reduce during confirmation of the shipment processing or the customer doesn't activate the confirm shipment functionality. When you run **End of day** processing, the system will close the sales order by putting the status as **999,** and create the invoice in the **Accounts Receivable** module. It will also create the journal entries based on your **DMAAI** setup—that is, the Cost of goods sold account, Revenue account, and Inventory account depending on the **GL** chart of accounts.

There's more...

The **End of Day** processing is used every day to maintain the most precise sales information. Subsequently, after running the **Sales Update** program, you can review, post, and print the other sales reports.

See also

- *Setting the end of the day processing*

Journal entry batch review and approval

The accuracy of the sales transaction records should be verified, by reviewing the **General Ledger** entries that the **Update Customer Sales** program creates, before you post them into the **General Ledger**.

Getting ready

You should run the **End of Day** processing (**R42800**) batch application in order to review the **Journal Entry** created by the sales order application.

How to do it...

1. Access the **Work with Batches** (**P0011**) application from **Fast Path**.
2. Enter the **Batch Number/Batch Type,** and then click on **Find**.

3. Select the appropriate batch type from among: **Unposted Batches**, **Posted Batches**, **All Batches** or **Pending**:

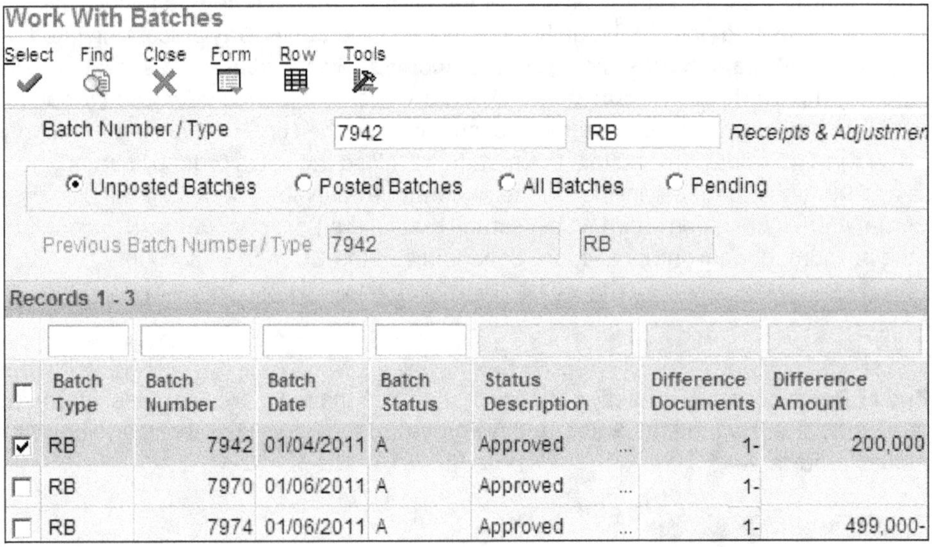

4. Select the batch that you want to review, and then click on **Select** on the menu bar.
5. Click on **Select** again, and review the **RI** sales invoices.

How it works...

When the **Update Customer Sales** program runs in the **Final** mode, it creates transactions in several batches, for posting into journals such as customer sales (batch type IB). The system creates batch type IB and summarized and detailed journal entries based on the processing option set up in the **Sales Update** program. The system creates batch type G for inventory and COGS entries. These transactions can be reviewed from **General batch review**, **Display batches by User ID**, **Batch Status**, **Batch Number**, and **Entry date range**. The batch detail can display journal entry header information, such as invoice number, document type, and gross amount for a single batch. These transactions will be posted to the **F0902** and **F0911** tables, reviewed in the **General Ledger Post** report **R09801**. The batch report can contain errors; the report also includes a text box, which will alert you if the program has found errors.

There's more...

When you review electronic mail messages, this will provide further information that will be useful in resolving errors.

See also

- *Setting up sales journal*

Reviewing electronic mail for messages

This recipe provides you with details of how to review the **Electronic Messages** that the system generates during batch application processing.

Getting ready

You should associate the employee address book with the JDE login ID in order to receive the **Electronic Messages** in the employee **Work Centre**.

How to do it...

1. Access the **Work with Work Center** from the **Action** menu.
2. Select **Electronic Messages,** and then click on the **Plus** sign.
3. Review the messages that are shown.
4. Resolve the issues as per the error messages:

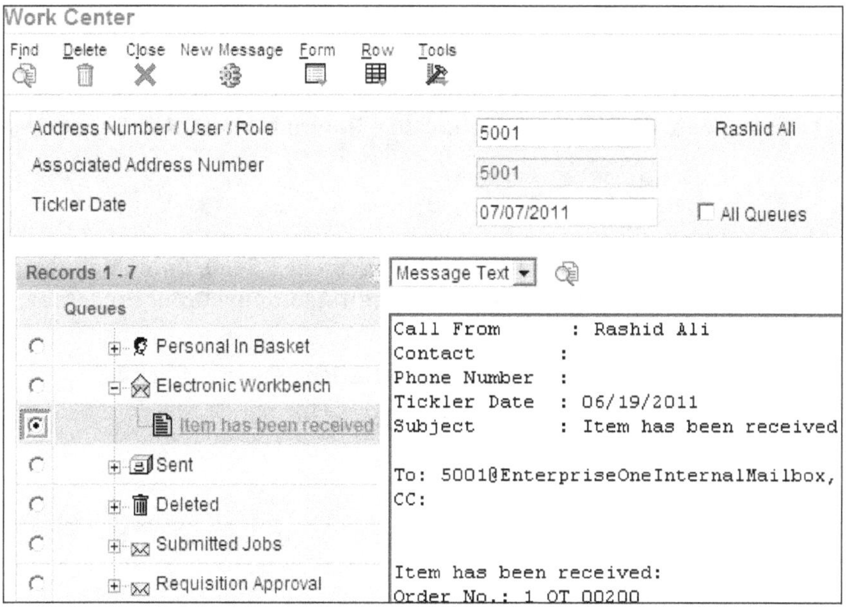

How it works...

When you run the batch application, the system sends messages via electronic mail to the **Employee Work Center,** both when errors occur and when the job has completed normally. Whenever you run the post program, you should review the electronic mail to determine the status of the job. If the job does not finish normally, the system generates error messages. Normally, an initial message notifies you that the job had errors; this will be followed by one or more detailed messages, each of which describes one of the errors.

There's more...

With the help of the error messages, you can access the Work with Batches, the which facilitates the location of the problems, and make the changes interactively.

See also

- *Running shipment confrmation in Chapter 11, Order Processing, Prepayments*

Returned material authorization

Returned Material Authorization is a process where approval comes from the supplier for the customer to return the inventory for credit, replacement, or repair.

Getting ready

You should create a **Sales Order** in order to create a **Return Material Authorization** (**RMA**).

How to do it...

1. Go to **EnterpriseOne Menus** | **Order Management** | **Sales Order Management** | **Daily Sales Order Management Processing** | **Additional Order Processes**, and click on **Returned Materials Authorization**.
2. On the **Work with Return Material Authorization** form, click on **Add**.
3. On the **Returned Material Authorization Revisions** form, enter the **Customer Number**.
4. Select **Sales Ledger** from the **Form** menu.
5. Enter the **Order Number** for the sales order that you previously entered for your customer.
6. Click on **Find**.

7. Select the row that contains a **Next Status** of **620,** select **Credit Memo,** and then select **Line** from the **Row** menu:

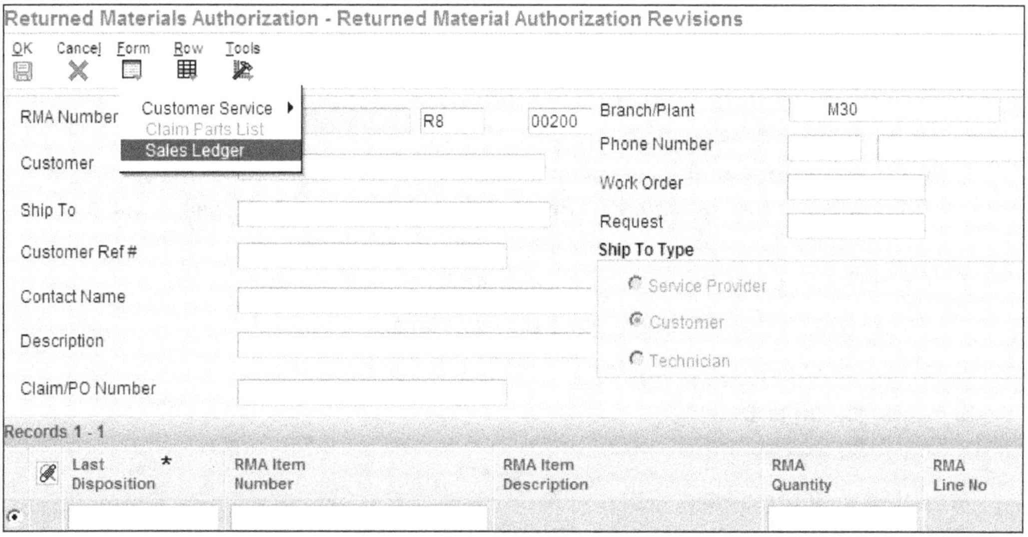

How it works...

When you create an **RMA**, the system creates an authorization number for the supplier to track the return of the inventory. When you create an RMA, a purchase order can be created to receive the products. This will also create a sales order to ship substitute items. Alternatively, instead of shipping a replacement item, a **Credit Order** can be created. You can specify how the system should create **Purchase Orders** and **Sales Orders** by setting up the processing options of **Sales Order** entry (**P4210**) and **Purchase Orders** entry (**P4310**), and specifying those versions in the **Return Material Authorization** Defaults (**P40052**).

See also

- *Running the end of day processing*

Interbranch and intercompany orders

This recipe provides the details of **Interbranch** and **Intercompany** orders in the order management system.

Getting ready

You should set up the **Order Activity Rule** in order to create an **Interbranch** or **Intercompany** sales order.

How to do it...

1. Go to **EnterpriseOne menus Logistics Management | Sales Order Management | Daily Sales Order Management Processing | Sales Order Processing**, and click on **Sales Order**.
2. On the **Sales Order Detail** form, click on **Add**.
3. Enter the **Sold To** party (the **Selling Branch Plant**).
4. Enter the **Ship To** party (**Customer Address Number**).
5. Enter the **Order Date**.
6. Enter the **Customer PO**.
7. Select the **Currency**.
8. Enter the **Quantity Order** information in the grid area.
9. Enter the **UoM**.
10. Enter the **Item Number**.
11. Enter the **Requested Date**.
12. Enter the **Unit Price**; the **Extended Price** will be calculated automatically:

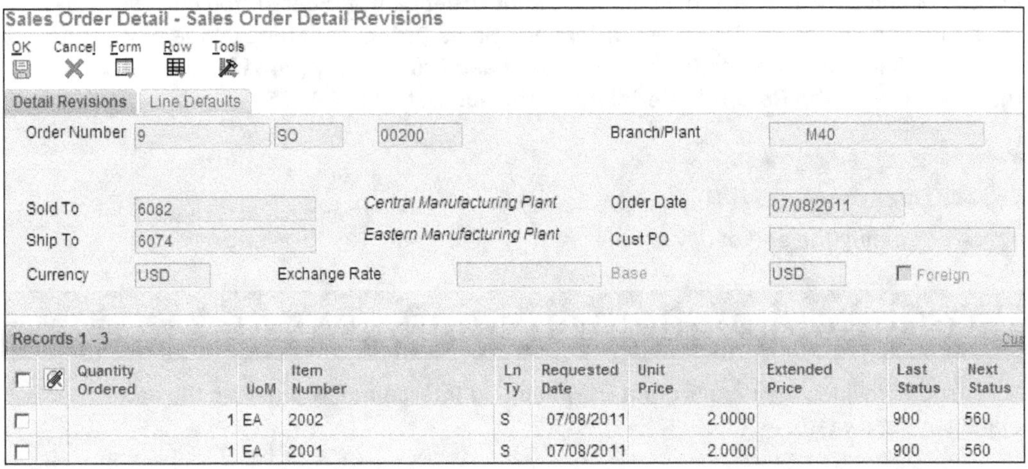

How it works...

When you create **Interbranch** orders, it is based on the document type and line type combination that you set up for **Interbranch** orders. An **Interbranch** order is used to load the orders for customers from inventory at a branch branch/plant that is not directly used for material sales. **Interbranch** orders are useful if the company sells from one location, but the order will load and ship from another location—that is, a central supply store. An **Intercompany** order is used to link the transactions of the selling branch/plant and the supplying branch/plant. Although the interbranch order is the sales order created for the customer, the intercompany order is created for the purchase order to the supplying branch/plant. The only differences between a direct ship order and an intercompany order are that the supplier number which is entered into the PO is that of the supplying warehouse or material-supplying branch/plant, the **Sold to Address** is the selling branch/plant, and the **Ship to Address** is the **Customer Number**.

There's more...

In addition, the **Intercompany** order is created only after running the **Shipment Confirmation**. **Interbranch** orders are processed based on the **Document Type** and line type blend, which you set up for **Interbranch** orders.

See also

- *Journal entry batch review and approval*

Reposting orders

The **Repost Active Sales Order** program is a batch application that is used to resolve the commitment problem that arises during the sales update. This recipe explains the method of reposting sales orders, and also describes how the process **Repost Active Sales Order** works.

Getting ready

You should run the **Customers Sales Update** (**R42800**) program in **Final Mode** in order to run the **Repost Sales Order program**.

How to do it...

1. Select the **Repost Active Sales Order** (**R42995**) from the **End of Day Processing** menu (**G4213**).
2. Select the **XJDE0001** version, and then click on **Select** from the menu bar.

3. Review the **Sales Order** status and **Item Availability** for those items whose quantity was not updated after the **End of Day** processing.

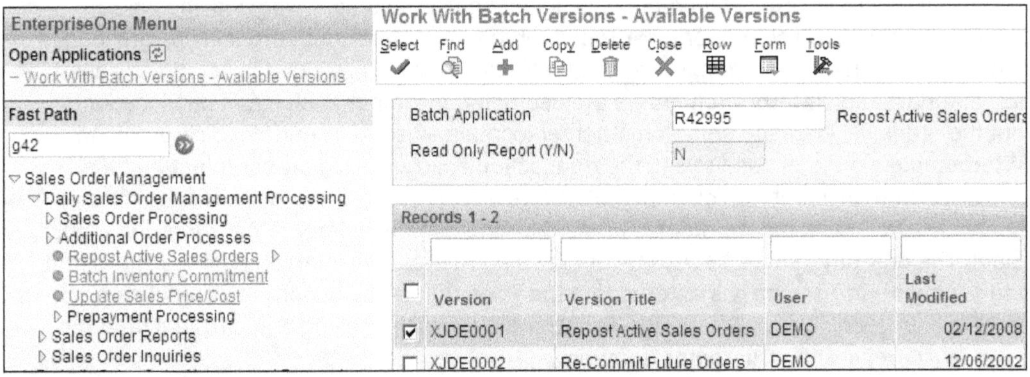

How it works...

The **Repost Active Sales Orders** program (**R42995**) is used to recommit the upcoming sales orders and repost the active **Sales Orders** that not closed during the **Sales Update** process. When you recommit upcoming **Sales Orders**, the system checks the customer's **Credit Limits** for future sales orders, and also verifies the **Hard-Commit** items. The system also compares the **Scheduled Pick Date** in **F4211** table with the current date, and adds this to the number of days—specified in the commitment days—that are set up in the **Branch/Plant Constants** program (**P41001**).

There's more...

When the agreed **Scheduled Pick Date** of the item is equivalent to the **Sales Order** entry date plus the added number of commitment days, the system relieves the **Future-Committed** order. Once the recommit process is completed, the report can be printed with the sales order detailed lines, and will also include future-committed items.

See also

- *Running the end of day processing*

Setting up sales journal

The system generates the **Invoice Journal** when you run the **Update Customer Sales** program. This recipe explains the details of how to set up the **Sales Journal**.

Getting ready

You should run the **Customers Sales Update** (**R42800**) program in **Final Mode** in order to run the **Sales Journal**.

How to do it...

1. Access the **Processing Options** of **Print Sales Journal** (**R42810**) program by entering **BV** on the **Fast Path**.
2. Enter **R42810** and click on **Find**, select the **Row** menu, and then click on the **Processing Option**.
3. On the **Default 1** tab, specify the **Update Status Codes** of sales orders.
4. On the **Default 2** tab, specify the **Override Status Code**—specify whether the system overrides the status code for a sales order.
5. On the **Print** tab, specify the **Currency Printing Mode** processing option in order to control the **Currency Printing Mode** for the report:

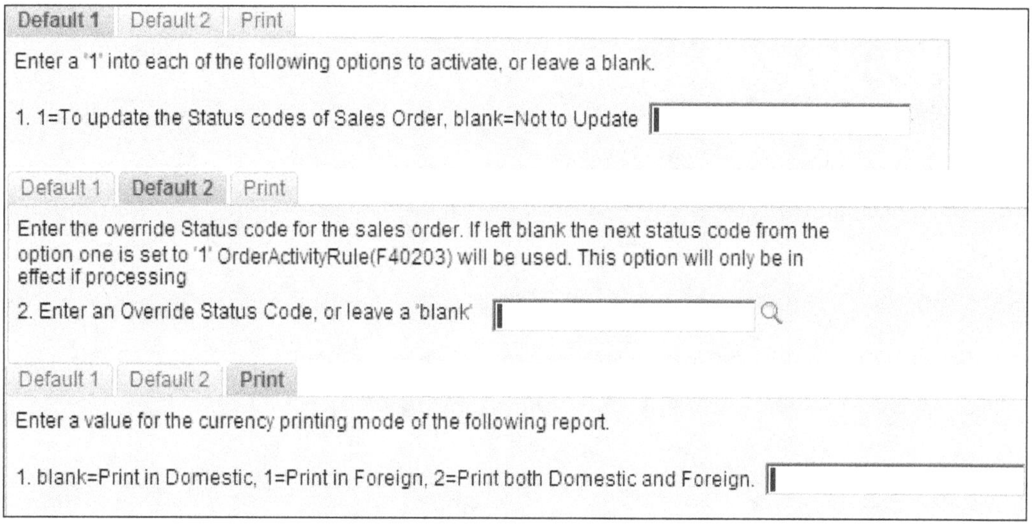

How it works...

When you run the **Customer Sales Update program**, the system generates the **Sales Journal** report automatically; the **Print Sales Journal** report can also be printed separately. When you run the **Sales Journal** report it is processed based on the **Processing Option** and data selection set-up criteria. The **Sales Journal** report is a supportive view used to review the **Sales Revenues** that are distributed. The sales journal contains only summary information; the report includes **Invoice Total Amounts**, **Cost of Sold**, **Profit Amounts**, and **Percentages**.

There's more...

When you set up the **Update Customer Sales** processing option to print the **Sales Journal** report before the sales update, you should not reference the version to **Print Sales Journal** (**R42810**). You should set up the same data selection as you specified for the **Update Customer Sales** (**R42800**) program.

See also

- *Journal entry batch review and approval*

13

SCM Customizations

In this chapter, we will cover:

- Developing the stock analysis report
- Creating the sales invoice report
- Creating the purchase order report
- Reconciliation of the item ledger with the account ledger report

Introduction

In this chapter, you will learn the fundamentals of SCM custom objects along with the technical specifications and code that technical consultants and application programmers will find useful. Technical consultants are expected to know the table structure, business views, and report design aids in order to develop SCM custom objects.

Developing the stock analysis report

The stock analysis custom report is developed in order to control the stock available in the warehouses. The report will show the stock items with their related current on-hand quantity. The current on-hand inventory must be classified according to the receiving date. The report should also show the time period as mentioned in the processing options, and the quantity related to the selected period. The report will show the record and calculate the total quantity according to the commodity.

Getting ready

You should install a fat client in order to use **JD Edwards Object Management Workbench** (**OMW**). Technical consultants should use the correct status for the development of new objects.

How to do it...

You should use the following technical specification in order to develop the stock analysis report. The following tables are used: **F0101**, **F0111**, **F0006**, **F42021**, **F4101**, **F4108**, and **F4102**. The developer should create the business view according to the report requirement:

1. Fetch the field from **F0111.NICK** (**F0111** table and **NICK** field) where **F0111.AN8** = processing option 1, and **F0101.ALPH** where **F0101.AN8** = processing option 1 by using the table design aid.
2. Enter **Stock Aging Analysis** (report title).
3. Print the "As of" and the description of the period will be entered in processing options 2 and 3.
4. Read the **Business Unit** number from processing option 4 and pass it to **F0006.MCU;** print the description from **F0006.DL01**.
5. Pass the **Business Unit** number from processing option 4 to **F4102.MCU** and get all the items that are based on their related **F4102.PRP1** values. Pass **F4102.PRP1** to **F0005.KY** (add seven spaces on the left for fetching the business unit code), where **F0005.SY = 41** and **F0005.RT = P1**.
6. Based on the condition mentioned in step 4, enter the **Business Unit** in processing option 4 to **F4102.MCU** and print **F4102.LITM**.
7. For each item selected in step 6, pass **F41021.LITM** to **F4101.LITM,** and print **F4101.DSC1** and **F4101.DSC2**.
8. For each item selected in step 6, pass **F41021.IMT** to **F4102.IMT** and sum (**F4102.PQOH**) &" "& (pass **F41021.IMT** to **F4101.IMT** and get **F4101.UOM1** then (pass **F4101.UOM1** to **F0005.KY** (add seven spaces on the left) and print the description from **F0005.DL01** where **F0005.SY = 00** and **F0005.RT = UM**)).
9. For each item selected in step 6, pass **F41021.ITM** to **F4105.ITM** and print **F4105.UNCS**, where **F4105.LEDG = 02** and **F4105.MCU** = the business unit selected in step 4.
10. Multiply Field 8 (**Current Quantity**) by Field 9 (**Unit Cost**).
11. To print the report headings, the report should have two sections, Months and Years. Also, store processing option 2 in variable X and execute the following formula:

    In the Month section:

    ```
    While X != 1
    {           Print X
                X-X-1
                Loop
    }           Print X
    ```

For the Years section, store processing option 3 in variable Y and print it in the column:

```
Y-1, Y-2, Y-3, Y-4, Y-5
```

For each item selected in field 6 (**Item Number**), get **F4102.ITM**; pass **F4102.ITM** and **F4102.MCU** to **F41021.ITM** and **F4102.MCU**. For each displayed row, if (*PQOH >0*), pass **F41021.LOTN**, **F41021.ITM**, **F41021.MCU** to **F41021.LOTN**, **F4108.ITM**, **F4108.MCU**, and get **F4108.DLEJ**.

Compare the date in the **DLEJ** field with the combination of processing options 2 and 3. If **DLEJ** year value = processing option 3 value, then show it (**F41021.PQOH**) and ((**F41021.PQOH**) * field 9 (**Unit Price**)) in the Month section in the proper `X` value.

If **DLEJ** year value ! = processing option 3 value, and then show it in the Year section in the proper `Y` value.

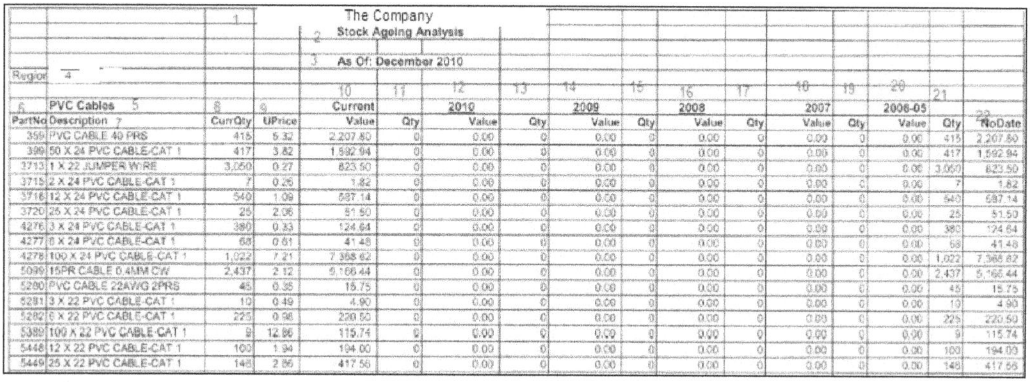

The Company

Stock Ageing Analysis

As Of: December 2010

Region

PVC Cables

PartNo	Description	CurrQty	UPrice	Current Value	Qty	2010 Value	Qty	2009 Value	Qty	2008 Value	Qty	2007 Value	Qty	2006-05 Value	Qty	NoDate
359	PVC CABLE 40 PRS	415	5.32	2,207.80	0	0.00	0	0.00	0	0.00	0	0.00	0	0.00	415	2,207.80
399	50 X 24 PVC CABLE-CAT 1	417	3.82	1,592.94	0	0.00	0	0.00	0	0.00	0	0.00	0	0.00	417	1,592.94
3713	1 X 22 JUMPER WIRE	3,050	0.27	823.50	0	0.00	0	0.00	0	0.00	0	0.00	0	0.00	3,050	823.50
3715	2 X 24 PVC CABLE-CAT 1	7	0.26	1.82	0	0.00	0	0.00	0	0.00	0	0.00	0	0.00	7	1.82
3716	12 X 24 PVC CABLE-CAT 1	540	1.09	587.14	0	0.00	0	0.00	0	0.00	0	0.00	0	0.00	540	587.14
3720	25 X 24 PVC CABLE-CAT 1	25	2.06	51.50	0	0.00	0	0.00	0	0.00	0	0.00	0	0.00	25	51.50
4276	3 X 24 PVC CABLE-CAT 1	380	0.33	124.64	0	0.00	0	0.00	0	0.00	0	0.00	0	0.00	380	124.64
4277	8 X 24 PVC CABLE-CAT 1	68	0.61	41.48	0	0.00	0	0.00	0	0.00	0	0.00	0	0.00	68	41.48
4278	100 X 24 PVC CABLE-CAT 1	1,022	7.21	7,368.62	0	0.00	0	0.00	0	0.00	0	0.00	0	0.00	1,022	7,368.62
5099	15PR CABLE 0.4MM CW	2,437	2.12	5,166.44	0	0.00	0	0.00	0	0.00	0	0.00	0	0.00	2,437	5,166.44
5280	PVC CABLE 22AWG 2PRS	45	0.35	15.75	0	0.00	0	0.00	0	0.00	0	0.00	0	0.00	45	15.75
5281	3 X 22 PVC CABLE-CAT 1	10	0.49	4.90	0	0.00	0	0.00	0	0.00	0	0.00	0	0.00	10	4.90
5282	6 X 22 PVC CABLE-CAT 1	225	0.98	220.50	0	0.00	0	0.00	0	0.00	0	0.00	0	0.00	225	220.50
5389	100 X 22 PVC CABLE-CAT 1	9	12.86	115.74	0	0.00	0	0.00	0	0.00	0	0.00	0	0.00	9	115.74
5448	12 X 22 PVC CABLE-CAT 1	100	1.94	194.00	0	0.00	0	0.00	0	0.00	0	0.00	0	0.00	100	194.00
5449	25 X 22 PVC CABLE-CAT 1	148	2.86	417.56	0	0.00	0	0.00	0	0.00	0	0.00	0	0.00	148	417.56

[**AN8** stores **Address Book Number** and **ALPH** stores the **Address Book Name.**]

How it works...

It is required to do the programming on OMW based on the given specification. The system generates the following code, which can be modified. In the `Initialize Section`, you will initialize the variable and in the `Do Section` you will do the main coding:

```
=====================================================================
    SECTION: STOCK AGING ANALYSIS [GROUP SECTION] ()
=====================================================================
    OBJECT:  SECTION
    EVENT:  Initialize Section
---------------------------------------------------------------------
--
```

```
0001 Set Selection Append Flag( <Yes>)
0002 If PO Company_CO is not equal to <Blank>
0003    Set User Selection(BC Company (F0006) (CO), <Equal To>, PO
Company_CO,  <And>)
0004 Else
0005 End If
0006 If PO CostCenter_MCU is not equal to <Blank>
0007    Set User Selection(BC Business Unit (F0006) (MCU),  <Equal
To>, PO CostCenter_MCU,  <None>)
0008 End If
0009 //
0010 If PO YearOrMonth_FLAG is not equal to "M"
0011    Stop Section Processing
0012 Else
0013 End If
-------------------------------------------------------------------
     EVENT:  Do Section
-------------------------------------------------------------------
     evt_CenturyFiscalYear_CFY
     evt_LotEffectivityDate_DLEJ
     evt_LotCenturyFiscalYear_CFY
     evt_LotPeriodNo_PN
     evt_LedgType_LEDG
     evt_AmountUnitCost_UNCS
0001 //
0002 // §§§      Fetching Lot date, F4108
0003 F4108.Fetch Single
        BC Lot/Serial Number (F41021) =  TK Lot/Serial Number
        BC Business Unit (F0006) =  TK Business Unit
        BC Item Number - Short (F4102) =  TK Item Number - Short
        VA evt_LotEffectivityDate_DLEJ <- TK Lot Effectivity Date
0004 // §§§-     Fetching Lot date, F4108
0005 //
0006 //       Unit Cost, F4105
0007 VA evt_LedgType_LEDG = "02"
0008 F4105.Fetch Single
        BC Item Number - Short (F4102) =  TK Item Number - Short
        BC Business Unit (F0006) =  TK Business Unit
        VA evt_LedgType_LEDG =  TK Cost Method
        VA evt_AmountUnitCost_UNCS <- TK Amount - Unit Cost
0011 //      Current Value
0012 RV CurrValue_MATH01 = BC Quantity on Hand - Primary units
(F41021)*VA evt_AmountUnitCost_UNCS
0013 //
```

```
VA evt_CenturyFiscalYear_CFY = concat(PO Century_CTRY,PO FiscalYear_FY)
VA evt_LotCenturyFiscalYear_CFY = date_year(VA evt_LotEffectivityDate_DLEJ)
VA evt_LotPeriodNo_PN = date_month(VA evt_LotEffectivityDate_DLEJ)
//
// §§§      January seperating QTY and VALUE
If VA evt_LotPeriodNo_PN is equal to "1" And VA evt_LotPeriodNo_PN is less than or equal to PO PeriodNo_PN And VA evt_CenturyFiscalYear_CFY is equal to VA evt_LotCenturyFiscalYear_CFY
    RV Month01Qty_PQOH = BC Quantity on Hand - Primary units (F41021)
    RV Month01Value_MATH01 = VA evt_AmountUnitCost_UNCS*BC Quantity on Hand - Primary units (F41021)
Else
End If
// §§§-    January seperating QTY and VALUE
//
// §§§     Febuary seperating QTY and VALUE
If VA evt_LotPeriodNo_PN is equal to "2" And VA evt_LotPeriodNo_PN is less than or equal to PO PeriodNo_PN And VA evt_CenturyFiscalYear_CFY is equal to VA evt_LotCenturyFiscalYear_CFY
    RV Month02Qty_PQOH = BC Quantity on Hand - Primary units (F41021)
    RV Month02Value_MATH01 = VA evt_AmountUnitCost_UNCS*BC Quantity on Hand - Primary units (F41021)
Else
End If
// §§§-    Febuary seperating QTY and VALUE
//
// §§§     March seperating QTY and VALUE
If VA evt_LotPeriodNo_PN is equal to "3" And VA evt_LotPeriodNo_PN is less than or equal to PO PeriodNo_PN And VA evt_CenturyFiscalYear_CFY is equal to VA evt_LotCenturyFiscalYear_CFY
    RV Month03Qty_PQOH = BC Quantity on Hand - Primary units (F41021)
    RV Month03Value_MATH01 = VA evt_AmountUnitCost_UNCS*BC Quantity on Hand - Primary units (F41021)
Else
End If
```

> This code is not complete as it covers only the main areas where you initialize the variable and where you must do the main coding under the `Do Section`.

There's more...

The following processing options need to be defined:

- **Company Address Book Number** (**AN8**)
- **Period number** (**PN**), if left blank, then current month
- **Year Number** (**FY**), if left blank, then current year
- **Business Unit**, if left blank, then all

See also

- *Reconciliation of the item ledger with the account ledger report*

Creating the sales invoice report

The company requires the sales invoice report to be customized in order to control the printing of sales invoices. This section contains two parts; one is the technical specification, and the other one is the report development coding.

Getting ready

You should install a fat client in order to use JD Edwards OMW object library workbench.

How to do it...

The following are the specification details. The specification details are linked with the screenshot of the customized report, which has been marked with the field number, and each of the steps in the text is identified in the screenshot. The sales analysis report's detailed technical information is as shown next:

Tables used are: **F4201**, **F4211**, **F0101**, and **F0111**. You can also create your custom business view from these tables as per the requirement:

1. Insert the Company logo and name in the page header.
2. **Sales Invoice** should appear on the report header after the company name and logo.

3. For the selected **Order Number** and **Order Type**, put the data selection **F4201.DOCO** and **F4201.DCTO**, and print **F4201.DOCO** and **F4201.DCTO**.
4. For the selected **Order Number** and **Order Type**, put the data selection **F4201.DOCO** and **F4201.DCTO**, print **F4201.DOCO** and **F4201.DCTO**.
5. For the selected **Order Number** and **Order Type**, put the data selection **F4201.DOCO** and **F4201.DCTO**, pass **F4201.DOCO** and **F4201.DCTO** to **F4211.DOCO** and **F0201.DCTO**, and print **F4211.IVD** where **F4211.SOQS > 0** for the selected **F4211.DOCO** lines (**F4211.LNID**).
6. For the selected **Order Number** and **Order Type**, put the data selection **F4201.DOCO** and **F4201.DCTO**, pass **F4201.AN8** to **F0101.AN8** and print **F0101.ALPH.**
7. For the selected **Order Number** and **Order Type**, put the data selection **F4201.DOCO** and **F4201.DCTO**, print **F4201.AN8**.
8. For the selected **Order Number** and **Order Type**, put the data selection **F4201.DOCO** and **F4201.DCTO**, pass **F4201.DOCO** and **F4201.DCTO** to **F4211.DOCO** and **Fr201.DCTO**, and print **F4211.IVD** where **F4211.SOQS > 0** for the selected **F4211.DOCO** lines (**F4211.LNID**). For the selected **Order Number** and type in the data selection **F4201.DOCO** and **F4201.DCTO**, pass **F4201.AN8** to **F0111.AN8**, and print **F0111.NICK**.
9. ***.
10. For the selected **Order Number** and **Order Type**, put the data selection **F4201.DOCO** and **F4201.DCTO**, and print **F4201.AN8**.
11. For the selected **Order Number** and **Order Type**, put the data selection **F4201.DOCO** and **F4201.DCTO**, and pass **F4201.DOCO** and **F4201.DCTO** to **F4211.DOCO** and **F4211.DCTO**, and print **F4211.AITM** where **F4211.SOQS > 0**.
12. For the selected **Order Number** and **Order Type**, put the data selection **F4201.DOCO** and **F4201.DCTO**, and for the printed item in field 14 (**Item Number**) pass **F4211.LITM** to **F4107.LITM**, and print **F4107.SDSC1**.
13. For the selected **Order Number** and **Order Type**, put the data selection **F4201.DOCO** and **F4201.DCTO**, and for the printed item in field 14 (**Item Number**) print **F4211.SOQS**.
14. For the selected **Order Number** and **Order Type**, put the data selection **F4201.DOCO** and **F4201.DCTO**, and for the printed item in field 14 (**Item Number**) print **F4211.UPRC**.
15. For the selected **Order Number** and **Order Type**, put the data selection **F4201.DOCO** and **F4201.DCTO**, and for the printed item in field 14 (**Item Number**) print **F4211.AEXP**.
16. For the selected **Order Number** and **Order Type**, **print F4211.DSC2**.
17. For the selected **Order Number** and **Order Type**, put the data selection **F4201.DOCO** and **F4201.DCTO**, print **F4211.DSC1** & **AEXP** where **F4211.LNTY = S1**.

18. For the selected **Order Number** and **Order Type**, **print F4211.AEXP**.
19. For the selected **Order Number** and **Order Type**, **print F4211.UPRC.**

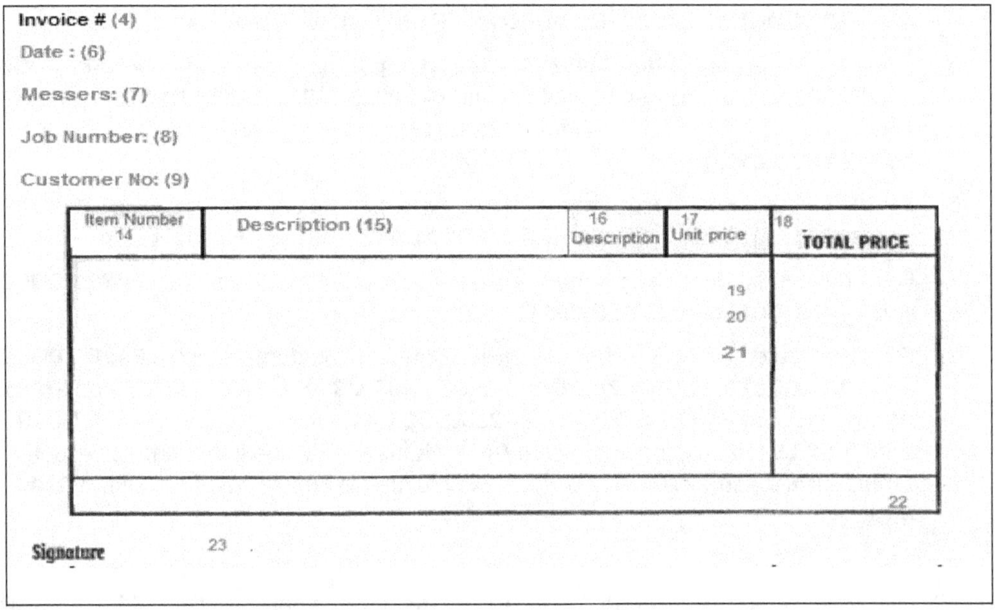

How it works...

The coding of this report is based on the given specifications; the system generates the following code on OMW. In the `Initialize Section`, you will initialize the variable, and in the `Do Section`, you will do the main coding:

```
======================================================================
     SECTION: Join Between F4201 & F4211 [GROUP SECTION] (S1)
======================================================================
     OBJECT:  SECTION
     EVENT:  Do Section
----------------------------------------------------------------------
     evt_PriceAdjustmentType_AST
     evt_UserDefinedCodes_RT
     evt_ProductCode_SY
     evt_AmtPricePerUnit2_UPRC
     evt_FactorValue_FVTR
     evt_AdjustmentReasonCode_ARSN
0001 If PO PrintAttachment_FLAG is equal to "Y"
```

```
0002    Media Objects(GT4211A,  <Get Text>, RV LineAttachment_DL01,
BC Document (Order No, Invoice, etc.) (F4201) (DOCO), BC Order Type
(F4201) (DCTO), BC Order Company (Order Number) (F4201) (KCOO), ...)
0003 Else
0004 End If
0005 //
0006 VA evt_PriceAdjustmentType_AST = "GEN"
0007 VA evt_ProductCode_SY = "40"
0008 VA evt_UserDefinedCodes_RT = "AR"
0009 ! F4074.Fetch Single
     !    BC Document (Order No, Invoice, etc.) (F4201) =  TK Document
(Order No, Invoice, etc.)
     !    BC Order Type (F4201) =  TK Order Type
     !    BC Order Company (Order Number) (F4201) =  TK Order Company
(Order Number)
     !    BC Line Number (F4211) =  TK Line Number
     !    VA evt_FactorValue_FVTR <- TK Factor Value
     !    VA evt_AmtPricePerUnit2_UPRC <- TK Amount - Price per Unit
     !    VA evt_AdjustmentReasonCode_ARSN <- TK Adjustment Reason
Code
0010 RV FactorValue_FVTR = VA evt_FactorValue_FVTR*-1
0011 RV UnitPrice_UPRC = VA evt_AmtPricePerUnit2_UPRC
0012 Get UDC Description (Obsolete)
        VA evt_ProductCode_SY -> BF szSystemCode
        VA evt_UserDefinedCodes_RT -> BF szUserDefinedCodes
        VA evt_AdjustmentReasonCode_ARSN -> BF szUserDefinedCode
        RV F0005Description_DL01 <- BF szDescription01
0013 RV SubTotalAmount_AA = BC Amount - Extended Price (F4211)+RV
UnitPrice_UPRC
0014 //
0015 If PO Language_FLAG is equal to "A"
0016    F4107.Fetch Single
           BC Item Number - Short (F4211) =  TK Item Number - Short
           RV ItemDesc_DL01 <- TK Short Description
0017 Else
0018    RV ItemDesc_DL01 = concat(BC Description (F4211),BC
Description - Line 2 (F4211))
0019 End If
```

There's more...

The following are the required processing options, which need to be incorporated:

- **Sales** or **Receivables**
- **Language**
- **Print Attachment**

See also

- *Creating the purchase order report*

Creating the purchase order report

The purchase order report should be developed in order to integrate system modules and minimize the data duplication and data entry. It will also control the electronic approval process.

Getting ready

You should install the fat client in order to use JD Edwards object library workbench.

How to do it...

This section provides the specification details of the purchase order report. The specification details are linked with the screenshot of the customized report, which has been marked with the step number from the text:

1. Insert company logo and for the selected document number **F4301.DOCO** and document type **F4301.DCTO** and put into data selection, pass the supplier number **F4301.AN8** and pass it to **F0101.AN8** and print **F0101.ALPH** supplier name.
2. Fetch the PO number **F4301.DOCO** and type **F4301.DCTO** in the data selection, pass **F4301.AN8** to **F0101.AN8** and get **F0101.ADD1** and **ADD2** and **CTY1** and **ADDZ**.
3. Pass **F0101.CTR** (add seven spaces on the left side), and print **F0005.DL01** where **F0005.SY = 00** and **F0005.RT = CY**.
4. For the selected PO number and Type **F4301.DOCO** and **F4301.DCTO** in the data selection pass **F4301.AN8** to **F0115.AN8** and print: Concatenate ((**F0115.PHTP** & : & **F0115.PH1**) where **F0115.RCK7** = 1 and **F0115.PHTP** = TEL) and ((**F0115.PHTP** & : & **F0115.PH1**) where **F0115.RCK7** = 1 and **F0115.PHTP** = FAX).

5. For the selected PO number and type **F4301.DOCO** and **F4301.DCTO** in the data selection pass **F4301.AN8** to **F0111.AN8**, and print **F0111.MLNM** where **F0111. IDLN = 1**.
6. Print the **Order Number** and order type selected in data selection **F4301.DOCO** and **F4301.DCTO**.
7. For the selected PO number and PO type **F4301.DOCO** and **F4301.DCTO** in the data selection, print **F4301.OORN** and **F4301.OCTO**.
8. For the selected PO number and PO type **F4301.DOCO** and **F4301.DCTO** in the data selection, print **F4311.SBL**.
9. For the selected PO number and PO type **F4301.DOCO** and **F4301.DCTO** in the data selection, print **F4301.TRDJ**.
10. For the selected PO number and PO type **F4301.DOCO** and **F4301.DCTO** in the data selection, pass **F4301.OORN** & **F4301.OCTO** to **F4301.DOCO** & **F4301.DCTO**, and print **F4301.TRDJ**.
11. ***.
12. Print: "Print Purchase Order".
13. ***.
14. The system will prompt us to enter a value for processing option 3 when this report will run.
15. The system will prompt us to enter a value for processing option 4 when this report will run.
16. The system will prompt us to enter a value for processing option 5 when this report will run.
17. The system will prompt us to enter a value for processing option 6 when this report will run.
18. The system will prompt us to enter a value for processing option 7 when this report will run.
19. The system will prompt us to enter a value for processing option 8 when this report will run.
20. Print **F0111.NICK** where **F0111.AN8** = processing option 1.
21. **F0101.ALPH** where **F0101.AN8** = processing option 2.
22. Print **F0101.ADD1** and **ADD2** and **CTY1** and **ADDZ** where **F0101.AN8** = processing option 3 and **F0101.AN8** = processing option 2. Pass **F0101.CTR** to **F0005.KY** (add seven spaces on the left side) and print **F0005.DL01** where **F0005.SY = 00** and **F0005.RT = CY**.
23. ***.

24. Fetch **F0115.AN8** = processing option 4.

    Concatenate ((**F0115.PHTP** & : & **F0115.PH1**) where **F0115.RCK7 = 1** and **F0115.PHTP = TEL**) and (**F0115.PHTP** & : & **F0115.PH1**) where **F0115.RCK7 = 1** and **F0115.PHTP = FAX**).

25. For the selected PO number and type **F4301.DOCO** and **F4301.DCTO** in the data selection, and print **F4301.DEL1&DEL2**.

26. Print **F0111.NICK** where **F0111.AN8** equals to **F4301.AN8**.

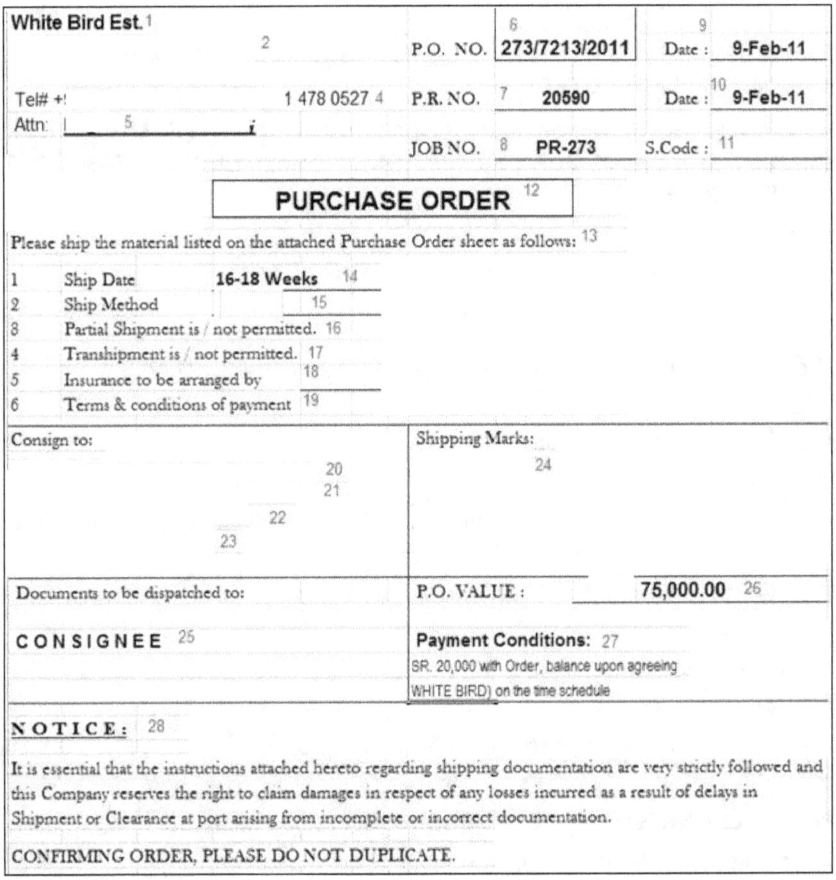

White Bird Est. 1

2

P.O. NO. 6 273/7213/2011 Date : 9 9-Feb-11

Tel# +! 1 478 0527 4 P.R. NO. 7 20590 Date : 10 9-Feb-11

Attn: 5

JOB NO. 8 PR-273 S.Code : 11

PURCHASE ORDER 12

Please ship the material listed on the attached Purchase Order sheet as follows: 13

1 Ship Date 16-18 Weeks 14
2 Ship Method 15
3 Partial Shipment is / not permitted. 16
4 Transhipment is / not permitted. 17
5 Insurance to be arranged by 18
6 Terms & conditions of payment 19

Consign to: 20 21 22 23

Shipping Marks: 24

Documents to be dispatched to:

CONSIGNEE 25

P.O. VALUE : 75,000.00 26

Payment Conditions: 27
SR. 20,000 with Order, balance upon agreeing
WHITE BIRD) on the time schedule

NOTICE: 28

It is essential that the instructions attached hereto regarding shipping documentation are very strictly followed and this Company reserves the right to claim damages in respect of any losses incurred as a result of delays in Shipment or Clearance at port arising from incomplete or incorrect documentation.

CONFIRMING ORDER, PLEASE DO NOT DUPLICATE.

How it works...

The development of this report is based on the preceding specification, the system generates the following code, which can be modified. In the `Initialize Section`, you will initialize the variable, and the main report coding will be written in the `Do Section`:

```
*********************************************************************
```

```
    GLOBALS: Global Variables
**********************************************************************
rpt_SuppressPrinting,  rpt_ChangeOrderNumber, rpt_
SelectChangeOrderFlag,      rpt_InventoryInterface,   rpt_
TextYN,  rpt_ErrorMessage,   rpt_PreviousLineType,     rpt_
QuantityInPrimaryUnits,
// ***********************************************************
//                                        Revision Log
// ***********************************************************
// 12/16/2004 - IC8872866 -7439649 - Ship to address incorrect on
P
// 05/20/2005 - IC8823626 -7664281 - Fix Media Object Corruption
// ***********************************************************
// SAR 7133527 Begin: Added Code For PO Dispatch of Ordes
Generated from eReqs
// ***********************************************************
//
If RI cPOGenSourceSystem_POGS is equal to "2"
   F4333WF.Select
      RI mnUniqueKeyIDInternal_UKID = TK Unique Key ID (Internal)
   While SV File_IO_Status is equal to CO SUCCESS
      F4333WF.Fetch Next
         VA evt_mnDispatchOrderNumber_DOCO <- TK Document (Order
No, Invoice, etc.)
         VA evt_szDispatchOrderType_DCTO <- TK Order Type
         VA evt_szDispatchOrderCo_KCOO <- TK Order Company (Order
Number)
         VA evt_szDispatchOrderSuffix_SFXO <- TK Order Suffix
      If SV File_IO_Status is equal to CO SUCCESS
         Set User Selection(BC Document (Order No, Invoice, etc.)
(F4311) (DOCO), <Equal To>, VA evt_mnDispatchOrderNumber_DOCO,  <Or>)
         Set User Selection(BC Order Type (F4311) (DCTO), <Equal
To>, VA evt_szDispatchOrderType_DCTO, <And>)
         Set User Selection(BC Order Company (Order Number)
(F4311) (KCOO), <Equal To>, VA evt_szDispatchOrderCo_KCOO, <And>)
         Set User Selection(BC Status Code - Last (F4311) (LTTR),
<Not Equal To>, "980", <And>)
         If VA evt_szDispatchOrderSuffix_SFXO is not equal to
<Blank> And VA evt_szDispatchOrderSuffix_SFXO is not equal to <Null>
            Set User Selection(BC Order Suffix (F4311) (SFXO),
<Equal To>, VA evt_szDispatchOrderSuffix_SFXO, <And>)
         End If
         VA evt_cUserSelectionSuccess_EV01 = "1"
      End If
   End While
   If VA evt_cUserSelectionSuccess_EV01 is not equal to "1"
```

```
        Set User Selection(BC Document (Order No, Invoice, etc.) (F4311) (DOCO), <Equal To>,  <Zero>, <And>)
        Set User Selection(BC Order Type (F4311) (DCTO), <Equal To>,  <Blank>, <And>)
        Set User Selection(BC Order Company (Order Number) (F4311) (KCOO), <Equal To>,  <Blank>, <And>)
    Else
        // Delete Records from F4332WF if User Selection Successful
        F4333WF.Select All
           UNDEFINED = UNDEFINED
        F4333WF.Delete
           RI mnUniqueKeyIDInternal_UKID =  TK Unique Key ID (Internal)
    End If
Else
    // SAR 7133527 End
    If RI Documentorderinvoice is not equal to <Null>  And RI Documentorderinvoice is not equal to <Blank>  And RI Documentorderinvoice is not equal to <Zero>
        Set User Selection(BC Document (Order No, Invoice, etc.) (F4,  <Equal To>, RI Documentorderinvoice,  <And>)
        Set User Selection(BC Order Type (F4311),  <Equal To>, RI Ordertype,  <And>)
        Set User Selection(BC KCOO (Order Company (Order Number)) (F4311), <Equal To>, RI Companykeyorderno, <And>)
        //
        // Do not display lines that were cancelled in entry-Status 980
        // SAR 6414845 begin
!         Set User Selection(BC Status Code - Last (F4311) (LTTR), <Less Than>, "980", <And>)
        Set User Selection(BC LTTR (Status Code - Last) (F4311), <Not Equal To>, "980", <And>)
        // SAR 6414845 end
        //
        If RI Ordersuffix is not equal to <Blank>  And RI Ordersuffix is not equal to <Null>
           Set User Selection(BC Order Suffix (F4311),  <Equal To>, RI Ordersuffix,  <And>)
        End If
    End If
End If
//
```

```
// ***********************************************************
// Get fields for EDI to insert into tables
// ***********************************************************
//
VA rpt_PreviousLineType = " "
VA rpt_EDER_SendReceiveIndicator = "S"
VA rpt_EDSQ_DetailRecordSequence = "01"
VA rpt_EDTY_DetailRecordType = "D"
VA rpt_EDSQ_DetailSequence2 = "02"
VA rpt_EDLN_EDILineNumber = "1"
//
If PO szEDISelectionvalue2 is not equal to <Blank>
   EDI Batch Number, Get Next Number
      VA rpt_EDBT_EDIBatchNumber <> BF szEdiBatchNumber
End If
// ***********************************************************
// Initialize Variables
// ***********************************************************
//
VA rpt_STA1_TaxAuthAmount1Total = "0"
VA rpt_STA2_TaxAuthAmount2Total = "0"
VA rpt_STA3_TaxAuthAmount3Total = "0"
VA rpt_STA3_TaxAuthAmount3Total = "0"
// ***********************************************************
// Get Audit Information to use to update tables
// ***********************************************************
//
Get Audit Information
   VA rpt_UserId <- BF szUserName
   VA rpt_Date <- BF jdDate
   VA rpt_Time <- BF mnTime
   VA rpt_WorkStationId <- BF szWorkstation_UserId
VA rpt_ProgramId = "ER43500"
//
If SL CountryCode is not equal to <Blank> And SL CountryCode is
not equal to <Null>
   R43500 - Plug And Play
      SL CountryCode -> BF szCountry
      "R43500" -> BF szProgramId
      "POPRN" -> BF szFormId
      "INI" -> BF szFormAction
```

```
          PO PrintFromSecondUBE <> BF szSecondUBEStd
          VA rpt_szSecondUBELoc_VL11 <> BF szSecondUBELoc
0110 End If
0111 //
0112 // SAR 7182994 Begin - Delete any junk workfiles
0113 If PO PrintFromSecondUBE is equal to "1"
0114    F43UI50D.Delete
          VA rpt_WorkStationId =  TK Work Station ID
          VA rpt_UserId =  TK Computer ID
0115    F43UI50H.Delete
          VA rpt_WorkStationId =  TK Work Station ID
          VA rpt_UserId =  TK Computer ID
0116    F40UI00T.Delete
          VA rpt_WorkStationId =  TK Work Station ID
          VA rpt_UserId =  TK Computer ID
0117 End If
0118 // SAR 7182994 End
0119 //
0120 // Get the purchasing Advanced Pricing flag
0121 ! Get Tag File
     !    "43" -> BF szSystemCode
     !    VA rpt_ADVP_AdvPriceFlag <- BF cSystemConstantsCode11
0122 // SAR 5214294 - Retrieve AdvPri Flag and UOM Conv by Branch Flag
0123 F4009 Get Distribution Constants
        VA rpt_cUOMByBranch <- BF cUoMConversionByBranch
        VA rpt_ADVP_AdvPriceFlag <- BF cAdvancedProcurementPricing
0124 //
0125 //
---------------------------------------------------------------------
     EVENT:  Do Section
---------------------------------------------------------------------
     evt_ForeignDescription_DSC1
     evt_ForeignDescription2_DSC2
     evt_szEDIDescription_DSC1
     evt_szEDIDescription2_DSC2
     evt_GeoCodeValid
     evt_F4311Updated_EV01
     evt_CUS_LineDescription_DL01
     evt_CUS_ItemDesc_MSGTEXT
0001 VA rpt_SuppressPrinting = " "
0002 VA rpt_SelectChangeOrderFlag = "0"
0003 VA rpt_cColumnarFooter_EV01 = " "
```

```
VA rpt_FormQuotSupp_EV01 = " "
VA rpt_CustSuppItemDes_DSC1 = " "
//
// BEGIN SAR 6101689
// SAR 7389629
! VA rpt_XPIMulOrderCounter_MATH01 = VA rpt_XPIMulOrderCounter_
MATH01+1
// END SAR 6101689
//
// SAR 6357546 BEGIN
VA rpt_EditItemMaster_YN = ""
// SAR 6357546 END
//
// SAR 6705837
VA rpt_AmountForeignExtPrice_FEA = 0
//
// SAR 3084166
If BC Purchasing Taxable (Y/N) (F4311) is equal to "Y"
   VA rpt_cTaxTestFlag_FLAG = "0"
End If
```

The coding that you are doing is called ER (Event Rule) in Oracle JDE.

There's more...

You should set up the following processing option details in order to set up the fetch criteria:

- **Company Address Book Number** (**AN8**)
- **Ship to Address Book Number** (**AN8**)
- **Ship Date**
- **Ship Method**
- **Partial Shipment**
- **Transshipment**
- **Insurance to be arranged by**
- **Terms and condition of payment**

See also

- *Creating the sales invoice report*

Reconciliation of the item ledger with the account ledger report

The account ledger report must be processed to any item ledger and account ledger discrepancies, based on the invoice number and the invoice document type.

Getting ready

You should install the fat client in order to use JD Edwards object library workbench.

How to do it...

The following steps are the detailed technical specifications that you need to follow in order to develop the item ledger and account ledger reconciliation report. Tables used are **F4111** and **F0901**:

1. **Business Unit**: Fetch from **F4111.MCU**.
2. **Doc Type**: Fetch from **F4111.DCT**.
3. **Document Number**: Fetch from **F4111.DOC**.
4. **GL Date**: Fetch **F4111.DGL**.
5. **Extended Cost**: Fetch from **F4111.PAID**.
6. **Document Number**: Fetch from **F0901.DOC**.
7. **Doc Type**: Fetch from **F0901.DCT**.
8. **Account Number**: **F0901.ANI**.
9. **Amount**: **F0901.AA**.

F4111					F0911			
Business Unit	Doc Type	Document Number	GL Date	Extended Cost	Doc #	Doc Type	Account Number	Amount

How it works...

The development of this report is based on the preceding specification. In the `Initialize Section` of the following code, you will initialize the variable, and in the `Do Section` you will do the main report coding:

```
Listing of ER for Report: Report: Sales Update Discrepancy between
Sales / Cardix / AR / GL (R574211I)
**********************************************************************
     GLOBALS: Variables (Global)
**********************************************************************
     rpt_CompanyKey_F0911_KCO
     rpt_DocumentType_F0911_DCT
     rpt_InvoiceNumber_F0911_DOC
     rpt_RevenueAmount_F0911_AA
     rpt_COGSAmount_F0911_AA
     rpt_InventoryAmount_F0911_AA
     rpt_SalesAmount_F4211_AEXP
======================================================================
     SECTION: Sales Order Detail - Integrity [GROUP SECTION] ()
======================================================================
     OBJECT:  SECTION
     EVENT:  Initialize Section
----------------------------------------------------------------------
     OPT: Using Defaults
0001 VA rpt_ErrorMsg01_DL010 = "ERROR: Integrated Module!"

----------------------------------------------------------------------
     EVENT:  Do Section
----------------------------------------------------------------------
     OPT: Using Defaults
0001 VA rpt_CompanyKey_F4111_KCO = BC Document Company (F4211)(KCO)
0002 VA rpt_InvoiceNumber_F4111_DOC = BC Document (Voucher, Invoice,
etc.) (F4211)(DOC)
0003 VA rpt_DocumentType_F4111_DCT = BC Document Type (F4211)(DCT)
0004 VA rpt_CostCenter_F4111_MCU = BC Business Unit (F4211)(MCU)
0005 VA rpt_ItemNumber_F4111_LITM = BC 2nd Item Number (F4211)(LITM)
0006 VA rpt_LineNumber_F4111_LNID = BC Line Number (F4211)(LNID)
0007 //
0008 // CARDIX, F4111
```

```
0022 RV COGS_F0911_FLAG = VA rpt_COGS_F0911_FLAG
0023 RV Inventory_F0911_FLAG = VA rpt_Inventory_F0911_FLAG
0024 RV Receivable_F03B11_FLAG = VA rpt_Receivable_F03B11_FLAG
0025 //
0026 // ☒☒☒ SO, SG, CO Documents types
0027 If BC Order Type (F4211)(DCTO) is not equal to PO OrderType1_DCTO
Or BC Order Type (F4211)(DCTO) is not equal to PO OrderType2_DCTO
Or BC Order Type (F4211)(DCTO) is not equal to PO OrderType3_DCTO Or
BC Order Type (F4211)(DCTO) is not equal to PO OrderType4_DCTO Or
BC Order Type (F4211)(DCTO) is not equal to PO OrderType5_DCTO Or BC
Order Type (F4211)(DCTO) is not equal to PO OrderType6_DCTO Or BC
Order Type (F4211)(DCTO) is not equal to PO OrderType7_DCTO Or BC
Order Type (F4211)(DCTO) is not equal to PO OrderType8_DCTO Or BC
Order Type (F4211)(DCTO) is not equal to PO OrderType9_DCTO Or BC
Order Type (F4211)(DCTO) is not equal to PO OrderType10_DCTO Or BC
Order Type (F4211)(DCTO) is not equal to PO LeaseOrderType1_DCTO Or BC
Order Type (F4211)(DCTO) is not equal to PO LeaseOrderType2_DCTO Or BC
Order Type (F4211)(DCTO) is not equal to PO LeaseOrderType3_DCTO Or BC
Order Type (F4211)(DCTO) is not equal to PO LeaseOrderType4_DCTO Or BC
Order Type (F4211)(DCTO) is not equal to PO LeaseOrderType5_DCTO
0028    If BC Line Type (F4211)(LNTY) is equal to "N"
0029       If RV Cardix_F4111_FLAG is equal to "N" And RV Receivable_
F03B11_FLAG is equal to "Y" And RV Revenue_F0911_FLAG is equal to "Y"
And RV COGS_F0911_FLAG is equal to "N" And RV Inventory_F0911_FLAG is
equal to "N"
======================================================================
     SECTION: Sales Order Detail - Integrity [GROUP SECTION] ()
======================================================================
     OBJECT:  SECTION
     EVENT:  Do Section
----------------------------------------------------------------------
     OPT: Using Defaults
0001 RV ErrorMsg_Sales_620_DL010 = "Error: Open sales orders!"
0002 RV Cardix_F4111_FLAG = "N"
0003 RV COGS_F0911_FLAG = "N"
0004 RV Inventory_F0911_FLAG = "N"
0005 RV Receivable_F03B11_FLAG = "N"
0006 RV Revenue_F0911_FLAG = "N"
======================================================================
     SECTION: Sales Order Detail - Integrity [GROUP SECTION] ()
======================================================================
```

```
     OBJECT:  SECTION
     EVENT:  Do Section
---------------------------------------------------------------------
     OPT: Using Defaults
RV ErrorMsg_Sales_620_DL010 = "Error: Open sales orders!"
RV Cardix_F4111_FLAG = "N"
RV COGS_F0911_FLAG = "N"
RV Inventory_F0911_FLAG = "N"
RV Receivable_F03B11_FLAG = "N"
RV Revenue_F0911_FLAG = "N"
```

See also

- *Developing the stock analysis report*

The Supply Chain Business Process

This appendix covers:

- Supply Chain Management—As-Is process
- Supply Chain Management—To-Be process
- Inventory Management—To-Be process
- Procurement Management—To-Be process
- Sales Order Management—To-Be process
- Supply chain standard reports

Introduction

This appendix explains a Supply Chain Management business process' live case study. The business process document comprise the As-Is and To-Be business processes, which are based on JD Edwards EnterpriseOne supply chain management application solutions. The As-Is process gives you the current business process of a client and the To-be business process comprise the future business processes and what solutions and features will be implemented for that client.

Supply Chain Management—As-Is process

A company's business process starts from the customer order, which could be the sales of a product or the manufacturing of a product based on a customer's request. In the case of the sale of a product, they create a sales order for the customer and issue the items from their stock, which results in accounting entries for this transaction in the system, and the update of the on-hand stock. For sales, which are based on a customer request, the company calculates the item cost plus the price to create the customer order and receive a partial payment from the customer. In the manufacturing business, some companies manufacture the material based on the customer request–for example, in the furniture business, the company also manufactures the material based on customer request. After that, a new item code is initiated for the ordered item and then a purchase order is created and sent to the supplier for material delivery. The company purchases the material from foreign suppliers as well as local suppliers. The supplier payment is made through Telex Transfer (TT) or Letter of Credit (LC). After they receive the material, they issue to Work in Process (WIP) to start manufacturing. Company manufacturing is based on discrete manufacturing; there is no process manufacturing in their current business process. After they finish the manufactured product, they transfer the finished product to the warehouses. Then, the warehouse creates a Good Transfer Note (GTN) and they deliver the finished goods to the showroom has received the customer request for this product. After this, the showroom creates a Good Issue Note (GIN) for the customer, which results in accounting entries in the system.

Customer order

When the customer requests a product that needs some modifications, the company creates a sales invoice and receives partial or full payment from the customer. Then a new item code is created with a calculated cost for the new item. In order to finish the product for the customer, the company creates a purchase order to the supplier for the required materials. After paying the supplier either through LC or TT, they issue the material to the WIP to begin manufacturing the product. When the finished product is ready, they send it to the showroom and issue the item through GIN to the customer.

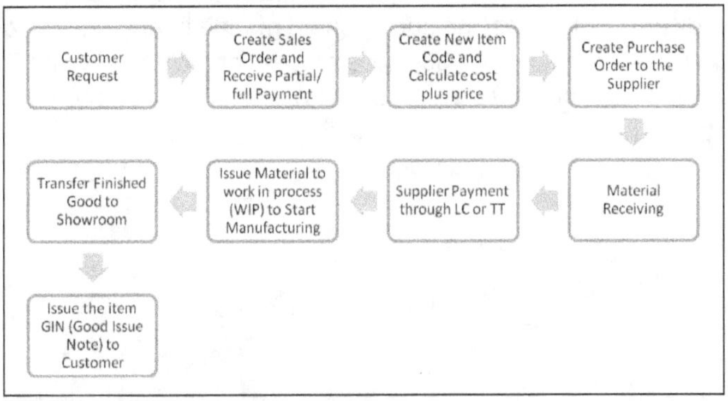

Sales order process

The sales order process begins with a customer's request for an item. Then the company creates a sales order and receives partial or full payment. Then they create **Local Good Order** (**LGO**) and send it to the warehouse that receives and sends the items and issues the GIN. The showroom receives the items and creates a **Good Receipt Note** (**GRN**) for the customer and prints the Customer Statement if requested.

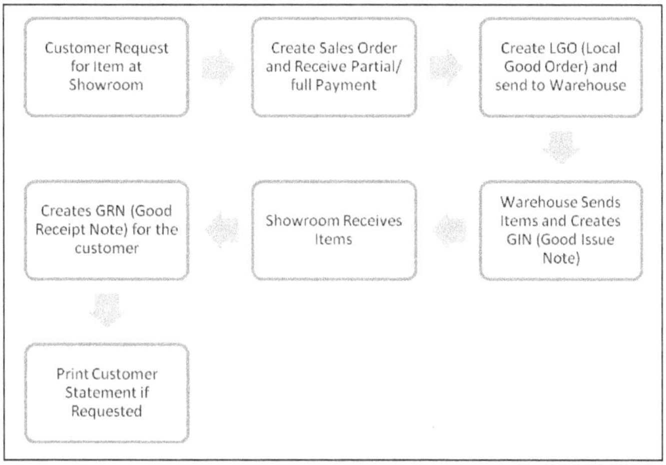

Inter-organizational transfers

The inter-organizational transfers are done among branches in various countries. An inter-organizational transfer starts with a requesting branch sending an internal purchase order to the other branch. The receiving branch then issues a GIN for the requested items and send this to the requesting branch and a GRN is created.

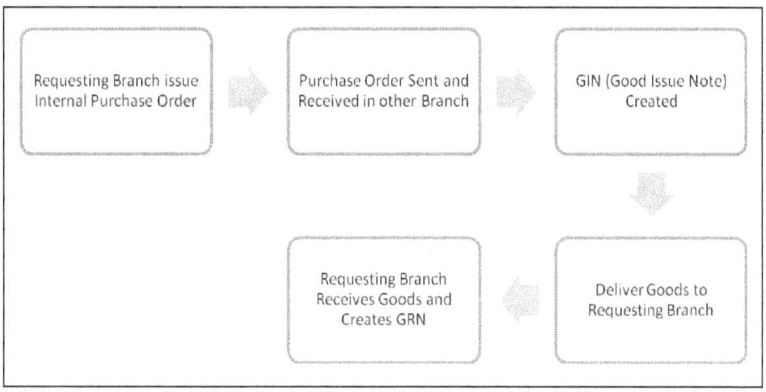

Sales order returns

Whenever the customer rejects the items, the company creates a sales return invoice against the funds returned, and they also create an **Item Return Note** (**IRN**) against the returned items.

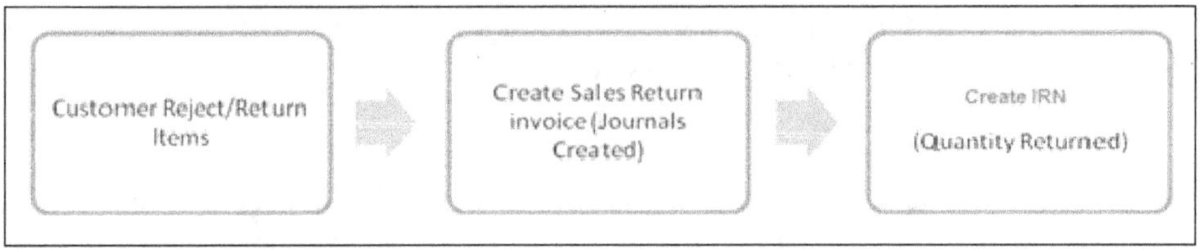

Sales quotation

When the customer requests a quotation, the company verifies if the item is available in their stock or needs some modifications, if it requires modification they calculate the actual cost plus profit margin, and they create the sales quotation that is sent to the customer. After receiving the customer PO, they create the sales order from the quotation.

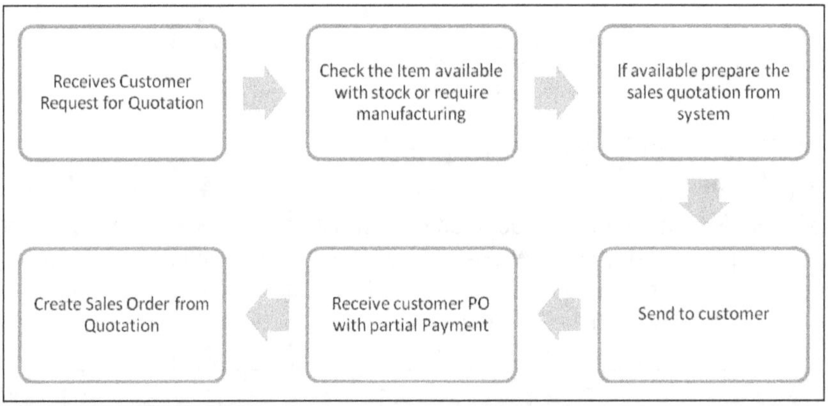

Supply Chain Management—To-Be process

The following is a suggested JDE SCM process that is advised to be implemented for that company.

To-Be simple process

In this process, the customer requests for an item, which is available in the stock and the following procedures for this can be viewed in Oracle JDE:

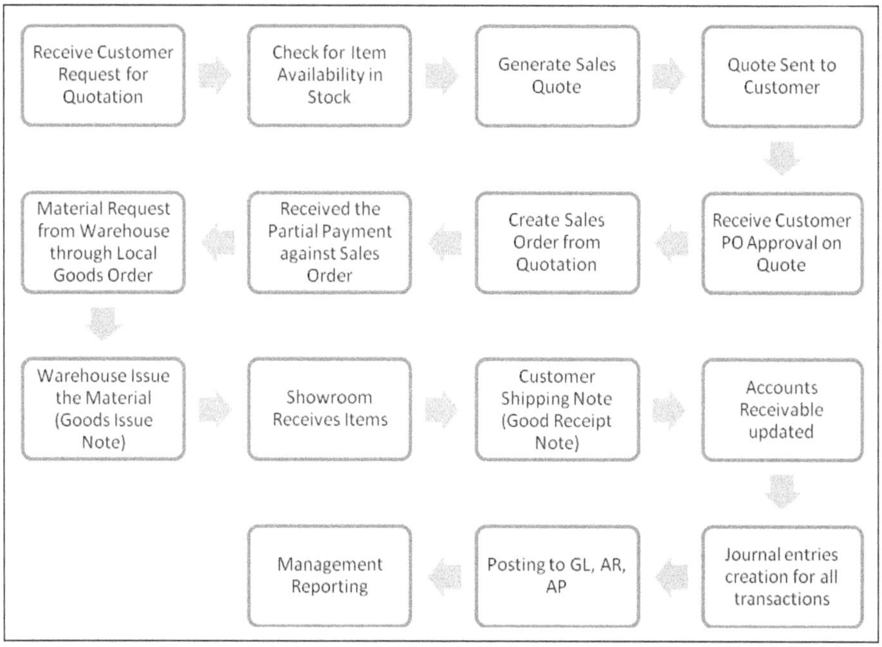

Inventory Management—To-Be process

This section provides the proposed "To-Be" process for Inventory Management. The following recommended solutions are the suggested solutions for Inventory Management implementation.

Branch/Plant address and search types

It is suggested that **Address Book Numbers** should be defined for all branch/plants to maintain detail information in the system. Each store must have an address book number to register all relevant information, such as storekeeper, other contact person, phone number, and store classification (if required).

> **Address Book – Search Type** (for branch/plants) should be entered as **F**.

Item master

The item master information can be defined for both stocked and non-stocked items. The item master information includes the item number, item name, description, and general information related with the item.

Item coding

Client material is represented by three numbers:

First identification—short number

This is a system-generated numeric counter for all items.

Second identification—product number

This is an alpha-numeric number. It is agreed during the business analysis to use the current item number for the client.

Third identification—catalog number

This is an alpha-numeric number and it will be used to maintain the supplier item number as the reference number.

Costing level

This is suggested that all stock items should have a costing level set at the store level and not by location. In the **Item Master Costing Method**, you should specify **2**, which is the **Item Cost at Branch/Plant Level**.

Average cost

The average cost will be calculated online during the processing of inventory receipts, adjustments, and transfer receipts. Average cost will be maintained at the store level.

Costing method

The client will use **Average Costing Method (02)** for all inventory transactions of purchased items, and this will be calculated automatically. **Last Purchase Price Method (01)** will be used for purchase requests and purchase orders. However, the following costing method will be defined for each item in the system:

- Last in
- Weighted average
- Purchasing cost
- Standard cost (this may not be required)
- Manufacturing last (for manufactured items only)

Procurement Management—To-Be process

This section provides the proposed "To-Be" process of procurement management. The following recommended solutions are the suggested solution for JDE procurement management implementation.

Purchase requisition

It is suggested that the client should process purchase requisition through JDE system to perform all internal formalities before creating purchase orders. It is the best practice to process purchase requisition. Being subject to approval by authorized persons, the purchase requisitions will be converted to **Request for Quotation** (**RFQ**) or directly purchase order (if there is a price list provided by the supplier). The request for quotation process will be performed, if required.

Suppliers quotation processing

Purchasing department/project manager will convert purchase requisitions after GM approval to RFQ through the system. RFQ can also be prepared in the system if the purchase requisition does not exist (if the scenario is applicable).

> The system will provide facility to split purchase requisition line item and convert to multiple RFQ for different suppliers. You can see the steps in *Generate Quote from Requisition*.

Long term contract or blanket order

Long term contract (if exists) should be defined as **Blanket Orders** to keep the track of all released purchase orders under the same supplier contract. The original contract will remain in the system and its number will be populated in supply orders.

Purchase order processing

The purchase order will be created in different ways:

- Release from contracts as purchase order
- Convert from quotation
- Directly entered in the JDE as per project planning and demand
- Order suggestion by re-order point

Purchase order approvals

JDE EnterpriseOne provides a facility for online approval of purchase orders through workflow. This can be used instead of or in addition to the hard copy approval. Based on the value of the purchase order, different authorized personnel will be set up for each purchase order type.

Electronic approval route

JDE EnterpriseOne requires the set-up of approval route codes to use electronic approval through the system. Approval route codes should have all the details of approving authorities and their approval levels for requisitions and purchase orders. It was decided to not use the approval for blanket orders.

Purchase order revisions

It is suggested to revise the purchase order in certain cases because of price changes or an additional request. Purchase requisition will be revised to be synchronized with the purchase order. For any revision, the authorized person's approval is required. All revisions will be tracked in the system and displayed by inquiry or printed by reports. The revision can be printed on the purchase order.

Goods received note (GRN)

GNR is entered by goods receiving staff at the warehouse. It will be identified by the "OV" document type and its number will be system generated. It is suggested that the OV number should be used as the GRN number.

Before processing a GRN, the following tasks must be performed:

- Related landed cost rules must be attached to the purchase order or entered during GRN entry. All fixed percentage and amount components should be mentioned in the landed cost rule during the setup. If revisions are required in future, it should be performed by the Finance team.
- Variable landed cost components should be revised for each GRN before the entry of GRN in the system. This can be done by the Finance team as per the company policy. All related accruals will be created automatically through the system and should be offset later against the actual invoice of the transporter or port authorities.

> Receipt Reversal (for mistakes/oversights, and so on) will be done by the authorized people.

Partial/full receipt

During material receipt, both the (partial and full quantity receipt) options are acceptable. If partial receipt is performed, the system provides the option to do keep the remaining quantities open in the PO until the supplier provides the materials and receive the quantities, or cancel the remaining quantities (if the supplier will not supply them at a later date).

- Receive the material and close the Purchase Order
- Receive the quantities into multiple locations

Supplier prices

It is suggested that periodic or yearly prices of certified suppliers will be maintained in the JDE system using the supplier catalog feature.

Payable voucher

Finance will create payable vouchers to close/open GRNs as per the requirements, subject to the submission of invoices by the suppliers.

Sales Order Management—To-Be process

This section provides the proposed "To-Be" process for sales order management. The following recommended solutions are the suggested solutions for Sales Order Management implementation.

Direct ship sales

Direct ship sales will be used to supply the material directly from the supplier to the customer (end-to-end), without updating the client stock. A purchase order will be created automatically from the direct ship sales order.

Cash sales

Cash sales will be used to sell products on a cash basis. No account receivables record will be created. Usually, one customer account will be created to process all cash sales orders. No approval process is required for the cash sales process.

Order acceptance

After receiving the order acceptance from the customer, the sale quotation will be converted into contracts or directly into sales orders as per the requirements of the sales process. At this stage, the Sales team will forward the request to the Finance section to maintain all required price groups for the customer in the system.

Sales quotation status

JDE provides online information about the following quotation statuses by customer/products combination:

- Open
- Rejected
- Closed (converted to sales order)

Client sales contracts or blanket orders (XB)

Blanket orders will be identified by separate document type of "XB" and a system-generated number. This feature will be used for long-term contracts with customers who request client product deliveries under the same contract. Based on each request, a sales order will be released from the contract. Alternatively, blanket orders can be used to prepare the current and future month delivery schedule and can then be forwarded to the customer. This will not affect the quantity commitment.

Sales hold order processing

During sales order entry, the order will be on hold if any of the following are true:

- Credit limit is exceeded
- Margin is insufficient
- Overdue invoices exist
- The sale is a credit sale

It has been agreed that all credit sales will be held automatically and a workflow message will be sent to the general manager in order to release (approve) the orders. A hold code will not be implemented for cash sales. This process will be taken care of by the Finance team.
It requires the set-up of hold codes along with the authorized person's employee number.

Confirm shipment

Shipment confirmation is the most critical process and needs to be re-engineered as follows:

- Product availability will be verified online.
- The Dispatcher will print the pick slip (material request) and verify physical availability of the material.
- If all is fine, then run JDE shipment confirmation/lot confirmation. This will reduce on-hand quantities from the JDE system.
- The system will pick the quantity from the lowest lot number to ensure compliance with the FIFO method. That is, the first quantity received, will be released first.

Delivery note

It is suggested that the delivery note should be printed separately (not with the invoice) to register the number in the system for future reference However, this will be a choice of the client team.

Invoice processing

An invoice will be printed for orders with items having the status "Shipment Confirmed". During this stage, the system will assign an account receivable record number. The invoice format must be developed as per the custom format.

Customer credit memo

It is suggested that the credit memo (CO) should be issued for invoice correction or cancellation or return sales. The credit memo can be entered directly into the system or it can be generated against the existing invoice (to be cancelled) in order to retrieve the same "sale price and cost". Both of these options will be set up for the user's convenience.

Sales branch—internal sales transfer

Inter-branch transfers can take place between all sales branches. It is suggested that the client use the JDE sale transfer program for this purpose, in order to maintain document controls. Quantities need to be released from the sender branch and these will be shown as "In transit" in the **Item Availability** (**P41202**). The application receiver branch will update the transferred quantities.

Product price

The product price will be the base sales price or net discounted price as per the customer pricing groups. The existing pricing set-up (price groups) will be done in the JDE EnterpriseOne new system, with additional requirements. The net prices are calculated by the system (base price minus discount). However, if the discount details are required to be printed on the quotation then this needs to be reflected in a separate line type called a Discount line.

Back order processing

It is required to set up the item by warehouse or customer level. A back order will be created if the available quantity is not enough to meet the demand.

Sales update

It is suggested that "End of Day Process" should be executed manually. It needs to be run frequently in order to get up-to-date AR and GL balances. It will be run by the Finance department, for orders with a status of confirm shipment.

Supply chain standard reports

The following are the JDE Supply Chain Management standard reports:

Report ID and report name	Description	Module
R41540 – Item Ledger Detail	This report lists the cumulative transactions from balance forward records before the G/L date that you selected in the processing options.	Inventory Management
R41530 – Stock Status	This report is used to list the location and status of the inventory items in a specific branch, plant, or warehouse.	Inventory Management
R41550 – Inventory Journal	This report is used to review the transactions against the inventory.	Inventory Management
R41590 – Valuation Report	This report is used to review the extended value of on-hand inventory.	Inventory Management
R41116 – Inventory Turn Report	This report is used to review the details of a cost center, item, and date range combination that you specify.	Inventory Management
R4051 – Supply and Demand Report	This report provides information about an item's demand, supply, and available quantities.	Inventory Management
R41700 – Margin Report	This report is used to identify the profit margin based on current information.	Inventory Management

Report ID and report name	Description	Module
R41580 - Cost Report	This report lists items that have a transaction cost that is different from the current average cost that you specified in the processing options.	Inventory Management
R41505 - Lot Trace and Track Print	This report provides trace and track information of the inventory items with lot number.	Inventory Management
R4152 - Buyers Guide	This report lists product and item performance information.	Inventory Management
R41560 - Item Master Directory	This report lists the item master records.	Inventory Management
R41510 - Price Book Report	This report lists the current prices for the inventory.	Inventory Management
R4164 - ABC Analysis Report	This report is based on the principle that a small number of items will account for the largest part of a company's business.	Inventory Management
R43530 - Request for Quotation	This report is used for quotations and shows the supplier information with order details.	Procurement Management
R43510 - Purchase Receiver Report	This report shows the details of purchases received at the customer warehouse.	Procurement Management
R43535 - Order Revisions History	This report is used to review the history of orders with all of their details.	Procurement Management
R43512 - Inventory Receipt Register	This report is used to review the details for received items with supplier and receipt details.	Procurement Management
R4401P - Order Detail	This report is used to review the details of orders that have been placed.	Procurement Management
R43632 - Open Purchase Order	This report is used to review the details of open purchase orders, by item.	Procurement Management
R43525 - Purchase Order Status	This report is used to review the status of purchase orders.	Procurement Management
R43415 - PO Summary by Supplier	This report is used to review purchase order information by supplier.	Procurement Management
R43420 - Purchase Ledger Report	This report is used to list the original detail line information and changes that have been made to the quantity or extended amount on each detail line.	Procurement Management

Report ID and report name	Description	Module
R43412 - Received/ Vouched Status Report	This report is used to review the received and vouchered quantities with open quantity and amounts.	Procurement Management
R43428 - Logged Voucher	This report shows the details of logged vouchers with invoice number, document number, due date, and amount.	Procurement Management
R43450 - Voucher Reconciliation	This is a report that shows orders received but not vouchered.	Procurement Management
R04602 - Supplier Analysis	This report shows supplier analysis details.	Procurement Management
R42640 - Held Sales Orders	This report is used to review the list of all sales orders that are on hold for these reasons: credit, profit margin, partial order hold, and price review.	Sales Order Management
R42810 - Sales Journal	This report is used to review the sales details by customer, invoice number, and invoice date.	Sales Order Management
R42620 - Open Sales Orders	This report is used to review the orders that have been picked but not shipped, orders that have been picked but not billed, and the open orders that have passed the customer's requested ship date.	Sales Order Management
R42600 - Sales Ledger	This report is used to analyze the sales history.	Sales Order Management
R42611 - Sales Analysis Summary	This report is used to review period-to-date and year-to-date sales amounts and sales margins.	Sales Order Management
R42632 - Open Sales Order by Item	This report is used to review the number of open orders for an item and determine how to fill them using availability information.	Sales Order Management
R42118 - Backorders Report	This report is used to review the back orders, with branch/plant, order number, item number, and quantity failed.	Sales Order Management
R42520 - Print Pick Slip	This report is used to print ordered items that need to be shipped, and from which location and lot number they should be picked.	Sales Order Management
R42535 - Print Delivery Note	This report is used to print shipping documents that should accompany the order to its destination. Delivery personnel can use these documents to compare what they are supposed to deliver with what they are transporting.	Sales Order Management

Report ID and report name	Description	Module
R42810 - Print Sales Journal	This report is used to print the sales order with the following information: total invoice amounts, cost of goods sold, and profit amounts.	Sales Order Management
R42950 - Batch Update Sales Price/Cost	This report is used to adjust item price/cost by the new amount.	Sales Order Management

Index

Symbols

A

B

D

J

K

L

M

O

P

S

V

W

Z

[PACKT] enterprise
PUBLISHING
professional expertise distilled

Thank you for buying
Oracle JD Edwards EnterpriseOne 9.0: Supply Chain Management Cookbook

About Packt Publishing

Packt, pronounced 'packed', published its first book "*Mastering phpMyAdmin for Effective MySQL Management*" in April 2004 and subsequently continued to specialize in publishing highly focused books on specific technologies and solutions.

Our books and publications share the experiences of your fellow IT professionals in adapting and customizing today's systems, applications, and frameworks. Our solution-based books give you the knowledge and power to customize the software and technologies you're using to get the job done. Packt books are more specific and less general than the IT books you have seen in the past. Our unique business model allows us to bring you more focused information, giving you more of what you need to know, and less of what you don't.

Packt is a modern, yet unique publishing company, which focuses on producing quality, cutting-edge books for communities of developers, administrators, and newbies alike. For more information, please visit our website: `www.PacktPub.com`.

About Packt Enterprise

In 2010, Packt launched two new brands, Packt Enterprise and Packt Open Source, in order to continue its focus on specialization. This book is part of the Packt Enterprise brand, home to books published on enterprise software - software created by major vendors, including (but not limited to) IBM, Microsoft and Oracle, often for use in other corporations. Its titles will offer information relevant to a range of users of this software, including administrators, developers, architects, and end users.

Writing for Packt

We welcome all inquiries from people who are interested in authoring. Book proposals should be sent to `author@packtpub.com`. If your book idea is still at an early stage and you would like to discuss it first before writing a formal book proposal, contact us; one of our commissioning editors will get in touch with you.

We're not just looking for published authors; if you have strong technical skills but no writing experience, our experienced editors can help you develop a writing career, or simply get some additional reward for your expertise.

www.ingramcontent.com/pod-product-compliance
Lightning Source LLC
LaVergne TN
LVHW080018210926
848481LV00011B/3053
* 9 7 8 1 8 4 9 6 8 1 9 6 4 *